Jews in the East European Borderlands

BORDERLINES:
RUSSIAN AND EAST EUROPEAN JEWISH STUDIES

Editorial board:

Mikhail Krutikov (University of Michigan)
Harriet Murav (University of Illinois, Urbana-Champaign), Series Editor
Alice Nakhimovsky (Colgate University)
David Shneer (University of Colorado, Boulder)
Anna Shternshis (University of Toronto)

JEWS IN THE EAST EUROPEAN BORDERLANDS

Essays in Honor of John D. Klier

Edited by EUGENE M. AVRUTIN
and HARRIET MURAV

Boston
2012

Library of Congress Cataloging-in-Publication Data:
A catalog record for this book is available from the Library of Congress.

Copyright © 2012 Academic Studies Press
All rights reserved
ISBN 978-1-936235-59-9

Book design by Ivan Grave
On the cover: The General map of Volynia province, 1820.

Published by Academic Studies Press in 2012

28 Montfern Avenue
Brighton, MA 02135, USA
press@academicstudiespress.com
www. academicstudiespress.com

Contents

List of Contributors 9

Acknowledgments 13

Introduction 14
Eugene M. Avrutin and Harriet Murav

Part 1: History, Culture, and Everyday Life

1. The Mariinsko Sergievskii Shelter for Converted Jewish Children in St. Petersburg
ChaeRan Y. Freeze 27

2. Yiddish in Imperial Russia's Civil Society
Gennady Estraikh 50

3. An-sky in Liozno: "Sins of Youth" and the Archival Diary
Gabriella Safran 67

4. In the Evil Kingdom of Things: Sholem-aleichem and the Writing of Everyday Life in Jewish Literature
Olga Litvak 83

5. A Paper Life: Model Letters and Real Letters as a Key to Russian-Jewish Aspirations at the Turn of the Twentieth Century
Alice Nakhimovsky and Roberta Newman 106

Part 2: Upheaval, Violence, and Antisemitism

6. Violence and the Migration of Ashkenazi Jews to Eastern Europe
Shaul Stampfer 127

7. Uses and Abuses: "Pogrom" in the Anglo-American Imagination, 1881–1919
Sam Johnson 147

8. Look! Up There in the Sky: It's a Vulture, It's a Bat . . . It's a Jew. Reflections on Antisemitism in Late Imperial Russia, 1906–1914
Robert Weinberg 167

9. Shots in the Back: On the Origin of the Anti-Jewish Pogroms of 1918–1921
Oleg Budnitskii 187

10. Between External Persecution and National Renaissance: Simon Dubnow's Lachrymose Vision of Russian-Jewish History
Joshua M. Karlip 202

11. Soviet Holocaust Photography and Landscapes of Emptiness
David Shneer 224

12. Transformed Myths in Verse: Boris Slutsky's Three Holocaust Poems and the Question of Violence
Marat Grinberg 246

A Bibliography of John D. Klier's Works 265

Index 272

List of Illustrations

Chapter 8. Look! Up There in the Sky...

Figure 8-1. Veche, 24 December 1906. "The Kike Locust in the Countryside Has Already Begun Its Activities before Elections to the State Duma" 179

Figure 8-2. Veche, 28 January 1907. "A Grim Dream, but Waking Up Will Be Sweet" 180

Figure 8-3. Znamia, 1 April 1914. "The Antedeluvian Beast—The Kikosaurus" 183

Figure 8-4. Znamia, 15 July 1914. "Who Is He?" 184

Chapter 11. Soviet Holocaust Photography and Landscapes of Emptiness

Figure 11-1. Ogonek Coverage of Nazi Atrocities, 25 June 1941. German "trophy" photograph. Caption: "Punishment in Poland. Those sentenced are forced to dig their own graves." 226

Figure 11-2. Dmitrii Baltermants, "Residents of Kerch Search for Their Loved Ones," 1942. Scanned from the maquette for Baltermants's unpublished book Tak eto bylo. Courtesy of Paul and Teresa Harbaugh. 227

Figure 11-3. Evgenii Khaldei, "Kerch," January 1942. Courtesy of Fotosoiuz, Moscow. 229

Figure 11-4a-b "Death Camp." Ogonek, 20 November 1943. 235

Figure 11-5. Mikhail Trakhman, "Local Visitors at Majdanek." August 1944. Courtesy of U.S. Holocaust Memorial Museum. .. 238

Figure 11-6. Unattributed, but most likely Mikhail Trakhman, "Poles Watching Germans Bearing Witness to Corpses," August 1944. Yad Vashem Archives 4212/16. 239

Figure 11-7. Mikhail Trakhman, Majdanek, July–August 1944. Courtesy of U.S. Holocaust Memorial Museum. 241

Figure 11-8. Mikhail Trakhman and Boris Tseitlin, "Majdanek Death Camp." Ogonek, 31 August 1944, 8–9. 243

Chapter 12. Transformed Myths in Verse

Figure 12-1. Slutsky's handwritten copy of
"I was a liberator of Ukraine." 255

Figure 12-2. Unattributed, "General View of the Shooting Area at Babi Yar." Source: Yad Vashem Archives, photo no. 4147/20.....261

Contributors

Eugene M. Avrutin is assistant professor of modern European Jewish history and Tobor family scholar in the program of Jewish Culture and Society at the University of Illinois. He is the author of *Jews and the Imperial State: Identification Politics in Tsarist Russia* (2010) and is currently working on a book project on ritual murder and small-town life in Velizh.

Oleg Budnitskii is professor of history and director of the Center for the History and Sociology of World War II at the National Research University Higher School of Economics, Moscow. He is also senior research fellow at the Institute of Russian History of the Russian Academy of Sciences and editor in chief of the annual *Arkhiv evreiskoi istorii*. His major books are *Den'gi russkoi emigratsii: Kolchakovskoe zoloto, 1918–1957* (2008) and *Rossiiskie evrei mezhdy krasnymi i belymi, 1917–1920* (2005).

Gennady Estraikh is associate professor of Yiddish studies, Skirball Department of Hebrew and Judaic Studies, New York University. He is the author of *Yiddish in the Cold War* (2008), *In Harness: Yiddish Writers' Romance with Communism* (2004), *Soviet Yiddish: Language Planning and Linguistic Development* (1999) and the co-editor of *Translating Sholem Aleichem: History, Politics, and Art* (2012).

ChaeRan Y. Freeze is associate professor in the Department of Near Eastern and Judaic Studies at Brandeis University. She is the author of *Jewish Marriage and Divorce in Imperial Russia* (2001).

Marat Grinberg is assistant professor of Russian and Humanities at Reed College in Portland, Oregon. He is the author of *"I am to be read not from left to right, but in Jewish: from right to left": The Poetics of Boris Slutsky* (2011), as well as numerous essays in English and Russian on literature and Jewish intellectual history and politics.

Sam Johnson is senior lecturer of modern European history at Manchester Metropolitan University. She is the author of *Peasants, Pogroms, Jews: Britain and Eastern Europe's Jewish Question, 1867–1925* (2011). Her current project focuses on antisemitic caricature and the visualization of Jews in Europe before World War I.

Joshua M. Karlip is assistant professor of history at Yeshiva University. Recently, Karlip was Harry Starr Fellow at the Center for Jewish Studies at Harvard University. Karlip's articles and his current book in progress analyze the ideologies of Yiddishism and diaspora nationalism during the first half of the twentieth century.

Olga Litvak is the Michael and Lisa Leffell chair of modern Jewish history at Clark University. She is the author of *Conscription and the Search for Modern Russian Jewry* (2006) and a forthcoming book on the Haskalah and Jewish romanticism in Eastern Europe (2012). Litvak specializes in the study of Russian-Jewish culture in the imperial period. She is currently working on a study of Marc Chagall, as well as a critical biography of Sholem-aleichem.

Harriet Murav is professor of Slavic Languages and Literatures and Comparative and World Literature at the University of Illinois at Urbana-Champaign. Her studies of Dostoyevsky, Russian law and literature, and nineteenth-century Russian-Jewish literature are complemented by her most recent work, *Music from a Speeding Train: Jewish Literature in Post-Revolution Russia* (2011).

Alice Nakhimovsky is professor of Russian and Jewish Studies at Colgate University. She has written extensively on Russian-Jewish literature and everyday life. She and Roberta Newman will revisit the subject of *brivnshtelers* in a book entitled *How to Live a Paper Life*, to be published by Indiana University Press.

Roberta Newman is an independent scholar, writer, and researcher in New York. She is the illustrations editor and director of Archival Research of both the print and online editions of *The YIVO Encyclopedia of Jews in Eastern Europe* and a special consultant to the new Russian-Jewish history museum now being developed in Moscow.

Gabriella Safran, professor of Slavic Languages and Literatures at Stanford University, is the author of *Rewriting the Jew: Assimilation Narratives in the Russian Empire* (2000) and *Wandering Soul: The Dybbuk's Creator, S. An-sky* (2010).

David Shneer is professor of history and director of the program in Jewish studies at the University of Colorado at Boulder. His most recent books include *Through Soviet Jewish Eyes: Photography, War, and the Holocaust* (2010) and *New Jews: The End of the Jewish Diaspora* (2005).

Shaul Stampfer teaches East European Jewish history at the Hebrew University of Jerusalem. He has worked on topics such as the history of education, family structure, demography, and migration in the context of East European Jewish history. He met with John Klier in Israel and in England, but most of all in Moscow.

Robert Weinberg teaches history at Swarthmore College and has written books on the 1905 revolution in Odessa and Birobidzhan. He is currently writing a book on the ritual murder trial of Mendel Beilis in 1913.

Acknowledgments

This volume is the product of an international academic conference in honor of John D. Klier's life and work held in April 2009 at the University of Illinois, Urbana-Champaign. The conference had generous financial support from the University of Illinois' Program in Jewish Culture and Society, the Department of History, the Department of Slavic Languages and Literatures, the Center for Advanced Studies, the Office of the Chancellor, the Hewlett International Conference Program, and the Russian, East European and Eurasian Center. The editors would also like to thank Michael Stanislawski and Jeremy Dauber of Columbia University's Institute for Israel and Jewish Studies, as well as Jeffrey Veidlinger of Indiana University's Robert A. and Sandra S. Borns Jewish Studies Program for their financial assistance. Helen Klier, Sam Johnson, Robert Weinberg, and Lars Fischer answered all of our questions. Faith Stein compiled the bibliography of John D. Klier's works. In particular, the editors would like to say a special thank-you to James Loeffler for reading the manuscript in its entirety and offering numerous constructive comments, as well as to Carolyn Pouncy for expertly editing the collection.

The Editors

Introduction

Eugene M. Avrutin and Harriet Murav

On 8 December 2003, at a lecture given at the inaugural conference of the International Center for Russian and East European Jewish Studies in Moscow, John Doyle Klier traced the crooked path by which Russian-Jewish history and culture developed—from a field restricted to a few lonely pioneers at major research universities to a thriving discipline boasting a solid institutional infrastructure, dynamic practitioners, and a surge in publications, book series, and conferences enriched by new approaches to scholarship.[1] Moscow, it turned out, was the ideal place to reflect on the state of the field. John came of age as a historian at a time when only a handful of scholars had made the transatlantic journey to work on Jewish topics in the former Soviet Union. For much of the 20th century, access to Jewish sources (either archival or published) was restricted or strictly forbidden. Over the years, John worked tirelessly to promote Jewish studies in the former Soviet Union, to build alliances among scholars who were separated as much by geography as ideology and methodology. After the implosion of the Soviet Union from within, John continued to extend the boundaries of the field by writing articles and books grounded in meticulous primary source research. When John passed away from cancer at the age of 62, on 23 September 2007, his broad range of publications had influenced an entire generation of new scholarship on Jews in the East European borderlands.

John was born on 13 December 1944 in Bellefonte, Pennsylvania, a small Victorian town located in the Nittany Valley of the Ridge and Valley Appalachians. His father, Eugene Klier, taught aeronautical engineering for several years at Penn State before moving on to the Catholic University in Washington, DC. When John was 11 years old, Eugene moved the family to Syracuse, New York, to take a position at Syracuse University. The Klier family was devoutly Catholic; and John, the oldest of six siblings, attended Catholic schools in Syracuse before taking his B.A. and M.A. in history at the University of Notre Dame. There he excelled in fencing, eventually earning

---

[1] John D. Klier, "'Otkuda i kuda idem': Izuchenie dorevoliutsionnoi istorii rossiiskogo evreistva v Soedinennykh Shtatakh v XX veke," in *Istoriia i kul'tura rossiiskogo i vostochnoevropeiskogo evreistva*, ed. O.V. Budnitskii et al. (Moscow, 2004), 40–65.

an all-America distinction for his skills in the sport. While pursuing his doctorate at the University of Illinois, he became captain of the fencing team and continued to fence nearly every week over the course of his career at Fort Hays State University and University College London (UCL), earning several medals in tournaments. Listening to opera and classical music, going to the theater, and reading world literature were other things that John enjoyed doing in his spare time.

At around the age of 19, while studying history at Notre Dame, John listened to a performance of Modest Mussorgsky's *Pictures at an Exhibition*. His enthusiasm for the music and the composer triggered a lifelong passion for 19th-century Russian culture and history. In 1968, after completing his M.A., John transferred to the University of Illinois to study Russian history. While working on his Ph.D., the civil rights movement that sparked violent, often deadly confrontations across the South made a deep impression on John, eventually influencing his decision to write a thesis on interethnic relations between Jews and Russians. At the time, this was a surprising and unorthodox choice. His advisers warned him of the tremendous difficulties of conducting research on a Jewish topic in the Soviet Union. But John remained true to his own intellectual interests and utilized one of the most comprehensive library collections in the United States on Russia and Eastern Europe to write "The Origins of the Jewish Minority Problem in Russia, 1772–1812," which he defended successfully in 1975.

Dissatisfied by the prerevolutionary historical interpretations of Russian Jewry, John set out to reexamine the gradual formulation of the Jewish question in the Russian bureaucratic mind. "My initial interest in the legal position of the Jews in the Russian Empire," John wrote in the preface to his thesis, "grew out of my personal dissatisfaction with the treatment accorded the subject by the standard histories dealing with the waning of the imperial regime. Much of the conventional wisdom, especially that treating the role of the government in the promotion of antisemitism, seemed to me to exist without real substantiation." As he began the research, John found himself "receding further and further into the past," until he recognized the necessity of reexamining the origins of the Jewish question in imperial Russia.[2] The relations between Jews and Russians, in all of their political, social, and administrative complexity, would captivate John for the rest of his life.

When John finished his thesis, Jewish history was rarely taught or researched in the United States, outside of a select group of scholars on the

---

[2] John D. Klier, "The Origins of the Jewish Minority Problem in Russia, 1772–1812" (Ph.D. diss., University of Illinois, 1975), iii.

East Coast who mostly specialized in classical Judaica.[3] Although Russian historians wrote important new studies on bureaucracy, law, and society, they published little, if anything, on empire and nationality. As a result, John's thesis fell through the cracks and failed to make an immediate impact on the field. In fact, it took nearly 11 years and at least 15 rejection letters from academic publishing houses before Northern Illinois University Press agreed to take a chance on the manuscript. One publishing house, after reviewing the book proposal, replied that it had already agreed to publish a book on the Jews of Russia and did not see any reason to publish a second one.[4] Yet as soon as it appeared, *Russia Gathers Her Jews* was immediately recognized as an ambitious reassessment of the contradictory policies—combining both rational and prejudicial elements—used by the Russian government to rule its Jewish population.[5] Fifteen years after its initial publication, at a time when interest in Jewish history had significantly increased in Russia and in Israel, *Russia Gathers Her Jews* was translated into Russian. John used the opportunity to incorporate newly available archival materials, as well as to expand and update the chapters and the bibliography to reflect the most current scholarship in the field.[6] In the spring of 2011, on the 25th anniversary of its publication, Northern Illinois reissued the book in soft cover—a fitting testament to the enduring importance of John's early scholarship to students of Russian and Jewish history.

For most of the 1970s and 1980s, John taught history at Fort Hays State University in Hays, Kansas. Located halfway between Denver and Kansas City in the Smoky Hills region of the great central plains, Hays was once a military outpost town, famous for its saloons and dance halls, railroad workers and tough guys. John began to teach at Fort Hays while writing his thesis and continued to work there, rising to the rank of full professor, until 1989. This was a significantly productive period in John's life. Working at a public university, with demanding teaching responsibilities and scarce library resources, John worked feverishly to publish over a dozen articles and book chapters. He spent many of his summers in Champaign at the Slavic and East European Summer Research Laboratory, working on his second book

---

[3] For a good overview of some of the most important changes in Jewish historical studies in the second half of the 20th century, see Paula Hyman, "The Ideological Transformation of Modern Jewish Historiography," in *The State of Jewish Studies*, ed. Shaye J. D. Cohen and Edward L. Greenstein (Detroit, 1990), 143–57. And for a personal perspective by leading Jewish studies scholars, see *AJS Perspectives* (Fall 2010): 55–59.

[4] Klier, "'Otkuda i kuda idem,'" 48.

[5] John D. Klier, *Russia Gathers Her Jews: The Origins of the Jewish Question in Russia* (DeKalb, IL, 1985).

[6] John D. Klier, *Rossiia sobiraet svoikh evreev: Proiskhozhdenie evreiskogo voprosa v Rossii* (Moscow, 2000).

project on Jews and public opinion during the Great Reform era. He received several grants from international funding agencies, including two from the International Research and Exchanges Board (IREX), to read newspapers, periodicals, and other published materials in Leningrad and Moscow libraries. To mask a politically sensitive topic, John applied to IREX—and was given the stamp of approval by Soviet authorities—to work on a project that proposed to examine the "growth and development of the Russian periodical press." Like so many American scholars who did research in the Cold War era, John adjusted his topic to appease the Soviet historical establishment, which he did at great personal and professional peril.[7]

In those days, John recalled, the Jewish question was "just one of an enormous number of topics which, for ideological reasons, constituted 'blank spots' which were off-limits for research or discussion by scholars, foreign or native, in the Soviet Union." While working in the Newspaper Reading Room of the Soviet Academy of Sciences in Leningrad, his fellow readers nicknamed John "The Page Turner."

> Whenever I left my desk in the Reading Room, I was always careful to turn past the page I was reading. Apparently no other reader was curious enough to actually turn the page back when I left the room. Had they done so, they would have found a recurrent word in the columns I was perusing. That one word, had the authorities discovered it, would have been sufficient to have me packed off home, international scholarly exchange or not. The one word was "Jew."[8]

The delights and frustrations of daily life in the USSR, however, were the source of many fond memories for John. Long after the fall of the Soviet Union, John enjoyed retelling his research adventures to his younger colleagues over lunch or a bottle of beer at scholarly conferences.

The research and writing of John's second monograph, *Imperial Russia's Jewish Question*, took 20 years to complete.[9] In a richly documented study based on a reading of nearly 200 periodical publications, many of the obscure provincial variety, John set out to examine the transformation of the Jewish question in public consciousness. If in the first half of the 19th century the Jewish question—centered on the themes of Jews' extreme cultural isolation and lack of social utility—was discussed behind closed doors, in the era of the Great Reforms it had become one of the burning questions of the day. By

---

[7] On the adventures and agonies of doing Russian historical research, see Samuel H. Baron and Cathy A. Frierson, eds., *Adventures in Russian Historical Research: Reminiscences of American Scholars from the Cold War to the Present* (Armonk, NY, 2003).
[8] John D. Klier, "Hunters' Notebooks," *East European Jewish Affairs* 27, 1 (1997): 87.
[9] John D. Klier, *Imperial Russia's Jewish Question, 1855–1881* (Cambridge, 1995).

the end of the reign of Alexander II in 1881, hundreds of newspaper stories and editorials appeared on Jewish themes. The debates in the press—on topics ranging from language, education, and military service to religious reform, economic productivity, and fears of Jewish conspiracy and exploitation—did not, John argued, constitute "mere rhetoric."[10] On the contrary, he demonstrated how public opinion—in all its ideological dimensions—helped shape official attitudes toward Jews. One of the most impressive achievements of the book was John's ability to tie the threads of empire around public discussions of Jews—to show, in other words, how the Jewish question emerged amid other prominent problems and concerns of the Great Reform era (such as the abolition of serfdom and the Polish insurrection of 1863). Equally impressive was John's sensitivity to the regional variations of the debates, which provided important new insights into popular local attitudes and expressions.

Imperial Russia's Jewish Question was an ambitious undertaking that solidified John's reputation as the world's leading authority on Russia's treatment of Jews. By the time the book appeared in print, John was teaching East European Jewish history at UCL. The move to London proved propitious, despite a steep drop in rank from full professor to lecturer. At UCL, John was able to rise rapidly through the academic ranks and assumed the Sidney and Elizabeth Corob Professorship in 1996, shortly after the publication of *Imperial Russia's Jewish Question*. Outside of an impressive publishing record and his work at *East European Jewish Affairs*, John played an influential role in the development of Jewish studies in England. He served as the chair of the Hebrew and Jewish Studies Department for nearly a decade and was president of the British Association for Jewish Studies for one year. Among his many other commitments, he served as a consultant to the Rothschild Foundation and the Avi Chai Foundation, two of the world's most influential philanthropic organizations committed to promoting research on and education in Jewish studies.

While in London, John witnessed the dramatic collapse of Soviet socialism, and as a result, many (but by no means all) of the institutional constraints that had made researching Jewish topics so problematic in the USSR. Suddenly, hundreds of thousands of archival files were opened to scholars, and John took advantage of the unexpected turn of events to do what he loved doing best—working with primary sources. In the summer of 1991, while writing *Imperial Russia's Jewish Question*, John spent three months at the Central State Historical Archives in Kiev. The archival treasures, John observed in a review article of newly published archival guides, "constitute a happy hunting ground of unbelievable richness for the contemporary scholar of Jewish history and

---

[10] Ibid., xv.

culture," even if the legacy of "past controls" continued to cast a dark shadow. "There is virtually no means of identifying the nature, variety, or dimensions of holdings of Jewish interest in any particular collection."[11] Whatever the challenges, John was one of the first scholars in the world to systematically examine Jewish documents in Moscow, St. Petersburg, Kiev, Vilnius, and Minsk archives. And while working in the archives or giving papers at academic conferences, John continuously reached out to his colleagues in the East. More than anyone else, John devoted himself to developing a new generation of Jewish studies scholars. Over the course of two decades, John was involved in almost every important Jewish studies initiative in the former Soviet Union. He served on numerous advisory councils and played an instrumental role in creating two Jewish studies centers: Sefer in Moscow and Petersburg Judaica at the European University in St. Petersburg. As the historian Viktor Kel'ner observed in a moving obituary, "Only now, several months after John's tragic death, have we in Russia begun to understand just how important his role was in shaping and developing the study of Jewish history in Russia's academic centers and institutions."[12]

After nearly 50 years of irrelevance, the largest Jewish population in the world began to matter, and not only to scholars trained in Jewish studies. The "imperial turn" in Russian historical studies made John's written work—on topics such as conversion, censorship, Russification politics, antisemitism, and pogroms—ever more relevant to current research concerns. John was invited to contribute numerous essays to journals and edited collections on questions of nationalism, ethnic classification, religious toleration, and violence.[13] At the time, he also began archival research on *Russians, Jews, and the Pogroms of 1881–1882*, an exhaustive study of the pogrom crisis that erupted shortly after the assassination of Alexander II. Finished only a few months before his death, the book zeroed in on a historical moment that proved as pivotal for the history of the Jews in Russia as for the entire imperial social order.[14] John's masterful reconstruction of the events of 1881–82 not only dispelled several enduring assumptions in the historical literature but also repositioned the pogrom paradigm within a wider body of scholarship on ethnic violence.

Ultimately, John was admired as much for his scholarship as for his exceptional generosity, kindness, and humility. Together with such pioneers

---

[11] Klier, "Hunters' Notebooks," 87.

[12] Viktor Kel'ner, "Obituary: Our Old Friend John Klier," *East European Jewish Affairs* 38, 3 (2008): 255.

[13] Klier also coedited a pioneering collection of articles on anti-Jewish violence. See John Doyle Klier and Shlomo Lambroza, eds., *Pogroms: Anti-Jewish Violence in Modern Russian History* (Cambridge, 1992).

[14] John D. Klier, *Russians, Jews, and the Pogroms, 1881–1882* (Cambridge, 2011).

in the field as Jonathan Frankel and Hans Rogger, John helped resurrect Russian-Jewish history from the ill-fated charge of parochialism. Unlike most academics whose work is largely determined by scholarly fashion, John continued to wrestle with a problem—the tortuous, often violent, entanglements between Jews and the imperial order—that intrigued him ever since he began writing his Ph.D. thesis. This is not to suggest that John succumbed to scholarly inertia. On the contrary, John's passion for history—his indefatigable desire for working with new primary sources, asking new questions, offering new interpretations based on a meticulous reconstruction of historical events, while immersing himself in the latest scholarly literature and debates—meant that he pushed himself to dig more and more deeply until his very last days.

Jews in the East European Borderlands is based on a conference in honor of John Klier held in April 2009 at the University of Illinois at Urbana-Champaign. John's work and John himself inspired and guided the research of many of the presenters. Since the collapse of the Soviet Union in 1991, the intersecting fields of Russian, East European, and Jewish studies have witnessed a remarkable outpouring of scholarship.[15] Utilizing newly discovered archival documents and previously untapped published sources, this collection showcases some of the most innovative research in the field of Russian-Jewish historical and cultural studies. Part 1 explores the intersections of history, culture, and the everyday. Collectively, the essays examine new forms of association, sociability, and intellectual activity that were made possible due to the monumental economic, social, and political changes that destabilized all facets of Jewish communal life and culture in the late imperial and early Soviet periods.

ChaeRan Freeze's "The Mariinsko Sergievskii Shelter for Converted Jewish Children in St. Petersburg" sheds light on the activities of Russian Orthodox social welfare services for converted Jews, a new development in the 1860s. Her essay reveals the barriers separating Jews from their fellow Russian Orthodox subjects in late imperial Russia. Freeze shows how the Mariinsko Sergievskii Shelter was both a launch pad for Jews seeking new points of entry into higher education and ultimately positions in government service and at

---

[15] For a selection of some of the most innovative research, see Benjamin Nathans and Gabriella Safran, eds., *Cultural Front: Representing Jews in Eastern Europe* (Philadelphia, 2008); Jonathan Dekel-Chen, David Gaunt, Natan M. Meir, and Israel Bartal, eds., *Anti-Jewish Violence: Rethinking the Pogrom in East European History* (Bloomington, IN, 2010); and Stefani Hoffman and Ezra Mendelsohn, eds., *The Revolution of 1905 and Russia's Jews* (Philadelphia, 2008).

the same time a battlefield for models of difference in Russian culture of the time. Conversion did not necessarily lead to acceptance, especially, as Freeze shows from her work with the documentary sources, since negative traits, such as clannishness, were considered innate and intractable features of Jews. A fascinating and subtle conflict unfolds between Jews seeking paths of upward mobility and Christians seeking the means to change the very characteristics that helped Jews succeed at social and economic mobility.

Philanthropy was not, of course, the unique province of the Russian Orthodox Church. Jews and non-Jews alike wanted to reform Jews. In "Yiddish in Imperial Russia's Civil Society," Gennady Estraikh shows that the work of Jewish philanthropic organizations, including, for example, ORT (Society for the Promotion of Artisanal and Agricultural Work among Jews in Russia) helped create a Jewish civil society. Estraikh's essay provides fresh insights into the rise of Yiddish as a language associated with high culture. Whereas most scholarship to date focuses on the part played by modern literature in this development, Estraikh shows how the use of Yiddish by Jewish philanthropic organizations contributed significantly to a new role for the language. A more standardized and proper Yiddish occupied a prominent place in the civic arena that these organizations fostered. The philanthropic associations contributed to a significant shift in the function and capacities of Yiddish, which no longer served merely as the daily life language "zhargon" of unassimilated shtetl-dwellers but also become the professional workplace language of educated St. Petersburg Jewish civic activists. Yiddish enjoyed a new mobility in new spheres of Jewish life.

Yiddish played a differential role in the public and private lives of Semyon Akimovich An-sky (Shloyme-Zanvl Rappoport), as Gabriella Safran reveals in "An-sky in Liozno: 'Sins of Youth' and the Archival Diary." The image of An-sky in his 1881 diary provides a startling contrast to the image of An-sky in the ethnographic expeditions. The man who said he was fulfilling his lifelong dream by going back to the Pale of Settlement to mine its Jewish cultural treasures was markedly different from the man who saw the Pale as a place where he was the only human being among "cattle," and the editor who insisted that Yiddish authors such as Der Nister agree to have their work translated into Russian in order to be published. In contrast to the dominant trend of An-sky scholarship, which relies on David Roskies's model of departure and return, Safran argues for a far more fluid and "restless" picture of the author. Safran's comparison of the early Yiddish diary, An-sky's later memoir, and An-sky's Russian-language fiction convincingly shows how the author used his writing to fashion himself as an appealing public figure whose "sins" could be forgiven.

No figure dramatizes the blurry line between the creation of an author's public image and its role in his reception than Sholem-aleichem. Olga Litvak's "In the Evil Kingdom of Things: Sholem-aleichem and the Writing of Everyday Life in Jewish Literature" decisively undermines the hackneyed image of the author as the champion of and servant to the Jews, particularly its "little people." Litvak, like other contributors to this volume, also changes the standard image of the Yiddish language itself, showing how Yiddish, characterized as the "uninhibited language of childhood" does not function as a transparent vessel of meaning, much less a tool of social reform in the work of this best-known Yiddish author. Sholem-aleichem's use of Yiddish and his characteristic highlighting of trivial objects, which serve as the locus of conflictual desire, transform Yiddish into a transgressive force. Litvak's comparison between the role of the knife in "Dos meserl" ("The Penknife") and in *Anna Karenina* and *The Idiot* opens up a dimension of Sholem-aleichem rarely seen in the critical literature: the way that the Yiddish author and the Russian authors use a common reservoir of images to signify forms of transgression that are all the more dangerous because they are concealed. Literature itself, in Litvak's reading of Sholem-aleichem, appears as a form of theft.

Writing as an instrument of self-fashioning is the object of study in Alice Nakhimovsky and Roberta Newman's "A Paper Life: Model Letters and Real Letters as a Key to Russian-Jewish Aspirations at the turn of the 20th Century." Letter writing, beyond the *Forward*'s "Bintl briv" is another significant, but overlooked dimension of Jewish daily life at the turn of the 20th century. Nakhimovsky and Newman's exploration of personal correspondence in this time period shows the hopes and fears of ordinary people, who wanted to fashion themselves according to new patterns of behavior but who lacked the education and confidence to do so without a little help from guidebooks. In contrast to Sholem-aleichem's destabilizing use of Yiddish, the authors of letter-writing guidebooks provided norms to stabilize their clients' language. Because they juxtapose model letters in both Russian (*pis'movniki*) and Yiddish (*brivnshtelers*) to actual correspondence, Nakhimovsky and Newman are able to track the interactions among historical forces, literary genres, and individuals in their daily lives and to tease out the subtle differences between the Russian and Yiddish texts. A striking contrast, for example, emerges in the relations between parents and children. Nakhimovsky and Newman find that Yiddish model letter anthologies offer a template that intensifies and dramatizes the parents' representation of their anxiety over their children, in contrast to the Russian, which mitigates the strength of parental feelings. The Yiddish model letter anthologies present immigration differently from the actual letters, which stress economic need as a reason for departure, not educational opportunity.

The questions of social, personal, and communal transformations, explored in part 1, are examined against the backdrop of ongoing political upheaval and anti-Jewish violence, the theme of part 2. Although scholars have long revised the lachrymose view of East European Jewish history, a rethinking of the question of violence and interethnic conflict remains a central concern in the borderland regions that are the subject of this book. Instead of seeing violence in terms of the total destruction of the Jewish lifeworld, however, the essays in part 2 explore its history in the context of daily life and the process of community building and reconstruction of individual and collective Jewish identity. Moving beyond traditional sources, including newspapers and other print material, the contributors draw on neglected belletristic literature, photography, and newly opened archives. The study of Jews in World War II in Russia and Eastern Europe—not as victims of Nazi genocide but as soldiers, journalists, and literary eyewitnesses—has been largely overshadowed and provides a point of focus for two essays.

But before turning to 20th-century events, part 2 looks back to the founding moments of the East European Jewish community. In "Violence and the Migration of Ashkenazi Jews to Eastern Europe," Shaul Stampfer disputes the established wisdom that large-scale factors—mainly, violence and expulsions—pushed Yiddish-speaking Ashkenazi Jews to migrate east. Rather, subtle, overlooked reasons such as differences in population growth rates between Jews and non-Jews, including, for example, low child mortality rates and high fertility rates, help explain why the largest Jewish population in the world formed in the east. According to Stampfer, when movement took place between 1500 and 1700, it was usually small-scale and regional. In a bold, revisionist interpretation, Stampfer concludes that there was no single, dramatic factor that led to the establishment of Jewish communities in the eastern borderlands of Europe.[16]

A cluster of essays explores new perspectives on anti-Jewish violence in the period 1881–1922. The most familiar form of violence against Jews in the East European borderlands is the pogrom, to which John Klier devoted considerable work. Sam Johnson's essay "Uses and Abuses: 'Pogrom' in the Anglo-American Imagination, 1881–1919," explores the changing meanings of the term "pogrom" in American and British press and literary sources. Johnson reveals how the myth of the pogrom, including the assumption that the government initiated the anti-Jewish violence—emerged and took on canonical form, persisting in the public imagination and in scholarship

---

[16] For two recent studies that interpret forced dislocation as the central factor for the development of Jewish life in Eastern Europe, see Robert Chazan, *Reassessing Jewish Life in Medieval Europe* (Cambridge, 2010), 90–106; and David D. Ruderman, *Early Modern Jewry: A New Cultural History* (Princeton, NJ, 2010), 29–33.

for decades. Building on Klier's new findings about pogrom perpetrators, Johnson corrects other misapprehensions about pogroms, particularly when the term entered the English language. She establishes a relation between the circulation of the term in the British press and a clear set of political motivations for the negative image of Russia and the tsarist government in the first decades of the 20th century.

In "Look! Up There in the Sky: It's a Vulture, It's a Bat... It's a Jew. Reflections on Antisemitism in Late Imperial Russia, 1906–1914" Robert Weinberg offers an analysis of antisemitic attitudes in the Russian press between the 1905 revolution and the beginning of World War II, drawing primarily on visual imagery. Religious and economic forms of Jew-hatred tended to be more prevalent in Russian culture than racialist views, but as Weinberg argues, the beginning of the 20th century already witnessed an inroad of racialist antisemitism. Weinberg's essay also demonstrates how Russian antisemitic ideology—in its symbolic form—crossed various geographic, cultural, and political boundaries. No matter how crude an antisemitic image may appear to be, as Weinberg shows, it relies on multiple and overlapping meanings and associations. Russian antisemitic visual images show that the boundaries among various types of antisemitism are not fixed.

Multiple factors were at work in anti-Jewish imagery and, as John Klier's work showed, in anti-Jewish violence. Oleg Budnitskii draws attention to the military nature of anti-Jewish violence during the time of the Russian Civil War in his essay, "Shots in the Back: On the Origin of Anti-Jewish Pogroms of 1918–21." Attitudes and behaviors formed and carried out by the Russian Imperial Army during World War I played a significant role in the violence that followed the Russian Revolution. During the war, the Imperial Army held the Jews in suspicion and deported hundreds of thousands to prevent acts of espionage. Violence against Jews and Jewish property had become a normal pattern before the political upheaval and social disarray of the Russian Civil War. The great war provided the training ground for the conflicting groups of the Civil War, including Whites, Reds, and the Volunteer Army, evidenced in the perpetration not only of brutal acts against Jews but also in the perpetration of the same myths about Jewish treason.

In a volume that repositions violence as a central theme in Russian-Jewish historical and cultural studies, it is fitting to reexamine its historiographical genealogy. Joshua Karlip's "Between External Persecution and National Renaissance: Simon Dubnow's Lachrymose Vision of Russian-Jewish History" shows how Dubnow's development of the lachrymose narrative fit the historian's nation-building project. The story of Russian and East European Jews offered a tragic counternarrative to the history of Jews in Western Europe, but the tragedy could be put to useful ideological purposes. Jewish suffering, as

Karlip interprets Dubnow, could lead to a national renaissance. Karlip shows how the religious/martyrological schema served Dubnow's secular goals, and how his historiography meshed with his political and cultural ideology. The expulsion of the Jews from Spain provided a particularly significant touchstone for Dubnow's interpretation of the 1891 edict expelling Jews from Moscow. Karlip finds that the popularity of Yiddish translations of 16th-century texts played a supporting role in Russian-Jewish appropriations of Spanish-Jewish history generally.

In December 1941, German troops murdered Dubnow, together with thousands of other Jews living in Riga. Scholars have largely overlooked Soviet-era representations and responses to the murder of Jews under German occupation. David Shneer's "Soviet Holocaust Photography and Landscapes of Emptiness" is one of the first explorations of this subject. Shneer shows the multiple functions of Soviet Holocaust photography as distinct from its role in the West: the photographs served to mobilize the population to fight against the enemy, and to provide forensic evidence against Nazis and their collaborators. The humanizing elements of Holocaust photojournalism in the West are often absent from Soviet-era images, because visual evidence of crimes, including Nazi crimes, was not aimed at telling a story of liberation and the end of suffering. The question of the specificity of Jewish victims is more elusive. As Shneer argues, there was a difference between the photographers' knowledge about who the victims were and the way they framed their images. Shneer raises an intriguing question about the ambiguity of the role of the spectator, thematized in photographs of local Polish inhabitants viewing the site of the Majdanek camp. He suggests that their spectatorship was a form of punishment.

For the Russian poet Boris Slutsky, World War II and the murder of the Jews was a singularly transformative experience, as Marat Grinberg shows in "Transformed Myths in Verse: Boris Slutsky's Three Holocaust Poems and the Question of Violence." The violence of the war, including specifically anti-Jewish violence, changed Slutsky's fundamental poetic method and his approach to poetic language, whose capacity to address violence falters. "I was a liberator of Ukraine," written before 1952, addresses the murder of the Yiddish language itself. "Now I often dream of Auschwitz," published in 1969, is, as Grinberg says, horrific in its rejection of horrific imagery, dreamlike in its slow pace; the poem accomplishes a prolongation of the lives of those deprived of human life even before they were physically exterminated. As Grinberg points out, "The Rabbis walked onto the plains" resonates with Soviet photojournalism depicting Nazi killing sites. The poem attempts to insert the distinctly Jewish narrative into a Russian landscape; the rabbis encounter the white blossoms of spring apples only on their way to their deaths.

In his groundbreaking *Russia Gathers Her Jews*, John Klier described a gap in Russian Jewish history, the "curious intellectual vacuum" into which prerevolutionary Russian-Jewish scholarship had fallen. At the time of the publication of his first book (1986), the work of his forerunners had not yet been subject to critical reappraisal.[17] In the intervening years, much has been done to fill in the vacuum, both in the tsarist and the Soviet periods; the "normal progression" of scholarly criticism, whose absence John lamented, has resumed an even course.[18] It is the hope of the editors that this volume of essays will contribute to the growing body of work on Jews in the East European borderlands, a field that John did so much to develop and promote.

---

[17] Klier, *Russia Gathers Her Jews*, xiii.

[18] The work of four of our contributors has recently appeared in book form. See Marat Grinberg, *"I Am to Be Read Not from Left to Right, But in Jewish: from Right to Left": The Poetics of Boris Slutsky* (Boston, 2011); Gabriella Safran, *Wandering Soul: The Dybbuk's Creator, S. An-sky* (Cambridge, MA, 2010); David Shneer, *Through Soviet Jewish Eyes: Photography, War, and the Holocaust* (New Brunswick, NJ, 2011); and Oleg Budnitskii, *Russian Jews Between the Reds and the Whites, 1917-1920* (Philadelphia, 2011).

Part 1

History, Culture, and Everyday Life

1. The Mariinsko Sergievskii Shelter for Converted Jewish Children in St. Petersburg

ChaeRan Y. Freeze

"After my arrival [at the Serafimova Women's Monastery in Arzamas (Vladimir province)], I was initially bored but then asked to help make hay [stacks] with the sisters at the home of the *matushka* [priest's wife]," wrote Vera Astaf'eva in 1869 to Nikandr Briantsev, the archpriest who directed the Mariinsko Sergievskii Shelter for Baptized Jewish Children.[1] "Little by little I have become accustomed to labor and monastery life. I am learning to sew and knit garments; I do not shun any kind of labor within my strength. I sometimes experience despair because of doubts, and sometimes for want of means. How difficult it still is for me to get used to monastery life!" The baptismal waters had done little to transform her old self into the Russian Christian woman who she desired to be; rather, the young Jewish convert struggled daily to perform a new set of scripts (i.e., different work ethics, modest dress, Russian language) at the convent that she had learned during her sojourn at the shelter.

The mission of the Mariinsko Sergievskii Shelter—which was originally founded by an English missionary, Mariia Noevna Birch, in 1864—was to serve as a "parental home" (Rus. *roditel'skii dom*) where converted Jewish children could receive a proper upbringing "in the spirit of Russian Orthodoxy and Russian life."[2] The goal was to prepare the converts for further education or to take up artisanal trades when they came of age, depending on their gender

---

[1] Tsentral'nyi gosudarstvennyi istoricheskii arkhiv, Sankt-Peterburga (TsGIA SPb), which was previously the Leningrad Oblast Archive, f. 542, op. 1, gg. 1869–1875, d. 16, ll. 1–58. The official name of the shelter was the Mariinsko Sergievskii Shelter for Jewish Children Who Are Preparing for or Have Converted to the Russian Orthodox Faith. For more on Jewish conversion, see John D. Klier, "State Policies and the Conversion of Jews in Imperial Russia," in *Of Religion and Empire: Missions, Conversion, and Tolerance in Tsarist Russia*, ed. Robert P. Geraci and Michael Khodarkovsky (Ithaca, NY, 2001), 92–115; Michael Stanislawski, "Jewish Apostasy in Russia: A Tentative Typology," in *Jewish Apostasy in the Modern World*, ed. Todd Endelman (New York, 1987), 193; ChaeRan Y. Freeze, "When Chava Left Home: Gender, Conversion, and the Jewish Family in Tsarist Russia," *Polin: Jewish Women in Eastern Europe* 18 (2005): 153–88; and Ellie Shainker, "Imperial Hybrids: Russian Jewish Converts in the Nineteenth Century" (Ph.D. diss., University of Pennsylvania, 2010).

[2] Rossiiskii gosudarstvennyi istoricheskii arkhiv (RGIA), f. 768, op. 3, d. 46, l. 2.

and talents. Reflecting imperial discourse on Jews as well as religious zeal, the shelter's staff and patrons sought to remake Jewish converts into useful Russian citizens, not simply faithful Christians, and thereby facilitate their integration into Russian society. This reeducation invariably underlined the converts' "differences"—poor hygiene, negative character traits (insincerity, greed, a sense of entitlement), and ties to troublesome Jewish relatives. Through reeducation, the shelter produced a "reformed, recognizable Other," who was "almost the same but not quite" (to borrow Homi Bhabha's words), invariably creating ambivalence, even suspicions, toward the Jewish convert.[3] To prove their sincerity, some graduates of the shelter denounced fellow converts who had fallen away from the Christian faith or penned zealous articles calling for the conversion of their former coreligionists. Embedded in these texts, however, was not abject submission, but a subtle challenge to the superiority of "native-born" Christians—after all, had Christ not come first to the "lost sheep of Israel"? To understand the relationship between the shelter and the converts, this chapter examines the shelter's assumed role as a "parental home" (which aimed to transform its wards into "useful members of the great Russian family"), the gendered projects of education and productivization, and the profile of the converts and their parents.

The Mariinsko Sergievskii Shelter as a Parental Home

The shelter's image as a "parental home" enabled both the converts and the staff to justify their relationship to the children. Converts who deposited their children at the shelter to acquire education or vocational training could rationalize that they were leaving their young with a good Christian "family." In fact, one founding narrative of the shelter, published in the Russian Orthodox journal *Strannik* (*The Pilgrim*), attributed its very origins to a convert's need for a substitute home.[4] When P. D. Dzagiler, a former Jewish schoolteacher in Minsk, discovered that he could not bring up his son at the St. Petersburg Ecclesiastical Seminary in 1864, he turned to Mariia Birch of the St. Petersburg Missionary Society.[5] She rented a small apartment and hired

---

[3] For more on postcolonial theories of Homi Bhabha and Russian-Jewish history, see Harriet Murav, *Identity Theft: The Jew in Imperial Russia and the Case of Avraam Uri Kovner* (Stanford, CA, 2003).

[4] Like Yaakov Brafman, a Jewish convert who wrote the judeophobic *Book of the Kahal* (1869), the author offered sharp criticisms of Jewish burial societies, the Talmud, and the stubbornness of the Jews. See "Chastnyi priiut v S. Peterburg dlia prisoedniamykh v pravoslavnoi Tserkvi evreev," *Strannik* (July 1870): 54–76.

[5] Dzagiler was admitted to the seminary prior to the reforms of 1867 and 1869, when the church opened up the St. Petersburg Ecclesiastical Seminary to nonclergy children. See

1. The Mariinsko Sergievskii Shelter for Converted Jewish Children in St. Petersburg

a caretaker for the sons of converted seminary students.[6] The following year, two philanthropists from Moscow "from the highest circles of Russian society" paid their expenses. While lauding the generosity of these donors, the author of *Strannik* criticized the St. Petersburg Missionary Society for its apparent indifference to the fate of the boys when the funds for their support ran out. Citing the Psalms, he declared faith in God's unwavering commitment even if others abandoned the Christian mission: "However, *if my father and mother forsake me* [Psalms 27:10], God said to his true firstborn Israel, *I will not leave you*. God did not abandon these innocent children, the true new Israelites and others like them who have come to Christ." In the author's eyes, the establishment of a permanent shelter was a sign of God's solicitous care of His true children. The author's deliberate use of the words "true" and "firstborn" contested the triumphalist Christian claim to have superseded the Jews as the chosen people. In this sense, the shelter was not just a physical place but a refuge (as the Russian term *priut* signified) sanctioned by God, a temporary sanctuary to help converts transition into their new life.

Under the guidance of Father Briantsev, the shelter developed from a transitory apartment into a permanent home at the corner of Baseinaia Street (in Liteinyi district). The shelter's daily regimen aimed at transforming converts into humble Russian Orthodox Christians. Much to the frustration of the staff, however, one scandal followed another, which they took as a sign of the converts' ingrained Jewish values. Vera Golubeva, who was in charge of the children's maintenance, expressed solicitous concern for her wards but waxed indignant at their parents, who complained about the food or seemed ungrateful. She wrote to Father Briantsev in a daily memo:

> I ask you to issue a strict reprimand to Lipska [Averbakh], whose impertinence is beyond measure. She complains about the poor care of her children, imagining what they will be when they grow up, and desires that they be fed rolls and tea. She allegedly had a stomachache from the milk at Sergei's. But the doctor was here today, examined all the children, and found nothing that resembled pain. Today after Lipska's outcry, all the children at tea refused milk on the grounds that they would have stomachaches and [claimed] that you would allow them to drink tea instead of milk like the Averbakhs.[7]

Another issue was the gap between the nutritional needs of children and church rules on fast days. In August 1870, for instance, Dr. Pavel Bakinovskii

---

Gregory Freeze, *The Parish Clergy in Nineteenth-Century Russia: Crisis, Reform, Counter-Reform* (Princeton, NJ, 1983), 319–29.
[6] *Strannik* (1870): 70; TsGIA Spb, f. 768, op. 3, d. 46, l. 1–1 ob.
[7] TsGIA SPb, f. 524, op. 3, d. 4 (1870–1878), ll. 1–28.

visited the shelter to examine the health of the children, voiced horror over the poor diet of the sick ones, and advised Father Briantsev to provide "more nutritious food, which can be modest." The latter immediately sent a petition to Mikhail Nikolaevich Chelishchev, a member of the Imperial Philanthropy Society: "Your Excellency, would it be possible to permit foods forbidden during fasts [i.e., meat and milk products] as the doctor so reasonably desires? In his opinion, the sick children absolutely need to be allowed to have a meat diet for their recovery." His request met with a sharp reproof from Chelishchev, who reprimanded Father Briantsev for placing the physical needs of his wards before their spiritual responsibilities: "I do not dare to take it upon myself to answer before God for permitting such foods during a fast." It was all the more incumbent on the shelter, which serviced Jewish converts, to observe the fasts of the Russian Orthodox Church in order to set the proper example. Chelishchev, citing the words of the apostle Paul that "every person ... is renewed internally," administered this warning to Father Briantsev:

> If one worries only about the body—without extreme necessity— and permits deviation from the teachings of Christianity that is detrimental to the soul, then the purpose of the shelter will not be achieved, neither during the ward's sojourn at the shelter, nor especially in the future. They will not forget the indulgence of the people on whom rested the duty not to allow them [to eat foods forbidden during fasts]. Permission for meat and even milk products will lead to doubts among the devout benefactors of the shelter, and perhaps the shelter will lose them. *However, for the dangerously ill*, perhaps a diet of [forbidden] foods will be tolerated during the fast in accordance with the demand of the doctor.[8]

The final clause left a small window for Father Briantsev to act, but with great circumspection for fear of alienating his pious patrons. One member of the Imperial Philanthropy Society cautioned: "I hope that the pious benefactress,[9] who insistently demands the observance of fasts, will understand the importance of the reason for the present order." With the assistance of a medical expert, Father Briantsev calculated that the shelter needed to order ten pounds of meat for the week. "Every day, we are to add to this a few pounds, approximately five, in order to restore the health of the children at the shelter who are *by nature sickly*" (emphasis added). He noted

---

[8] TsGIA SPb, f. 542, op. 1, d. 22, gg. 1870–1874, ll. 1–21.
[9] Menandr Semenovich Sushinskii may have been referring to Empress Maria Aleksandrovna Romanova, the shelter's royal patron.

1. The Mariinsko Sergievskii Shelter for Converted Jewish Children in St. Petersburg

that the additional quantity of meat would also help to "prevent whooping cough which is now appearing among children in the city."[10]

The image of "sickly" Jewish children regularly surfaced at every physical exam of incoming wards. A typical evaluation by Dr. Bakinovskii read: "Most honorable Fr. Nikandr Ivanovich. I was at the shelter yesterday and examined one girl, Mariia Gutman, 16 or 17 years old. It was impossible to make a positive conclusion about her condition. She complains about a headache and general weakness." To be sure, the doctor did find a few exceptional children who came with a clean bill of health. For instance, after his examination of Ruman Kan's son, Dr. Bakinovskii wrote: "[The] son of the retired Jewish soldier Ruman Kan is ten years of age, of good build with a properly developed chest and other parts of the body ... In general, he has not been exposed to any illness or symptoms." Indeed, the shelter's mission was not only to save the souls of Jewish children but also to transform them into healthy able-bodied Russians, who could engage in productive labor or enroll in an educational institution. To this end, the staff had to pay close attention not only to proper nutrition but also to their wards' hygiene. When Mariia and Elizaveta Iakobson came to the shelter, for instance, the doctor found that "as a result of scrofula [*zolotykhi*], they have many matured embryos of insects (lice) on them." He gave the staff instructions on "how to remove them gradually and to destroy them completely."[11]

As in any extended "family," the shelter came complete with its black sheep—the drunken overseer (*diad'ka*). When Vera Golubova could no longer tolerate his behavior, she "humbly" demanded that Father Briantsev fire the overseer immediately:

> [He] has drunk himself into oblivion three times after his recovery from cholera and has been missing from the institution for entire days at a time. Today, he excused himself again on business from 10:00 to 12:00. By 1:00, he had returned and then immediately disappeared again to some unknown place. Here it is already 6:00 PM. I do not know what to do with this person. For God's sake, if it is possible, obtain a noncommissioned officer who is recommended by a doctor as the manager; do not give in to generosity, and dismiss Perovskii from his duties since there is absolutely no possibility of reform.[12]

Briantsev heeded Golubova's demands and hired a new overseer, the converted Jew and noncommissioned officer Matvei Trotskii, who pleased his

---

[10] TsGIA SPb, f. 542, op. 1, d. 22, gg. 1870–1874, l. 20.
[11] Ibid.
[12] Ibid., d. 55, gg. 1872–1874, ll. 1–16.

employer with "his good morality, irreproachable behavior, and conscientious fulfillment of his responsibilities."[13]

In 1870, the shelter came under the patronage of Empress Maria Aleksandrovna Romanova, Grand Duke Sergei Aleksandrovich, and the Imperial Philanthropy Society—elevating the metaphor of the "parental home" to new heights. Just as foundling homes established by the imperial court "stood as an expression of concern . . . by the mother of the fatherland" for her children, so too did the shelter symbolize the imperial family's beneficence for Jewish converts.[14] The regular allocation of funds to the shelter represented a symbolic connection between the imperial family (more specifically, the "most august mother," as the empress was called in the correspondence) and Russia's new Christians. While imperial patronage gave the shelter greater visibility and resources, it also brought the shelter under greater bureaucratic control. As one official report of the Imperial Philanthropic Society put it, until now, the shelter did not have "any official significance."[15] For the first time, the society drew up an official charter that defined the shelter's specific mission. As David Ransel has pointed out, the government regularly published the charters of institutions such as foundling homes and even translated them into foreign languages to "advertise [its] enlightened policies."[16] While the original intent of the shelter was to service Jewish converts, the new statutes included "both Jews and Russians . . . especially the children of fallen and injured soldiers." While Father Briantsev was still alive, the majority of the wards were of Jewish origins; after his death in 1887, however, the shelter ceased to give special preference to Jewish converts. In fact, a brochure about the shelter published in 1892 completely omitted any ethnic distinctions: "The purpose of the shelter is to provide charity and education for children of both sexes from ages 7 to 12, with preference for orphans and children of poor parents of the Russian Orthodox confession without distinction of rank or status."[17] The list of wards suggests that the shelter began to accept more Russian children than Jewish converts. For instance, in 1894, out of eighteen boys, only four had identifiable Jewish surnames; of the twenty-three girls, only three had possible Jewish surnames.[18]

The 1870 charter adopted strict rules regarding legal documentation, which placed the shelter under the surveillance of the state. Specifically,

---

[13] Ibid.
[14] David Ransel, *Mothers of Misery: Child Abandonment in Russia* (Princeton, NJ, 1988), 50–51.
[15] TsGIA SPb, f. 768, op. 3, d. 46, l. 2 ob.
[16] Ransel, *Mothers of Misery*, 51.
[17] TsGIA SPb, f. 542, op. 1, d. 833, g. 1892.
[18] TsGIA SPb, f. 542, op. 1, d. 835, gg. 1893–1894, ll. 100–101 ob. These children's Jewish backgrounds are discussed in another file (d. 834, ll. 22–24, 73–74).

anyone seeking conversion or assistance from the shelter had to present the following documents: "a passport or other document of residency, a metrical certificate of birth, and a certificate attesting that the petitioner is preparing to adopt the Orthodox faith." Those already baptized in the Orthodox faith needed to present a passport or other residence permit, as well as a certificate of conversion. Jews who did not enjoy the right of residency in the empire's capital were to obtain a proper passport to cover the duration of the time required to prepare for holy baptism, "through the intercession of the shelter's committee or the local police chief."

The thorniest legal issues arose when Jewish women showed up in St. Petersburg without a proper passport or parental consent to convert as explicitly required by Russian law. One sensational case involved Gita Taube Zil′bershtein, who appeared at the shelter in 1869 on someone else's passport, a document belonging to a soldier's wife, Gitlia Abelevaia Ozerova. Zil′bershtein was illiterate and had no inkling that the passport listed Ozerova as residing in a Vilna brothel. When the priest preparing Zil′bershtein for conversion asked whether she intended to remain in her "previous unworthy way of life," she did not understand what he meant. The priest took her denials and confusion as a sign of her "extreme, irrevocable moral decay and inordinate shamelessness." Zil′bershtein managed to maintain her false identity despite the stigma of prostitution until a former teacher (a Jewish convert) of the State Rabbinical School of Vilna at the shelter recognized her. Only then did she admit the truth: "Desiring to adopt the Russian Orthodox faith, based on the example of my aunt who was baptized a long time ago and lives in St. Petersburg, and being convinced that my father would prevent me from doing this, I decided to run away from Vilna to St. Petersburg." She had obtained the passport from a *faktorka* (broker) in Vilna and had come secretly to the capital. Despite efforts by the shelter to intercede, state authorities arrested Zil′bershtein and sent her to prison for traveling illegally on someone else's passport.[19]

Whereas Father Briantsev had decided whom to accept into the shelter, the new statutes required the approval of the "shelter's committee with confirmation of the most august patron of the shelter [Grand Duke Sergei Aleksandrovich Romanov]." Official stationery, regular meetings of the committee, and a chain of command from the imperial family down to the servants transformed the shelter from a grassroots organization that assisted converted Jews into a modern philanthropic institution under the gaze of the state.

---

[19] *Strannik* (September 1870): 195. The journal offers no information about her fate after completion of her prison term.

The Shelter as a School

The shelter represented more than a parental home for baptized Jewish children; it was also a classroom where teachers inculcated knowledge about the Russian Orthodox Church, modernity, and productive citizenship. A few zealous converts also expressed their hope that the shelter would prove that the conversion of the Jews was not a lost cause, a sentiment found in both official documents and popular writings.[20] The education of new converts at the shelter consisted of two components: religious classes and vocational training in a skilled trade. According to *Strannik*, Christians often berated Jewish converts for their lack of conviction in their new faith and even accused some of continuing to observe their old Jewish ways. "It is even sadder," the author remarked chidingly, "that converts return to the faith of their fathers, eliciting from Christians nothing more than cold indifference—not the love that constitutes the essence of Christianity." To counter charges of insincerity and to prevent a return to Judaism, the author urged the shelter to provide its wards with a proper "religious-moral education." Four Russian Orthodox seminary graduates, P. D. Dzagiler (a Jewish convert), P. I. Kedrov, and V. Sol'skii (a priest at the Khristorozhdestvenskaia Church in St. Petersburg) devoted themselves to providing instruction in the faith (*zakon Bozhii*) and liturgy. Until 1868, the ordained monk and Jewish convert O. Veniamin helped Father Briantsev perform daily services at the shelter. Before he returned to his monastery, Veniamin conducted an all-night vigil and public service that accompanied the conversion of the wards. He expressed a sense of deep emotional kinship to these Jewish converts, which went beyond their new spiritual ties:

> I was moved to tears upon seeing the wards of the shelter perform and hear the Psalms and prayers with such emotion, with such sincere feeling . . . I could not hold back the tears as I gazed upon these fortunate ones, who were radiant. I have always grieved on finding my fellow brothers, who are so dear to my heart by nature and habit, but who are lost and ignorant of the truth. Thus it is with great emotion that I rejoiced at last upon seeing that the path [to salvation] is now before them, and the gates of salvation are open. I shed tears of happiness with them and prayed together for the further success of the shelter.[21]

In addition to teaching the children to say daily prayers and attend church services, the shelter sought to instill a deep sense of morality, especially for

---

[20] For instance, see RGIA, f. 796, op. 121, g. 1840, d. 601, ll. 13–76.
[21] *Strannik* (September 1870): 190.

wards with "bad parents," ensuring that they would turn into "honest and useful members of society."[22] According to *Strannik*, the shelter provided moral education for Jewish children who had been baptized under its auspices but no longer resided there.[23]

The shelter's curriculum not only included classes on religion and Church Slavonic (so that children could read the prayers) but also emphasized good citizenship and other worldly skills. Children studied the Russian language, reading, handwriting, arithmetic, singing, and gymnastics. Girls also learned needlework.[24] The goal was to place graduates (eleven-year-old boys and twelve-year-old girls) of the shelter in educational institutions that were commensurate with their abilities and ascribed gendered interests. For instance, by 1870, the shelter had placed three students on state stipends at the Lisin Forestry School in St. Petersburg. The Gur´ev children, who showed greater intellectual promise, received an elite gymnasium education: Nikolai at the St. Petersburg Gymnasium no. 3 and his sister Ekaterina at the Institute of Princess Ol´denburgskaia—both recipients of stipends from Her Imperial Majesty, Grand Duchess Aleksandra Petrovna. Others studied at specialized institutions: Lina Zetel enrolled in a midwifery institute on a stipend provided by the shelter, while Petr Lipkin matriculated at the Medical-Surgical Academy.[25] In 1887, the shelter also succeeded placing its wards at a St. Petersburg elementary diocesan school, the Trade School of Tsarevich Nicholas, and the music school of the Eighth Naval Company.

The shelter also found jobs and apprenticeships for children who showed no aptitude for formal study. There was no shortage of wealthy families in St. Petersburg who needed domestic servants and could perform a charitable deed by hiring a ward from the shelter. Sof´ia Iablonskaia wrote to Father Briantsev in 1869: "They told me that a young boy at your shelter, Pavel [Soganovich] desires to enter service as a servant. I am prepared to take him on probation."[26] Iablonskaia inquired whether they had succeeded in placing "poor Ritvo" in the service of Aleksandr Pavlovich Rep´er, the preceptor at the Kazan Theological Seminary. "He wanted to offer [Soganovich] work, if only temporarily," she reminded Father Briantsev and wished him "complete success in your apostolic deeds."[27]

Apprenticeships, however, did not always work out. Problems occurred in the case of Anna Gotz and her employer, the noblewoman Kaspara

---

[22] Ibid., 192.
[23] Ibid.
[24] TsGIA SPb, f. 542, op. 1, d. 833, g. 1892.
[25] Ibid., 196.
[26] TsGIA SPb, f. 542, op. 1, d. 2, g. 1869, l. 1.
[27] Ibid.

Kimbarova, whose husband acted as a patron of the shelter. In the summer of 1879, Kimbarova (who owned a seamstressing workshop) inquired about the possibility of hiring one of the shelter's wards on her graduation: "I agree to take her into my shop with the responsibility of maintaining her on full support and to teach her to sew underclothes for men, women, and children. Moreover, based on the provisions of a six-year-term, I will give her a diploma with the rank of artisan through the artisanal board on the completion of the term." The shelter drew up a formal contract that spelled out the moral and financial obligations of both sides. During her apprenticeship, Anna Gotz was to be "totally obedient" and occupy herself diligently to her work. The shelter expected her "to conduct herself decently and honestly, to fulfill strictly the rules and rites of the Orthodox Church, and no less than once a year to make confession and take communion primarily during Lent." For her part, Kimbarova was obliged to teach Gotz the seamstressing trade with a specialization in making underclothes by both hand and machine. She also promised to provide the child with "satisfying, substantial, and healthy food," and "decent clothes and shoes that correspond with the time of year." In the event that Gotz fell ill, Kimbarova was to treat her at home at her own expense or to send her to a public hospital. Most important, the employer was "to supervise the moral behavior of the girl, inspiring her to good behavior and conscientiousness at every opportune chance through example and advice." She was not "to tolerate reprehensible conduct." In the event that Gotz strayed from the Christian path through some serious misdeed, Kimbarova was to bring it to the attention of the shelter's committee so that it could "rectify the morality of the above-mentioned girl." At the end of the five-year term, Kimbarova was to grant Gotz a diploma of apprenticeship or twenty-five rubles, as well as a set of new clothes and shoes.[28]

Barely four months passed before Kimbarova returned Gotz to the shelter. She had nothing but bitter complaints about the girl: "On 16 June 1879 the twelve-year-old Anna Gotz was brought to me from the shelter to learn the seamstresses' trade. However, as it turns out, she—Anna Gotz—is sickly and has to be treated quite often at the children's hospital of Prof. Ol′denburgskii, where they performed an operation on the ear (polyps)." As if poor health were not enough, the girl had a poor work ethic ("she constantly needs to take breaks and has become more of a burden for me"). Kimbarova declared that she could find nothing in her personality that showed any promise: "In addition, Anna Gotz is a stubborn, disobedient girl and, more important, does not have the slightest aptitude for needlework. That is why I humbly ask

---

[28] TsGIA SPb, f. 542, op. 1, d. 131, gg. 1873–1879, ll. 1–9.

1. The Mariinsko Sergievskii Shelter for Converted Jewish Children in St. Petersburg

the shelter's committee to free me from the contracted terms and take Anna Gotz from me."[29]

The shelter also placed male wards in a wide range of "useful occupations" (*poleznye zaniatiia*) that could facilitate their integration into Russian society. In the 1870s, for example, Andrei Portukh and Mikhail Konevskii embarked on promising careers in the military. Others found jobs in Russia's rapidly expanding railway system. A few, such as Nikolai Bekker and Grigorii Ritvo, took up professions that had been closed to them as Jews: the former as a clerk in the State Senate, and the latter as a policeman.[30] In many respects, the shelter functioned as a halfway house and school linking the Jewish and Christian worlds in the Russian Empire. It treated the education and placement of its wards with utmost seriousness. As one article in *Strannik* claimed, the shelter never let its wards go into the world "without providing for their future." At the very least, it provided basic gendered skills—for example, sewing for women and text copying for men. In this way, "all those who receive charity made up one common family in which every member labors for the common good as best as possible."[31]

Profiles of the Wards and Their Parents

Jews who turned to the Mariinsko Sergievskii Shelter for assistance fit into four main categories: (1) impoverished families (mainly retired Jewish soldiers or artisans) who sought to unburden themselves of children they could no longer support; (2) parents who needed child care while they pursued a higher education; (3) parents seeking to provide their children with a free Russian education; and (4) students who had been baptized at the shelter and had received financial assistance for a higher education but no longer resided there. In the first three cases, the majority of parents had converted to Christianity or were preparing to do so. A few, however, refused to convert after they availed themselves of the shelter's assistance—much to the dismay and indignation of its staff and benefactors. The extant financial records show that the shelter housed no more than fifty wards in any given year. In 1887, for example, twenty-three boys and twenty-one girls resided there full time (even though Father Briantsev had baptized seventy-eight children that year); in 1892, the shelter had housed twenty-five boys and twenty-one girls.[32] The transition of these Jewish converts to the Christian world took place

---

[29] Ibid.
[30] *Strannik* (September 1870): 197.
[31] Ibid.
[32] TsGIA SPb, f. 542, op. 3, d. 1, g. 1888, ll. 1–2; f. 542, op. 3, d. 833, g. 1892.

amid constant reminders of their Jewish past; to qualify for charity (as most inevitably did), the wards needed to emphasize to their patrons that they were indeed Jews who had been baptized at the shelter. Moreover, in accordance with imperial law, they could change their given names but had to retain their Jewish surnames, which inevitably marked them as "Other" even as the shelter sought to promote their assimilation into Russian society.[33]

Petitioners usually cited poverty as the reason for seeking assistance from the shelter. In a letter dated 8 August 1873, Pelageia Ivanovna Gots cited her inability to support her child: "After the death of my husband this past 21 July, I have been left with my daughter Anna, who is seven years old, without any means to live. That is why I take the liberty to appeal to the committee of the shelter ... to assign my daughter a place at the aforementioned shelter at the state's expense."[34] Father Briantsev related the plight of another widow of a retired Jewish soldier, Vasil´evna Kan, who requested the baptism of her son Ruman because she could not afford to keep him at a Jewish shelter: "The documents about the ten-year-old boy, who has studied up till now in a Jewish shelter, have been delivered to me. The widow Kan herself works at a factory for a wage of 35 kopecks a day. Having removed her son from the Jewish shelter, she finds it impossible to keep him with her for a single day."[35] Similarly, Ivan Semenovich Shimanovich, a retired noncommissioned officer, applied in 1880 with the hope of giving his children, Nikolai (eight years old) and Anastasiia (six years old), a "warm corner" (*teplyi ugol*) and a proper education that he was not in the position to provide.[36]

Some impoverished families had already converted to the Christian faith, albeit of a different confession, and now sought to convert their children to Orthodoxy in order to qualify for material assistance. Thus in 1872, Iulius Kan inquired whether the shelter would be willing to take two of his eight children (a six-year-old son Vladimir and twelve-year-old daughter Elizaveta) into its care.[37] While Kan and his wife chose to remain Lutheran for the present (because "it facilitates my work"), the parents wanted the two children to be raised in the Orthodox faith. With the understanding that the parents would convert in the future, Father Briantsev decided to accept the son, Vladimir.

---

[33] On the Jewish surnames of converts, see RGIA, f. 1412, op. 1, g. 1905, d. 208, ll. 1–37 ob.; Andrew M. Verner, "What Is in a Name? Of Dog-Killers, Jews, and Rasputin," *Slavic Review* 53, 4 (1994): 1046–1070; and Eugene Avrutin, "Racial Categories and the Politics of (Jewish) Difference in Late Imperial Russia," *Kritika: Explorations in Russian and Eurasian History* 8, 1 (2007): 13–40.
[34] TsGIA SPb, f. 542, op. 1, d. 131, gg. 1873–1879, ll. 1–9.
[35] TsGIA SPb, f. 542, op. 1, d. 57, g. 1873, ll. 3–6.
[36] TsGIA SPb, f. 542, op. 1, d. 514, g. 1880, l. 1–1 ob.
[37] TsGIA SPb, f. 542, op. 1, d. 57, gg. 1872–1879, ll. 1–11.

1. The Mariinsko Sergievskii Shelter for Converted Jewish Children in St. Petersburg

Considering "the numerous members of the Kan family," he wrote, "I believe it would be unfair to deny him charity."

In some cases, neighbors or even strangers brought the plight of a converted Jewish family to the attention of the shelter. In 1884, Natal'ia Mikhailovna Glotovaia asked Father Briantsev to extend Christian charity to the "unhappy family of the artisan Pavlov [Rybakov]," who were "strangers" to her but whose extreme poverty was well known to everyone:

> The Rybakov family lives in a tiny, wretched shack that affords protection from neither the cold nor rain. The young children, from ages 1.5 to 14, barefoot and almost naked, frequently sit hungry because the eternally drunk father hauls off everything to the tavern, even the last shirt from the shoulders of his own children. The oldest daughter (age 18), who suffers from an eye [disease], and the ailing mother, burdened with five minor children, are in no condition to feed the starving family by their own toil. In general, hunger, cold, and filth are the conditions in which the family lives. I hope that the guilt of the father will not be transferred to his innocent children. I earnestly beseech you to take if only one of the unfortunate Rybakov sons from this alarming, ever more destructive situation: do accept the young Fedor (eight years old) at the Shelter for Baptized Jewish Children.

An investigation found that the Rybakovs, with six children, were indeed destitute artisans living in a small room that the father was renting for six rubles a month. There was nothing in their cramped quarters (2.3 square meters [1.5 square sazhen] for all eight people) except for "a locksmith's bench made of three boards, which in all likelihood serves as a bed for the children, night lights (but not lamps) by which they work, small stools, a table, and bed on which two small blankets are barely noticeable." The investigator recommended that the shelter, as soon as vacancies appeared, accept two children: Vasilii, who was to turn nine years old on 22 September; and Mariia, four years old. The remaining children did not qualify due to their age, being either too young or over eleven.[38]

Although the shelter's staff and its benefactors were usually sympathetic to tales of poverty, some expressed annoyance in their daily interaction with Jewish converts, whom they found troublesome and importunate. A certain Polisadov, who was assisting Father Briantsev to find appropriate godfathers for prospective converts, described his frustrations in a letter on 7 August 1868: "The petitioner Liubova Ivanovna Gol'dinger earnestly asks me to intercede with you to allow her to find refuge for a short time at your shelter.

---

[38] TsGIA SPb, f. 542, op. 3, d. 8, gg. 1884–1886, ll. 1–9.

Fulfill her petition along with the attached request. These Jews are a lot of trouble. You sense this, of course; and to be honest, I have experienced this 'pleasure.'[39] Gol´dinger's son should have been baptized a long time ago, but I have not been able to come across a good godfather."[40] Significantly, even though Gol´dinger had converted, Polisadov nonetheless refers to her as a troublesome "Jew."

Still more problematic were Jews who obtained charity from the shelter based on their declared intent to convert but then reneged on their promise. One such case even ended up in court. In 1868, Father Briantsev informed the procurator of the St. Petersburg Court that Illarion Sergeevich Snipishinskii, who had lived at the shelter for a month while preparing for holy baptism, had begged for funds to make a trip with his eight-year-old daughter Shifra to Vilna so that she could convert there to Orthodoxy. However, she returned unbaptized and lived at the shelter's expense for another month. In the meantime, Father Briantsev had invited Princess Ekaterina Alekseevna Vasil´chikova and her son to serve as her godparents. Snipishinskii suddenly announced to the shelter that he had reconsidered the promise to convert his daughter. In Father Briantsev's view, this change of heart was either due to the "threats of his parents or the seduction of money that an unconverted Jew have given him to leave his daughter a Jew." To add insult to injury, Father Briantsev reported that Snipishinskii "facilitated her escape from the shelter, handing her over to the Jews," and attacked Madame Sheremet´eva's apartment with some Jewish coconspirators, allegedly for the purpose of abducting another girl, Vita Davidova. He asked the court to try Snipishinskii for "profaning the Orthodox faith" by expressing a desire to convert with his daughter and then reneging on his promise, deceiving the shelter to receive "charitable resources," and participating in a physical assault on the shelter with the intent to kidnap two potential converts. While the file does not indicate whether Father Briantsev recovered the money that he had "squandered on Snipishinskii and his daughter," he clearly portrayed the deception as a "Jewish" act, even though it had been committed by a Christian.

Letters from the godparents of Jewish converts also express "fatigue" over financial burdens they had assumed. The correspondence between Nikandr Briantsev and Aleksandr Petrovich, for instance, reveals that the latter accepted responsibility for a Jewish girl, Vitka, who was renamed Mariia Davidovich at her baptism in 1868. The letters indicate that she suffered from poor health and had to be hospitalized on multiple occasions. By 1871, the girl had a new

---

[39] I have added the single quotation marks to reflect Polisadov's exasperation and obvious sarcasm.
[40] TsGIA SPb, f. 542, op. 2, d. 2, gg. 1867–1868, ll. 1–10.

guardian, A. Kuznetsova, who seized on her relocation to ask Father Briantsev to take Davidovich back into his custody: "I will be leaving St. Petersburg shortly [and] can no longer take care of Davidovich. She would be left without supervision and without a place—in a word left to the mercy of fate. When I lived in St. Petersburg, I did everything possible for her; I gave her shelter, paid money for her, and in general, took care of her for more than two years. But now with my departure from St. Petersburg, I do not have anyone to leave her with here. She would be left on her own if you refuse assistance."[41] In the case of Vera Astaf'eva, a novice at the Serafimova Women's Monastery, Father Briantsev intervened when her godfather refused to provide support: "Now, in particular, she is in need of assistance because she has not had a single kopeck for quite a while for bread [and] tea, let alone for obtaining clothes for herself. Astaf'eva's godfather has not turned out to be any help to her. I have the honor to request the committee of the shelter to send a certain sum to Astaf'eva."

As the shelter's files indicate, Father Briantsev responded generously to financial requests from the children whom he had baptized. In a few cases, however, he admonished those who he believed had taken advantage of the charity of godparents and other patrons, as in the case of Ivan Bassevich, a student at the Imperial Medical-Surgical Academy. In August 1869, Bassevich informed Father Briantsev that he regularly received a monthly stipend of eight rubles from his godmother Maria Aleksandrovna Kruzenshtern and another ten rubles from his godfather Musin-Pushkin. The former had entrusted him with twenty-four rubles until September, while the latter went off to his estates, advising him to live on this money until he returned in the fall. However, his godfather fell ill at his estates and left straight for the Carlsbad spas, forgetting "of course, that there is a student in St. Petersburg who is in need of his stipend. Thus I have lived from 1 July without a kopeck." When he turned to Mariia Aleksandrovna for assistance, she explained that she could not help at this time but advised him to visit Vasilii Ivanovich Ovchinnikov, who had access to Count A. P. Tolstoi's fund for converted Jews at the shelter. All Bassevich needed was written permission from Father Briantsev to receive the requested sum. In the most pitiable tone, Bassevich implored the archpriest to approve the twenty-five rubles, which would spare him the landlady's daily harassment for his delinquent rent payments (for she "does not give me peace") and allow him to fix his boots, which had completely fallen apart: "Father, dear, do not refuse me charity. You need only to write to Vasilii Ivanovich; he, in his own words, will give out [the money] with pleasure."[42] He signed his name, "the converted Jew, the student Bassevich," as though to remind Father Briantsev

---

[41] In the final resolution of the case, Vitka Davidovich was placed in the care of Anna Ivanovna.
[42] TsGIA SPb, f. 542, op. 1, d. 9, gg. 1869–1875, ll. 1–2 ob.

of his humble origins and the promise of what he could become as a Christian; this appellation also served a constant reminder that he was indeed "almost but not quite" like native-born Christians.

While the archival file does not indicate the outcome of this petition, it shows that Bassevich's next request for money (in 1873) met with a cold rebuff from Father Briantsev, who had, in the interim, learned that his ward had not been entirely truthful. Bassevich openly admitted his guilt before his spiritual mentor:

> I found out from Maria Aleksandrovna Kruzenshtern that you were very displeased with me for requesting your intercession before Sushkin. I did not tell you candidly that I receive 15 rubles a month from the heiress Mariia Aleksandrovna. I would have liked to set out to your place to ask your forgiveness; however, I knew that you were very busy with [your] service during the fast and I have no spare time on account of exams; I preferred to explain the matter to you better through writing. Allow me first to ask your forgiveness for my dishonest deed.[43]

At the same time, Bassevich appealed to Father Briantsev's tolerance for the weaknesses "inherent" in Jewish converts: "Turn your gracious pastoral attention to these circumstances." He proceeded to explain that "obviously it was impossible to live" on the fifteen rubles that his godmother's brother, A. A. Stakovich, provided each month: eight rubles went to pay the rent for his room, and seven rubles for his board, tea, sugar, laundering linens, and other expenses. That is why he kept this sum secret and sought supplemental assistance from the shelter. "I would have liked to confess to you before and ask forgiveness, but somehow I have put it off from day to day," Bassevich repented. "Forgive me, kindest father archpriest; indigence forced me to act so." He quickly added that he hoped that the error on his part would not prevent the shelter from continuing to grant him a monthly stipend, as he had only five more courses left before he completed his studies.[44] In this case, the shelter's patrons denied his request, citing the lack of honesty toward his benefactors.[45] Only when Bassevich completed his course at the Imperial Medical-Surgical Academy with the rank of physician did the shelter come to his aid again. Until he found employment, he was to receive eighty rubles: forty from the shelter and forty from the personal funds of Grand Duke Sergei Aleksandrovich Romanov. His patrons were willing to overlook his previous

---

[43] Ibid., ll. 7–8.
[44] Ibid.
[45] Ibid., l. 13.

1. The Mariinsko Sergievskii Shelter for Converted Jewish Children in St. Petersburg

financial misdeeds and to reward his academic accomplishments, which represented a fulfillment of the shelter's mission.

The second category of Jews who turned to the shelter were those who sought to pursue a higher education in St. Petersburg but had nowhere to place their children. As mentioned above, the need for child care was the main impetus for creating the shelter in the first place. The shelter was an especially attractive option for Jewish women like Ernestine Shlomovich of Riga, who had to navigate their way through a new city alone. In correspondence with Father Briantsev, she vouchsafed her sincere desire to convert to Russian Orthodoxy and to study midwifery, confident that she possessed a "clear intellect about everything that I undertake." Yet she was not entirely candid about her real family circumstances, as Briantsev learned from Nikolai Nikolaevich Goffman, a Jewish convert who resided in Riga. While Shlomovich asserted that she was divorced and that her three children (a seven-year-old daughter, six-year-old son, and three-year-old daughter) were in her custody, this was far from the truth.[46] Goffman met with the prospective convert at the tobacco factory of Mindel and Co. in the summer of 1869. "Ever since I have sympathized with and adopted the Christian Orthodox faith, I am especially glad when Orthodoxy is magnified even further," explained Goffman. "[Thus] I took upon myself the task to go with her to the archpriest at the Pokrovskii Church and explained her sincere desire." He learned that Shlomovich's wealthy parents, who were prominent in the community of Riga, opposed her decision: "Her parents knew about her [wish earlier] because of her minority."[47] Although she was now twenty-five years old, she was "wary of all troubles." Even the archpriest, who was well aware of her family's position in the city, "advised us that if it was possible [for her] to leave for the city [of St. Petersburg] and convert to the Orthodox faith there, so much the better." Another obstacle was her husband "who does not live with her but is not divorced." In fact, Goffman observed that she knew no peace, "for [the husband] keeps coming around." Finally, even if he were to secure the family's safe passage to St. Petersburg, Goffman would have to obtain a passport with the children registered under the mother, a bureaucratic challenge since only the oldest daughter possessed a birth certificate. As if to answer the unasked question, he added that Shlomovich refused to leave without her children and was determined to obtain a higher education.

Perhaps to counter any doubts about the motives for her conversion, Shlomovich assured Father Briantsev that this desire preceded her aspirations

---

[46] TsGIA SPb, f. 542, op. 1, d. 15, g. 1869, ll. 1–9.
[47] According to Russian law, priests were required to inform Jewish parents about their children's desire to convert to Orthodoxy and gain their consent.

to study midwifery: "My soul and my whole way of life from very early youth have been attached with love to the truth of the Orthodox faith; only I am not to blame that I was not in position to carry this out because I was under the strict supervision of my parents and was hampered with an early marriage against my will. Now I have decided resolutely to calm my heart and to carry this out with the help of God and kind people."

Although the file does not indicate the final resolution of her case, in general, Father Briantsev was willing to provide travel assistance (i.e., train tickets to St. Petersburg), help with bureaucratic procedures (i.e., securing a passport and residency permits), and room and board at the shelter. For Jewish women like Shlomovich who could not obtain a legal divorce from their husbands, the opportunity simply to leave town and convert was very appealing.[48] Moreover, navigating the bureaucratic maze was especially difficult for women. Russian law ascribed a woman's legal status according to first her father and then her husband ("unless, in the latter instance, she belonged to a higher estate than her husband").[49] It denied wives the right to reside apart from their husbands or gain employment without their permission. The only way to circumvent the law was to apply for a separate passport from His Imperial Majesty's Chancellery for the Receipt of Petitions, which was established in 1884, some fifteen years after Shlomovich's first petition to the shelter. Even had the chancellery existed earlier, her petition might have been rejected: this office granted separate passports to women only in "exceptional cases of abuse and neglect."[50]

The third reason cited in seeking the shelter's assistance was a desire to provide children with a proper Christian and Russian education. As Pavel Mikhailovich Kliott explained in 1869, he had graduated from the Vilna rabbinical school and had converted with his wife (renamed Ol'ga Vladimirovna) and three minor children in order to enter state service: "However, so much about Christian life is unfamiliar to us, and that is why I would consider it my great happiness if my children were able to receive an education in the true Christian principles and Orthodox Russian life." Although Kliott expressed modest aspirations for his children ("I will be content with whatever God sends in terms of their education"), he clearly saw the shelter as a stepping stone to a brighter future. He had attempted to enroll his son Petr at the Artisan School of Tsarevich Nicholas when Petr turned thirteen; when the young boy failed the entrance examination, however, the father requested the

---

[48] On Jewish divorces and conversion, see ChaeRan Y. Freeze, "When Chava Left Home."
[49] William Wagner, *Marriage, Property, and the Struggle for Legality in Late Imperial Russia* (Oxford, 1994), 63.
[50] See ChaeRan Y. Freeze, *Jewish Marriage and Divorce in Imperial Russia* (Waltham, MA, 2002), 161–62.

1. The Mariinsko Sergievskii Shelter for Converted Jewish Children in St. Petersburg

shelter "to assign Petr to any educational institution where he would receive at least a little education." Kliott also expressed dissatisfaction at his daughter Mariia's education at the shelter and transferred her to the *pansion* of Sergei Aleksandrovich in 1874.[51]

In a few exceptional cases, minor Jewish children showed up at the shelter and expressed a desire to convert to Russian Orthodoxy. In 1867, for instance, the mayor of St. Petersburg issued a notice about a missing Jewish girl, Vitka Davidovich, who had lived with her brother, David Davidovich, on Konnogvardeiskaia Street in the house of Vasil'ev, no. 28. According to the latter, she disappeared on 24 September.[52] The description of the missing girl read: "16 years old; medium height, light brown hair, gray eyes, a clean face, dressed in a brown summer blouse, coffee-colored woolen skirt, a gray scarf on [her] head. He [David Davidovich] requests a search and her return to her parent's home." In fact, Vitka Davidovich had run away to the shelter with the intent of converting but had fallen ill and was hospitalized. Her Jewish family refused to accept her conversion and even attempted to kidnap her along with Illarion Sergeevich Snipishinskii's daughter, Shifra (as discussed above)—not an uncommon response.[53]

The final category of individuals who received assistance from the shelter (in the form of financial stipends or letters of recommendation) were former wards who went on to study at trade schools or institutions of higher education. Letters to Father Briantsev show that the Jewish converts followed similar paths as their former coreligionists in terms of educational choices: women studied to become seamstresses or midwives, while men pursued pharmaceutical, medical, and engineering professions. Elizaveta Lazareva, for instance, who had initially studied to become a seamstress in Moscow, decided to study midwifery at a maternity institution in St. Petersburg in 1874. She credited the shelter, especially Father Briantsev, with setting her on the right path: "Having neither mother nor father, and being completely helpless, I would have absolutely perished had the archpriest Briantsev and the shelter's committee not lent me assistance," Lazareva wrote. Now she requested further funds to help pay for her room and board until the end of her courses.[54] As if anticipating some admonition about her lack of frugality, Lazareva added that she would "not buy linens or books which are demanded at the institution" but would live modestly. As was customary, the committee

---

[51] TsGIA SPb, f. 542, op. 3, d. 5, gg. 1869–1881, ll. 1–47.
[52] TsGIA SPb, f. 542, op. 2, d. 5, gg. 1867–1871, ll. 1–5.
[53] For a case involving an attempted kidnapping of a convert, see Gosudarstvennyi arkhiv Rossiiskoi Federatsii (GARF), f. 102, 3 d-vo, d. 1, ch. 18, g. 1904, ll. 18–28 (case of Gitlia Korn of Lublin).
[54] TsGIA SPb, f. 542, op. 1, d. 46, gg. 1871–1878, ll. 1–68.

conducted an investigation of Lazareva's circumstances and found that she did indeed live in poverty at her sister's home. While it decided to support her studies, it issued a strict reprimand to change her "extremely quarrelsome disposition" (the cause of bitter complaints from her sister).[55]

In another case, Sof'ia Gofman petitioned the shelter to support her studies in medical gymnastic massage. According to the records, her mother had suffered from mental illness and had her daughter baptized as a young girl. The widow Ekaterina Feliksovna Nikitina (perhaps her godmother) placed her in the Aleksandrovskii Orphanage, an institution that emphasized the teaching of crafts so that graduates would pursue an independent trade. Gofman had excelled in her classes and was especially "well adapted to female needlework." The orphanage had recommended that she choose embroidery as her trade. As Gofman explained in a letter to the shelter's committee, she embarked on a different path when she left the orphanage, enrolling instead in a midwifery course, which she completed on 7 May 1892. Due to her poverty, she did not have any money to pay for her degree, let alone the expensive midwifery instruments. Gofman also wanted to go beyond her midwifery training to add new skills to her repertoire: "I have a strong desire to study massage in the medical gymnastic massage establishment on Kazan Street, where the fee is 70 rubles." The shelter decided to provide only part of the requested sum (thirty rubles).

Male graduates of the shelter, like Mikhail Markuson, who chose to study pharmaceutics, received assistance in finding housing and navigating the bureaucracy after leaving St. Petersburg. In 1872, Markuson sent a letter requesting to be released from the ranks of the St. Petersburg townspeople so that he could take the examinations for a pharmaceutical assistantship in Moscow.[56] Bret Egorovich, the president of the Moscow Board of Guardians, found him to be a diligent student employed at the Sushevskii Pharmacy at the edge of the town of Sushevin, which was located at a great distance from the university. "This forced him in August to prepare his lessons at the pharmacy and move into the home of our benefactor Liapin, where 100 students receive a free apartment, heat, light, water, and bedclothes," Egorovich explained. He was so moved by the student's modesty and unassuming demeanor that he recommended a stipend for Markuson, even though he had not requested any funds: "As soon as I saw the young man and recognized [him], observing his embarrassment, I gave him 5 rubles. When I gathered information about him from the pharmacist, with whom he was residing, and from others, I

---

[55] Ibid.
[56] TsGIA SPb, f. 542, op. 3, d. 3, gg. 1869–1875, ll. 1–21.

recommended that the committee give him 30 rubles for October and November."⁵⁷

Other men like Vladimir Nikolaevich Veksler found jobs in the railway industry. Veksler began his career as an inspector at the Korsakovka-Varshavskoi Railway Station in 1869 and received a promotion from clerk to assistant chief the following year. In 1872, he transferred to a station in Ostrov (Pskov province) where he married a merchant's widow, Mariia Pavlovna Matskeeva.⁵⁸ "I celebrated the wedding fabulously," he informed Father Briantsev. "At the present time, I have already entered [my] post and work even more diligently. My wife and her parents accepted the grand duke's presents with great reverence." The problem was that his current position did not generate the income that he needed to support his new family. As a former ward of the shelter, Veksler requested a letter of recommendation that would assist in his promotion: "I humbly ask Your Grace to intercede before my chief so I will be given a better position with a little larger salary than I am receiving now. The position of cashier at the first-class station pays 600–720 rubles a year and even more; I have the full right to such a position. But without Your intercession it would not be possible for me to receive such a promotion." Either because Father Briantsev failed to write the letter or for some other reason, Veksler wrote again the following year with the same request, this time with news that they were expecting a child, making his promotion all the more urgent: "I now live as a family man . . . Up till now, I barely was able to live on 40 rubles a month and made use of only the essentials. But in the present time I live daily with a growing family. Reluctantly, I ponder that in the future, I will have to give up much to feed and raise another member of the family." He reminded Father Briantsev that the railway administration did not welcome requests for promotions from their own agents but might accept recommendations from the outside: "Your personal petition to Mr. Al'kis or his assistant, Barin Kayl'bars, even Sergei Romanovich Nizguritser may be absolutely enough for me. For the sake of Christ, I ask you not to refuse me this time in my petition; I no longer have anyone to whom I can turn."⁵⁹ The next year, Veksler repeated his appeal to Father Briantsev, stressing the urgency to his request: "My health has been ruined severely due to my increased engagement with affairs at work but equally from the worry of supporting the family." His poor health required treatment at mineral spas abroad, preventing him from working for two months. "If it is God's will that I regain my health abroad," Veksler continued, he would stop by St. Petersburg to visit. In the

---

⁵⁷ Ibid.
⁵⁸ TsGIA SPb, f. 542, op. 1, d. 14, gg. 1869–1874, ll. 1–19.
⁵⁹ Ibid., ll. 17–18.

meantime, he reminded his spiritual father of his "request for promotion in work and transfer from Ostrov. My family remains in Ostrov." The file did not include a response from Father Briantsev; whatever the outcome, however, Veksler obviously believed that his spiritual mentor had the right connections and influence to intercede on his behalf—a belief rooted in the shelter's royal patronage, which he invoked in his first letter describing the grand duke's wedding presents.

Word of the shelter's ties to the imperial family prompted some Jewish converts who had no connection to the shelter to appeal for intervention. For instance, in 1873, Lev Poliak sent a letter to Father Briantsev's successor (Father Aleksandr), recounting the difficult work that he performed as the locksmith-roller at the Beryoz depot on the Moscow-Brest railway line: "I would describe to you my biography, if only the calloused hand would have sufficient strength and perhaps capacity. But believe me, Father, it is now [weak] from [gripping] a vice." The strenuous labor was only half the problem. Having suffered "persecution on all sides from the Jews" after his conversion, he was shocked when the "Christians took it into their heads to push me around." In particular, Poliak complained about the Germans, who "are preparing to devour me but for my good fortune that the boss likes me for my good behavior." Clearly, his conversion had not changed the ethnic tensions at work; if anything, he claimed that he was a target of the Germans who had created their own "kingdom" at the depot. Poliak had heard through "hearsay" that the shelter responded to "all requests as far as possible" and requested a recommendation to enroll in a state mechanical school. As in most cases, the shelter's board wrote back that while it sympathized with Poliak's plight, it was *"primarily concerned with those people who have been baptized under the auspices of the shelter"* (emphasis in the original).

"The words of the Lord to his disciples and apostles: 'Go instead to the lost sheep of the house of Israel' (Matthew 10:6)." With this verse, in 1870, an anonymous author writing in *Strannik* penned his response to the public debate on the Jewish question in tsarist Russia. In his view, state efforts "to make Jews into useful members of the great Russian family" through secular education, agricultural colonies, and expansion of legal rights had failed. The time was ripe for more serious consideration of Jews' conversion to Christianity. Yet he was struck by the Christian neglect of the Jews in Russia: "Until now, we have done practically nothing to facilitate the conversion of the Jews to Orthodoxy. We have had neither missionaries nor literature . . . to enlighten the Jews. Moreover, we have not even been concerned enough about

1. The Mariinsko Sergievskii Shelter for Converted Jewish Children in St. Petersburg

the Jews who themselves seek Christianity and are found in need of urgent material and moral assistance." The author conceded that it was "even harder for Jews than for heathens" to leave their religion, but dismissed critics who claimed that attempts to convert the Jews were in vain. He pointed to famous converts, such as Yaakov Brafman and Aleksandr Alekseev who had paved the way for their former coreligionists to join the Christian faith.[60] In his view, one of the most important steps in Russia's civilizing mission was the creation of the Mariinsko Sergievskii Shelter in St. Petersburg, which served the most elementary needs of Jews who desired to embrace Christianity.

Fr. Nikandr Briantsev, who played a central role in shaping the mission of the shelter, saw himself in almost prophetic terms: "I was predestined to stand as an intermediary between good Christians and those seeking holy baptism, as well as newly baptized Jews in the Orthodox faith." He envisioned the shelter as a substitute parental home, one that could provide Jewish converts with a "refuge from the persecution of their former coreligionists [and provide] a livelihood at the time when they are preparing for holy baptism." With the assistance of Tat'iana Borisovna Potemkina, a "mother figure" for many converts according to *Strannik*, Father Briantsev transformed the shelter from a tiny apartment into a large home, complete with a staff of Jewish converts and prominent Christian benefactors. While the shelter's primary goal was to teach the "principles of faith and Christian life to the fullest extent," it also sought to remake Jews into "honest" and "useful" Russian citizens who would engage in productive labor—whether in an artisanal trade or a respectable profession. Employing the language of state reform, the staff and patrons emphasized the need for converts to abandon old Jewish vices (greediness, insincerity, and entitlement) and occupations (namely trade) and embrace a new moral code and lifestyle. During reeducation, the shelter invariably reminded the Jewish converts of their roots and otherness, making them "almost the same" but not the same as the native-born Russian Christians, with whom they were to merge. The discourse used by the shelter and its Orthodox patrons reflected a trend toward racialization—that is, treating converted Jews not on the basis of confession but as a separate ethnic racial group with deeply ingrained traits regardless of any real or nominal conversion. With the growing prestige of racial anthropology in Russia starting in the late 1870s,[61] Jewish converts found it increasingly impossible to unburden themselves of their "innate Jewishness," even at the Mariinsko Sergievskii Shelter, which promised them refuge.

---

[60] "Chastnyi priiut v S. Petersburg dlia prisoediniaeshchykh k pravoslavnoi Tserkvi evreev," *Strannik* (July 1870): 55–56, 58, 61–81.
[61] Avrutin, "Racial Categories and the Politics of (Jewish) Difference"; for more on Jews who returned to Judaism, see his "Returning to Judaism after the 1905 Law on Religious Freedom in Tsarist Russia," *Slavic Review* 65, 1 (2006): 90–110.

2. Yiddish in Imperial Russia's Civil Society

Gennady Estraikh

The transformation of Yiddish into a language of high modern culture—in Simon Dubnow's words, "from 'jargon' to Yiddish"[1]—is usually associated with remarkable achievements in such domains of Jewish life in late imperial Russia as literary and journalistic creativity (especially of the classical triumvirate, Mendele Moykher Sforim, Sholem Aleichem, and I. L. Peretz), and the socialist labor movement. This chapter, however, focuses on the impact of Jewish philanthropic and mutual-aid organizations, whose role remains largely neglected in academic discourse concerning the history of Yiddish culture in the nineteenth and twentieth centuries. Such neglect is hardly surprising given that thousands of voluntary organizations that existed in the empire in its last decades remain the least researched elements of Russia's civil society.[2] Yet the picture of Yiddish in Russia remains unfinished without these components of Jewish life. Although the raison d'être of Jewish philanthropic and mutual-aid organizations had little to do with Yiddish, and many of their activists even maintained that there was no such thing as the Yiddish *language*, they ultimately became a central force in defining its modern functions and status.

As the core of Jewish civil society in Russia, voluntary organizations contributed enormously to the national consolidation of various groups of Yiddish-speaking population divided by distinct dialects, customs, religious traditions, economic circumstances, and vectors of cultural gravitation. The consolidation also had a language-planning dimension, in particular for Yiddish, because the Jewish organizations had no choice but to use it in their activities and, as a result, facilitated standardization, lexical development, and—most important—recognition of the language. This essay looks into the growth of Yiddish in the environment created by Russian-Jewish civil society.

---

[1] See Simon Dubnov, *Fun "zshargon" tsu yidish* (Vilna, 1929).
[2] Joseph Bradley, "Subjects into Citizens: Societies, Civil Society, and Autocracy in Tsarist Russia," *American Historical Review* 107, 4 (2002): 1106.

Pillars of Jewish Philanthropy

The Russia-wide consolidation of Jewish activities, initially in the form of lobbying before the state (*shtadlanut*), was facilitated by Emperor Alexander II's edict of March 1859, which permitted the upper crust of Jewish financiers and industrialists, or "first-guild merchants," to settle outside the Pale of Jewish Settlement. This edict inadvertently advanced the appearance of a St. Petersburg-based Jewish national elite of wealthy men and their intellectual entourages. From the 1860s onward, the capital housed several Jewish-owned banks, including that of the Gintsburgs, an enlightened Westernized "royal family" of Russian Jewry. The "Gintsburg Circle," to borrow John Klier's term, exercised control over the Petersburg Jewish community and had an impact on Russian-Jewish life as a whole.[3] To a significant degree, the Petersburg elite formed the nucleus of Russian-Jewish consolidation.

Coincidentally, 1859 also brought government relaxation in its policy toward private charities.[4] It is no accident that the Gintsburg Circle founded the Society for the Promotion of Enlightenment among the Jews of Russia (OPE, according to its Russian initials), in St. Petersburg in 1863. The emergence of this first national, secular Jewish organization fit neatly into the climate of Alexander II's reign, with its educational experiments aimed at promoting loyal citizenship among ethnic and religious minorities.[5] Benjamin Nathans writes about "selective integration," or "the process by which the tsarist state hoped to disperse certain categories of Jews into the Russian social hierarchy."[6]

Petersburg's Jewish sophisticates tended to internalize the criticism leveled at the "nonproductive" dweller of the Pale.[7] At the same time, many members of the Gintsburg Circle were sincerely perturbed by the economic predicament of the Pale, particularly of artisans, who made up one-third of the empire's Jewish population. Tailors, shoemakers, and other craftsmen were "productive." As such, they were nearer and dearer to the hearts of enlightened Jews

---

[3] John Doyle Klier, *Imperial Russia's Jewish Question, 1855–1881* (Cambridge, 1995), 22, 460; Benjamin Nathans, *Beyond the Pale: The Jewish Encounter with Late Imperial Russia* (Berkeley, 2002), 65, 169; Boris V. Anan'ich et al., *Kredit i banki v Rossii do nachala XX veka: Sankt Peterburg i Moskva* (St. Petersburg, 2005), 244–49.

[4] Adele Lindenmeyr, *Poverty Is Not a Vice: Charity, Society, and the State in Imperial Russia* (Princeton, NJ, 1996), 121–22.

[5] See Dov Yaroshevski, "Empire and Citizenship," in *Russia's Orient: Imperial Borderlands and Peoples, 1700–1917*, ed. Daniel R. Brower and Edward J. Lazzerini (Bloomington, 1997), 64–65.

[6] Nathans, *Beyond the Pale*, 78, 311.

[7] See Tamar Bermann, *Produktivierungsmythen und Antisemitismus: Eine soziologische Studie* (Vienna, 1973), 150.

than marketers, brokers, leaseholders, moneylenders, or people of indeterminate occupation, labeled later, at the turn of the century, as *luftmentshn*. The Russian government, too, viewed craftsmen as a useful segment of the Jewish population and made mastery a metric for their integration/amalgamation. A law of 1865 permitted Jewish master craftsmen to reside outside the Pale, in the so-called internal provinces of Russia, if they provided the necessary legal evidence of proficiency in their crafts.[8]

In reality, Jewish master craftsmen, whose number was rather limited, usually lived quite well in their hometowns, among their relatives and friends, and did not want to face the challenges associated with eastward migration. In contrast to the state apparatus and enlightened Jews, traditional Jewish society placed artisans low in the traditional hierarchy. Successful artisans, intent on gaining respectability, often used their accumulated wealth to move from handicraft to "nonproductive" merchandising. Meanwhile, the vast majority of artisans lacked sufficient skills to be allowed to leave the Pale and lived there in a vicious cycle of penury, often dependent on the unofficial charitable organizations that honeycombed every small Jewish community.[9] By the end of the nineteenth century, up to one-fifth (in towns, one-third) of Russia's Jews received ongoing support from various charities.[10] Poor artisans could not afford the advanced education or training that ultimately might entitle their children to be "selectively integrated" into the larger society. Under such circumstances, support of general and vocational education could be seen as a panacea—one that until the 1880s went hand in glove with the governmental policy of using education as a means of struggle against Jews' "harmfulness."[11]

In 1880, Nikolai (Noah) Bakst, an established scholar in the field of physiology, persuaded several wealthy members of the Gintsburg Circle to set up the Society for the Promotion of Artisanal and Agricultural Work among the Jews in Russia (ORT, according to the Russian initials). (Scientists with social-reform aspirations generally contributed a great deal to building civil

---

[8] G. Samoilovich, *O pravakh remeslennikov* (St. Petersburg, 1894); T. N. Tikhonov, *Evreiskii vopros v Rossii i Sibiri* (St. Petersburg, 1906), 62; Isaac M. Rubinow, *Economic Condition of the Jews in Russia* (New York, 1975), 489.
[9] Iulii Gessen, *Istoriia evreiskogo naroda v Rossii* (Leningrad, 1926), 2:159; Lindenmeyr, *Poverty Is Not a Vice*, 121–22.
[10] Il'ia Orshanskii, *Evrei v Rossii: ocherki ekonomicheskogo i obshchestvennogo byta russkikh evreev* (St. Petersburg, 1877), 21–22; Yitskhok Leybush Peretz, *Iber profesyonen* (Warsaw, 1894), 22; S. Gepshtein, *Ekonomicheskaia struktura evreiskogo naseleniia Rossii* (St. Petersburg, 1906), 36.
[11] See, e.g., F. Gets, "Shkol'noe obuchenie u russkikh evreev," *Zhurnal Ministerstva narodnogo prosveshcheniia* 51 (1914): 2.

society in Russia.)[12] Bakst exemplified the integration trajectory of Russian-Jewish intellectuals born into enlightened families. His father, Isaac Bakst, owned the Zhitomir-based Jewish publishing house that brought out the pioneering Yiddish dictionaries compiled by Yeshue-Mordkhe Lifshits—a man of wide culture, whose outlook combined devotion to the language of the Jewish masses with a strong desire to make them productive.[13] Nikolai Bakst's brainchild, the ORT, derived from the OPE—which supported university students, writers, and scholars—but its original charter did not include the goal of educating craftsmen. The fact that the new society was modeled on the Prussian Gesellschaft zur Verbreitung der Handwerke und des Ackerbaus unter den Juden reflected the general tendency in Russia to borrow German patterns.[14]

With the OPE and the ORT already in place, the Jewish Colonization Association (JCA) formed the third—and ultimately most influential—centralized constituent of Russian-Jewish civil society. The JCA's prehistory was also associated with Bakst, under whose influence Baron Maurice de Hirsch, a West European Jewish businessman and philanthropist, had developed the idea of establishing schools for Jewish youth in Russia. Ultimately, the Russian government blocked that project, and Baron Hirsch's attention turned to the Jewish colonization of the Argentine steppes. Bakst, a Russian patriot, could not bring himself to justify emigration and remained at odds with the JCA until the end of his life (in 1904). He remained unconvinced even when the leadership of the Russian branch (established in 1892) persuaded the international board of the JCA to place more emphasis on improving the economic situation of Russian Jews.[15]

In the aftermath of the 1907 constitutional coup, which saw the dissolution of the Russian parliament and the persecution of its socialist depu-

---

[12] Elizabeth A. Hachten, "In Service to Science and Society: Scientists and the Public in Late-Nineteenth-Century Russia," in *Science and Civil Society*, ed. Lynn K. Nyhart and Thomas Broman (Chicago, 2002), 175–76.

[13] Zalman Reisen, *Leksikon fun der yidisher literatur, prese un filologye* (Vilna, 1930), 2:180–88; Dmitry A. El'iashevich, *Pravitel'stvennaia politika i evreiskaia pechat' v Rossii, 1797–1917* (St. Petersburg and Jerusalem, 1999), 273, 283, 637; Max Weinreich, *History of the Yiddish Language*, ed. Paul Glasser, trans. Shlomo Noble with the assistance of Joshua A. Fishman (New Haven, 2008), 287.

[14] Nikolai Bakst, *K stoletnemu dniu konchiny Moiseia Mendel'sona* (St. Petersburg, 1886), 45; Steven M. Lowenstein, "Governmental Jewish Policies in Early Nineteenth-Century Germany and Russia: A Comparison," *Jewish Social Studies* 16, 3–4 (1984): 303–20; Angelica Kipp, *Jüdische Arbeits und Berufsfürsorge in Deutschland 1900–1933* (Berlin, 1999), 25; Brian Horowitz, *Jewish Philanthropy and Enlightenment in Late-Tsarist Russia* (Seattle, 2009), 69–70.

[15] Genrikh B. Sliozberg, "N. I. Bakst kak obshchestvennyi deiatel'," in *Otchet Obshchestva remeslennogo i zemledel'cheskogo truda sredi evreev v Rossii za 1908 god* (St Petersburg, 1909), 74–77.

ties, numerous activists became disillusioned by direct political activism and found a new home in civil society organizations—including the ORT, which had been taken over by a group of politically liberal intellectuals. Bakst and his contemporaries saw productivization and correction of other "defects" among Jews as prerequisites for integration into Russian society. The younger generation of activists had similar tactical objectives, but strategically they usually aimed at modern Jewish nation building.

Some younger activists moved to the ORT from the JCA. Among them were Leon Bramson, the director of the JCA's central committee; and Boris (Ber) Brutskus, head of the agricultural department. Bramson and Brutskus believed that the JCA, despite its impressive achievements, remained a remote, undemocratic, and bureaucratic structure. Bramson, a liberal politician who, in 1906, was one of the Jewish deputies elected to the First Russian Duma, took part in formulating the ORT's new statute, which simplified procedures for opening a provincial branch and allowed people with low incomes to join. Nonetheless, a complete transformation of the ORT from a philanthropic entity into a mutual-aid mass organization remained a pipe dream.[16]

The St. Petersburg-based JCA, OPE, and ORT built a centralized Jewish civil society, whose components closely interacted with Jewish political groups and formed a modern alternative to traditional Jewish communities. Most civil-society activists belonged to a new stratum that had developed in the Pale. Some of them were known as "conscious, or intellectual, workers" (*soznatel'nye rabochie/bavustzinike arbeter*), who had connections with illegal party groups. While "intellectual workers" usually came from poor families, many offspring of more affluent (*balebatishe*) parents were Talmudic students who became secular "semi-intellectuals" (*poluintelligenty/halb-inteligentn*)—a term "proper," university-educated intellectuals used to refer to the "slightly educated" autodidacts. Both groups of activists had already severed their links with the traditional community but due to their socioeconomic position, education, and outlook had difficulty finding a place in the larger society.[17] The civil-society network also attracted numerous Jewish intellectuals steeped in Russian culture, who sought to find a place and purpose in the country that had reared them for integration but ultimately treated them as second rate.[18] The institutions of civil society competed with the old Jewish charities, *hevras*, which fulfilled many social functions in local communities.

---

[16] Gennady Estraikh, "Changing Ideologies of Artisanal 'Productivization': ORT in Late Imperial Russia," *East European Jewish Affairs* 39, 1 (2009): 3–18.
[17] El'iashevich, *Pravitel'stvennaia politika i evreiskaia pechat' v Rossii*, 469.
[18] See S. M. Dubnov, *Kniga zhizni: Materialy iz istorii moego vremeni* (Moscow, 2004), 249.

Jewish Cooperatives

Jewish activists paid particular attention to credit cooperatives, or savings-and-loan associations. Traditionally, young Jewish men, including artisans, based their own family and business life on a dowry. A character in David Bergelson's 1909 story "At the Depot" explains: "When you get your dowry, then you have your capital." Nonetheless, from the 1870s onward, craftsmen often needed additional start-up capital to purchase modern equipment.[19] Receiving credit at reasonable rates could secure an artisanal or merchandizing business and protect it from loan sharks, known among Yiddish speakers as *protsentniks* or *vokherers*.[20] No-interest-loan associations, *gmiles khesed*, which operated with capital donated by more affluent members of the community, usually did not have sufficient resources and, as a result, were of very limited effectiveness for financing a business project.

In the 1880s, an unofficial savings-and-loan association, called in Yiddish *aktsye* (share) or *be(y)nkl* (small bank), formed part of Jewish life in many areas inside the Pale. Such associations often emerged on the basis of a previously existing *gmiles khesed*.[21] In June 1895, a special law facilitated the formation of small societies offering mutual credit in the Russian Empire. In the next year, the first such Jewish voluntary society was established in the shtetl of Parichi (Parech) in Belorussia. In Vilna, "where the pulse of [Jewish] civic life [was] ... stronger than in anywhere else in the Pale,"[22] a similar society emerged in 1898. Several towns, such as Dvinsk (Daugavpils), Białystok, Gomel, and Mogilev, soon copied the model. Russia became the first and only country where the cooperative movement (most notably, credit cooperatives)

---

[19] Israel Sosis, *Di geshikhte fun di yidishe gezelshaftlekhe shtremungen in Rusland in XIX y"h* (Minsk, 1929), 126; Ruth R. Wisse, *A Shtetl and Other Yiddish Novellas* (Detroit, 1986), 117. On the role of the dowry for starting an artisanal business in Western Europe, see James R. Farr, *Artisans in Europe, 1300–1914* (Cambridge, 2000), 57. Dowries played a less significant role or even completely disappeared among the proletarians, who depended on wages rather than capital—see Jack Goody, *The European Family: An Historico-Anthropological Essay* (Oxford, 2000), 137.

[20] To bypass the biblical and Talmudic injunction against charging interest on loans offered to Jews, lending for profit was legalized through the *heter iska* (literally "exemption contract"), or a *partnership* (rather than a loan agreement) between creditor and debtor—see, e.g., R. J. Lister, "The Composition of Interest: The Judaic Prohibition," *Accounting, Business, and Financial History* 16, 1 (2006): 121–27. For the etymology of *vokherer*, or *vokhernik*, see Dov Sadan, "Vokher," in *Yuda A. Yofe-bukh*, ed. Yudel Mark (New York, 1958), 269–73.

[21] Solomon O. Margolin, *Evreiskie kreditnye kooperatsii* (St. Petersburg, 1908), 8–14; Khaim Dov Hurwitz, *Zelbst-hilf far hantverker* (St. Petersburg, 1912), 23.

[22] B. Rubshteyn, "Der ekonomisher kamf in Galitsyen," *Di Yidishe Velt*, no. 3 (1913): 134.

developed into a Jewish mass movement.[23] By 1912, over six hundred cooperatives provided credit to over four hundred thousand Jewish members. By the beginning of World War I, 450,000 Jewish members of savings-and-loan associations and their families encompassed about three million people, or half of the empire's total Jewish population. The appearance of independent funds reflected the increasing cultural and political maturation of Russian-Jewish society and created links between corporate craft traditions and early forms of socialism.[24] Indeed, early Jewish savings-and-loan associations often gave rise to illegal trade unions, whose (*kamf-*)*kases*, or (struggle-)funds, provided means of support during strikes.[25] The Bund, founded in 1897 in Vilna, eventually turned into a social-democratic party, but in its embryonic form, it was a union of *kases* and *krayzlekh*, workers' education circles.[26]

The cooperative movement, with its unprecedented number of participants and its relative independence "from outside interference by either local authorities or orthodox elements of Jewish society," became one of the principal secular agents in traditional communities, building a modern social and economic armature for Jewish life in Russia.[27] Cooperatives had more than economic utility. They often sponsored libraries, schools, and medical positions; met other social needs; and created an organized (through institutional links, conferences, and periodicals) environment for voluntary, part-time, or even full-time job positions for Jewish activists and professionals.[28] This became particularly important after 1890, when Jews were deprived of the right to vote in elections for the *zemstvo*, an elected local self-government,

---

[23] Eugene M. Kayden, "Consumers' Coöperation," in *The Cooperative Movement in Russia during the War* (New Haven, 1929), 4–10; Boris Halpern, *Pinkes fun yidishn bank tsum 40-yorikn yoyvl fun der 1ter vilner yidisher lay- un shpor-kase far hantverker un kleynhendler* (Vilna, 1936), 7–23; Joseph Jaszunski, "Di kooperatsye biz tsu der ershter velt-milkhome," *Algemeyne entsiklopedye: Yidn. Alef* (Paris, 1939), 533; Anita B. Baker, "Community and Growth: Muddling through with Russian Credit Cooperatives," *Journal of Economic History* 37, 1 (1977): 143.

[24] Farr, *Artisans in Europe*, 287.

[25] Jonathan Frankel, *Prophecy and Politics: Socialism, Nationalism, and the Russian Jews, 1862–1917* (Cambridge, 1981), 172, 225; Nathan Weinstock, *Le pain de misère: histoire du movement ouvrier juif en Europe*, 1 (Paris, 1984), 1:87.

[26] Henry J. Tobias and Charles E. Woodhouse, "Political Reaction and Revolutionary Careers: The Jewish Bundists in Defeat, 1907–10," *Comparative Studies in Society and History* 19, 3 (1977): 367–96; Yoav Peled, *Class and Ethnicity in the Pale: The Political Economy of Jewish Workers' Nationalism in Late Imperial Russia* (New York, 1989), 50.

[27] Christoph Gassenschmidt, *Jewish Liberal Politics in Tsarist Russia, 1900–14: Modernization of Russian Jewry* (Houndmills, UK, 1995), 79.

[28] I. A. Blium and Lev S. Zak, eds., *Kooperatsiia sredi evreev (po dannym 1911 i 1912 gg.)* (St. Petersburg, 1913), 58–59; Jeffrey Veidlinger, *Jewish Public Culture in the Late Russian Empire* (Bloomington, 2009), 42, 59–60; For illegal "craft libraries" established by *kases*, see David Shavit, "The Emergence of Jewish Public Libraries in Tsarist Russia," *Journal of Library History* 20, 3 (1985): 244–46.

whose institutions employed thousands of doctors, teachers, agronomists, and other qualified personnel.[29]

Meanwhile, from the 1880s onward, "[c]ontinuing economic development and the inroads of secularism were preparing even larger numbers of Jews to give up their traditional ways and live a more 'modern' life, just as the policy makers of 'amalgamation' had hoped, but the tsars were no longer encouraging Jews to become part of Russian society."[30] Eugene Avrutin has shown that between the 1880s and 1917, racial categories increasingly replaced estate and religion and, as a result, even conversion to Christianity did little to improve the Jews' status in society. Perhaps because of this shift, hundreds of baptized Jews returned to Judaism after 1905.[31] As John Klier's research demonstrates, the Russian authorities were, in general, not particularly committed to converting Jews to Christianity.[32]

In an atmosphere defined by a state ideology of nationalism and anti-semitism, disaggregation from larger society rather than integration into it dominated Russia's Jewish civil society. Thus, according to Natan Meir's case study, "[i]n the last decade before World War I, ethnic segregation in the realm of charitable work seemed increasingly to be true in Kiev."[33] Even the type of cooperatives reveals clear signs of ethnic segregation in the Pale: Jews usually did not organize consumer cooperatives, while this kind of association became popular among non-Jewish residents, notably peasants, and was widely seen as a means of struggle with Jewish shopkeepers. In some areas of Eastern Europe, consumer cooperatives had a devastating effect on Jewish trade, stimulating an increase in emigration.[34] At the same time, savings-and-loan associations mainly had Jewish members. Despite various restrictions (e.g., preventing the registration of savings-and-loan associations established

---

[29] No zemstvo of any kind had been introduced in the provinces of Vilna, Kovno, and Grodno. See Theodore R. Weeks, *Nation and State in Late Imperial Russia: Nationalism and Russification on the Western Frontier* (DeKalb, IL, 1996), 150.

[30] Lowenstein, "Governmental Jewish Policies in Early Nineteenth-Century Germany and Russia," 314.

[31] Eugene M. Avrutin, "Racial Categories and the Politics of (Jewish) Difference in Late Imperial Russia," *Kritika: Explorations in Russian and Eurasian History* 8, 1 (2007): 13–40.

[32] John D. Klier, "State Policies and the Conversion of Jews in Imperial Russia," in *Of Religion and Empire: Missions, Conversion, and Tolerance in Tsarist Russia*, ed. Robert P. Geraci and Michael Khodarkovsky (Ithaca, NY, 2001), 92–112.

[33] Natan Meir, "Jews, Ukrainians, and Russians in Kiev: Intergroup Relations in Late Imperial Associational Life," *Slavic Review* 65, 1 (2006): 489.

[34] P. Libman [(Peysekh-)Liebmann Hersch], *Tsu der kooperativer bavegung* (Vilna, 1911), 57–58; Rubshteyn, "Der ekonomisher kamf in Galitsyen," 121; A. Litvin [Shmuel Hurvitz], "Yidisher kleynhandl un kooperatsye," *Di yidishe velt*, no. 6 (1913): 40, 46. For a unique example of a Jewish producers' cooperative, a tobacco factory in Grodno, see Moyshe Olgin, "Di eyntsike yidishe kooperative fabrik," *Forverts*, 5 July 1910, 5.

by shopkeepers), only about 10 percent of such cooperatives' members in pre–World War I Ukraine were non-Jewish. Even a decade later, in the early Soviet period, their average non-Jewish membership did not exceed 20 percent.[35]

At that time, many group of Jewish socialists embraced "democratic forms of nationalism" and rejected assimilation, arguing that they accepted that Jews must one day relinquish their distinctive ethnocultural traits and blend into the international community (*chelovechestvo*) of the future but could not justify the assimilation of Jews by other nations.[36] The integrationist idea that artisans should move from the Pale to the internal provinces also became less popular over time. In February 1914, during the ORT conference in St. Petersburg, the economist theorist Boris Brutskus argued that because resettling Jewish artisans was almost impossible under current circumstances, it was much more practical to concentrate efforts and resources on supporting Jewish craftsmen inside the Pale, finding jobs for them, and assisting them in selling their products.[37]

The Language of Separation

John Klier analyzed attempts to integrate Jews into the Russian state system and concluded that the "well-intentioned" state-sponsored experiments had failed because they "derived from abstract views of the Jews as 'urban commercial elements,' or 'unproductive exploiters,' or as a dichotomous group of 'good and bad subjects.' [...] Reforms rooted in such caricatures could not but fail, and failure produced disillusionment and counter-reform."[38] Failure also changed the vector of activities of Jewish civil-society institutions, which had been established to facilitate integration of Jews by making them "productive" and, generally, "good." From the beginning of the twentieth century, local and national Jewish organizations increasingly concentrated on building a parallel ethnic society and economy. The expansion of cooperatives and other voluntary organizations and the appearance of political (notably socialist) groups altered the fabric of Jewish society, reinforced the ethnic separation of Jews, and left a lasting mark on language politics and practice.

---

[35] A Soykher [Khaim Dov Hurwitz], "Fun ekonomishn lebn," *Der Fraynd*, 27 April 1909, 2–3; Sh. Gurevitsh, "Di lay- un shpor-kases af Ukraine," *Di Royte Velt* 15 (1926): 80.

[36] Bazin [Moyshe Zilberfarb], *O evreiskom voprose na stranitsakh sotsialisticheskoi pechati* (Mozyr, 1906), 5, 32.

[37] *Otchet o soveshchanii Komiteta: Otchet Obshchestva remeslennogo i zemledel'cheskogo truda sredi evreev v Rossii za 1914 god* (Petrograd, 1915), 9.

[38] John D. Klier, "The Concept of 'Jewish Emancipation' in a Russian Context," in *Civil Rights in Imperial Russia*, ed. Olga Crisp and Linda Edmondson (Oxford, 1989), 144.

2. Yiddish in Imperial Russia's Civil Society

Yiddish, which according to Bramson "more than anything else contributed to the isolation of the Jewish masses from the remaining population,"[39] found recognition as an important marker of ethnic separation. According to John Keane, "civil society can be conceived as an aggregate of institutions whose members are engaged primarily in a complex of non-state activities [...] and who in this way preserve and transform their identity by exercising all sorts of pressures of controls upon state institutions." Russia's Jewish civil society was an important factor in shaping Russia's Jewish ethnic society, exercising all sorts of control on its institutions.[40] In this new climate, the status of Yiddish was transformed from a patois ("jargon") to a national language.

During the 1900s, Yiddish began to appear in political platforms of the Bund, Zionist Socialists, Folkists, and even Labor Zionists. At the same time, the practical need to use Yiddish exerted greater pressure than political discussions and resolutions. According to Max Weinreich (himself a Bundist in his youth): "The excess of practical achievements over theoretical clarification can best be seen among the Jewish socialists. Their role in strengthening Yiddish as a written and spoken cultural language is enormous, but they arrived at their role not so much by the logic of a preconceived program as by the logic of events. In the first circles [i.e., *krayzlekh*] ... the language of instruction was exclusively Russian. When the movement ... counted its followers in the hundreds," it moved to "written and spoken agitation in Yiddish."[41] As early as the mid-1890s, interactions among intellectuals, semi-intellectuals, and intellectual workers brought to life the so-called *zhargon* committees, aimed at producing and distributing Yiddish literature in socialist-leaning proletarian circles.[42] Committee activists usually joined the Bund, following its foundation in 1897. Some of them ultimately became committed Yiddishists, or Ashkenazic nationalists, dreaming about realizing a diasporic or territorial strategy of building a modern Yiddish-speaking nation. The 1897 census also unwittingly raised the standing of the *evreiskii iazyk*, "Jewish language" (which usually implied Yiddish), by listing it among other languages spoken in the empire.

To a considerable degree, Yiddishism developed amid admiration of the "quasi-state" Jewish civil society, based on the belief that behind its scaffold, one could already see the edifice of modern Jewish nationhood. In 1907, Vladimir Grossman, who later made a career in Yiddish journalism and in working for the ORT, joined the office of the JCA in St. Petersburg. He was surprised to encounter such an association in the Russian capital, playing a

---

[39] Cited in Horowitz, *Jewish Philanthropy and Enlightenment in Late-Tsarist Russia*, 109.
[40] John Keane, *Democracy and Civil Society* (London, 1988), 14.
[41] Weinreich, *History of the Yiddish Language*, 291.
[42] A. Litwak [Khaim Yakov Helfand], *Vos geven: etyudn un zikhroynes* (Vilna, 1925), 69–115.

dominant role in the life of Russian Jewry and enjoying the respect of government circles. A "component of organized Jewish public life, the Petersburg chapter of the JCA was led and financed by the JCA's central office in Paris [. . .] and was, in fact, a Jewish government of sorts. [. . .] The ORT organization emerged and developed from this close cooperation with the JCA."[43] In 1910, Jacob Lestschinsky, then considered the most serious social economist in the Zionist Socialist Workers' Party (which encouraged emigration with the ultimate goal of building a modern Yiddish-speaking socialist state), also detected components of a "Jewish government":

> It is remarkable that without having our own state or state institutions we still have our own bureaucrats who sit in their [state] "departments": a ministry of finance and industry (JCA), a ministry of education (OPE) [. . .]. It would be wrong to underestimate the role of these "departments." This is a very original, rather than only peculiar, phenomenon, when organizations that have emerged on the basis of random heirloom bequests and exist thanks to the sponsorship of several rich people make, nonetheless, such an impact on the economic and cultural conditions of a whole community.[44]

Wolf Latski-Bertoldi, one of the founders and leaders of the Zionist Socialist Workers' Party, wrote that although the Jewish people did not have its own state, it had a sprawling bureaucracy whose members had not been democratically elected to their positions.[45] Although Lestschinsky, Latski-Bertoldi, and many other advocates of Yiddish language and culture criticized the Jewish administrative apparatus, they also appreciated its quasi-state role, because it dovetailed with Simon Dubnow's scheme of Jewish communal autonomy.[46] (As Lestschinsky admitted half a century later, their projects of diasporic Jewish life were based on an "almost child-like faith in the steady advance of human progress and the impending triumph of Democracy throughout the world.")[47] Given the restrictions of the tsarist regime, the parties, which after 1907 shrank to small circles of diehards, often living in emigration, could not compete with the "departments" and other institutions of civil society for key roles in Jewish life in late imperial Russia.

---

[43] Vladimir Grossman, *Amol un haynt* (Paris, 1955), 18–19.
[44] Jacob Lestschinsky, "Profesyon-froyen-shule oyf dem Vilner tsuzamenfor," *Der Shtral*, 21 January 1910, 2.
[45] [Wolf Latski-]Beltoldi, "Fareynikn oder boyen?" *Der Fraynd*, 21 June 1909, 2.
[46] See David E. Fishman, *The Rise of Modern Yiddish Culture* (Pittsburgh, 2005), 67–71.
[47] Jacob Lestschinsky, "Dubnow's Autonomism and His 'Letters on Old and New Judaism,'" in *Simon Dubnow: The Man and His Work*, ed. Aaron Steinberg (Paris, 1963), 89.

2. Yiddish in Imperial Russia's Civil Society

The debate over the role and status of Jewish languages expanded from the political arena to affect most of Jewish civil society. Admittedly, discussions about the relative merits of Yiddish, Hebrew, and other languages had limited practical value, because in fact, Russia's Jewish civil society could not function without Yiddish. Activists of various political persuasions realized that they needed Yiddish if their ideas were to reach the general population. It was no coincidence that the 1906 Zionist Congress in Helsinki resolved to support education and other public functions in both Hebrew and Yiddish.[48] The cooperative movement, with participants in the hundreds of thousands, was even less fastidious. The movement had to use the dominant language of the masses to distribute circular letters, pamphlets, and books.

Although Russian made impressive inroads in the Pale of Jewish Settlement, for most Jews, it remained a foreign language. For instance, a pre–World War I survey of 657 artisans who owned workshops (a group that was usually better educated than their mates and apprentices), conducted in the Belorussian town of Bobruisk, showed that 339 of them could not read Russian. Moreover, the activists who had conducted the survey took its results with a pinch of salt, because some artisans were ashamed to reveal their Russian illiteracy.[49] Jewish troupes that performed in Russian and Hebrew (from 1883 on, the Yiddish theater was banned in Russia and had to disguise itself as "German") usually attracted a rather narrow audience.[50]

A Jewish artisan could find interesting material in the Yiddish press. The Petersburg Yiddish newspaper *Fraynd*, which emerged in 1903 as the "first Russian daily in *zhargon*," featured a regular rubric titled "Arteln un kredit-khevres" (Cooperatives and Credit Associations). Khaim Dov Hurwitz (Horowitz)—known also as "A Soykher" ("A Merchant"), a pioneer of economics journalism in Yiddish and head of the JCA's Department for Savings-and-Loan Associations—edited the paper's economic section. A year after the tsar's October 17, 1905, manifesto, which significantly liberated the press, five Warsaw-based Yiddish dailies had a combined circulation of ninety-six thousand.[51] All Yiddish periodicals regularly covered events and discussions in cooperatives and other voluntary organizations. In 1913, the editors and publishers of the Warsaw-based Yiddish daily *Moment* founded a Jewish artisans'

---

[48] M. R—n, "Di yidishe natsionale shprakhn," *Di Proletarishe Velt* 4 (1907): 39–54.
[49] Abraham Kizhnits, "Yidishe bal-melokhes (des sakh-hakl fun an ankete)," *Di Yidishe Velt* 9 (1913): 108–17.
[50] Evgenii Bunevich, *Istoriia evreiskogo teatra v Rossii, 1875–1918* (Baltimore, 2009), 295–301, 374–81.
[51] See Daniel Gutwein, "Economics, Politics, and Historiography: Hayyim D. Horowitz and the Interrelationship of Jews and Capitalism," *Jewish Social Studies* 1, 1 (1994): 94–114; Gennady Estraikh, *In Harness: Yiddish Writers' Romance with Communism* (Syracuse, NY, 2005), 18–19.

club, similar to the club established in Łódź in 1911 by the Zionist activist Jan Kirschrot.[52]

The press also paid attention to problems of general and vocational education. Until 1914, the Russian authorities did not allow secular schools to use Yiddish as a language of instruction. Yet the issue of introducing Yiddish into the secular schools became a topic for discussion in the early 1900s.[53] In 1905, *Der Tsayt-gayst*, the weekly supplement of the New York Yiddish daily *Forverts*, wrote: "under the powerful impact of reality, the *zhargon* has occupied the most important place in intellectual life of Russian Jews. The rise of the language reflects the rise of the nation."[54] The Duma election in 1906 and its associated debate about education and languages of instruction also raised the profile of Yiddish.[55] Initially, the Jewish intelligentsia's drive to promote instruction in Yiddish often had little to do with any nationalist programs or ideas. Rather, the intelligentsia followed the example of other ethnic groups in the empire.[56] Gradually, however, Yiddish attracted hundreds of enthusiasts who saw the language as an important, even the most important, ingredient of modern Jewish nation building. The August 1908 Yiddish Language Conference in the then-Austro-Hungarian town of Czernowitz signaled that Yiddish had found advocates who subscribed to various ideologies. In 1909 and 1910, the rise in the status of Yiddish triggered "language wars" between Yiddishists and Hebraists. The December 1909 Hebrew language conference in Berlin, convened on the eve of the Ninth Zionist Congress in Hamburg, was one of the first episodes in the "war."[57]

Following a 1909 Vilna conference of educators from vocational schools for Jewish girls, Lestschinsky—who advocated teaching in the mother tongue—wrote: "The language problem forms the foundation of our national life, and one cannot avoid it in any discussion of our society."[58] The civic activist and journalist Joseph Roitberg reported a strong interest in Yiddish educa-

---

[52] Elimelech Rak, *Zikhroynes fun a yidishn hantverker* (Buenos Aires, 1958), 17–21.

[53] See, e.g., Ia. Sh., "Zhargon, kak sredstvo prosveshcheniia," *Evreiskaia shkola*, April 1904: 18–30; Dov-Ber Slutski, "Yidish," *Fraynd*, 6 February 1905, 3. See also Gennady Estraikh, "Dov-Ber Slutski—a goyrl fun a yidishn intelektual," *Forverts*, 30 March 2008, 12–13.

[54] "Der zshargon un der zshargonizher lezer in Rusland," *Der Tsayt-gayst*, 22 September 1905, 8.

[55] Cf. Wayne Dowler, "The Politics of Language in Non-Russian Elementary Schools in the Eastern Empire, 1865–1914," *Russian Review* 54, 4 (1995): 516–38.

[56] Abraham Golomb, "Pedagogishe problemes fun der yidisher shul," *Shriftn far psikhologye un pedagogik* 1 (Vilna, 1933): 299.

[57] See, e.g., Moyshe Olgin, "'Zshargon': tsum shprakh-shtrayt in der yidisher gas," *Forverts*, 5 February 1910, 4; A. Litvin, "Di yidishe kultur-frage un der Berliner 'kongres,'" *Forverts*, 6 February 1910, 4.

[58] Lestschinsky, "Profesyon-froyen-shule oyf dem Vilner tsuzamenfor," 6.

tion in Kiev.[59] By 1909, some Jewish vocational schools for girls taught Yiddish "to introduce them to modern Yiddish literature."[60] During sessions of the "parliament of Jewish women," as the 1909 Vilna conference was dubbed, the "question of Yiddish as a language of instruction had provoked hot debates. Some participants even demanded that instruction take place only in Yiddish, but they remained a minority. Still, the sessions decided that Yiddish, the students' mother tongue, should be used for explaining complex questions."[61]

From the late 1900s on, the JCA and the ORT published "how to" literature in Yiddish.[62] More than two years before the Czernowitz Yiddish Language Conference, the OPE decided to consider Yiddish equal to Hebrew and Russian. Liberals and Zionists initiated the OPE's decision, but without support from the Bundists, who refused to cooperate with the "antiquated bourgeois" OPE.[63] No doubt, the decisions of essentially non-Yiddishist educators and their sponsors, such as the OPE and the ORT, had greater effect than the resolutions of the Czernowitz conference, whose immediate practical impact was quite limited.[64] Granted, OPE activists continued to favor Hebrew in its practical work. Thus, the pioneering Yiddish school in Demievka, then a Kiev suburb with a large Jewish population, could not win financial support from the OPE, because the school did not give in to the OPE's demands to introduce Hebrew lessons.[65]

In August 1913, two hundred members of Jewish cooperatives were among the 1,300 delegates attending the Second Congress of All-Russian Cooperatives in Kiev. The Jewish delegates influenced the congress resolutions, especially those on the forms of coordination of the cooperative movement. Together with the Ukrainian delegates, the Jewish representatives successfully championed the autonomy of each national group. Although the Ukrainians preferred territorial autonomy, the final resolution reflected the Jewish delegates' predilection for nonterritorial autonomy.[66] The Jewish delegates met separately at the congress and decided to establish a commission

---

[59] Joseph Roitberg, "Vegn der yidisher shul un der yidisher shprakh," *Der Fraynd*, 3 May 1909, 4.

[60] *Trudy s"ezdov po evreiskomu professional'nomu obrazovaniiu*, 1 (St. Petersburg: JCA, 1911), 251.

[61] A. Litvin, "Der 'parlament' fun yidishe vayber in Vilne," *Forverts*, 11 February 1911, 4.

[62] See, e.g., *Di takones (der muster-ustav) fun a lay- un shpor-kase* (St. Petersburg, 1909); and *Di praktik fun lay- un shpor-kases* (St. Petersburg, 1909).

[63] Fishman, *The Rise of Modern Yiddish Culture*, 45–46; Brian Horowitz, "Victory from Defeat: 1905 and the Society for the Promotion of Enlightenment among the Jews of Russia," in *The Revolution of 1905 and Russia's Jews*, ed. Stefani Hoffman and Ezra Mendelsohn (Philadelphia, 2008), 85–95; Horowitz, *Jewish Philanthropy and Enlightenment in Late-Tsarist Russia*, 186.

[64] See, e.g., Barry Trachtenberg, *The Revolutionary Roots of Modern Yiddish, 1903–1917* (Syracuse, NY, 2008), 70.

[65] Estraikh, *In Harness*, 13.

[66] Khaim Dov Hurvits, "In der yidisher velt," *Di Yidishe Velt* 8 (1913): 158–59.

to promote Jewish cooperatives, among other things. The participants voted to adopt Yiddish in all publications, including a journal (thirty-two, including the JCA representative, supported this resolution, whereas twenty-four voted for both Yiddish and Russian, and ten preferred Russian alone). As a temporary measure, the group decided to use the journal *Handl un Melokhe* (Commerce and Trade), edited by the socialist educator and journalist Abraham Hersh Kotik (only two issues of this periodical came out in 1913).[67] According to Christoph Gassenschmidt, an earlier journal, *Der Kooperativer Kredit in Mayrev-kant* (Cooperative Credit in the [North-]West Region), was published in Minsk after the 1913 congress.[68] In 1914, a new monthly journal, *Di Yidishe Kooperatsye* (Jewish Cooperation), appeared in St. Petersburg.

By that time, the new generation of Jewish activists, whom Barry Trachtenberg calls "the generation of 1905," had become increasingly visible within Jewish civil society. "This was the first generation to take seriously the possibility that Yiddish could serve as a means through which to communicate the entire range of human thought."[69] Representatives of that generation staffed the Jewish relief network established during World War I under the umbrella of the Central Jewish Committee for the Relief of War Victims (EKOPO), which combined the efforts of such organizations as the JCA and the ORT.[70] Employees of this relief organization included scores of enthusiasts of Yiddish, among them Wolf Latski-Bertoldi and Jacob Lestschinsky. During the war, which saw the development of Yiddish schooling, many intellectuals of "the generation of 1905" became educators. In general, the spectacular achievements of Yiddish culture in the 1920s and 1930s would have been impossible without this group. "Children" of the 1905 revolution, they were also products of Russia's Jewish civil society, which created an environment where the *zhargon* of the shtetl community developed into the Yiddish language.

Organizations and institutions established in imperial Russia laid the foundation for Jewish civil societies in post–World War I Eastern Europe. The ORT, which in 1921 morphed into the World ORT Union, an international

---

[67] A. Slutski, "Di yidishe baratung oyf kooperativn tsuzamenfor," *Fraynd*, 12 August 1913, 2.
[68] Gassenschmidt, *Jewish Liberal Politics in Tsarist Russia*, 125.
[69] Trachtenberg, *The Revolutionary Roots of Modern Yiddish 1903–1917*, 3; see also Khaim Abraham Finkel, "ORT," *Di Royte Velt* 9 (1926): 94.
[70] For discussion of EKOPO's activities, see Steven J. Zipperstein, "The Politics of Relief: The Transformation of Russian Jewish Communal Life during the First World War," in *The Jews and the European Crisis, 1914–1921: Studies in Contemporary Jewry IV*, ed. Jonathan Frankel (Oxford, 1988), 22–40.

organization, became a stronghold of Yiddishism. The educator Israel Rubin, an activist of the Zionist Socialist Workers' Party, contended that his party had effectively taken over the ORT.[71] In the 1920s, some activists tried to advance an ideology of "ORTism" that attached paramount importance to Jewish economic emancipation.[72] A product of decades-long debates among Russian-Jewish intellectuals, ORTism combined Jewish Diaspora nationalism, "productivization" theories, and Yiddishism. David Bergelson, who, in the autumn of 1924, went on an ORT-sponsored mission to Bukovina and Bessarabia, wrote to Lestschinsky hailing the ORT as "a national movement."[73] Like many Yiddish intellectuals, Bergelson looked for a mass Yiddishist movement that had an economic and social basis. In reality, Yiddishism never developed into a mass movement with independent values that transcended political divisions but remained a mere niche in Jewish life—a passion of those literati and intellectual workers who regarded Yiddish and Yiddish culture as life-giving components of Jewish nation building. Seeds of the language's decline could be detected even at the time of its success around 1910. A. Litvin, then the *Forverts* correspondent in Russia, wrote about "a triumph and a tragedy" of Yiddish. On the one hand, many socialist and liberal intellectuals responded to the widening scale of activities by embracing the language of the Jewish masses. When Litvin visited St. Petersburg in 1910, he was pleasantly surprised to see that even OPE functionaries were happy to speak with him in Yiddish. On the other hand, Yiddish had little value among ordinary people, who perceived it as a "low" language, especially in comparison with such "high" languages as Russian, Polish, and Hebrew.[74]

Yiddish cultural activities always relied heavily on civil-society organizations, which were particularly successful in the artisanal sector and at those enterprises (e.g., in the apparel trades) whose workforce was to a great extent Jewish. Even in the Soviet Union, the artisanal sector formed the most propitious environment for preservation of traditional cultural, religious, and communal life. In the 1920s, some Soviet trade-union branches (e.g., of tanners) in Ukraine and Belorussia remained predominantly Jewish.[75] By 1927, in the Soviet Union there were 233 *kases*, established and supported by the American Jewish Joint Distribution Committee (JDC) and the JCA. These

---

[71] Israel Rubin (Rivkai), *Fundanen ahin: retrospektsye-eseyen un zikhroynes* (Tel Aviv, 1972), 206.

[72] Leon Shapiro, *The History of ORT: A Jewish Movement for Social Change* (New York, 1980), 169.

[73] See Gennady Estraikh, "Jacob Lestschinsky: A Yiddishist Dreamer and Social Scientist," *Science in Context* 20, 2 (2007): 224.

[74] A. Litvin, "Yidish, yidish, yidish: der kurs fun mame-loshn heybt zikh in Rusland," *Forverts*, 2 July 1910, 5.

[75] Gennady Estraikh, "From Shtetl to the City of the Sun Calling at the Schools of Communism: Yiddish in Soviet Ukrainian Trade Unions of the 1920s," *East European Jewish Affairs* 29, 1–2 (1999): 51–60.

credit cooperatives had over sixty thousand members, providing service to about three hundred thousand people, or 10 percent of the entire Soviet-Jewish population.[76] In the post-Holocaust period, separate cooperatives sponsored by the JDC and the ORT reemerged in Poland. Again, these cooperatives' membership created the social basis for Yiddish culture.[77]

It is also no accident that the longest-lived Yiddish newspapers often cultivated their own civil-society network. In the United States, *Forverts* was established in 1897 as a forum of Jewish trade unionists linked (from 1900) with the Workmen's Circle, whose split organization, the Jewish People's Fraternal Order, later nourished the communist daily *Morgn-Frayhayt*. The American Jewish workmen's organizations drew, "of course, their members principally from the ranks of artisans."[78] Clubs and various organizations of supporters kept left-wing Yiddish dailies afloat in Paris and Buenos Aires.[79]

No doubt, one could write a convincing history of the rise and decline of modern Yiddish culture in Eastern Europe and elsewhere by examining the developments in Jewish civil society, whose dominant language, Yiddish, fulfilled numerous functions, making many people believe that this modern ideological and cultural environment could be maintained as a stable Yiddishland. (In the mid-1930s, Joseph Opatoshu, a Yiddish prose writer with a taste for theorizing, concluded that "'Ashkenaz' had become 'Yiddishland,' or an ideological rather than a geographic notion.")[80] Ultimately, however, such organizations faced generational shifts in their membership and gradually changed the language of their activities (for instance, from Yiddish to English), lest they shrink dramatically or decline.

---

[76] Joseph Rosen, "Report," in *After Three Years: The Progress of the Jewish Farm Colonies in Russia* (New York, 1927), 8.

[77] See, e.g., Hersh Smolar, *Oyf der letster positsye mit der letster hofenung* (Tel Aviv, 1982), 248–50; David Sfard, *Mit zikh un mit andere* (Jerusalem, 1984), 251–52; and Daniel Blatman, "Polish Jewry, the Six-Day War, and the Crisis of 1968," in *The Six-Day War and World Jewry*, ed. Eli Lederhendler (Bethesda, MD, 2000), 291–310.

[78] Samuel Koenig, "The Social Aspects of the Jewish Mutual Benefit Societies," *Social Forces* 18, 2 (1939): 271.

[79] Leonardo Senkman, "Repercussions of the Six-Day War in the Leftist Jewish Argentine Camp: The Rise of Fraie Schtime, 1967–1969," in *The Six-Day War and World Jewry*, 175–76; Aline Benain and Audrey Kichelewski, "*Parizer Haynt* et *Naïe Presse*, les itineraries paradoxaux de deux quotidiens parisiens en langue Yiddish," *Archives juives* 1, 36 (2003): 52–69.

[80] *Ershter alveltlekher yidisher kultur-kongres* (Paris, 1937), 26.

3. An-sky in Liozno

"Sins of Youth" and the Archival Diary

Gabriella Safran

When the Russian and Yiddish writer Semyon Akimovich An-sky (Shloyme-Zanvl Rappoport, 1863–1920) described his own life, he imagined it in quintessentially literary terms. In his 1910 memoir, "Sins of Youth and Sins of Age" (Grekhi molodosti i grekhi starosti, later published as simply "Sins of Youth," Grekhi iunosti), one of his most familiar texts in English, he describes the few months he spent in 1881 in the Belorusian shtetl of Liozno (known as the birthplace of Shneur Zalman, the founder of Hasidism).[1] The seventeen-year-old hero (whom I will call, anachronistically, An-sky) survives by tutoring local Jewish children in Russian, but his secret goal is to lead them astray toward Haskalah and revolution. He pretends to the pious townsfolk that he is one of them, but he tells his diary—which he keeps in the form of a letter to a close friend, the eventual diaspora nationalist Chaim Zhitlowsky—the truth about his scorn for them and their beliefs. When the daughter of his landlady finds his diary, she reads it aloud to her friends, and the next day, some of the hapless tutor's erstwhile employers, stung by his criticism, turn him away. Eventually, Liozno youth are discovered reading the tutor's forbidden books—

I am grateful to my colleague Monika Greenleaf and to the many other kind Slavists who replied to my SEELANGS query looking for examples of the public reading of diaries and letters. I also thank the editors of this volume.

[1] "S. An-skii, "Grekhi molodosti i grekhi starosti," *Evreiskii mir* 2, 10–11 (1910). My citations are from a slightly later Russian edition, "Grekhi iunosti (stranichka iz vospominanii)," in S. An-skii, *Sobranie sochinenii* (St. Petersburg, 1911–13), 2. The text has been translated into English from a later Yiddish version, "Hatos neurim," Sh. An-ski, *Gezamelte shriftn* (hence *GS*), 10 (New York: An-ski, c1920s), and published twice, as "I Enlighten a Shtetl" in Lucy S. Dawidowicz, *The Golden Tradition: Jewish Life and Thought in Eastern Europe* (London, 1967), and as "The Sins of Youth," in S. Ansky, *The Dybbuk and Other Writings*, ed. David G. Roskies (New York, 1992) (hence *DOW*).

in particular, Moshe Leib Lilienblum's 1873 memoirs, *Sins of Youth*—and soon he is forced out of town.

The downfall of the careless secret agent who writes too much down and then leaves the evidence lying around is familiar from literature. Many Americans would recognize this scene as the central moment of Louise Fitzhugh's 1964 children's classic, *Harriet the Spy*, whose young heroine, an aspiring writer, notes down her frank observations about her classmates and is then ostracized by them after they read her notebooks aloud. For Russian adults and children of An-sky's time and since, the scene is equally familiar from act 5 of Nikolai Gogol's 1836 play, *The Inspector General* (Revizor), where the postmaster brings the townsfolk a purloined letter proving that Ivan Alexandrovich Khlestakov is not a government inspector but a good-for-nothing, cheerfully exploiting the local officials whom he describes to a friend in mocking terms. An-sky himself knew perfectly well that this scene was a literary cliché. Just the year before, in the 1909 story "Behind a Mask" (Pod maskoi), he had a shtetl maskil scornfully describe big-city maskilim such as he himself had been. "They like to talk a lot, and especially to write long letters about everything one shouldn't mention, and those letters almost always end up in the hands of the rabbi or the head of the yeshiva. They also love to carry heretical books in all their pockets, and these often give them away."[2]

It is tempting to dismiss An-sky's recollection of the theft of his diary as too good to be true, most likely exaggerated if not simply invented. He knew which incidents in his life played well, and he retold them often and effectively, embroidering them to suit whichever audience he faced.[3] Dismissal of this incident is complicated, though, by the recent rediscovery of the diary in question. In 1924, Frida Shargorodskaia described the An-sky archive located at the Jewish Historical-Ethnographic Society as containing a letter to Zhitlowsky written in the form of a diary and dating from the early 1880s.[4] This document was taken with much of the rest of that archive to the Vernadsky National Library in Kiev. The 2006 catalogue of the Vernadsky An-sky collection refers to a 16-page document, "A Melamed's Diary: A Novella" (A melameds tagebukh. A povest). The first nine pages of this document are in fact an unfinished story in Yiddish about a melamed, while the last seven (front and back) are the diary-letter mentioned by Shargorodskaia.[5]

---

[2] S. An-skii, "Pod maskoi (Rasskaz starogo 'maskila')," *Evreiskii mir* 1, 6 (June 1909): 85.

[3] I discuss such a case in Gabriella Safran, "An-sky in 1892: The Jew and the Petersburg Myth," in *The Worlds of S. An-sky: A Russian-Jewish Intellectual at the Turn of the Century*, ed. Gabriella Safran and Steven J. Zipperstein (Stanford, CA, 2006), 68–74.

[4] F. Shargorodskaia, "O nasledii An-skogo," *Evreiskaia starina*, no. 11 (1924): 307.

[5] Viddil fondiv Iudaiki, Institut rukopisi Natsional'noi biblioteki Ukrainy imeni V. I. Vernads'koho (VFU IR NBUV) f. 339 (An-sky papers), od. zb. 73 (A melameds tage bukh. A

3. An-sky in Liozno

The rich collection in An-sky's Kiev archive includes documents from the 1880s through the 1917 revolution; it contains papers that he appears to have kept with him throughout his life, including many that must have survived the devastating 1909 fire in his boarding house. Thus, it is possible that the writer had this fragmentary adolescent diary with him when he composed "Sins of Youth" (and "Under a Mask"), and that as he drew in his writings on his youthful experiences, he consulted his own early composition. We cannot know whether he did so, but regardless, the juxtaposition of the 1881 Liozno diary and An-sky's later memoir offers material to consider how he fashioned himself and his writerly persona over time, how he conceptualized his audience, and how he manipulated his sources and, perhaps, his memories in order to achieve the results he desired.

A picture emerges of An-sky as something other than what he pretended to be. He tended to present himself to Jewish audiences as a returner: a person who, having flirted with assimilation in his youth, had realized the error of his ways and returned, repentant, to the Jewish people. This narrative of return dominates his published Yiddish writing, much of the memoir literature, and the scholarship that has relied on these sources. But close examination of archival sources, such as the diary, and comparison of them with his various versions of his own works, suggests that he was more a restless self-fashioner than a true returner. Even while he would sometimes insist that he longed only to devote himself selflessly to the cause of Jewish cultural revival, the evidence I investigate shows that he remained a canny self-promoter, always conscious of the effect of his words on his audience—a discovery that does not negate but complicates the notion of an intellectual's "return" to the folk. He chose, at times, to fashion himself as a returner, when he sensed that that guise would serve him best.

Liozno

The 1881 diary has much in common with other letters that An-sky actually sent to Zhitlowsky.[6] The handwriting is messy and the Yiddish replete with Russian words, whose spelling reveals An-sky's Litvish Yiddish

---

povest); see Irina Sergeeva, *Arkhivna spadshchyna Semena An-skoho u fondakh Natsional'noi biblioteky Ukrainy imeni V. I. Vernads'koho* (Kyiv, 2006), 118.

[6] Zhitlowsky's archive at the YIVO Institute for Jewish Research contains some 215 letters written by An-sky in Russian and Yiddish between 1883 and 1920. YIVO Institute for Jewish Research, RG 208 (Zhitlowsky papers).

pronunciation (he spoke "sabesdike losn," that is, with /s/ in place of /sh/).[7] The tone is confessional and emotional, with frequent references to the writer's loneliness and his difference from those around him. "Börne, Börne!" he wrote in Liozno, referring to the German-Jewish writer Karl Ludwig Börne (1786–1837), one of the favorites of the maskilim. "Correctly did you write, 'It is hard to be a human being among cattle!' Not a single human being! Not a word! Not a familiar word, as it should be, according to me."[8] He is explicit about the diary's function as a place to record impressions and ideas. "My head is full!" he began. "Scene after scene, each one better than the next [. . .] but I'm so busy that I can't manage to write it all down in the diary that I'm writing you. Certainly a lot is missing and I will certainly forget a lot." He was sure that to record everything he saw would require "an artist's pen," and he feared that his efforts would be inadequate.[9] He recorded things that he had never seen before—such as a woman's death—as well as recounting his dreams, his anxieties, and his vows to be more frugal.[10] He used this document, as he used later letters and diaries, to work through his own emotions.[11]

His emotions in Liozno were those of an angry, isolated adolescent. Although he had been born in a shtetl himself, he was now a big-city kid from Vitebsk, scornful of the shtetl folk. In Liozno, he noted gloomily, smiling at a Jew who was not wearing a skullcap would qualify you as a liberal, reading secular books instead of studying rabbinic texts made you a heretic, and thinking that learning Russian was as important as studying Talmud made people see you as an apostate.[12] To convince the traditional townspeople to hire him as a tutor, An-sky found out that he would have to play the role of an observant, synagogue-going young man. "'You have to go to shul,' the landlord said to me. To shul? Yes . . . to shul. You have to . . . you must go to shul!"[13] An-sky went to shul. He was unimpressed: "The shul was like a stable where there are horses." As for the ark holding the scrolls of the Torah, even to describe it would be to "desecrate the holy places." When he went door to door to find tutoring work, An-sky found the householders unappealing. He wrote scathingly of one father in his diary: "The householder was sitting by

---

[7] [Mikhail Krutikov], "Sh. An-ski, fun 'Hatos neurim,'" *Forverts*, 27 May 2005, 12. This issue contains a publication of a section of the archival diary as well as a brief linguistic analysis.
[8] "A melameds tage bukh," l. 10.
[9] Ibid.
[10] Ibid., ll. 15 ob., 16 ob.
[11] I discuss the similarities between An-sky's correspondence with Roza Ettinger and *Khurbn Galitsye* (Destruction of Galicia) in the ninth chapter of my biography of An-sky, *Wandering Soul: The Dybbuk's Creator, S. An-sky* (Cambridge, MA, 2010). In the seventh chapter, I discuss the unsent letters to Edia Glezerman in which he grapples with his feelings about their divorce.
[12] "A melameds tage bukh," l. 10.
[13] Ibid., l. 11.

the table and eating, wearing just an undershirt. A small face […] a stubbly beard […] a cunning smile. What to say? What to begin with? Brrrr! 'I heard that you need … a … tutor for your children. I am a tutor from Vitebsk.' I said the words and turned red, my head began to spin."[14]

While An-sky mocked some of the shtetl folk, others turned out to be on his side. Having gone to synagogue, he started to pray, then noticed two boys giving him funny looks. "They started to pull each other by their coattails and say 'look!' and giggle. The *gabbai* came up to them and yelled, 'Pray!'"[15] The boys were not the only ones to guess that An-sky was out of place in the shul. Another man who sensed his true inclinations revealed himself as a secret ally.

> On the other side of the table was a young man of about 30 […] he offered me his hand.
>
> "Do you already have some lessons set up?"
>
> "Very few. Almost none."
>
> "It would have to be hard here. People are cursed here. Come, I'll try to do something about it."
>
> We went away. As we walked, he told me a bit about Liozno. […] One must be shrewd with them. […] He is a melamed and must dance to their tune; someday he will tell me his life story. We came to his place […] small but perfectly clean. We spoke a little; he made me a list of the householders that I will try to go to. He said in a few places he would also go in with me. I said that I didn't want to trouble him. "You think you're so smart," he said, "sure!" But I understood that he wouldn't refuse to help me.[16]

The diary shows that this seemingly sleepy shtetl was a land ripe for rebellion, where insurgents lurked everywhere, recognizable to each other through subtle signs. Even while An-sky stood in the shul and mouthed the prayers, something in his tone, stance, or style made it obvious to the boys pulling each other's coattails and to the thirty-year-old melamed that he was one of them, as opposed to the "cattle." They could tell that although he billed himself as a Russian tutor, he really wanted to teach the children of the town to rebel—to read the heretical books of the maskilim and the Russian radicals, to abandon the code of religious regulations governing their parents' lives,

---

[14] Ibid., l. 12 ob.
[15] Ibid., l. 11 ob.
[16] Ibid., ll. 11 ob.–12.

and to dedicate themselves to ideals and a lifestyle their parents would find abhorrent.

"Sins of Youth," the memoir that An-sky wrote ten years later, has episodes that appear to come straight from the diary: the forced synagogue attendance, the need to pretend to his pupils' parents that he was as pious as they, the scornful depiction of the townsfolk. He describes his contact with fellow young rebels in terms that recall the two boys in his diary who pick him out in synagogue and giggle: "No matter how out-of-the-way the shtetl was, it already had some secret freethinkers, gripped by a confused yearning for light and knowledge, hungering for a living word, advice, teaching. They immediately guessed that I had the same views, and wordlessly, just by their glances, which were silent, reverently loyal, entreating and inviting, they made me understand that they thirsted to meet me and speak with me."[17]

Finally, the diary itself—which in a later Yiddish edition of the memoir he identified explicitly as the one he kept in the form of letters to Zhitlowsky—appears in the memoir as one of the sources of his undoing:

> I kept my diary in Yiddish. Of course, I hid it away carefully, but one day I forgot to lock my box and the landlady's daughter, a curious person, came in during my absence, fished out the diary, began reading, and finding my descriptions of the people she knew interesting, assembled a few of her girlfriends for a literary soirée. The next day, the contents of my diary were known all over town.
>
> Unaware of all this, I went as usual to give my lessons. When I arrived for the first lesson, the lady of the house greeted me at the door with this welcome: "Listen here, you teacher! I hired you to teach my girls to read and write, but not for you to write down that my Yakhninka's nose is dirty, and that my Fridinka has big teeth, and that I go about in a bedraggled dress. I can assure you that even if I wear a bedraggled dress, whatever I put in the garbage is worth more than you and your fine learning. And you can go back where you came from! Teachers like you I don't need!"
>
> The same scene was repeated at the next lesson. I was beside myself with despair, not knowing what had caused this misfortune. I expected that I would find the same reception at my other lessons, but apparently my dear first reader had no time to read the whole diary or forgot to tell everything. At the other homes, I was received not only without anger and abuse but

---

[17] "Grekhi iunosti," 245.

with even more friendliness than usual. These women, rolling with laughter, begged me to let them read how I described their neighbors.[18]

The exposure of his diary was only the beginning of An-sky's troubles, as recounted in "Sins of Youth." The year of 1881 was a time of political drama and violence in the empire. The assassination of Tsar Alexander II on 1 March provoked a wave of pogroms in the south of the empire that lasted for over a year. There were no pogroms in Vitebsk province, but when the Liozno elders learned of the violence against Jews elsewhere, they became convinced that the real cause was the growing disregard among the young for religious traditions and observance: in His anger, God had sent pogroms to punish the people. Meanwhile, some of the teenage boys in town, having deduced An-sky's identity, had begun to meet in his room late on Friday nights to discuss their ideas. He lent them books, which they read secretly. Among them was *Sins of Youth*, Lilienblum's recently published and highly scandalous Hebrew memoir.[19] One of An-sky's young friends stayed up all night reading Lilienblum's account of the alienation from the religious worldview of his father and his community that eventually provoked his own rejection by that community. The boy brought *Sins of Youth* to the study house in the morning to read it under the cover of the Gemara, then fell asleep. The forbidden book was discovered by a yeshiva student who happened upon the line, "Who can prove that God exists?"[20] Although the boy awoke and snatched the volume away, the damage had been done. In the ensuing furor, as An-sky recalled, a dozen secular books were found in people's homes and publicly burned, and the tutor was forced out of town.

Lilienblum

When An-sky published his own "Sins of Youth" in October 1910, Lilienblum and his autobiography were on his mind. Lilienblum had just died in March of that year, and An-sky began his first publication of the memoir with a paean to Lilienblum and the impact of his *Sins of Youth* on the Jews of An-sky's generation. "They didn't just read it but studied it piously, like a book of the bible, a symbol of our faith. The more bitterly it was persecuted by the elders, the holier it became for the youth. […] The influence of this book was

---

[18] Ibid., 247. Translation adapted in some places from *DOW*, 73.
[19] For a useful English summary, see Leon Simon, *Moses Leib Lilienblum* (Cambridge, 1912).
[20] "Grekhi iunosti," 249.

simply magic. Under its influence people sometimes were reborn overnight."[21] By titling his essay "Sins of Youth," An-sky paid homage to Lilienblum, emphasized the significance of the moment in the memoir when Lilienblum's book is read, and suggested an organic tie between himself and the recently deceased Hebrew writer.

When An-sky hinted in the title of his essay that his youth was analogous to Lilienblum's, he adopted a conceit that Lilienblum himself had used. As part of his defense of the genre of autobiography in general, Lilienblum had compared his own work to another Hebrew autobiography, Mordecai Aaron Guenzburg's *Aviezer* (1864). Because *Aviezer* tells the story of the writer's childhood and youth, Lilienblum announced that his own autobiography would start at the end of adolescence, where Guenzburg's left off, as though their lives were so similar that one description would suffice for both.[22] This narrative device created the sense of a community of Jewish radicals like the writer, all with shared experiences and goals: a single plot shaped all their lives.[23] The "sins" of Lilienblum's youth—committed not by Lilienblum himself but by the family and community who urged him to devote his mental energy to the Talmud alone, married him off young, and made it impossible for him to leave the Jewish world—were repeated in Guenzburg's youth and in the youths of many other Jewish men.

At first glance, it seems the conceit might work for An-sky too. Indeed, the bare outlines of the narrative of An-sky's life for his months in Liozno echoed elements of Lilienblum's life as he retold them in *Sins of Youth*. Having started to question his faith in God, Lilienblum began writing articles advocating religious reform, and his fellow townsmen responded by branding this yeshiva teacher an unbeliever and an atheist. He was persecuted and threatened with exile to Siberia. Finally, he left his home for the more liberal city of Odessa, where he supported himself as a tutor and a clerk. There he read Dmitrii Pisarev and other Russian radical writers and turned into a yet more severe critic of Judaism. He began to write articles asserting that secular sciences would not be enough to resolve the problems of the Jews: instead, their entire economic structure would have to change, and young people would have to study real crafts rather than musty tomes. An-sky shared Lilienblum's fascination with Pisarev and practical work, and he too was branded an unbeliever and chased out of a shtetl.

More careful examination shows, however, that An-sky's childhood was very different from Lilienblum's. An-sky could hardly complain that the "sins"

---

[21] Ibid., 243.
[22] Moshe Leib Lilienblum, "Hatot-neurim," *Ktavim otobiografiim* (Jerusalem, 1970), 1:95.
[23] For an analysis of this device, see Alan Mintz, *"Banished from Their Father's Table": Loss of Faith and Hebrew Autobiography* (Bloomington, IN, 1989), 29.

that ruined Lilienblum's life had marred his own as well. Where Lilienblum had no mother (she died when he was very young) and a father who brought him up within the bonds of tradition, An-sky had an absent father and an indulgent mother; where Lilienblum read only Hebrew and Yiddish, An-sky was reading Russian novels in his teens; and where Lilienblum reserves special wrath for the institution of early marriages and criticizes his family harshly for marrying him off at fourteen to a girl three years younger than he was, An-sky was unbetrothed not just at seventeen but into his thirties. An-sky belonged to a later generation (Lilienblum was born two decades before him), and a deep cultural gap separated the two men. Whereas Lilienblum experienced the loss of belief in God as a trauma and spent his life searching for a faith to replace his former one, An-sky, in his voluminous writings, rarely touched on God or religious faith. Where Lilienblum turned from a convinced maskil to a passionate Zionist, An-sky frustrated friends and colleagues with his unwillingness to hew to any Jewish party line. But with his retrospective analogy between his childhood and Lilienblum's, An-sky claimed membership in a fellowship of Jewish writers that included Lilienblum.

If An-sky's implicit analogy between his own life and Lilienblum's was factually shaky, it had an ideological import that would have been clear to contemporaries. By the time of his death, Lilienblum played a specific role among Russian-Jewish cultural activists. He was not seen as the angry narrator of *Sins of Youth*, bitter about the father, the in-laws, and the entire Jewish culture that had prevented him from acquiring an education and doing anything useful for himself or anyone else, but rather as the Zionist activist that he later became, the author of the 1899 *Derekh Teshuvah* (The Way Back), an account of his rejection of the ideal that assimilation would solve the problems of the Jews. Thus, An-sky's "Sins of Youth" could be read as signaling not the maskilic bitterness about the constraints of traditional Jewish life from the first part of Lilienblum's memoirs, but a move away from the Haskalah and the embrace of new possibilities for Jewish community, which are associated with the second part of Lilienblum's memoir. Certainly An-sky's "Sins of Youth" suggests a cynicism about his own youthful idealism. The notion of a community that is collectively guilty and that then suffers collectively is implied in the Hebrew word that Lilienblum uses: a reader immersed in Jewish religious tradition might associate the *hattot* (sins) of his title with one of the central prayers of Yom Kippur, the confession in which the congregation chants in unison, "Hattanu" (we have sinned). But An-sky's "sins" were not the communal *hattot* to which the Jewish congregation confesses on Yom Kippur, but rather the individual sins that the Russian word of his title, *grekhi*, implies, remembering that Russian Orthodoxy knows individual but not collective confessions of sins. While the Hebrew title of

Lilienblum's *Sins of Youth*, "Hattot Neurim," could refer to the sins against youth of which the entire community is guilty, the Russian title of "Grekhi molodosti" would more likely mean the sins of which a single young person is guilty. Given the irony in the story about the protagonist's attempts to lure his students away from tradition, the primary sin to which the title refers may be the Christian sin of pride.

If An-sky was using his memoir in 1910 to atone for his youthful maskilic pride and to claim that he now held communal loyalties analogous to Lilienblum's, then his audience may have been his fellow Jewish writers. In the fall of 1908, An-sky had asked a number of well-known Yiddish writers to contribute to *Evreiskii mir* (Jewish World), a new journal where he would work through mid-1911.[24] His goal in editing the literary section, as he explained, was to familiarize the Jewish public that read only Russian with "the best works of Jewish literature in all languages," including new stories and poems by Yiddish and Hebrew writers. He offered to pay forty rubles per signature for new, never-before-published Yiddish stories: the *Evreiskii mir* editorial office would organize and pay for the translation, and after the stories came out in Russian, the writer would be free to republish them in the original.[25] With these conditions, he successfully recruited the best-known Yiddish writers of the time. The first issue (January 1909) contained memoirs by Mendele Moikher Sforim, a dramatic poem by Peretz (translated by An-sky himself), and a new story by Sholem Aleichem about Tevye the dairyman.[26]

For some Yiddish writers, though, the notion of having their Yiddish work appear for the first time in Russian translation was unappealing. Der Nister (Pinkhes Kahanovitsh, 1884–1950) explained his reaction in a December 1908 letter to Shmuel Niger: "I got an invitation from An-sky to participate in his *Evreiskii mir*. Among other conditions, he insists that what I give him must not have been published already in Yiddish or Hebrew: that is, to release first in Russian something that was born and raised in Yiddish . . . Well, how could

---

[24] The journal was monthly through 1909. The first eighteen issues of its newspaper version came out more or less weekly from 8 January 1910 until 6 May 1910, under the name *Evreiskoe obozrenie (Jewish Review)* from mid-May through August 1910, and from 10 September 1910 again as *Evreiskii mir* until 30 April 1911 (although issue no. 10 of 1911 was confiscated by the censors and destroyed). On the history of these publications, see U. G. Ivask, *Evreiskaia periodicheskaia pechat' v Rossii* (Tallinn, 1935), 56–66.

[25] Letter from An-sky to Dinezon, 20 November 1908, Petersburg, in *Fun Yankev Dinezons arkhiv: Briv fun idishe shriftshteler tsu Yankev Dinezon*, ed. Sh. Rozenfeld (Warsaw, 1921), 20.

[26] Mendele-Moikher-Sforim, "Istoriia odnoi zhizni (vospominaniia pisatelia)"; I. L. Peretz, "'Na pokaiannoi tsepi.' Dramaticheskaia poema v trekh chastiakh"; Sholem-Aleikhem, "Tev'e-molochnik uezzhaet v Palestinu," *Evreiskii mir* 1, 1 (January 1909). A partial list of contributors appears in the front cover of the first trimonthly supplement to *Evreiskii mir*, no. 1 (January–March 1910).

one feel? I would feel like a person bringing his only child to be baptized, but what else can you do? But it's just not possible. I'm not even talking about money, but where can you find a place to publish in Yiddish?"[27] Der Nister knew that Russian occupied a privileged position relative to Yiddish, and because An-sky offered a path into Russian publication, he had to agree, however reluctantly, to his terms.

Ultimately, for a cohort of Yiddish writers of the younger, more militant generation, some of whom An-sky published in *Evreiskii mir*, he became a symbol of the irritation that Der Nister articulated about the subordination of Yiddish culture to Russian, and a target for their anger at what they saw as an assimilationist's willingness to betray his Jewish heritage. Their resentment is apparent in memoirs they wrote after An-sky's death. Shmarye Gorelik described An-sky as living in Vilna in early 1908 as though he were a Russian political exile sent to Irkutsk: he may have been an honorable and admirable person with charmingly old-fashioned Yiddish, but he was a mediocre writer, hopelessly committed to the ideals of the Russian Populists, and a member of a generation that "had understood literature wrong."[28] Alexander Mukdoyni (Alexander Kapel, 1878–1958), a theater critic in Peretz's circle, insisted that An-sky, though a warm personality, was a "fifth-rate writer" who became popular among the Jewish public only because he had made a career in Russian and had such strong connections to famous figures in Russian literature and culture.[29] Even when An-sky publicly embraced Yiddish and Jewish culture in his ethnographic work, Tsvi Hirshkan saw him as unable to overcome his own deep-rooted Russianness, his fateful assimilationism: just as he could only dance a Russian dance, the Kamarinskaya, "Hasidic-style," so he could only dance real Hasidic dances Russian-style.[30]

These young writers were not the only ones who felt uncomfortable with An-sky's request that they have their Yiddish texts translated into Russian; this anxiety was expressed on the pages of *Evreiskii mir* as well. An-sky's friend and editor Arkady Gornfel'd, writing in the first issue of 1909, expressed discomfort with the idea of the translation of Yiddish literature into Russian. Even while such translation could be useful to keep the Russian-Jewish intelligentsia informed about currents in shtetl life, and even while it made economic sense for Yiddish writers to want their work to reach a broad

---

[27] Letter from Der Nister to Niger, 13 December 1908, in "Igrotav shel Der Nister al Shmuel Niger," ed. Avraham Novershtern, *Khuliot* 1 (Winter 1993): 179.
[28] Shmarye Gorelik, *Eseyen* (Los Angeles, 1947), 336–39.
[29] Dr. A. Mukdoyni, *I. L. Peretz un dos yidishe teater* (New York, 1949), 252–53.
[30] Tsvi Hirshkan, "Der rusish-yidisher yid (Sh. A. Anski)," *Unter eyn dakh* (Warsaw, 1931), 73–74. Hirshkan's correspondence with An-sky is at VFU IR NBUV, f. 339, od. zb. 1013–25.

Russian audience, Gornfel'd wrote, "From my perspective, the perspective of a linguistic nationalist [...] not a single significant work was created or could be created in an atmosphere of national effacement and calculated attempts to appeal in various languages, that is, various modes of thought."[31] An-sky himself voiced similar ambivalence on a number of occasions. For instance, in 1913, after the journal had folded and another of the same name but in Yiddish had appeared in Vilna, he wrote to Yankev Dinezon, "Don't forget, my friend, that Petersburg is now, thank God, a Jewish town. Even the goyish *Evreiskii mir* has converted into a *Yidishe velt.*"[32] Given the atmosphere and given An-sky's own ambivalence about his editorial work at the time, it makes sense to read An-sky's "Sins of Youth" as a conciliatory move, an attempt to diminish the sense that he was somehow disloyal to Jewish or Yiddish culture, and to link himself to communal loyalists such as Lilienblum.

"Writers Like You I Don't Need"

Having drawn on his diary to write his 1910 memoir, An-sky put the text aside for a few years. He republished the memoir in Yiddish translation in 1919.[33] As he translated it, he revised it to serve different functions. He removed the introductory section on Lilienblum and the significance of his *Sins of Youth* and rewrote the scene of the discovery and public reading of his diary. The landlady's daughter is now described as "a lover of literature." Where in the 1910 Russian version of the text, the people of Liozno see An-sky primarily as a "teacher"; in the 1919 Yiddish version, they refer to him as a writer: "Listen, you writer!" says his student's offended mother. "Writers like you I don't need."[34] The 1919 text, more than the 1910 one, indicates that although An-sky may never have been a very successful conspirator, he had found his true calling in literature. The bumbling secret agent who spills his heart to his diary and then leaves the incriminating evidence in an unlocked box surely deserves the reader's scorn, but his misadventure unexpectedly brings him an appreciative audience. From the landlady's daughter to her

---

[31] A. Gorenfel'd, "Zhargonnaia literatura na russkom knizhnom rynke," *Evreiskii mir* 1, 1 (January 1909): 74.

[32] Letter from An-sky to Dinezon, 15 March 1912, *Fun Yankev Dinezons arkhiv*, 28. I discuss An-sky's correspondence with Shmuel Niger, in which he makes even more such conciliatory moves, in Gabriella Safran, "'Reverse Marranism,' Translatability, and the Theory and Practice of Secular Jewish Culture in Russian," in *Jewish Literatures and Cultures: Context and Intertext*, ed. Anita Norich and Yaron Eliav (Providence, 2008), 189–91.

[33] Sh. An-ski, "Hatos neurim," *Lite* 2 (Vilna 1919), reprinted in *GS*, 10.

[34] *GS*, 10:8–9.

friends at the "soirée" and the laughing mothers enjoying his mockery of their neighbors, the people of Liozno concurred with the evaluation of the student's mother. First and foremost, it would seem, An-sky was indeed a writer.

The changes that An-sky made to the 1919 text add to the relative weight of the diary-reading scene, the most literary moment of the memoir. They thereby increase the connection that An-sky was claiming to writers who used such scenes before him in Russian and Yiddish literature. The scene of the public reading of the stolen, insult-filled private document was linked in both languages to claiming one's identity as a writer. In Gogol's *Inspector General*, one of the last lines in Khlestakov's letter—after "The director of charities is a pig in a skullcap," "The superintendent of schools reeks of onions," and "Judge Liapkin-Tiapkin is the ultimate in *mauvais ton*"—is, "So long, Triapichkin, old pal. I intend to follow your example and take up literature. Life's dreary, my friend. In the long run a man hungers for spiritual nourishment. I'll just have to devote myself to the higher things in life."[35]

Another canonical Russian drama, the fantastically popular Aleksandr Ostrovskii's 1868 *Even the Wise Can Err* (Na vsiakogo mudretsa dovol'no prostoty), centers on a similar figure: the young social climber Yegor Dmitrich Glumov, a nimble-tongued hypocrite. Even as he schemes to secure the favor of a rich uncle and the hand of a wealthy maiden, he describes his own machinations and the reactions of those around him in his notebook. The notebook is stolen, of course, and read aloud to those whom he lampoons. They react, astonishingly, by recognizing their own foolishness: the liberal Ivan Ivanovich Gorodulin agrees that Glumov is a better writer than he, and says, "You are a delightful young man. Here is my hand. All that you say about us—that is, about me, I don't know about the others—is the absolute truth."[36] Glumov defends himself by arguing that he provides a crucial service to society.

> You cannot get on without men of my sort; if it is not me, it will be another. [...] There is one thing I do know, gentlemen—so long as I circulated in your society, the only honest moments I knew were those in which I wrote this diary. No honest man could take any other view of you than that recorded in these pages. You raised my gorge. What did you find in my diary that offended you? What did you learn about yourselves that was new to you? You say the very same things about one another every

---

[35] Translation adapted from *The Theater of Nikolay Gogol: Plays and Selected Writings*, ed. and trans. Milton Ehre and Fruma Gottschalk (Chicago: University of Chicago Press, 1980), 127.
[36] A. N. Ostrovskii, "Na vsiakogo mudretsa dovol'no prostoty," *P'esy* (Moscow, 2006), 371–72. Translation adapted from Alexander Ostrovsky, *Plays*, trans. Margaret Wettlin (Moscow, 1974), 365.

day, only behind one another's backs. If I had privately read to each one of you what I wrote about the others, you would have applauded me.[37]

In these scenes from Gogol and Ostrovsky, the illicit public reading of the theoretically private text demonstrates the appeal of a previously unrecognized writerly voice; these scenes also show that honesty is possible even for a hypocrite living in a hypocritical society. That possibility of honesty is connected both to art and to spite: to people's appreciation of a well-turned phrase, and to people's nasty pleasure when they hear others put down. It is easy to situate these texts in the realist tradition of art as social critique, as epitomized in nineteenth-century Russian literature by Mikhail Saltykov-Shchedrin's 1869–70 satire *History of a Town* (Istoriia odnogo goroda), and in Yiddish by maskilic satires, such as Aizik-Meyer Dik's 1868 "The Panic, or the City of Herres." Social satires such as these are meant, as critics of Gogol's and Ostrovsky's time recognized, to make readers recognize their own faults and reform.[38] That satiric model, though, is not sufficient to explain the literary scenes of the public reading of the private document, where the satirical judgment is voiced not by an omniscient narrator but by an individual whose authority is already compromised. The duplicitous Khlestakov and Glumov use their capacity for invention to their own advantage and the detriment of others until they are exposed. Even as they claim the identity of writer, that identity is revealed as morally flawed.

A similar scene appears in the Yiddish canon, in Sholem-aleichem's unfinished 1915 autobiographical novel *From the Fair* (Funem yarid), where it again confirms the young writer's professional identity.[39] Fascinated by his foul-mouthed new stepmother's language, the young Sholem writes down and then alphabetizes her curses, titling his composition "A Stepmother's

---

[37] Ibid., 366–67.

[38] An-sky's once-favorite critic Dmitrii Pisarev exemplifies this attitude.

[39] Literary history, Russian and other, abounds with other situations in which theoretically private documents become public. Sometimes writers themselves would allow certain people to see their insult-filled letters or diaries. See William Mills Todd, *The Familiar Letter as a Literary Genre in the Age of Pushkin* (Princeton, NJ, 1976), on how Romantic writers wrote letters meant to be shared with an exclusive group of readers beyond the addressee. Mikhail Kuzmin, An-sky's Petersburg contemporary and reviewer, was known for reading his diary out loud to a select group of people. Lev Tolstoy and his wife showed each other their diaries. Clearly, the idea of these writings as private or meant for a single addressee was fictional; indeed, in all these cases, the idea that the reader was getting access to a text that should be off-limits made it only more attractive. In English literature, scenes in which theoretically private writings are read publicly occur in Lucy Maud Montgomery's *Emily of New Moon*, in Neil Simon's *Biloxi Blues*, and elsewhere. My discussion of this is not meant to be exhaustive; I am primarily interested in cases where this literary trope is connected both to the possibility of societal reform and to the claiming of a writerly identity.

Invective," which the narrator calls "the future Sholem Aleichem's first work." His father confiscates it and reads it aloud to the stepmother, who is delighted, especially by the terms "pipsqueak" and "visor head": "A miracle occurred. It was hard to determine if she was in a fleeting good humor or was just ashamed to show anger. In any case, a strange frenzied laughter overtook her. She almost got apoplexy from shrieking."[40] Sholem Aleichem was undoubtedly in debt to Gogol and Ostrovsky, but his text is yet further away than theirs from the purely satirical mode. The point is not the hypocrisy of the society described or the possibility of honest criticism, but the inevitability of Sholem's eventual literary career and his choice to write not in Hebrew or Russian but in a Yiddish replete with oral elements.

An-sky's diary-reading scene also drew on the model of satire offered by Saltykov-Shchedrin and Dik, but like Gogol, Ostrovsky, and even more so Sholem Aleichem, he stepped away from pure satire. Like Khlestakov and Glumov, his narrator is a truth teller, but simultaneously a hypocrite and a figure of dubious authority. Like Sholem Aleichem, An-sky, in his memoir, distanced himself from the maskilic tradition of satire represented by Dik and from his own 1881 adolescent self, claiming to be a postmaskilic, less morally self-confident kind of writer.

It is useful to consider An-sky's diary and the various drafts of his memoir in light of Michael Stanislawski's insistence, in his recent book *Autobiographical Jews*, that memoirs should not be viewed as transparent historical sources. Instead, they reflect the author's needs of the moment; they are "artifacts of individuals' quests, tempered by the constraints of our all-too-human embodiment, to make sense of their lives, first and foremost for themselves and then, if possible, for their readers."[41] Clearly, the story of An-sky's memoirs confirms Stanislawski's assertion; as I have shown, An-sky used the retelling of an episode from his own life to make a specific kind of sense of himself—to one purpose in 1910 and to a slightly different purpose in 1919.

Now that we have access not only to these fictionalized accounts of An-sky's time in Liozno but also to the archival diary itself, should we privilege the diary over the various versions of the memoir, assuming that the diary, at least, gives us unmediated truth? I think not. The Russian writer Iurii Olesha noted in a 1930 diary entry: "There are no absolutely honest diaries. People pity their friends. They are ashamed. There is always the fear that the diary may be read by someone. People get smart, put it in code. [...] The diary also contains belletristic features. Their writers simply lie, make things up. (And

---

[40] Sholem Aleichem, *Funem Yarid, Oysgeveylte verk* (New York, 1923) 6:12–13. Translation adapted from Sholem Aleichem, *From the Fair*, trans. Curt Leviant (New York, 1985), 140.

[41] Michael Stanislawski, *Autobiographical Jews: Essays in Jewish Self-Fashioning* (Seattle, 2004), 17.

there is the desire to seem intelligent for posterity.)"[42] An-sky's youthful diary was also a letter—and so, Olesha argued, are all diaries: the possibility of being read is recognized by their writers, who are motivated, even at the time of writing, by artistic considerations.

The comic literary trope of the public scene of the reading of a private text, by its very popularity, confirms the fallacy of accepting the diary or letter as truly private. An-sky's 1881 diary, like the memoirs that draw on it and mention it, should be seen as an artistic product meant to attract readers and produce a calculated effect. In that context, the actual diary, valuable though it is as a biographical document and a record of life in Liozno in 1881, is in some ways inferior to the memoirs he produced later. The insults in the actual diary—the scornful words about Liozno's shul and the householder who sits at his table in his undershirt—are not nearly as funny as the put-downs of Khlestakov or Glumov. By structuring his memoir around the reading of his diary, without ever quoting the diary itself, An-sky accomplished something more important than he had managed in his 1881 text. He transformed the lonely, angry seventeen-year-old he had once been—a young person not unlike Harriet the spy—into a writer with an audience that could appreciate him in spite of all his sins. In the process, he made himself over—as he had so many times throughout his life—into the kind of artist and intellectual whom people might like.

---

[42] Iurii Olesha, "'My dolzhny ostavit' mnozhestvo svidetel'stv . . .' Dnevniki," *Znamia*, no. 10 (1996): 171. Cited in David Gillespie, "First Person Singular: The Literary Diary in Twentieth-Century Russia," *Slavonic and East European Review* 77, 4 (1999): 225.

4. In the Evil Kingdom of Things

Sholem-aleichem and the Writing of Everyday Life in Jewish Literature

Olga Litvak

Chiefly devoted to public history, John Klier's work manifests an abiding concern with the politics of Jewishness in the Russian Empire. In his pioneering monograph on the formative period in the making of Russia's Jewish policy, as well as in his magisterial *Imperial Russia's Jewish Question* and his manifold studies of Russian antisemitism, Klier explored various dimensions of the Russian-Jewish encounter in legal discourse and in the Russian-language periodical press. Students of the Jewish condition in Russia owe John Klier an immeasurable debt of gratitude for bridging the conventional divide between the history of the Jews in Russia and the history of Russian attitudes toward Jews.

Klier's prodigious bio-bibliography also offers a variety of examples of his inspiring ability to stretch as a scholar. Always deeply attentive and sensitive to the critical significance of literary and visual sources, John Klier was, for all of his rigorous training as a political historian, prepared to grapple with the

---

The conventional English spelling of Sholem-aleichem is Sholem Aleichem, which suggests that "Aleichem" is the author's last name. This is deeply misleading, not to mention just plain wrong, because "Sholem-aleichem" is actually a single phrase that means "How-are-you." Sholem-aleichem's actual last name was Rabinovich; to refer to him as "Aleichem-comma-Sholem" is to perpetuate the confusion between the person and the persona. For the sake of stylistic uniformity and historical transparency, I have chosen to transliterate Russian-Jewish names in accordance with their Russian transcription—rather, as in the case of Abramovich and Ravnitskii, Yiddish and Hebrew respectively. No matter what language Sholem-aleichem and company chose to use, all of them lived and worked in Russia rather than in the invented country of Yiddishland.

methodological implications of informed engagement with the modern Jewish imagination. To those of us whose interests lie at the intersection between the history of the Russian state and society and the evolution of Russian-Jewish culture, John Klier's appreciation of the importance of stories and pictures that often escape the radar of his fellow Russianists provided much-needed professional encouragement and intellectual support. Prompted by Klier's reflections on the "use of fiction . . . for the understanding of Jewish history," this chapter interrogates the writing of everyday life in the literary world of Sholem-aleichem, a place where John Klier glimpsed the "maturity" of Russian-Jewish self-consciousness—a "maturity," Klier wrote, "that may be witnessed in the position of Yiddish literature itself. Far from being the outcast daughter," of Jewish writers, in Sholem-aleichem's work, Yiddish had grown into a "national treasure" to become "an integral part of Jewish culture."[1]

For all that Yiddish served as the primary medium of Jewish expression and the first language of most nineteenth-century Russian Jews, descriptions of everyday life in Yiddish literary fiction remained heavily stylized. The founders of modern Yiddish literature limited their use of the vernacular to satire, ostensibly the most effective weapon against popular folly and vice. According to one critical reading, the social "utility" of Yiddish literature considerably attenuated the possibility of dispassionate observation and realistic representation because satire demanded the recourse to "caricatures and grotesques designed [. . .] to teach."[2] Jewish writers did not take for granted the choice to express themselves in Yiddish and often saw fit to provide elaborate ideological justification for stooping to the language of the masses.

> What profit accrues to a writer [wrote Sh. J. Abramovich, the creator of Mendele the Book Peddler] [. . .] if he does not serve his people? The question—for whom do I toil?—brought me no peace and caused me great perplexity. In my time, the Jewish language was an empty vessel, containing naught but gibes, nonsense, and fiddle-faddle, the jabber of fools who could not talk like human beings and had nothing to say. Women and vulgar folk read it without understanding; and the rest of the people, although they knew no other languages, were ashamed to read it so as not to expose their ignorance. [. . .] Our writers, masters of language, were interested only in the Holy Tongue and not in the people. [. . .] How great then was my dilemma when I considered that if I were to embark on writing in the shameful tongue, my honorable name would be besmirched! [. . .] But my

---

[1] John Klier, "From 'Little Man' to 'Milkman': Does Jewish Art Reflect Jewish Life?" *Studies in Jewish Civilization* 6 (2005): 222.
[2] Ibid., 218.

desire to be useful overcame my hollow pride; and I decided, come what may, I will write in Yiddish, that cast-off daughter, and work for the people.[3]

By the time Sholem-aleichem had discovered his own Yiddish muse, this kind of apology had become standard in rationalizations of the peculiar virtues of the vernacular. Constantly looking over their shoulders, writers turning to Yiddish conventionally placed themselves at a considerable imaginative remove from the life of the people whom their work was meant to improve and instruct. Abramovich and the equally popular Ayzik Meyer Dik both adopted hortatory alter egos to steer the reader through their imaginative landscapes of human perversity. Authorial strategies of self-estrangement involved the creation of native informers, like Abramovich's Mendele and Dik's modern "preacher" who claimed only to report the unvarnished truth of what they saw. Actually, the recourse to narrative mediation reflected the tension between a "theatrical" tendency toward deliberate disfigurement and well-established conventions of "formal realism," argues Dan Miron in his definitive study of the ideological origins of Yiddish fiction.[4] According to Miron, it was, paradoxically, the intimacy of the relationship between Yiddish and the immediacy of East European Jewish life that effectively compromised the capacity of the "language of the Jewish present" to function as a "natural medium [of] conscious artistic use."[5]

Sholem-aleichem, by contrast, had "felt no need to apologize for writing in Yiddish."[6] In his very first Yiddish story, a short masterpiece called *The Penknife* (Yid. Dos meserl), he constructed a different literary genealogy of his own turn toward Yiddish. In *The Penknife*, Sholem-aleichem's coming of age as a Russian-Jewish writer—his creative "maturity," as it were—entailed the discovery that Yiddish constituted the uninhibited language of Jewish childhood and, implicitly, the personal idiom of resistance to the reforming project in which his predecessors were so deeply invested. His radical disengagement from the pedagogical poetics of Jewish writing provided the entry of everyday Jewish life into Jewish literature with a new etiology. Although the writers associated with the beginning of the Hebrew Renaissance quickly seized on Sholem-aleichem's confessional artlessness

---
[3] Sh. J. Abramovich, "Notes for My Biography [1889]," trans. Gerald Stillman, in *Selected Works of Mendele Moykher-Sforim*, ed. Marvin Zuckerman, Gerald Stillman, and Marion Herbst (Malibu, 1991), 41–42. Translation slightly altered. For the original, see "Reshimot letoldotai," *Kol kitvei mendele mokher-sfarim* (Tel Aviv, 1947), 4.
[4] Dan Miron, *A Traveler Disguised: The Rise of Modern Yiddish Fiction in the Nineteenth Century* (Syracuse, 1996), 54–55, 207–14.
[5] Ibid., 34.
[6] Klier, "From 'Little Man' to 'Milkman,'" 222.

as an expression of their own affirmative commitment to truth in art, *The Penknife* ultimately resists any programmatic reading and subverts the dominant critical tendency to misread Sholem-aleichem as an artless realist. Sholem-aleichem's "confessional" revolt against the aesthetics of deformation does not constitute a polemic on behalf of naturalism. Neither does it strive to represent the parlous condition of Russian Jewry. Instead, *The Penknife* offers a brilliant defense of lying.

The Penknife first appeared as a separate book in St. Petersburg in the spring of 1887 as a supplement to Alexander Tsederbaum's *Jewish People's Gazette* (Yid. Dos yudishes folksblat), the empire's only Yiddish paper, to which Sholem-aleichem contributed regularly between 1883 and 1888. The story purported to offer an unvarnished and frankly disturbing look at traditional Jewish education. The account, initially presented by its author as a "trivial but sad event from [his own] childhood," might well have served the contemporary polemic about the lamentable state of elementary Jewish schooling.[7] It is not immediately obvious, however, that Sholem-aleichem's avowal of confessional truthfulness actually promotes progressive Jewish education; the story fails to locate its main source of narrative tension in the conflict between the innocent child and his adult oppressors. Despite its vividly rendered fascination with the brutality of traditional educational methods, the state of the schoolroom remains peripheral to the moral drama being relived by the protagonist in the course of recounting a critical turning point in his autobiography. The highly self-conscious act of confession relegates the representation of the social circumstances that constitute the donnée of his life to the status of a foregone conclusion rather than to an immediately urgent dilemma liable to a cure. Furthermore, the "trivial" nature of the psychological event that takes center stage in *The Penknife* implicates the power of representation in the ineluctable subjectivity of memory and desire. The narrative exposes itself as partial and self-serving and implicitly hostile to the possibility of realism. The game of autobiographical transparency, as any writer who lived in the age that followed Rousseau's *Confessions* might have known, reveals an infinite series of obstructions to knowledge of the whole truth. "Perhaps," writes Lionel Gossman, "in autobiography [...] there are two impulses. One is to release a discourse that has been suppressed, to permit what could not be said, was not said, and is indeed unsayable—the thing that is at the heart of the writer's activity as a writer—to be said, or rather to be

---

[7] For the quotation, see Sholem-aleichem's original subtitle on the frontispiece of *Dos meserl* (St. Petersburg, 1887). On the contemporary debate about Jewish education, see Steven J. Zipperstein, "Transforming the 'Heder': Maskilic Politics in Imperial Russia," in *Jewish History: Essays in Honour of Chimen Abramsky*, ed. Ada Rapoport-Albert and Steven J. Zipperstein (London, 1988), 87–109.

approximated. The other impulse is to imprison it again, to disguise it, to keep it at arm's length, by means of substitutions and displacements."[8]

Looming over the plot, the ever-present image of the penknife/pocketknife, literally "little knife," signifies the symbolic contraction (Heb. *tsimtsum*) of historical reality to the equivocal and self-serving position of individual conscience, driven, it would seem, by its own eminently antisocial and perverse appetites. The knife divides the narrator from himself and initiates him into the potentially hostile but eminently tempting place beyond the control of moral authority, an evil kingdom of things where all is permitted. Explicitly contrasted by the narrator's father with a "holy book" (Heb. *sefer*), the knife makes its initial appearance as a dangerous distraction that diverts a growing Jewish boy from the serious occupation (Yid. *der takhlis*) of learning and his proper vocation as his father's heir (Yid. *kaddish*) and threatens to turn him into an "apostate" (Yid. *sheygets*) and a "gentile punk" (Yid. *goyets*): "'What is this? Knives?' Father coughed taking the knife and the whetstone away from me. 'What a young lout! Too lazy to pick up a book and study, hah?'"[9] Following *The Penknife*, Sholem-aleichem wrote many comparable stories in which the outside world obtruded on a fragile and fractious Jewish ego in the form of small, seemingly insignificant, and mostly unnecessary objects, like hats, shawls, clocks, and playing cards—all, in various ways, echoing the master image of the knife. Like the penknife, these unexpected indices of everyday life awaken fantasies and trigger anxieties that defy all efforts at social control and self-restraint.

Sholem-aleichem effectively wrote two stories called *The Penknife*, the first in 1887 and the second in 1901; the latter was published in the first volume of the 1903 edition of the *Collected Works*, itself a first for Sholem-aleichem.[10] This text, with only minor corrections, appeared in the canonical posthumous Folksfond edition, in the volume dedicated to children's stories, and became the basis for all subsequent reprints.[11] Despite the continuity between the 1887 and the 1903 versions of *The Penknife*, there are good reasons to argue that the significant but subtle differences are ultimately as important as the similarities for understanding the nature of Sholem-aleichem's achievement. When Sholem-aleichem returned to *The Penknife* in December 1901, he removed the knowing and mildly self-deprecating subtitle, which referred to the story as

---

[8] Lionel Gossman, "The Innocent Art of Confession and Reverie," *Daedalus* 107 (Summer 1978): 66.
[9] Sholem-aleichem, "The Penknife," in *Some Laughter, Some Tears: Tales from the Old and the New*, trans. Curt Leviant (New York, 1968), 115. For citations of the original, see *Dos meserl*, ed. Chone Shmeruk (Jerusalem and Cincinnati, 1983).
[10] *Sholem-aleichems ale verk*, 4 vols. (Warsaw, 1903–4), 1:75–98.
[11] Sholem-aleichem, *Ale verk*, 28 vols. (New York, 1917–1921), 8:7–32.

a "trivial, yet pathetic event" (Yid. "nareshe, nor a troyrige geshikhte") drawn from the "history" of the author's own childhood—and replaced it with the naive "tale (Yid. *mayse*) for Jewish children," calling attention to a substantive shift in genre and tone.[12] Heightening the new-found moral, he also added a biblical epigraph, "Thou shall not steal!" both in Hebrew and in Yiddish; this heavy-handed authorial intervention runs counter to the way in which Sholem-aleichem first presented himself to his public in the 1887 edition of *The Penknife*. The 1901 attempt to translate the potentially scandalous plot into the affective register of Jewish children's literature turned the scriptural injunction into self-parody because, as we shall see, the disquieting resolution of *The Penknife* actually subverts the exhortation against theft.

Unlike the first version, which Sholem-aleichem pointedly claimed to have composed in a single night, the second version was the poorer result of an unsatisfying collaboration.[13] The rewriting stalled for a year and a half (uncharacteristically for a writer who normally worked very quickly), probably because Sholem-aleichem remained ambivalent about the ways in which the demands of revision undermined a groundbreaking original. Commissioned by Sholem-aleichem's good friend and Odessa publisher Y. Kh. Ravnitskii, along with Ahad ha'am among the founders of the Jewish national revival, the new story was meant to be translated into Hebrew and included in a series of children's books.[14] In this context, the biblicism of the epigraph exemplified the genetic connection between ancient Scripture and the new Jewish literature of the Hebrew "revival" (Heb. *tehiyah*). Six months later, writing to Bialik and Ravnitskii about the revisions, Sholem-aleichem referred half-jokingly to the "writing [of] pen-knives," in the plural (Yid. *meserlekh*); by this point in the editorial process, Sholem-aleichem had come to think of the stories as two distinct *meserlekh* rather than two versions of the same one.[15] Ambivalent about the prospect of rewriting, Sholem-aleichem insisted on the distinction, which, as it were, kept the first *Penknife* separate and intact. What we have here is a trace of Sholem-aleichem's ambivalence about graduating into the ethical and political responsibilities of serious authorship. Flattered by the possibility of partnership with the modern "sages of Odessa," whom Sholem-aleichem both revered and envied, he embarked on the changes that Bialik and

---

[12] The Russian translation of the original subtitle, which likewise appeared on the front cover of the 1887 edition of *The Penknife*, brings the irony of the language out nicely: "Nichtozhnoe, no pechal'noe sobytie iz moego detstva."

[13] See Sholem-aleichem's 1904 letter to Y. Kh. Ravnitskii, in *Tsum ondenk fun Sholem-aleichem*, ed. I. Zinberg and Sh. Niger (Petrograd, 1917), 95.

[14] See Sholem-aleichem's letter to Ravnitskii, 4 December 1901, in *Letters of Shalom-aleichem* [Yid.], ed. Abraham Lis (Tel Aviv, 1995), 348.

[15] Sholem-aleichem's letter to Bialik and Ravnitskii, 26 May 1902, in *Letters of Shalom-aleichem*, 384.

Ravnitskii demanded. Yet the process was attended by psychological struggle, which expressed itself in constant delays to produce the requisite manuscript.

When *The Penknife* finally made its second appearance in the debut edition of *Collected Works*, the changes had come to represent a shift in the evolution of Sholem-aleichem's authorial persona. Like the first part of the *Tevye* cycle, published alongside the new version of *The Penknife* in the first volume, the "penknife" now stood for Sholem-aleichem's ostensible pedagogical concerns as a modern Jewish author—empathy for children and for other "little people, with their small-time triumphs" (Yid. *kleyne mentshelekh mit kleyne hasoges*), a class of individuals represented by the dairyman, the quintessential long-suffering Jewish father, Sholem-aleichem's little man with a big heart and an epic national conscience. But the implied analogy between the epideictic function of children and "little people" in the world of Sholem-aleichem involved a creative misreading of *The Penknife* that its rewriting as a "story for children" and its inclusion in the *Collected Works* encouraged. The grown-up secular *geshikhte* of 1887, completely overshadowed by the paradigmatic little Jewish *mayse* to which it subsequently lent its name and plot, presents an alternative point of entry into Sholem-aleichem's imaginative universe. The original "penknife" haunts all its eventual retellings.

The parallel between Sholem-aleichem's innocent Jewish children and equally ingenuous Jewish fathers suggested by the juxtaposition of *Tevye* and *The Penknife* is not at all self-evident in the first version of the story, written before the famous correspondence with the "grandfather" of Yiddish literature, Sh. J. Abramovich, before the publication of *The Jewish People's Library* (Yid. *Dos yudishes folks-bibliotek*), before the Jewish novels, before *Shomer on Trial* (Yid. *Shomers mishpet*)—that is, before Sholem-aleichem had undertaken to turn himself into the good son of the Jewish people as well as the respectable paterfamilias of modern Jewish culture. In fact, the primal text of Sholem-aleichem's literary career comes far closer to the dark, orphaned sensibility of his late, post-1905 masterpieces, such as the second half of the *Tevye* cycle, the monologues, the *Railroad Stories*, and *Motl, the Cantor's Son*.[16] While the two early Tevye stories, "Modern Children" (1899) included in the *Collected Works*, and "Hodl" (1904) written less than a year afterward, are sentimental Jewish comedies aimed at the heartstrings of secular readers, *The Penknife*, like *Motl*, is a gothic fantasy of filial revenge.

Positioned at the intersection between the first awakening of illicit desire and the beginning of the making of books (in 1887, *The Penknife* actually

---

[16] On the shift in tone, theme, and subject matter in Sholem-aleichem's late work, see Olga Litvak, "Khave and Her Sisters: Sholem-aleichem and the Lost Girls of 1905," *Jewish Social Studies*, n. s., 15, no. 3 (2009): 1–38.

constituted Sholem-aleichem's first book), the little knife recalled two other pocketknives in contemporary Russian literature, Anna Karenina's and Parfen Rogozhin's in Dostoevsky's *The Idiot*. Anna uses hers to cut the pages of an "English novel" during the train journey back to St. Petersburg that follows the electric meeting with Vronsky in Moscow. Impatient with the conventional love story she is reading, Anna embraces the urge to live out her own impending romance. In a telling gesture that foreshadows her eventual self-destruction under the wheels of the locomotive, she presses the cold steel blade of the little knife, used to cut the pages of her novel, to her overheated face, as the train clatters on the tracks below:

> The hero of the novel was already beginning to achieve his English happiness, a baronetcy and an estate, and Anna wished to go with him to this estate when suddenly she felt that he must be ashamed and that she was ashamed of the same thing. [...] She remembered the ball, remembered Vronsky, [...] and the feeling of shame became more intense. [...] She smiled scornfully and again picked up the book but now she was decidedly unable to understand what she was reading. She passed the paper-knife over the glass, then put its smooth and cold surface to her cheek and nearly laughed aloud from the joy that suddenly came over her for no reason. She felt her nerves tighten more and more, like strings on winding pegs. [...] She kept having moments of doubt whether the carriage was moving forwards or backwards, or standing still.[17]

Here the ominous presence of the knife points to the lethal consequences of taking fiction for life and alludes to the connection between Anna and Flaubert's notorious female fantasist Emma Bovary.

In *The Idiot*, Rogozhin's infamous "small gardening knife," also used to cut the pages of a new book and spotted by Myshkin in the course of his first visit to Rogozhin's apartment, eventually ends up inside the body of Rogozhin's would-be mistress and Myshkin's would-be wife, the lost woman Nastasya Filippovna.

> [Myshkin] had absently taken up the knife a second time, and again Rogozhin snatched it from his hand and threw it down on the table. It was a plain-looking knife with a bone handle, a blade about eight inches long, and broad in proportion; it did not clasp. Seeing that the prince was considerably struck by the fact that he had twice seized this knife out of his hand, Rogozhin caught it up

---

[17] Leo Tolstoy, *Anna Karenina*, trans. Richard Pevear and Larissa Volokhonsky (New York, 2002), 100–101.

4. In the Evil Kingdom of Things

with some irritation, put it inside the book, and threw the latter across to another table.

"Do you cut your pages with it, or what?" asked Myshkin, still rather absently, as though unable to throw off a deep preoccupation into which the conversation had thrown him.

"Yes."

"It's a gardening knife [Rus. sadovyi nozh], isn't it?"

"Yes. Can't one cut pages with a gardening knife?"

"It's quite new."

"Well, what of that? Can't I buy a new knife if I like?" shouted Rogozhin furiously, his irritation growing with every word.[18]

This "Garden-of-Eden" knife that separates the open and closed pages of a history book" is itself a kind of *corpus delicti,* the tool of Rogozhin's murderous jealousy, initially hidden from himself but not from the prescient *Lev Nikolaevich* (who shares his first name and patronymic with Lev Nikolaevich Tolstoy) Myshkin. The prince, an acute listener as well as a preternatural visionary, can hear through the lies that pass for stories and see directly into people's souls. Here, as in *Anna Karenina,* the knife inside the book provides the key to the fateful power of literary narrative as a seductive form of self-deception.[19]

These striking sources for the principal topos of *The Penknife* point to the implications of Sholem-aleichem's designs on Jewish literature. For Tolstoy and Dostoevsky, the striking proximity of books and knives symbolizes the struggle for personal freedom from the moral law of the Bible, otherwise known as *the* Book, the reading of which presumably keeps people from running off with their lovers, throwing themselves onto the train tracks, killing their mistresses, lying, stealing, and wishing their fathers dead. Both Tolstoy and Dostoevsky envision secular "readers"—Karenina reads novels and Rogozhin reads history—as narcissistic and dangerous rule breakers, governed entirely by the force of their own undisciplined and irresistible passions. Their titanic effort to bend other lives to their own will mirrors the creative risks attendant on the secularization of authorship, similarly governed by the conflict between social responsibility and the boundless drive toward wish fulfillment. In *The*

---

[18] Fyodor Dostoevsky, *Sobranie sochinenii v desiati tomakh* (Moscow, 1967), 6:246.
[19] On the "knife inside the book" in *The Idiot,* see Michael Holquist, *Dostoevsky and the Novel* (Princeton, NJ, 1977), 118.

Penknife, Sholem-aleichem associates the birth of literature with the principled abrogation of textual authority in the name of desire and with the potentially pathological consequences of writing for nothing but pleasure.

The subject of *The Penknife*, apparently without precedent in nineteenth-century Jewish literature, drew the attention of the historian and sometime literary critic, S. M. Dubnow, the first to make note of the young author's work in the Russian-Jewish press. Commenting on the story in St. Petersburg's preeminent Jewish weekly *Dawn* (Rus. Voskhod), Dubnow expressed his hesitation about the "seeming strangeness" of the "main subject"—the young hero's "odd obsession with little knives."[20] Indeed, the story capitalizes on the uncanny quality of perfectly ordinary, "trivial" matters. The narrator's insistence in the opening lines that the account was "not a concocted tale, but a real one that actually happened to me" heightens the shock value of the immediate introduction of the main theme: "There was nothing in the world for which I had a greater desire (Yid. *heyshek*) than for a pocketknife."[21] Immediately, the psychologically loaded line sets in motion all sorts of speculations about the nature of this mysteriously powerful *heyshek*, a word that endows "trivial" desire for a "pocketknife" with the force of near-mystical, erotic longing, usually reserved for the divine.[22] In the language of Jewish neo-Platonism, *heshek* means Eros, the yearning for ultimate knowledge. Some commentaries identified "Solomon's delight" (Heb. *heshek shlomo*) with the Song of Songs, a love poem that rabbinic tradition ascribed to King Solomon and interpreted allegorically to refer to the love between Israel and God. In *The Penknife*, the "pocketknife" represents a similarly charged "delight of Solomon," an allusion to Sholem-aleichem's real name, Solomon Naumovich Rabinovich.

---

[20] S. M. Dubnow, "Literaturnaia letopis': novye svidetel'stva o bednosti sovremennoi evreiskoi literatury," *Voskhod* 7 (1887), no. 7–8, sect. II, 36–37.

[21] Sholem-aleichem, *Dos meserl*, 1. All translations from this edition are mine.

[22] On the philosophical significance of the Hebrew word *heshek*, see Steven Harvey, "The Meaning of the Term Designating Love in Judeo-Arabic Thought and Some Remarks on the Judeo-Arabic Interpretation of Maimonides," *Judeo-Arabic Studies*, ed. Norman Golb (Amsterdam, 1998), 175–96. Sholem-aleichem's more immediate source may have been the *Autobiography* of the radical enlightener Solomon Maimon, where Maimon mentions his own unpublished manuscript called *Heshek shlomo*, apparently like *Dos meserl* a first book and devoted to the attempt at reconciling the teaching of Maimonides with Kabbalah. See the discussion in Abraham P. Socher, *The Radical Enlightenment of Solomon Maimon: Judaism, Heresy, and Philosophy* (Stanford, CA, 2006), 52–84. This subtle connection between the "confessional" text of *Dos meserl* and Maimon's work is suggestive, especially given that Maimon's *Autobiography* imported the conventions of Rousseau's *Confessions* into Jewish literature, a subject treated with great care and prodigious erudition in the work of Marcus Moseley, *Being for Myself Alone: Origins of Jewish Autobiography* (Stanford, CA, 2005). I hope to have the opportunity to explore Sholem-aleichem's affinity for Maimon more fully on another occasion.

4. In the Evil Kingdom of Things

The apotheosis of desire gives way to the admission of destructive and self-seeking urges for revenge. The narrator dreams of "cutting whatever I wanted [Yid. *vos ikh vil*]—and let my friends know all about it [Yid. *lozn mayne haveyrim vissen*]!"[23] Dubnow attempted to explain away the boy's curious "obsession with knives" as a perfectly understandable, if futile, "protest" against the "coercion of parents and teachers," but the knife is never aimed directly or entirely at adult "oppressors." The "knife-mania" does not affirm the child's "natural" sense of justice, affronted by unreasonable and degenerate dictates of compulsory "education." In fact, there is no suggestion in *The Penknife* that the world of children is any less corrupt or any more innocent than that of the adults. Initially aimed at the narrator's peers, the pocketknife is a classic weapon of ressentiment, the hidden aggression of a perpetually bruised and entitled ego that demands ceaseless admiration and courts envy.

The adult narrator virtually caresses the word *meserl* as he relives the pleasure of hiding the beloved object in his pocket and "taking it out whenever I wanted" (Yid. *ven ikh vil*). The suggestion of masturbation and aggressive exhibitionism that Sholem-aleichem here chooses to attach to (of all things!) a pocketknife links the act of confession with "indecent exposure" and "self-gratification."[24] And yet, what's most discomfiting is not so much the drama of the juxtaposition but the flattened, unambiguous diction that seeks to scale down the violence of the imagery to the level of everyday language. As the plot elaborates the growth of the boy's desire, the initial sense of the grotesque only deepens, and the presence of the pocketknife becomes more and more *unheimlich*. The recourse to realistic storytelling to naturalize the unexpected irruption of weirdness (which in other stories also takes on the form of everyday objects, a technique that distinguishes some of Sholem-aleichem's best stories, such as "On Account of a Hat" and "The Pot") in the lives of completely ordinary people characterizes some of Sholem-aleichem's most inventive work.[25]

The opening section ties the awakening of illicit desire for a pocketknife to the beginning of socialization into the male Jewish world, the entry into the more dangerous ground of the adolescent schoolroom where all sorts of horrors await.

---

[23] Sholem-aleichem, *Dos meserl*, 1.

[24] On the connection between the "genre of literary confession" and "acts of indecent exposure and masturbation" in nineteenth-century Russian literature and elsewhere, see Robin Feuer Miller, "Transformations, Exposures, and Intimations of Rousseau in *The Possessed*," in her *Dostoevsky's Unfinished Journey* (New Haven, 2007), 89.

[25] See David Roskies, "Sholem-aleichem: Mythologist of the Mundane," in *A Bridge of Longing: The Lost Art of Yiddish Storytelling* (Cambridge, MA, 1995), 168–90.

> How I loved that knife! How I adored it! I came home from school dead tired, hungry, sleepy and beaten up. (You see, I had just begun studying with the Talmud teacher, Motti, the Angel of Death. We were on the chapter "An Ox That Gored a Cow," and since one animal gored another, naturally I had to get whacked.) First, I removed the little knife from under the black cupboard where I had hidden it. (I couldn't take it to school, and I didn't dare let anyone know that I had a knife at home.) [. . .] Later, before going to sleep, I cleaned the knife, scoured and polished it, took the whetstone I had found in the attic, spit on it and quietly set to work sharpening the blade, sharpening and sharpening ... [Yid. *sharfn dos meserl, sharfn, sharfn*].[26]

The various lost "knives" that the narrator fashions out of household materials and that anticipate the "penknife" at the center of the story signify stages in the transition from the protective world of the mother to the dangerous domain of men, marked by verbal violence, associated primarily with the father, and by the regular doses of corporal punishment administered by the Talmud teacher. "They threw my little penknife so far I couldn't find it even after an intensive eight-day search. I sincerely mourned my misshapen knife, my good little knife. How dark and bitter was my lot in *kheder*! I came home day after day with swollen cheeks, with red ears mercilessly tweaked by the hands of Motti the Angel of Death—all because an ox gored a cow."[27] The raw material for the first two "knives" derives from increasingly intimate items of decidedly feminine inventory, a goose feather from a duster and a piece of metal broken off from mother's crinoline hoop, sharpened on one of her kitchen pots.[28] These homemade, makeshift "knives" represent the infantile longing for the mother's protection and the ever-present threat of paternal censure, a conflict accompanying the boy on his journey into the adult world.

The hero comes into possession of his own real knife, the originary object of ecstatic worship—"How I loved it! Oh, how I adored it!" he exclaims—upon graduation from his first *heder* and the beginning of his formal study of the Talmud, with a teacher known in the 1903 version of *The Penknife* as "Moti, the Angel of Death." In 1887, the teacher had been called "Moti, the despoiler" (Yid. *hagazlan*); this is one of the two changes introduced into the passage in the second version. In 1887, Sholem-aleichem provided an immediate explanation of the nickname, edited out in 1903: "Oh boy, how he used to hit! How he used to whip us! To the point of making us bleed!

---

[26] Sholem-aleichem, "The Penknife," 114. Translation slightly altered. See Sholem-aleichem, *Dos meserl*, 4.
[27] Sholem-aleichem, "The Penknife," 115.
[28] Ibid., 113.

As if to kill us! On top of it all, he was a drunk, a violent drunk."[29] More important, the 1903 version introduces the exemplary Talmudic passage "When an ox gored a cow" (TB, Bava' kamma', 46a) as a way of alluding to the connection between brute violence in the Talmud and beastly violence in the schoolroom. But in the 1887 adult version of the story, the relatively obscure passage that the narrator is studying, "A woman fell off a roof and onto a tree branch" (TB, Ketubot, 11a and TB, Yevamot, 54a), has a manifestly erotic content. The text here refers to the case of a virgin who loses her maidenhead due to impaling herself accidentally on a stick. The transparent reference to violent penetration, which results in the unexpected loss of innocence, links the blood in the description of Moti's beatings with the blood of defloration, elicited by the "despoiler" from his innocent charges. Meanwhile, at home, the boy stealthily "sharpens and sharpens" the blade of his recently acquired weapon until he's discovered in the act and disarmed by his furious father. The rhythmic masturbatory movement of sharpening the blade represents a form of futile, infantile resistance to the "accident" of painful initiation into the fellowship of Jewish manhood. The loss of the knife does not result in effective socialization into the group—the awakening of desire inspires narcissism and envy—and serves only to heighten the narrator's magnified sense of personal injury:

> To whom could I turn? I was as lonely as an orphan without my little hunchback of a knife. And no one, no one saw the tears that I silently shed when I came back from school and lay in my little bed. I would quietly have my cry, dry my eyes, fall asleep, and return to school all over again, back to the ox that gored the cow, back to Moti's blows, back to father's anger, father's coughing, father's curses. Never a moment of freedom, never a happy face, never a little smile from anyone, from anyone at all—alone, by myself, all alone, all alone in the entire world [Yid. *ayner aleyn, elent, elent oyf der velt*]![30]

This primal scene of thwarted desire and boundless self-pity continues to haunt the narrator—"All my childhood years were predestined to be cursed with pocketknives," he says—and demands reparation.[31] The ambiguous fulfillment of his wish, both a blessing and a "curse," unfolds over the course of the remainder of the story, devoted to the fate of a "beauty of a knife": "There

---

[29] Sholem-aleichem, *Dos meserl*, 21.
[30] Sholem-aleichem, "The Penknife," 115. Translation altered; see Sholem-aleichem, *Dos meserl*, 5.
[31] The original reads, "Es vayzt oys, az iz ober ongetseykhnet gevoren min-hashamayim, az mayne ale kinderishe yoren zol ikh opkumen far meserlekh." See Sholem-aleichem, *Dos meserl*, 5.

was nothing like it. It had a white bone handle, two expensive razor-sharp steel blades, and it came in a brass case, studded with red brass tacks. The genuine article, the real thing, a Zavyalov!"[32]

This is the knife that puts all previous knives in the shade; its acquisition represents the narrator's coming of age, a story of ambiguous possession and symbolic merger with the original owner of this "dear [Yid. *tayere*, alt. expensive]" penknife. Enter "Hertz Hertzenhertz," the "jew-goy" who does not wash his hands before eating, who has no beard and wears a short coat, and who speaks in a vaguely Germanic-sounding Yiddish. A boarder at the boy's house, Hertz Hertzenhertz plays the role of the familiar stranger, a foil for the narrator's irascible father and intemperate, cruel teacher. A man who is all "heart," he is the literary embodiment of forbidden romance in a world suffused by the harsh discipline of Talmudic learning.

For the narrator, Hertz Hertzenhertz presents an overwhelming set of temptations personified by his "thick, black, aromatic cigars" and by the objects on his desk. Here, the *meserl*, which had been simply a "little knife," makes its first appearance explicitly as a "*pen*knife," strewn among other writing and reading implements: "a big silver inkwell, and several fine pens . . . as well as several knickknacks—and a penknife. And what a beauty!"[33] These material accessories of cultivation and masculinity, self-evidently phallic and related to the process of *writing*, pose a curious contrast with books, the conventional focus of the life-changing confrontation between a young protagonist and an older, tutelary figure. Compare, for example, the meeting between Hershele, the protagonist of Abramovich's *The Wishing Ring*, and the maskil Rafael, who introduces the boy to *reading*. In the work of Abramovich, the paradigmatic liminal figure who mediates between the world of tradition and the world of enlightenment is not someone who writes (like Herr Hertzenhertz) but a book peddler.

The source of the boy's interest in Hertz Hertzenhertz has nothing to do with the arousal of his intellect but with the potent pleasures of the body exemplified by smell, sight, and touch. Knowledge here is explicitly erotic. Hertz Hertzenhertz does nothing to awaken the intelligence of the narrator, but everything about his person, including the sounds he makes, stimulates the boy's aesthetic sense to the point of irresistible physical excitement. Drunk with the power of his new-found desire, the boy swipes the penknife off the desk and slips it (where else?) inside his pocket. This act of theft constitutes a moment of erotic wish fulfillment, a potential union of the heart, cast

---

[32] Sholem-aleichem, "The Penknife," 116. Translation altered; see Sholem-aleichem, *Dos meserl*, 5–6.
[33] Sholem-aleichem, "The Penknife," 117.

in pointed contrast to the symbolic rape perpetrated by Moti, the Talmud teacher. While Moti initiates the boys into the dialectic of Talmudic morality, which provokes actual punishment for the "sin" of the imaginary woman who has lost her imaginary virginity, the real violation of Hertzenhertz's privacy represents the narrator's illicit attempt to breach the garden of distinctly earthly delights. At this point, the narrator's sin ceases to be an abstraction and begins to pursue him nearly unto death.

But the moral consequences of this theft, the staple subject of literary confessions since Rousseau's "little pink and silver ribbon" are not nearly so transparent.[34] As in Rousseau, the physical punishment and public humiliation meant for the narrator are actually visited on someone else—here, on the unlucky Berel, the fatherless boy who steals pennies from the charity box to buy sweets. But where his cunning is at best pathetic and infantile, the narrator's is a feat of derring-do, a breathtaking venture into foreign territory. Whereas Berel's ambitions do not extend beyond the charity box, the narrator aspires to feast at the table of the princely Hertz Hertzenhertz. Thanks to the hapless and dumbstruck Berel, the narrator experiences a vicarious crisis of conscience, becomes ill, and miraculously recovers, to end up rescued from the evil Moti and placed under the benign tutelage of Reb Hayim Koter. In the second version of the story, he is brought back from the side of the "Angel of Death" and enters "life" (Yid. *hayim*), idiomatically linked to adult male sexuality, suggested by the last name *Koter,* which means "tomcat."

Unlike his double, "Berel, the thief," the narrator neither undergoes the ordeal of facing the social consequences of his wrongdoing nor restores the knife to its rightful owner. Instead, he throws it into the river to rid himself of the nagging presence of the guilty body. Finally, he keeps the lie to himself until he makes his confession as an adult. The case does not really persuade the reader of the evils of dishonesty, since the narrator not only gets away with stealing but also actually profits from the lesson learned at the expense of a much more pathetic victim conveniently forgotten by the end of the tale. Worse still, the spectacle of Berel's punishment, in which all of the boys are made complicit, considerably attenuates the narrator's belated admission of guilt. He reassures the reader of his reform and of his resolve to be "always honest." But, as in the case of Rousseau, this self-serving avowal of lifelong psychological remorse in comparison with Berel's immediate physical punishment makes a poor case for the narrator's moral courage.

Berel's exposure and passive acceptance of suffering seems, instead, to absolve the narrator of his ethical responsibility and makes him (rather than Berel) the hero of the hour. In effect, Berel gets the punishment, but the

---

[34] Jean-Jacques Rousseau, *The Confessions,* trans. J. M. Cohen (New York, 1953), 86–88.

narrator gets the rewards of contrition and reintegration into the fold. At last, he is not alone and gets the attention he has claimed from the beginning. The inescapable inconsistency of cause and effect finds expression in the formal rupture of the last paragraph. Trailing ellipses and hysterical repetition puts the moral awakening in doubt: "I pressed my Talmud close to my heart and ran eagerly to school. I swore on the Talmud that I would never, ever swipe things that didn't belong to me, never ever steal, never ever deny anything, would always be honest, honest, honest . . ."[35] The language here has the feel of an incantation; the obsessive repetition provides a mantra *against* dishonesty on the part of a grown-up narrator who is nostalgic for his childhood resolve because he, as an adult, remains all too open to temptation. The trace of original guilt, associated not so much with remorse but with the absence of true contrition—the denial—underscores the sweet pleasure of a confession, enabled by the successful evasion of punishment.

Even as the concluding lines insist that the drama has ended, the ellipses suggest the persistence of the urge to relive again and again the blissful moment of crisis and rebirth that finally ushers in its wake the hot rush of communal love—the erotic bliss of union first suggested by the word *heyshek*—that the narrator has craved from the beginning:

> People swarmed around me; they stared at me. Each person came near me and tapped me on the head. They said charms over me, they whispered over me, they licked my forehead and spat. They tended me. They poured hot soup into me and stuffed me full of jam. Everyone hovered over me, caring for me like the apple of their eye. They fed me broths and duckling like a little baby, they wouldn't leave me alone. Mama always sat next to me and repeated the entire story. I had fallen to the ground virtually lifeless, and they had to lift me up. [. . .] They thought that I was quitting this world, God forbid. Then suddenly I sneezed seven times and returned from the dead to life.[36]

Compare this description of the child-as-fetish with the exposure and "trial" of Berel, the thief:

> Berel stood there as naked as the day he was born. All the blood had drained out of his face. He did not move. His eyes were lowered. He looked like a dead man. A corpse. [. . .]

---

[35] Sholem-aleichem, *Dos meserl*, 17.
[36] Sholem-aleichem, "The Penknife," 126–27.

"And now, children, pronounce judgment," [the rebbe says.] "You know what to do. [. . .] Let each one declare what punishment should be meted out to a thief who steals kopecks from a charity box with a tar-tipped straw. Little Hershele, you begin."

The rebbe cocked his head, closed one eye, and cupped his right ear. Little Hershele answered loudly.

"A thief who steals kopecks from a charity box should be whipped until the blood begins to flow."

"Moshe, what do you say?"

"This is what should be done," said Moshe plaintively, "to a thief who steals money from a charity box. He should be stretched out on the ground. Two boys should sit on his hands, two on his feet, and two should beat him with well-salted rods."

"What do you say, Kopele?"

Kopele wiped his nose and squeaked out his judgment.

"A thief who swipes kopecks from a charity box should have all the kids come up to him and sing right into his face loud and clear: You're a crook, you're a crook, you're a big fat crook."[37]

The elaborate sadistic fantasies of the boys called up to judge their schoolfellow provide a foil for the masochistic scenario of the protagonist, pummeled by his enthusiastic admirers and smothered in their unrelenting embraces. The narrator's near-death experience followed by the miraculous return to life represents a narcissistic victory over his fatally ill father. Illness pushes him to the forefront of his mother's attention, where he becomes the near-mythical subject of her storytelling. This scenario anticipates the final drama of confession in which he, again, becomes the object of limitless self-love and public adoration.

This shameless wallowing linked explicitly to the repetition of the "entire story [. . .] about whippings and knives," makes clear the nature of the narrator's investment in the elliptical conclusion of *The Penknife*. The normative—logical—reading of this tale demands some sense of an ending, an effective ethical resolution, but the realistic—psychological—reading forces us to grapple with the implications of the narcissistic need to experience abjection

---

[37] Ibid., 123–24.

over and over and over again. To be so good as to keep earning the most coveted prize, his father's "sweet words" and his mother's unadulterated attention, by the end of the story, the narrator must always already be very, very bad at its beginning. This is why the final paragraph sounds like a kind of magic spell, an attempt not to ward off the more obvious temptation of stealing for the sake of gaining the desired object (this is what poor simple-minded Berel does) but to engage the much more ingenious compulsion, "discovered" by the winsome, precocious "Sholem, son of Reb Nokhem" who is also Sholem-aleichem, the author, in the course of writing *The Penknife*—to keep stealing for the sake of confessing. The penknife, the original object of desire, must be made to fall into the void of the river to highlight the fact that its acquisition was never the point; Berel eats the fruits of his crime, and they disappear, but the narrator loses his so that he may keep it forever. The displacement of the real knife by the infinite fantasy represents the literary simulation of real objects as akin to theft, a striking parallel with the invocation of narrative design as a cover story for the crimes of adultery (*Anna Karenina*) and murder (*The Idiot*).

The uncanny weapon of the weak, which signifies death, followed by the orgiastic bliss of rebirth, points to the aggressive impulse implicit in the child's desire to avenge himself first on other children and eventually on adults, not by making the latter jealous like the former but by subjecting them to the terrifying fantasy of his own death. A double image, the "little knife" both exemplifies the impotence of the child against adults and the possibility that this impotence, in and of itself, constitutes a very effective means of disarming authority altogether. Himself initially seduced and overcome by the material signs of Hertz Hertzenhertz's virility, manifest in the objects on his desk, the boy, in the irresistible vulnerability of his illness, ultimately makes a captive of the erotic stranger who suddenly acquires both masculine *and* feminine attributes of the cigar and the clean-shaven face. In this passage, Hertz Hertzenhertz is the seducer who finds himself seduced: "Even the German Jew, that is, the Jewish German, Herr Hertzenhertz, with the cigar between his teeth, bent over my little bed with his clean-shaven mug, stroked my cheek and said in German: '*Gut, gut, gesund, gesund!*'" Again, a few lines down: "Even the German presented me with a few pennies along with a pinch on the cheek, saying '*Hübscher knabe! Gut, gut!*'"[38] The word "even," repeated twice, underscores the note of triumph, underlying the description of the special attention that Herr Hertzenhertz now sees fit to bestow on the narrator. In the first of the two passages, performing a gesture of submission, he "bends over" the "little bed"—the crèche—of the young god. The image of the "clean-shaven mug" (Yid. *gegalter morde*), with its insistently protruding cigar,

---

[38] Sholem-aleichem, *Dos meserl*, 16–17.

highlights the patently erotic, rough but gentle touch, which comes pretty close to consummating the narrator's yearning for this familiar stranger. In the second passage, Hertzenhertz presents him with a token of devotion and calls him "pretty boy." The intimacy of the physical contact, initiated by the older man in response to the charming weakness of the "pretty" (Ger. *hübsche*) convalescent, presents a pointed contrast to "father's cold hand on [the narrator's] forehead." The knife seems to have done its work in more ways than one; the corpselike "cold hand" signifies the imminent demise of the constantly coughing, consumptive, rejected by the son who can well afford to laugh at the prospect of kissing his own father, as he revels in the caresses of the other "father" expressly won over by his charms. By the end, the power dynamic shifts, forcing Reb Nokhem to live in the shadow of his own irresistible offspring. Sholem, having lived through his imaginary death, effectively survives to escape the clutches of *Reb* Nokhem, doomed to an early grave. The pointed rejection of the "cold hand" of the dying father and his erotic displacement by the Jewish-gentile "lover," *Herr* Hertzenhertz symbolizes the colder triumph of youth over adulthood, the latter always operating on borrowed time.

The confessional claims of *The Penknife* beg all sorts of questions about the autobiographical sources of this victory. Does this *heder* story commemorate Sholem-aleichem's own conflict over the pursuit of a secular education? To what extent does the opposition between the attractions of Hertz Hertzenhertz and the pathetic rage of Reb Nokhem reflect the state of Sholem-aleichem's feelings about his own father? In fact, Rabinovich senior never stood in the way of his son's cultural aspirations; on the contrary, Nahum Rabinovich was himself something of a Jewish intellectual. He not only actively supported Solomon's matriculation at the local Russian gymnasium, despite the burdensome costs to the family purse, but also encouraged his early experiments as a Hebrew writer. Unlike many of his contemporaries, Sholem-aleichem did not have to make a choice between enlightenment and banishment from his father's table. What's more, Sholem-aleichem apparently idolized his father. When Nahum Rabinovich died in 1888, the author, appointed his father's executor, not only mourned him in private but also dedicated a volume of Hebrew verse to his memory. If other Hebrew or Yiddish writers of his generation experienced similarly profound feelings of loss following the death of a parent, they left no comparable trace of it in their writing.[39]

---

[39] See the private note "In memoriam," reproduced in *Dos sholem-aleichem bukh*, ed. Y. D. Berkovich (New York, 1926), 34; and Sholem-aleichem, *A bintel blumen oder poezye on gramen* (Berdichev, 1888).

The discrepancy between the autobiographical posture of *The Penknife* and other sources does not, however, imply that the confessional character of the story should be altogether dismissed. The artfully constructed scenario of the penknife is essential to the truth that Sholem-aleichem intended to confess to the first readers who would come to embrace him as an author. The language of fantasy allowed him to move beyond the dialectical bilingualism of contemporary Hebrew and Yiddish literature and to give expression to what the Dostoevsky scholar Robert Louis Jackson in another context called the "*secular imagination,* imagination responsive chiefly to a despiritualized and disintegrated material world."[40]

What is the relationship between the loving father of Sholem-aleichem's family history and the enraged invalid who apparently took possession of his imagination? Why did Sholem-aleichem associate his literary debut with an act of rebellion that may have never happened? At the end, the story itself pulls back from the scenario of conflict with the father and withholds its expected resolution in favor of the "libidinous energy" of the son. According to Ruth Wisse, the son "sacrifices his desire to own a penknife in deference to his sickly father." Charged with guarding the tradition, the boy returns to *heder* and "assumes responsibility for what his father is too weak to protect."[41] Here, Wisse offers a neat rationale for Sholem-aleichem's poetics of "renunciation" and his embrace of a humble vocation as a "mere Jewish humorist," an interpretation of the principal purpose of the story that also conforms to the biographical evidence. For Wisse, the anti-Oedipal "repaternalization" of the narrator at the conclusion of *Dos meserl* exemplifies the moral triumph of the Jewish reality principle over the gentile delights (Yid. *goyim-naches*) of the pleasure principle signified by the knife (and, as we have seen, by its problematic connections with Russian literature).

Wisse's normative reconstruction seems to explain everything about the consequences of the theft—except for the fact that *the narrator gets away with it.* His "renunciation" may just as well be interpreted as the dubious public atonement of a successful criminal who profits from his "repaternalization" directly at the expense of Berel, the fatherless boy for whom there is no happy ending. The point here is not to privilege one reading of *The Penknife* over the other; Sholem-aleichem's self-serving fiction is perfectly plausible. The ambiguity of the "renunciation"—throwing the knife in the river looks suspiciously like the disposal of evidence *as well as* a supreme act of sacrifice—makes the narrator's repentant father, along with all the other

---

[40] "Gogol's 'The Portrait': The Simultaneity of Madness, Naturalism, and the Supernatural," in *Essays on Gogol: Logos and the Russian Word,* ed. Susanne Fusso and Priscilla Meyer (Evanston, IL, 1992), 109. Emphasis in the original.

[41] Ruth Wisse, *The Modern Jewish Canon* (New York, 2000), 48.

adults, including the enlightened Hertz Hertzenhertz, look like a softhearted fool who has been duped by his too-clever son. Indeed, by the end of the story, the father, in his new-found gentleness, is made to look not merely "weak" but deliberately ridiculous, a source of gleeful "embarrassment" for the narrator. In the absence of "persecution"—all that hitting and cursing—the father has been reduced to "nothing at all" (Yid. *gornisht oyf der velt*), a pathetic object of snide and decidedly unfilial snickering, the insidious "hee-hee-hee" of the future "Jewish humorist" for whom nothing is sacred.[42] Shielded by his "trivial" alter ego—embodied in childlike innocence and folksy, familiar humor—Sholem-aleichem infuses Jewish literature with the "anarchic breeze" of radical freedom.[43] Beneath the mask of a little sneak thief (Yid. *gonef*) hides the nature of an anarchic despoiler (Yid. *gozlen*), a scourge of God, an angel of death, a good boy who is also a demonic agent provocateur, armed with the perfect weapon—a sharp little pen/knife, lifted from the desk of an authentic, that is, "German" writer, a concealed stiletto ready to cut up whatever he wants, whenever he wants.

Thus there are two confessions in *The Penknife*. On the one hand, there is the confession of the theft, for which—the confession, not the theft—the adult author expects to be loudly and universally applauded; the repetition compulsion that the story performs virtually dictates this response, exacts it, one might say, at knifepoint. On the other hand, the figure of the imaginary bad father in *The Penknife* itself constitutes a confession of Sholem-aleichem's own guilt about the burden of paternal expectations—and his devious revenge on Jewish literature with which those expectations were inextricably bound up. Sholem-aleichem inherited a literary ethos in which the vernacular necessarily played second fiddle to Hebrew; the immediate social uses of Yiddish actually served the moral and aesthetic goals of Hebrew authorship. With the possible and crucial exceptions of Linetskii and Aksenfeld, none of Sholem-aleichem's immediate predecessors or contemporaries who wrote Yiddish prose wrote exclusively in that language. Joseph Perl, Isaac-Baer Levinsohn, Abraham Gotlober, Judah Leib Gordon, even Ayzik Meyer Dik, but most especially Abramovich, all tied their experiments in vernacular satire to the transcendence of biblical Hebrew. Sholem-aleichem had no "father" in his attempt to create a secular model of Yiddish authorship, divorced from the idealism of its Hebrew counterpart. His own fathers-in-literature identified the natural fulfillment of literary aspirations with Hebrew and other

---

[42] Sholem-aleichem, *Dos meserl*, 17.
[43] Gershom Scholem first used the phrase "anarchic breeze" to describe the revolutionary current of "freedom" that flows through the Jewish mystical tradition. See Gershom Scholem, "Toward an Understanding of the Messianic Idea in Judaism," *The Messianic Idea in Judaism and Other Essays in Jewish Spirituality* (New York, 1971), 21.

European languages of high culture—but certainly not with the native Jewish vernacular. Rebellion against tradition in the high-minded pursuit of Hebrew had, by 1887, a distinguished cultural pedigree in the Jewish republic of letters. Rebellion in the name of vernacular authorship was, literally, inconceivable. What would have been the point? In fact, the most popular Yiddish writer of Sholem-aleichem's day, the socially conservative and perfectly pious Dik, successfully domesticated his educational agenda by adopting the patriarchal persona of a household preacher.[44]

Sholem-aleichem's self-consciousness as a vernacular writer developed not in the shadow of modern Jewish biblicism but against the background of Russian realism, consumed with the problem of bearing witness to truth in the language of an unsanctified, fallen world. Most Jewish writers retained a romantic view of language; even when they bowed to the corrupted Jewish present, the idealized image of Jewish collective futurity, personified by the transcendent presence of scriptural Hebrew, remained always before their eyes. The dialectical relationship between the Judaic "holy tongue" and its profane Jewish counterpart virtually precluded the secularization of authorship in which Russian naysayers, like Gogol, Tolstoy, and Dostoevsky, found a source of unparalleled creative freedom, tainted by a sense of almost unbearable responsibility that sometimes resulted in the burning of manuscripts.

Sholem-aleichem began his career as Russia's first secular Jewish author with his "moral apostasy" from the pervasive Hebraism of nineteenth-century Jewish literature, a consummate act of rebellion against the authority of Jewish writing. The figure of the bad father in *The Penknife* represents his own bad conscience about the abandonment of his personal intellectual genealogy and the fortunate fall involved in the disappointment of paternal high hopes. Transforming his own good father into an ineffectual defender of a dying faith, Sholem-aleichem eviscerated the implicit commitment to the spiritual givenness, what we might call the *emes*—the truth—of the text that modern Jewish literature appropriated (stole) from rabbinic tradition. A triumph of indirection, *The Penknife* is a story in which every statement insinuates the opposite of what it says, expressly affronts the sensibilities of the listener and denies the possibility of authoritative, credible utterance. This is language as intentional *mis/communication*—oral, unstable, contingent, extravagant, ill tempered, lacking in every measure of fixity that Jewish writers and gentile philologists attributed to Hebrew, the sublime "language of paradise"—a language fit only for the real world, an unredeemable, immanent kingdom

---

[44] See Roskies, "The Master of Lore," in *A Bridge of Longing*, 56–98. For more on the conservative temper of Yiddish literature for the masses, see Nokhem Oyslender, "Varshever mekhabrim in di 1850er–1860er," *Di yidisher literatur in nayntsetn yorhundert*, ed. Chava Turniansky (Jerusalem, 1993), 241–88.

of things bereft of the promise of transcendence.[45] In this place, to open one's mouth is to lie.

Unlike the Yiddish of contemporary Hebraists, rooted in the carnivalesque poetics of inversion, Sholem-aleichem's native tongue does not bear witness to the ethical aspirations of the Bible. Yiddish authors, claims Dan Miron, lied explicitly in order to expose the credulous reader to the truth, otherwise self-evident to the well-trained, rational reader.[46] *The Penknife* exposes the impossibility of transparent speech in a fallen world where nothing that anyone says can be trusted and where every assertion is a deliberate exercise in obfuscation and evasion. In that final image of the boy running back to *heder*, holding on to his *gemore*, intoning the dual-edged formula that promises a commitment to honesty all the while reveling in the delights of a perfect lie, we have the autobiographical source of all the self-serving, manipulative narrators that Sholem-aleichem eventually invented. To extract the truth from such convincing and ingenuous liars requires the forensic skill of a police detective or a psychoanalyst. And even then, the enterprise is fraught with frustration and doubt. Catching the reader in the act of interpretation, Sholem-aleichem alerts every Jewish reader to the power of semiotic transgression, exposing us to the innumerable clever ways we ourselves devise to invite understanding and yet to avert the terrifying possibility that we might actually be understood.

---

[45] On the European roots of nineteenth-century Hebraism, see Maurice Olender, *Languages of Paradise: Aryans and Semites, a Match Made in Heaven* (Cambridge, MA, 1992), esp. chaps. 3–4.

[46] For the clearest example of the uses of Yiddish literature as a form of vernacular masquerade in the service of rationality and virtue, see Yisroel Aksenfeld's 1842 novella "The Headband" (Yid. *Dos shterntikhl*), in *The Shtetl: A Creative Anthology*, ed. and trans. Joachim Neugroschel (New York, 1979), 49–172.

5. A Paper Life

Model Letters and Real Letters as a Key to Russian-Jewish Aspirations at the Turn of the Twentieth Century

Alice Nakhimovsky and Roberta Newman

Parallel to the real lives of Russian Jews at the turn of the twentieth century was a life in paper: a life of correspondence. People wrote letters—business letters and courtship letters—to recipients nearby, though they also wrote to far-flung family members. Even within the Russian Empire, sons left home to study, to make a living, to board with in-laws, or because they were drafted. Daughters left with husbands or went alone to seek opportunities in bigger cities. And few families were unaffected by emigration to the United States.

Letters presented all sorts of opportunities: to boast, to cajole, to present yourself as you wanted to be and make others act in ways that matched your expectations. But to take advantage of these opportunities, you needed skills that lower-middle-class Jews often lacked. You needed fluency in writing Yiddish and sometimes Hebrew and Russian, and you needed examples of how to express your feelings and construct arguments that worked. For that, people turned to the *brivnshteler*, an anthology of model letters for business and private correspondence. This paper examines the *brivnshteler* in two ways. In part 1, we compare the Jewish *brivnshteler* to its Russian equivalent, the *pis'movnik*, with the aim of seeing how the Jewish compilers structured their letters to reflect specific Jewish concerns and behaviors. In part 2, we use the topic of emigration to America as a case study for comparing model Yiddish letters with real family letters, written by Jewish immigrants to America to their families in Eastern Europe.[1]

The authors would like to offer their thanks to Professor Robert M. Seltzer of the Graduate Center, City University of New York, for his suggestions and assistance; to Brad Sabin Hill, George Washington University, for his helpful bibliographic suggestions; and to Dr. Paul Glasser, YIVO Institute for Jewish Research, for consulting on the translations in this article. Thank you to Jon Zimman for granting us permission to quote from his family's collection of Yiddish letters.

[1] Family correspondence constitutes perhaps the largest body of documentation of the mass emigration of Jews from Eastern Europe to America ever to have existed, since millions of such

The *Brivnshteler* as a Way of Reading Yiddish-Speaking Russian-Jewish Society

The *brivnshteler* was an ephemeral text of the cheapest sort. It can be seen from the sometimes eccentric paginations that letter anthologies were often cobbled together from earlier materials. The results could include everything from accounting information to word games. But the central part of each *brivnshteler* was its model letters.

Who wrote these books? Most nineteenth- to twentieth-century *brivnshtelers* appear to have been written by *maskilim* or members of the postmaskilic intelligentsia. Many of these writers and journalists had to moonlight at other jobs and commissions to supplement whatever living they might be eking out from their more serious writing.[2] They may have seen *brivnshtelers* as cash cows and nothing more. Nevertheless, most *brivnshteler* authors, even those who expressed disdain for the Yiddish language, approached seriously the task of teaching their readers how to write Yiddish properly.[3]

Judging from the subjects taken up in these books, as well as from comments in memoirs and fiction, we can assume that readers of *brivnshtelers* were uncertain about their skills in either Yiddish or Hebrew or Russian or all of the above and wanted to write letters that portrayed them as respectable and educated. Business people needed to write correctly in a language that did not come naturally, a category that would include elevated (*daytshmarish*) Yiddish as well as Russian. Others sought the right prose to address old problems, such as anxiety over a child, and to tackle new ones, like romance. Reflecting the preoccupations of the authors and some readers are occasional letters with maskilic subtexts and modernizing agendas. Other letters, sometimes in the same *brivnshteler*, rail against modern temptations. These eclectic mixes reflect the disparate forces that were tugging at families and pulling individuals in contrary directions. Compilers, concerned with sales, may have been trying to satisfy everyone.

---

letters must have passed back and forth across the Atlantic during the height of the emigration. But they can be examined only anecdotally, since most have not survived; and those that have are scattered in individual family collections. Here we cite examples from two family letter collections—that of the Zimman family, based in Butrimonys, Lithuania; and the Weinberg family, based in Warsaw. Observations in general are based on about a dozen other family letter collections translated by Newman.

[2] See David Fishman, *The Rise of Modern Yiddish Culture* (Pittsburgh, 2005), 90.

[3] For instance, N. M. Shaykevitsh (better known by his pen name, Shomer) insisted in the introduction to *Shomer's briefenshteler* (Vilna, 1898) that "the *zhargon* does not have any rules of grammar."

While the model letters in *brivnshtelers* reflect many of the social and economic upheavals that Jews in Eastern Europe were undergoing at the turn of the twentieth century, they also omit some significant preoccupations of Jewish life during this period. They maintain, for instance, a near-total silence on political issues of the day, notably antisarist sentiment and activities. There are no mentions of political parties, such as the Bund, the Russian Social Democratic Labor Party, and other revolutionary organizations to which many Jews belonged. This is not surprising, given the stringent censorship of Yiddish books at the time.[4] Much more puzzling is the short shrift given to emigration to America. More than two million Jews immigrated to the United States from Eastern Europe between 1881 and 1914, and an estimated 1.6 million came from the Russian Empire.[5] Yet, as we will examine later, very few model letters broach this theme.

Russian Concerns and Jewish Ones: The *Brivnshteler* and the *Pis'movnik*

By the turn of the twentieth century, the primary focus of the non-Jewish letter manual in Europe was business, social behavior, and romantic love. The *pis'movnik* embodies all these interests, but it was nonetheless quite different from the *brivnshteler*. While Jewish compilers took some material directly from the *pis'movnik*, more often the content is decidedly Judaized. The aim of the first part of this essay is to examine how the *brivnshteler* differs from the *pis'movnik* in reflecting specifically Jewish expectations.

Let us focus first, as the *brivnshteler* tends to do, on learning to write. There is no point in spending much time on the *pis'movnik*, where learning to write, if it appears at all, is relegated to children's letters, as in this example from *Obraztsy pisem" vsiakago roda c" riadom" pomeshchennym" nemetskim" tekstom"* (1907):

---

[4] About the closest that some *brivnshtelers* come to politics is their affinity for Zionism. For instance, Mordechai Betsalel Shnayder's *Kobets sipurim v'mikhtavim* (Vilna, 1901) cautiously promotes a Jewish home in Palestine as well as official policies aimed at Russification.

[5] Eli Lederhendler, "America," in *The YIVO Encyclopedia of Jews in Eastern Europe*, ed. Gershon Hundert (New Haven, 2008), 1: 34. See also Alice Nakhimovsky and Roberta Newman, "'Free America': Glimpses of Jewish Life in the Pages of American *Brivnshtelers*," *American Jewish Archives* 61, 2 (2009), for a discussion of *brivnshtelers* published in the United States.

5. A Paper Life

Dearest Mother, Dearest Father,

My teacher wanted me to show you an example of my penmanship for the New Year, and I applied myself as diligently as I could so that this New Year's greeting would be well-written. Please be assured, dear parents, that I will try always to be obedient, so that you will be satisfied with me.[6]

A teacher, an obedient child, and the obligatory parental greeting on 1 January: a picture of upper-class order. The combination doesn't say anything about the actual purchasers of *pis'movniks*—indeed, since we know these books were sold alongside other cheap editions for the newly literate, it is a fair guess that the home in which the *pis'movnik* ended up was far from upper class.[7] But in the *pis'movnik*, learning to write comes in the natural course of a happy childhood.

Not so the *brivnshteler*. Jewish memoirs that trace a route from poverty to education focus on the acquisition of literacy as a means of "awakening," to quote Jeffrey Shandler in the introduction to *Awakening Lives*.[8] Learning to write was not an automatic part of a *heder* education. For that reason, it was often the object of great desire, a childhood achievement that took special effort to pull off if you were a girl, or even a boy, in a poverty-stricken family.[9] In one of the autobiographies in *Awakening Lives*, Khane writes her first postcard and is "the happiest person in the world." In another, Henekh's father "instructed us boys in sacred texts and how to write correspondence in Yiddish," a phrase that unintentionally pairs sacred texts with the *brivnshteler* as the gateways to Jewish adulthood.[10] As important as the acquisition of writing was, it was not free of anxiety. A number of writers begin their autobiographies by apologizing for spelling mistakes and poor style.[11]

---

[6] P. Fuks and S. Mandel'kern, *Obraztsy pisem" vsiakago roda c" riadom" pomeshchennym" nemetskim" tekstom"* (Berlin, 1907), 40. This bilingual German-Russian edition is based on a French original and reflects cross-European practice. Part of its function is as a language text.

[7] Jeffrey Brooks, *When Russia Learned to Read* (Princeton, NJ, 1985), 93.

[8] Jeffrey Shandler, ed., *Awakening Lives: Autobiographies of Jewish Youth in Poland before the Holocaust* (New Haven, 2002), xxvii.

[9] In his essay-length entry "Brivnshtelers" in *Dertsiungs Entsiklopedie*, ed. H. B. Bass (New York, 1957), 467–88, Y. Birnboym emphasizes both the joy and importance of this achievement, which often occurred outside the framework of traditional education, and describes how writing was taught with the aid of a *brivnshteler*.

[10] Shandler, *Awakening Lives*, 113.

[11] See Kh. Sh. Kazdan, *Fun kheyder un "shkoles" biz tsisho: dos ruslendishe yidentum in gerangl far shul, shprakh, kultur* (Mexico, 1956), 76–108, for a discussion of the important role played by *brivnshtelers* in the teaching of Yiddish writing and spelling in *heders* and other alternatives to crown schools in the Russian Empire in the nineteenth century.

It is this anxiety that the *brivnshteler* seeks to allay. Its primary focus is to teach its readers how to write "reyn zhargon."[12] The phrase "pure jargon" sounds like an oxymoron but really was not. *Zhargon* had rules; native speakers did not feel that they knew them. The *brivnshteler* filled not only that gap but also others, providing the proper spelling, along with translations, of Hebrew salutations and other words and phrases appropriate for the formal opening of a letter.

The mere fact of bi- or trilingualism does not make the *brivnshteler* special. European letter-writing manuals are, in general, cross-linguistic. Model letters traveled from one language to another, and bilingual editions served as textbooks of foreign language, business language, and upper-class styles of behavior that reveal themselves in language. That being said, it remains true that the *pis'movnik*, in general, has nowhere near the Jewish obsession with languages.

Many *brivnshtelers* feature Hebrew and Russian in addition to Yiddish. Sometimes the Russian is a useful primary text, like a congratulatory telegram. Occasionally the letter has no practical use at all, and the content is so strikingly non-Jewish that the only possible use is language instruction. In a trilingual *brivnshteler* of 1889, a Russian-language letter advises the recipient to cut down on his drinking.[13] Difficult words are footnoted and glossed in Hebrew, after which the whole outrageously *goyishe* text is translated into Yiddish. The same *brivnshteler* teaches Hebrew writing, but in an entirely different emotional key. Letters from Hebrew learners are awash in desire and anxiety, sometimes justified: in a response to one letter, the writer is told that his Hebrew has so many errors, it is hard to fix.[14]

Some *brivnshtelers* stress the practical use of language learning. In a letter from a 1904 compilation, the writer is saved from disaster because he can write Yiddish and Russian (and do arithmetic):

> Ach, what a misfortune I've met with these past few days. It's painful for me to be silent, and screaming won't help me either . . . This week the last 300 rubles I had left from my wedding money after three years of boarding with my father-in-law and mother-in-law was stolen out of my bag. Now I'll have to throw myself off a bridge . . . The money was in five-ruble coins covered in fat and there was a gold watch made in a factory in London engraved with the number 300 . . . My good fortune is this: while I was

---

[12] N. M. Shaykevitsh, *Shomer's briefenshteler* (Vilna, 1913), title page.
[13] Shalom ben Jacob Cohen, *Sefer mikhtav meshulash* (Vilna, 1889), 8–9.
[14] Ibid., 18.

boarding with my in-laws I learned to write Yiddish and Russian and [to do] arithmetic.[15]

While the *pis'movnik* has no equivalent to the Jewish focus on learning to write, it spends a lot of time on *social* literacy. The understanding of writing as a kind of self-presentation is hardly foreign to the Yiddish—why else would readers need to know the proper spelling of Hebrew salutations? But the Russian has a special interest in style as the sign of a good upbringing. Particular attention is given to the writer's place in a social hierarchy. Some letters look down, to nannies, teachers, and similar hirelings who need to be thanked. Some look up to a variety of "excellencies."

At its extreme, the *pis'movnik* hits a social note entirely foreign to the Yiddish: an aristocratic sense of honor. An example from 1900, from a *pis'movnik* meant for American immigrants, tells readers how to call someone out to a duel.[16] This is not a subject taken up by the *brivnshteler*. But two of the most assimilatory, Harkavy's *Amerikanisher Briefen-Shteler* (New York, 1902)[17] and Frishman-Paperna's *Igron shalem* (Warsaw, 1911),[18] do include hierarchical letters, approaching the *pis'movnik* as a guide to "upper-class conduct."[19]

The emotional center of the *pis'movnik* is romance in all its stages: declarations of love; proposals and responses to proposals; and reproaches for coldness. Here is an example of a reproach from 1900:

---

[15] H. Poliak-Gilman, *Der nayer obraztsover brifenshteller, Hebreyish-russish, zhargon-daytsh. Mit vikhtige briev fun mandzhuryen un yapan. Mit eynige perevodin fun B. Kresin* (Berditshev, 1904), 34–35. Here and elsewhere, translations are from the Yiddish text. The Russian often differs slightly. Here, characteristically, the first sentence of the Russian is less calamitous ("Look what happened to me!" [U menia vot chto sluchilos'!]) Other differences, like Russian "Last night" versus Yiddish "this week," are hard to explain. Perhaps the translator took whatever phrase came to mind. Differences of this kind will not be noted further.

[16] *Novyi russki pis'movnik" v" 5 otdelakh" spetsial'no prisposoblennyi dlia Russkikh, zhivushchikh" v" Amerike.* (New York?, 1900s), 61.

[17] Harkavy, *Amerikanisher Briefen-Shteler* (Amherst, MA, 1999); repr. of Harkavy's *Amerikanisher Briefen-Shteler, English un Yidish* (New York, 1902).

[18] Dovid Frishman, Avrom Paperna, and Mrs. Hess, *Igron shalem: 'Ivrit, Rusit, Polanit ye-Ashkenazit: mikhatavim shonim le-khol tsorkhe ha-ḥayim* (Warsaw, 1911).

[19] Harkavy goes further, presenting a template for congratulating a parent on the secular new year, a ritual that reflects Russian rather than American practice. His letter reproduces the classic *pis'movnik* formula for spontaneous feeling: "Not because it is customary, but because my heart prompts me" (*Amerikanisher Briefen-Shteler*, 12). Here are some Russian examples: *Noveishii samyi polnyi i podrobnyi pis'movnik"* (St. Petersburg, 1822), "Ne odin Novyi god" zastavliaet" menia svidetel'stvovat' vam", pochtenneishii roditel'!" 58; *Novyi russki pis'movnik"* (1900s), "Ne odin" Novyi god" zastavliaet" menia svidetel'stvovat' Vam" moiu blagodarnuiu prizanatel'nost'. Ona v dushe moei vsegda prebudet", kak iskrennee synovnee chuvstvo," 16.

Dear Zina, close to my heart!

The coldness of your recent letters turns my heart to ice and casts into my soul the terribly unbearable feeling of doubt and fateful premonitions. If this isn't the delirium of my sick imagination, then this is terrible. I said "sick imagination." Yes, my soul is sick, because, I repeat, the most dreadful premonitions have tormented me. Warm my soul with a kind word that will restore it, like noble balm to the wounded heart of a suffering man. Do this if only because it is your simple Christian duty.[20]

Love letters occupy a much smaller percentage of *brivnshteler* real estate. But the incursion of modern forms of courtship into Jewish life created a need for some kind of correspondence. One 1900 *brivnshteler* parodies the genre's role in the process:

A young man of low intelligence wanted to write his girlfriend a letter but didn't know how to start it. So he bought a *brifshteller* and right away found just the letter he wanted. He wrote it down exactly the way he found it and sent it on its way. The girlfriend also had the same *brifshteller*; and when she came upon the letter there, she answered him on the spot: *Mein herr!* I have received your letter, and I am sending you the page on which you can find my reply.[21]

Readers who consulted *brivnshtelers* for letters useful both before and after marriage found a wide range of possibilities. The most traditional is represented by this message from a husband (note that he asks for a letter back):

To my dear wife Devoyre, may you live,

I just now received a letter from your dear father with his mazel tov over your having, thank God, gotten through it and with good fortune given birth to a son. I wish you, my dear wife, a mazel tov and that we may live to have nakhes from the newborn and also from the other children. Please, my dear wife, later, in a few days when you feel better, write me a letter by your own hand.

Your husband
Yitskhak Zak[22]

---

[20] *Novyi russkii pis'movnik"*, 102–3.
[21] *Eyn nayer brifenshteler in dray abtheylungen* (Vilna, 1900), 147.
[22] Ibid., 41.

In a letter like this—or in the decorous and flowery *khosn/kale* letters provided in some *brivnshtelers*—we are far from the unbridled passion of *pis'movnik* courtship. But the winds of modernity do blow through the *brivnshteler*, and sometimes strongly.

Modernity appears most strikingly in Poliak-Gilman's *brivnshteler* (1904) in a pair of friendship letters between young men. Both provide a Jewish twist on a classic *pis'movnik* genre. "Dear brother-in-law," begins one, "How sweet was the time when we were together and sat together at the table. It never occurred to me that you would leave us so soon. I thought there would still be a lot of time to tell each other our biographies and I had not gotten my fill of you when the time that my father was going to look after you flew by and you left together with your wife, my sister, to your parents."[23] The other letter is completely maskilic:

> Thank you for the present... When I began to read the book, I can't describe to you the pleasure I got from it, more than from the best theater... Your book opened my eyes, but I have to read it so that my comrades don't see because they would tell my father-in-law and mother-in-law. You must understand, my father-in-law is a Bratslaver Hasid, and when I'm with him, I have to play the role of today's Hasidim... But no one can find out that I am reading a [secular] book because right away I would get the reputation of being an apikoyres and be thrown out by my in-laws. Don't think that I am such a good friend of yours just because you sent me the book. I have always held you in high esteem. Write me letters often from your parents' about your parents, don't forget our love and friendship, and I will not forget you either. Your friend forever.[24]

Letters between unmarried couples also reflect the incursion of modernity. Some bilingual Yiddish-Russian *brivnshtelers* simply reproduce sections from *pis'movniks*. The provenance becomes obvious when a turn of phrase unlikely for a Jewish speaker appears in combination with a non-Jewish name. Consider the following declaration from the Russian half of a bilingual manual: "Only you, dear Maria, represent all that I seek: intelligence without pretense, beauty without coquettishness, and in general charm and modesty that delight all who know you." In the Yiddish, "dear Maria" is excised, but the

---

[23] Poliak-Gilman, *Der nayer obraztsover brifenshteller*, 11.
[24] Ibid., 32. The Russian also says "*apikoyres*." Gershon Hundert alerted us to another peculiarity of this letter: there were never more than a few hundred Bratslaver Hasidim (see Ada Rapoport Albert, "Bratslaver Hasidim," *The YIVO Encyclopedia of Jews in Eastern Europe*, 1:230–31).

"pretense" and "coquettishness" remain.[25] Other *brivnshtelers* combine Jewish romantic restraint with modern expectations. In *Miller's nayer brifenshteller in tsvey theyl* (1911), Sore Sneurzohn is surprised at how coldly her fiancé, Dovid, behaved to her during his visit and how trivial his conversation was. But his letter, she says, has cleared all that up, revealing that he is a strong character who does not like to speak of what is in his heart.[26] In the same *brivnshteler*, Yerukhem Fishelzohn apologizes to Fraulein Zonenshayn for not writing. Her father, he says, told him that in his very first letter, he must declare his intentions, and he could not make such a life-changing decision. He suggests they meet again. She agrees. Despite her great respect for her father, "as a daughter of the 20th century" she cannot accept that meeting two or three times is sufficient for such an important decision.[27]

Another modernizing staple is parental opposition. The following example from 1911 uses the language of battle:

> As you know, the terrible war that we had from all sides with our opponents and enemies until we achieved our desired goal—it's a fact that we have now become bound together with an eternal bond, so significant that it can bring a person to the surprising realization that aside from our having achieved our hearts' desire, we have had an even stronger victory over our opponents.[28]

From love to trouble is a short distance. Bernshteyn (1905) takes up the problem of the young man who has left not only the shtetl but also his shtetl sweetheart:

Dear beloved Rokhl!

> I can't find any words with which to defend myself—you are completely correct. It is true that I have received two letters from you which I haven't answered. But it would not be very clever on your part to conclude from this that I have become completely disinterested in my home town and my small-town girlfriends. Believe me, dearest, that the whole time I have lived here in the big city, I still haven't met a single person with whom I can be so close in life as I am with you.[29]

The Poliak-Gilman *brivnshteler* (1904) highlights different issues. Note the young man's fancy name (Mozes in Yiddish, Moisei in Russian), the young

---

[25] Frishman et. al., *Igron shalem*, 86.
[26] A. Miller, *A. Miller's nayer brifenshteller in tsvey theyl* (Piotrkow, 1911), 71–73.
[27] Ibid., 73–75.
[28] Ibid., 77–78.
[29] Arn Dovid Bernshteyn, *Bernshteyn's nayer yudisher folks-briefenshteler* (Warsaw, before World War I), 44–46.

lady's romantic self-presentation as "weakened," and the Jewish complication of another match:

> Dear and beloved Mozes!
>
> How quickly did the wheel of fortune turn for us without our noticing, and how quickly did misfortune arrive without our expecting it... When a cloud hides the sun, it sometimes becomes dark and sometimes light, and that's the way it was with you, dear Mozes. When I met you, it became light and then a bad person came and our destiny was cloaked in darkness. He expects me to marry his son... Please, dear Mozes, have compassion for your bride to whom you swore eternal love. Don't delay. If you write me, a letter, you will save my life... Dear Mozes, two years have passed since you left and you haven't written to anyone, not even to your parents... Have compassion for your weakened sweetheart, who has barely the strength to sign her name.[30]

Moses's answer declares undying love but fails to explain why he didn't write for two whole years. At the same time, the letter reveals some serious problems: as proof of his devotion, Moses mentions that he has broken with his parents and divorced his wife of three years. Though the "Bintl Brif" had not yet been invented—that scandal-filled advice column from the New York *Forverts* began appearing in 1906—the focus on broken marriages and modern complications is present in the Poliak-Gilman *brivnshteler* in full force.

A final subject of comparison is parents and children. Relations between parents and children are not a matter of particular importance to the *pis'movnik*. Templates are provided for children to express their devotion at the New Year, sometimes with prototypes of parental replies; similar formulations are provided for birthdays and holidays, like Easter or Christmas. The 1822 *Noveishii samyi polnyi i podrobnyi pis'movnik* has examples of letters by and to a prodigal son, a cross-European theme that did excite considerable passion. By the turn of the twentieth century, interest in prodigal sons had dwindled, though some *pis'movnik*s provide all-purpose letters of apology:

> My dear father!
>
> I am full of grief and suffering that my unworthy conduct called forth your anger. My heart is full of anguish; my soul has no peace; my conscience, aware of its crime, is not clean. I fall to your feet and with heartfelt repentance ask your parental

---

[30] Poliak-Gilman, *Der nayer obraztsover brifenshteller*, 36. The Russian "kogda ia uznal tebia" for "when I met you" is substandard and has sexual connotations of which the writer was likely unaware.

pardon. You gave me the gift of life. I owe my existence to your parental solicitude and care. Do not render me unfortunate; do not abandon your son to the vagaries of fate; replace your anger with kindness and allow me, in my moral torment, to appear before you and ask your forgiveness in person.[31]

Sons go astray in *brivnshtelers* too, but in a wholly different style. A *brivnshteler* apology is generally a response to a specific complaint letter: the son has not studied, has not learned a trade (including writing and arithmetic), is not pursuing business, has not notified his parents of his ill health, has not written, or (occasionally) is spending his time on amusements, of which theater looms with particular prominence. In general, the *brivnshteler* puts more emphasis on the complaints than the apologies. If the underlying sentiment in the Russian apology is the father's anger, an anger so great that the son cannot count on a personal audience, the Jewish mode combines scolding with unconditional love:

Volkovishki, 6 May 1903

Beloved son, Shloyme!

Your letter did not bring us any pleasure. Don't think that we expected anything else from you—we always said that this would be how your quest would end. You have robbed yourself of time and us—our health! What is it that you are running after? Do you lack for anything in your parents' home, do we fall short in our service to you? We always told you: stay at home, study science [kentenise], look after business, and get out of your head your fantasy about earning money on your own and the free life. But you were stubborn and went off. Nu, what do you have to say now? . . . We wonder only why you are so foolish and ask you yet again, "Where will you turn and what will you do?" Come home, to your parents. Depend on them and heed what they tell you to do. We are sending you fifteen rubles in this letter for travel expenses and enough with all this foolishness.

Your parents,

Ezriel and Toyve Pozen[32]

In a situation where an adult child is far away—for instance, in America—a Russian *pis'movnik* has him stressing the superiority of home but attempting

---
[31] *Novyi russkii pis'movnik"*, 56.
[32] Oyzer Bloshteyn, *Der nayer rikhtiger Bloshteyn's briefenshteler. Mit fil fershiedene geshribene brief fun di greste shriftshteler* (Warsaw, ca. 1905), 31.

to allay parental anxiety. Parting with the motherland has meant rushing into a "crowd of people who are alien, unfamiliar, indifferent, and cold." Fortunately, he has found shelter "in the bosom of a quiet and kind family."[33]

Templates for Jewish sons who are far away sometimes also try to calm parental nerves, particularly if the worry is about health. But other kinds of unhappiness are aired freely. In Miller's 1911 *brivnshteler*, Yerakhmil complains that he is "lonely, alone in a big world, in a sea of people, with no one interested in me, nor I in anyone. It's possible that I will become used to the present situation, but I don't see any happiness for myself."[34] His father replies, saying how empty the house is without Yerakhmil and bemoaning the fact that fate has ripped him from his loving family.

The point of Jewish parent-child templates is not to hide anxiety but to embellish it. In a letter from Miller, Naftule says that he and mother are out of their minds with worry—when their son was last passing through town, they both noticed that he didn't look well. There is a detailed description of their emotional pain.[35] In another letter, Matisyahu tells his son that he is behaving terribly toward his parents. Even if some misfortune has befallen him, he must let his parents know: "Your mother and I, she should live and be well, cannot rest from great worry and aggravation . . . Our minds picture various scenes that we don't want to commit to paper."[36] Letters that reach this peak of anxiety are often followed by replies that attempt reassurance. Take Gamaliel: he didn't write because he was unconscious, though he's now recovered.[37]

Perhaps the most striking of all this parent-child correspondence—and the most unthinkable in a *pis'movnik*—is the following template for writing to a son who has been drafted:

> 14 July 1904
>
> Dear beloved son Yoyl Moyshe Kostetski!
>
> Ever since we accompanied you to the Zdolbonover railway station, the tears have not dried from our eyes. We live in great anxiety, nothing in the world can make us forget you. If you saw your mother, you already wouldn't recognize her. Imagine, beloved son, compared to her, I'm a hero, my heart is full enough of blood, and I still have to give her strength. Sometimes she looks so terrible that I am simply afraid that I will lose her, too—so, dear child, we ask you, please, if you write to us about your

---

[33] *Novyi russkii pis'movnik"*, 7.
[34] Miller, *A. Miller's nayer brifenshteller*, 5–7.
[35] Ibid., 8–9.
[36] Ibid., 10.
[37] Ibid., 11.

health and courage, you will bring back our courage until God has mercy on us and brings you back to us.

From us,

Your father Yerakhmiel and your mother Khane

The son's reply showcases an entirely different set of values:

8 August 1904, Tshifu [R. Chifu]

Dear and highly esteemed parents!

What did you hope to accomplish with your letter? Until now, I have been cheerful and happy, and your letter caused me so much pain that it is impossible for me to bear. Why are you carrying on this way? Why do you allow yourselves these fantasies? It is, thank God, not bad for me. On the contrary, nothing has happened to me. I am healthy and feel, blessed be God, in the best shape. I have everything, do not lack for anything. At the end of July, we had a battle. The Japanese advanced on our right flank and our regiment repelled them in such a way that he [sic] is thankful to be alive. Since then, it has been so quiet for our regiment that you can't imagine. The officers live with us as well as if they were our own brothers. So, beloved parents, please don't worry and don't be sad. You are squandering your health needlessly and have made me anxious as well. Be cheerful and happy and I will soon write you another letter.

From me, your son,

Yoyl Moyshe Kostetski[38]

Yoyl Moyshe's template beautifully portrays a young man caught between Jewish behavioral patterns—he knows how to dig at his parents, even as he reassures them—and Russian ideas of heroism in battle.

---

[38] Poliak-Gilman, *Der nayer obraztsover brifenshteller*, 44–46. The Russian in the first letter is substandard in parts.

5. A Paper Life

Emigration as Depicted in *Brivnshtelers* and in Real Letters

The theme of separation from loved ones is ubiquitous in *brivnshtelers*. It is more commonly played out in letters from and to men (less commonly, women) who have left their hometowns as a result of marriage or to pursue business, work, and educational opportunities in large cities. Wives worry that they will never see their husbands again, and parents worry over their loss of influence over their children's moral lives. In one letter in *Bernshteyn's nayer yudisher folks-briefenshteler* (n.d., pre–World War I), a wife says that she is "scared of the paper life" she is now forced to live with her husband, who has gone away to America. In another letter from the same book, a woman worries that her husband's infrequent letters mean that he has forgotten her and their children.[39] Model letters like these are both a response to the real anxieties of people encountering these situations in real life and a suggestion on how to manage the anxiety and contain it in writing. In short, the model letters provide instruction on how to live "a paper life."

While very few model letters treat emigration to America, those that do are revealing, especially when compared to real letters between Jewish immigrants and their families back home in Eastern Europe. They also help explain possible reasons for the *brivnshtelers'* neglect of this mass communal phenomenon.

The duty of reforming Jews and Jewish life in keeping with maskilic ideals was presumably never far from the minds of the authors of *brivnshtelers*. But their focus was on the reformation of Jews and Jewish life in situ, in the Russian Empire or Austro-Hungarian Empire—or on a Zionist solution, on the dream of building a new, modern Jewish life in Palestine. America did not fit neatly into this agenda.

When America does make an appearance in model letters, it often does so in a way that openly expresses maskilic concerns. In the following letter from *Eyn nayer brifenshteler in dray abtheylungen* (1900), a father in Vilna links his son's emigration to America to the young man's failure to live up to maskilic educational ideals:

> Dear son Efroym, esquire, may he flourish,
>
> I received your letter. You blame yourself for your bad circumstances. And even though I know that you yourself are responsible for it, as your father, of course, I also have deep regrets. But how can I help you? You yourself know the truth, that I have done everything for you that was possible for me. I

---
[39] Bernshteyn, *Bernshteyn's nayer yudisher folks-briefenshteler*, 64–65.

have paid teachers to teach you everything essential and have demonstrated and explained how education brings a person good fortune and how unsuccessful an ignorant person is . . . I have told you this so many times, but you wouldn't listen to me. Now it is bad for you! You can't find a profession for yourself because you can't write or do arithmetic, and you also didn't want to learn a craft, so what are you good for? . . . Nonetheless, if you truly have regrets about your bad behavior, all is not yet lost. You can come home and I will do everything on your behalf.[40]

America is portrayed as a purgatory for those who have committed the sin of being uneducated or unskilled, a punishment for those who have not pursued a secular education (the preferred solution to the problems of modern Jewish life) and thus are ill suited to survive in the changing economy.[41] Castigation of an unsuccessful son is a familiar *brivnshteler* genre, usually directed at a boy who has left the shtetl for the big city to pursue better educational and/or business opportunities. It has been updated in this case to include exile in a strange land as an additional punishment for neglecting one's studies and failing to heed the sage advice of one's elders.[42]

While examination of real family correspondence can provide only anecdotal evidence for Jewish immigrant attitudes toward America, the samples consulted for this article reveal sentiments starkly dissimilar to those expressed in *brivnshtelers*.[43] The immigrants' families acknowledge that adjusting to a strange new world is hard for their children and express their longing to see them again, but America is generally depicted as an opportunity,

---

[40] *Eyn nayer brifenshteler in dray abtheylungen*, 9–20. An additional letter in the same vein can be found in this same *brivnshteler* on 20–21 and appears to be an almost word-for-word copy of a model letter printed earlier in Ts. H. Goldshteyn-Gershonovitsh, *Yudish-daytsher morall brifensheller. In fir thayl* (Berditshev, 1890), 17.

[41] For instance, horror over the hard work and fast pace of America is expressed in a letter from A. Miller's *nayer brifenshteller in tsvey theyl* in which Avsholem complains to his mother: "God has cast me out in a distant land where life is very hard—the worry, the business is dreadful, indescribable. No one who hasn't seen this sort of life with his own eyes can't imagine what a hell it is; life itself wears you out, forcing a person to work like our ancestors in Egypt, beyond your capabilities, and there is no time to take a breath" (18–20).

[42] Castigation of unsuccessful sons is also, in fact, a common theme in real family letters. For instance, in the following letter, Tsvi Dov, a grain merchant complains to his son Meyshe Abbe (who is known as Morris in the United States), that another son, Yitskhak (or Izzie), has not yet reimbursed him for his traveling expenses to America: "But please, dear Morris, speak with him, and tell him that he should reimburse us little by little for the travel expenses. Let's not be worse than the peasants. Every *sheygets* [non-Jewish boy] reimburses his parents for his travel expenses in the very first year. And [Izzie] is already three years in America. But he sends us only jokes and writes like a smart aleck in every postcard." Collection of Zimman Family, Letter 262, 23 July 1910.

[43] See note 1.

not a misfortune. Thus Alte Tsine (nee Zemkropska, married name unknown) in the Lithuanian town Prienai writes to her brother in the United States that she is toying with the idea of eventually joining him there:[44]

> Thank God, we are all in good health and we are making a living, but, of course, not the sort of living one makes in America. My dear husband also still thinks very well of America. Of course, it will take time, but, as one knows, we won't stay here forever. Business is, as we know, the way it is in Russia, and there is also not much that one can do for children here... If only I could actually go to America, then one could finally forget all these troubles! No more slaving away like horses and what do we have here! Dear brother, you can believe me, you should be happy that you are in such a precious land. Of course, I know quite well that you would like to see our parents, but one must be happy![45]

For most of those who emigrated to North America, formal higher education in the sense that it was envisioned by the *brivnshtelers* did not appear to have been an option; nor was its absence a motivation for emigration. Real family correspondence is often explicit about the more likely reasons for millions of Jews leaving for America: lack of economic opportunity, the desire to avoid military service, and, occasionally, the need to flee in order to avoid punishment for antitsarist activities.[46] The first two reasons are mentioned in the following letter, sent by Meyshe Abba Zemkropski from the Lithuanian town Butrimonys to his brother Izzie, who had emigrated a couple of years earlier and, for some unexplained reason, does not seem to want his brother to come to the United States:[47]

> Dear brother, I have written to you about how I am planning to come to America... but you have not replied at all. I really don't understand why you are angry at me, why you don't write to me. After all, we are brothers. My coming to America won't cost you a single kopek but because army service is coming up and I'd have to do four miserable years of duty and only then be able to come to America, well, you can certainly see the situation I'm in. As you know, Father won't spend a single kopek on me and I don't mean anything by this, I feel no resentment toward him. He can't spend anything on me—he is a sick man and has

---

[44] Prienai is 54°38' N 23°57' E, 54 miles west of Vilna.
[45] Collection of Zimman Family, Letter 270, n.d.
[46] For instance, the private family letter collection of Jaime Weinberg contains several letters from Polish Jewish anarchists and members of the Socialist Revolutionary Party writing from Paris and the United States, whence they had apparently fled in the wake of the revolution of 1905.
[47] Butrimonys is 54°30' N 24°15' E, 44 miles WSW of Vilna.

no business to enable me, as a young man, to stay in Baltrumonts [Butrimonys] ... Fayfke Khayim Shuel is also going to America today because there is nothing to do here ... It feels as if in Baltrumonts we go to sleep from Friday night to Saturday night, and afterwards there is nowhere to go anyway.[48]

Jewish desire to avoid army service would, of course, have been off-limits to the authors of the *brivnshtelers*, who therefore were prevented from honestly confronting the emigration phenomenon in model letters. But America was also a political topic for another reason: the civic equality that Jews enjoyed there. In the following letter from *Yudish-daytsher morall brifenshteller* (1890), an advertisement for America is slipped in between the curses. Aaron writes in desperation to his mother in Warsaw from New York, where he has just arrived:

> First of all I want to let you know, dear Mother, that on 20 December arrived safely in America and immediately realized what a bad deal I made, because I didn't take your advice, and I let myself be misled by frivolous people and I believed that in America gold rolled around in the streets and that one only had to bend down and pick it up. In the end, I have seen that it is not at all like that, though certainly this is a very free land where the Jew has all the same human rights as any other nationality, but to cross into such a distant part of the world one must ... almost forever become separated from one's homeland, where every bit of land, every blade of grass, every tree is beloved; and never again have the opportunity to see one's parents and acquaintances [emphasis added].[49]

The characterization of the United States as a country where Jews had full civil rights is an implicit, if not explicit, comment on the Russian Empire; and it is interesting to consider whether, in this case, it missed the notice of the censor. In one of the few other positive portrayals of America, a *brivnshteler* author avoids criticism of Russian policy toward the Jews by substituting a social critique of the Russian-Jewish community. In *Der nayer prakitsher brifenshteller* (1891), Dov Arye Friedman has Khayim Yoyne, newly arrived in New York, write to his wife Khane:

---

[48] Collection of Zimman Family, Letter 143, 17 October 1908. Other letters from this collection include stories about schemes for bribing officials and doctors to get young men exempted from the draft, about people purposely maiming or poisoning themselves to get out of military service, and about Jews who were killed in the course of army service or who attempted to flee their units.

[49] Goldshteyn-Gershonovitsh, *Yudish-daytsher morall brifenshteller*, 17.

> I am now based at your brother-in-law's, and after I have rested up a bit, I will also begin to look around for a way to make a living... I have run into Khaym Yekl, Grune's son. You would not recognize him at all; he is quite an aristocrat, going around in a fine coat and a top hat, and already speaking German and English. He earns bars of gold. Borekh too doesn't have it too badly. True, one must work with all one's strength here, but something can come of it. I also won't be lazy, I won't be embarrassed to do anything, because here one isn't ashamed to do any sort of work; only thievery is looked down on. But honest hard work is free and open to everyone, and that is what is really good about America. If at home among us, people wouldn't be ashamed to do anything, it would be America by us, too.[50]

In her reply to this letter, Khayim Yoyne's wife worries that he has made a mistake and that he will, like others, "come back from America with empty hands." But this only prompts another, even more glowing letter from her husband:

> If you could see the big pack that I shlep on my shoulders and must carry up to the sixtieth floor [sic], I am sure that tears would flow from your eyes. But despite this, I am happy. However, the skilled workmen do much better here. They sit restfully and earn real money. Now our high-status people, the yudlakh; Abraham, Isaac, and Jacob's grandchildren, who don't want their children to learn any craft, see how they make their children unfortunate. They are eating each other up and remain paupers, poor men, lying in dirt and living in muck and thereby darkening their years with chaos. If you could see how cleanly and tidily one lives here, you would say that the Americans are angels compared to the Russian Jews. The most impoverished person lives so cleanly that their floors shine like mirrors. And the clothing they wear! How cleanly and beautifully they dress when they go out!... I tell you the truth, that sometimes the idea comes into my heart of sending you a ship's ticket and bringing you and children here... What do you think, Khane?[51]

Khane prudently answers that he should first establish himself, and then she will come with the children.

---

[50] Dov Arye Fridman, *Der nayer praktisher brifenshteller* (Berditshev, 1891), 58. Shaykevitsh (1849?–1905), whose pen name was Shomer, was a well-known Yiddish author and playwright, who emigrated to the United States in 1889. This entire *brivnshteler* was later plagiarized, appearing in Vilna in 1908 as *Shomer's briefenshteler: mit dem pinkes tsu zammen fun dem gresten zhargonishe shrayber oykh mit fil briv.*
[51] Ibid., 59–60.

Both Khaym Yoyne's critique of Jewish shtetl life and Aaron's acknowledgment of the civil rights Jews enjoyed in America are echoed in a real letter from Morris Zimman (formerly Meyshe Abba Zemkropski), who was quoted above in a 1908 letter before his emigration to North America from Lithuania. Now known as Morris after several years in the United States, he responds to a letter from his fiancée informing him that his parents are being criticized by other Jews in their Lithuanian shtetl for renting a building to a non-Jew:

> America is a golden land where one should kiss every pebble. Here, no one gives me any flak. Whether I rent to a non-Jew or a Jew, everyone is equal . . . I'm sure the town already considers them sinners. Don't let the tailor's son read the Torah in the synagogue because he rents to a non-Jew. I guess they can even take it one step further and excommunicate him . . . like in some benighted little towns. I don't think I would be able to live in Baltremonts [Butrimonys] anymore.[52]

The perception that America was a brand-new world with vastly different social and economic norms is revealed in both the *brivnshtelers* and real correspondence through the anxiety of parents over loss of influence over their children. In a letter in *Shomer's briefenshteler* (1913), Devoyre writes to her daughter in America from Lutsk:

> You have delighted me, my child, with the news that you are in good health, thank God, and that you hope to find happiness in the new world, because you are being courted by many worthy young gentlemen.
>
> To tell the truth, the expression "many worthy young gentlemen" leaves a bad taste in my mouth. I would have been more pleased if you had written me that one manly worthy young man was seeking to win your love, because from many young gentlemen, a young girl's head can spin, so that she doesn't know what to do, who from among them to choose. My child! Do you understand that a young girl must be careful these days when she is surrounded by so many suitors? Are you familiar with sort of people that most of these suitors are?
>
> I must admit that that I have just asked you a stupid question. How would you know about such things? You are still a young child, you were brought up in a small town and you are still unskilled in the ways of the wider world, so I consider it

---

[52] Collection of Zimman Family, Letter 137, n.d. Draft of a letter by Morris Zimman.

my responsibility to make you aware of a few important matters that can help you protect you against great misfortune. You should know, my daughter, that big city young gentlemen are not stingy with their compliments to a pretty girl. Most of them do not really feel as they say, so you shouldn't believe every one of them. Even if one of them kneels before you and swears that his love for you is great and eternal, you should thoroughly, very thoroughly investigate whether his vow is true, because there are many scoundrels in the world who in order to attain their own dark ends will not hesitate to swear to anything.[53]

In a reply, Khane reassures her mother that she is not as naive as she thinks and that her fears are unfounded: "In the short time I have been in America, I have already had plenty of opportunities to become acquainted with the characters of today's young gentlemen, because many of my friends have met with tremendous misfortune at the hands of ill-intentioned parties. For me, this was the best education, and so the compliments that the young gentlemen of my acquaintance bestow on me leave me cold. Be assured, beloved Mother, that God will protect me from the sort of misfortune that you imagine."[54]

While similar parental anxieties appear in real letters, so does respect for the new world. Tsvi Dov, Morris's father, often offers business advice.[55] But he is careful to balance advice and criticism with respect for the modern ways of the world his son now lives in. He adopts his sons' American names right away, addressing all his letters to "Morris and Izzie," and, on occasion, uses English words, which he has presumably picked up from their letters. How else to explain phrases such as "*Vifl makhstu evri viks?* [How much are you earning every week?]" and *"olrayt"* [all right] from someone who has never been to America himself?[56] Surviving Yiddish letters between Jewish immigrants in America suggest that English words and terms very quickly insinuated themselves into their everyday Yiddish speech and no doubt found their way into letters sent back home to family and friends.

Tsvi Dov turns to tradition to counsel his sons, drawing on biblical passages, parables, and long story-jokes to make his points.[57] Sometimes, he seems a bit shocked at his sons' new way of life, as when he chides Izzie

---

[53] Shaykevitsh, *Shomer's briefenshteler*, 31–34. He wrote a number of *brivnshtelers* in New York, which were commissioned by a printer in Vilna, as well as one published in New York by the Hebrew Publishing Company. The model letters in his *brivnshtelers*, are, in a sense, *fictional* letters written by a *real* immigrant.
[54] Ibid.
[55] Ibid., Letter 118, 18 August 1911.
[56] Ibid., Letter 88, 7 March 1909.
[57] For example, in one letter, he relates a long joke involving business losses and dogs to express his skepticism about an investment his son is contemplating. Ibid., Letter 103, 30 August 1913.

in a 1908 letter for taking a photograph hatless.⁵⁸ But he also seems to take pains to present himself too as a modern Jew, one who has been, perhaps, left behind in Europe by his sons but not entirely left behind by history. In the same letter about the hatless portrait, he seems to make fun of the traditional wedding he has just thrown for one daughter: "The wedding was very fine, with everything prepared. It lacked only some of the family. But my head is still spinning because I spun the bride around the groom a few times as is the silly fashion among us here in Europe and also that they make the groom break a glass with his foot and have them drink from the cup that they used for the *shevebrokhes* [seven blessings recited at the wedding ceremony]. I'd do away with all of this, but one has to do as everyone else does."⁵⁹

We have explored here some aspects of the complicated interplay that *brivnshteler* authors negotiated—first between Russian manuals and the actual needs of a Yiddish-speaking public, and then, in regard to immigration to North America, between the experiences of their readers and the political realities of living in the Russian Empire. While both *brivnshtelers* and *pis'movnik*s were marketed to people uncertain about their literacy and longing for self-improvement, they present two different worlds: one quasi-aristocratic, with an emphasis on romantic love, and the other fraught with anxieties about education and children. *Brivnshtelers* mirror the dislocations of their modernizing, mobile readers.

The reliance on correspondence was a necessity for East European Jews separated from their families. For those forced by circumstances to enjoy only "a paper life" with spouses or children, *brivnshtelers* suggested the right words to maintain these overwhelmingly important ties. That the term "a paper life" also appears in real letters is a testament to the shared reality of the letters in *brivnshtelers* and real correspondence. As a young woman writes to her fiancé in America shortly before World War I, "I too want to put an end to the paper life. As the women say, 'They take people and they exchange them for paper.'"⁶⁰

---

⁵⁸ Ibid., Letter 212/213, 26 June 1908.
⁵⁹ Ibid.
⁶⁰ Collection of Zimman Family, Letter 123/125, n.d.

Part 2

Upheaval, Violence, and Antisemitism

6. Violence and the Migration of Ashkenazi Jews to Eastern Europe

Shaul Stampfer

At the beginning of the modern period, let us say in the fifteenth or the beginning of the sixteenth century, there were hardly any Jews in Eastern Europe. At the end of the nineteenth century, there were millions of Yiddish-speaking Ashkenazi Jews in Eastern Europe, and they were the vast majority of world Jewry. This is clear. What is not clear is who were the ancestors of these Jews, when did they come to Eastern Europe, and above all—why? It is widely believed that waves of Jewish migrants fled to the east in the wake of anti-Jewish violence in the German-speaking lands. This fits a standard image of Jewish history: time after time, persecution led entire Jewish communities to put their packs on their backs and seek a safe refuge—a haven that would ultimately prove to be temporary as well. One of the main difficulties in testing this view that links violence to migration to Eastern Europe is that there are almost no explicit sources from the early modern period that relate to the timing of the migration, the numbers involved, the motives of the migrants, and their place of origin. It is also highly unlikely that many such source materials exist or will be discovered. Nonetheless, it is possible to deal with these questions by considering the context, examining the dynamics of migration, and analyzing some basic cultural characteristics of East European

---

When I was just beginning this study, Prof. Jacob Goldberg gave me valuable advice. Gershon Bacon, Tomasz Jankowski, Alexander Kulik, Jerzy Mazur, Sergio della Pergola, Yohanan Petrovsky, Moshe Rosman, Jona Schellekens, Mark Tolts, Michael Toch, and Dan Yardeni read various versions and made valiant efforts to force me to write clearly, to be comprehensive, and to document my thesis. I received instantaneous help from Agnieszka Jagodzinska and Marcin Wodzinski when I needed it. My readers did not agree with everything I have written, but I value friendship far more than agreement. I hope to deal with this topic in greater detail in the future and to build a more precise reconstruction of Jewish population growth. I would be grateful for comments and suggestions by readers.

Jewry.[1] It is my claim that the evidence indicates that there was no mass migration, that antisemitism was not a major factor in migration, that the migrants who came did so mainly because of demographic and economic pressures, and that the large numbers of Jews in the nineteenth century were the result of high fertility and low mortality. In the following pages, I will show why this is the most reasonable explanation. Many of the details, I hope, will be fleshed out in future research, but all the data lead to the same conclusion.

Before going in detail into the nature of Ashkenazi migration to Eastern Europe, it is important to discuss a well-known alternative to the thesis that migration from German-speaking lands was at the root of East European Jewry. I am referring to the theory that large Jewish communities existed in Eastern Europe already in the medieval period and that the subsequent Jewish population was descended largely or mainly from these communities. The proponents of this theory do not deny that there was some migration of Ashkenazi Jews to Eastern Europe, and they would agree that this migration was significant culturally and linguistically. However, they would claim that the bulk of Eastern European Jews were not descended from migrants from Central European lands but from different populations—either of Slavic converts, Khazar converts, or Jewish migrants from further east. There is no question that some and, perhaps, most of the early Jewish settlers of the Polish lands were Jews of Byzantine origin that came from Crimea. They founded the medieval Jewish communities in Kiev, Vladimir, and probably elsewhere. These communities do not seem to have survived the Mongol invasion of Eastern Europe in the mid-thirteenth century, and thus the descendants of these settlers could not have been the source population of later East European Jewry. It may well have been the case that individuals or small groups of Jews survived and were able to integrate with the Jewish migrants from the west.[2]

---

[1] Contemporary court records that have not been utilized until now should offer more information on the life of Jews at the time—and on some aspects of their migration. See Jerzy Mazur, "Border Jews: Jewish Life on the Medieval Frontier of Europe" (Ph.D. diss., Brandeis University, 2009) for cases of this kind. He has been kind enough to inform me that his findings on migration of Jews from Regensburg eastward in the thirteenth century are consistent with my findings in this article.

[2] There are some fine surveys of references to early Jewish settlement in Eastern Europe. For the most recent and comprehensive, see Michael Toch's forthcoming book *Economic History of Early Medieval European Jews*, chap. 7, "East European Population." See also Aleksandr Kulik, "Evrei Drevnei Rusi: istochniki i istoricheskaia rekonstruktsiia," in *Istoriia evreiskogo naroda v Rossii: ot drevnosti do rannego Novogo vremeni*, ed. Kulik (Jerusalem and Moscow, 2009), 189–213; and Vladimir Petrukhin, "Evrei v drevnerusskikh istochnikakh XI–XIII vv. (in ibid., 214–39). Another important study by Kulik in English is Alexander Kulik, "Judeo-Greek Legacy in Medieval Rus'," *Viator: Medieval and Renaissance Studies* 39, 1 (2008): 51–64. For a classic formulation of sources, see Majer Bałaban, "Kiedy i skąd przybyli Żydzi do Polski?" *Miesięcznik Żydowski* 1, 1 (1930): 1–12, 1, 2: 112–21; Salo Baron, *A Social and Religious History*

6. Violence and the Migration of Ashkenazi Jews to Eastern Europe

However, there are absolutely no references to large autochthonous Jewish populations in Eastern Europe at the beginning of the fourteenth century—neither in Jewish sources nor in general sources. Had such populations existed, they would certainly have been given attention. There would have been references to the legal status of such populations, and their size would have had an impact on religious issues. One cannot posit the existence of a community just because it would solve a problem.[3] As we shall see, the genetic evidence seems to contradict this theory.

Before I examine the migration that created East European Jewry, as it was known from the seventeenth century on, I need to clarify the terms that will be used. In this case, that means defining "mass migration" as well

---

of the Jews, 2d ed., vol. 3 (New York and Philadelphia, 1957), chap. 19, esp. 213–20; and Bernard Dov Weinryb, "The Beginnings of East European Jewry," in *Legend and Historiography: Studies and Essays in Honor of Abraham A. Neuman*, ed. Meir Ben-Horin, Bernard Dov Weinryb, and Solomon Zeitlin (Leiden, 1962), 445–502. There is an important survey of Ashkenazi migration in Hanna Zaremska, "*Migracje Żydów aszkenazyjskich* w średniowiecznej Europie," in *Wędrówka i etnogeneza w starożytności i średniowieczu*, ed. Maciej Salamon and Jerzy Strzelczyk (Kraków, 2004). Many of the sources are surveyed in Kevin Alan Brook, "The Origins of East European Jews," *Russian History/Histoire russe* 30, 1–2 (2003): 1–22, but his emphasis is more on citation than on critical analysis. A more recent article by Jerzy Mazur, "The Late Medieval Jewish Settlement in Red Ruthenia: The Case of Krosno," appeared in *Studia Judaica* 13, 2 (26) (2010): 237–52. His findings fit my thesis as presented below. Jits van Straten, in *The Origin of Ashkenazi Jewry: The Controversy Unraveled* (Berlin, 2011), concludes, "The genetic background of East European Jewry . . . is probably very heterogeneous and to a large extent has its origin in people who lived in areas now called Ukraine, Belarus, Lithuania, and Poland and to a lesser extent in Jews from Byzantium and the Middle East" (194). This conclusion is quite original, but it is based, as far as I understand, on a misunderstanding of demographic dynamics and of the sources. Although Jews often converted slaves, Van Straten provides no real evidence for mass conversion of Slavs to Judaism and does not explain how large-scale Jewish *proselytization* among the Slavic peoples went unnoticed and unreported. I obviously think that my thesis, though less earth shaking, is more reasonable, has more textual support, and is closer to reality.

[3] Jits van Straten's analysis led him to conclude that "the size of the Jewish population in 1500 in Poland (Eastern Europe) must have been between 460,000 and 860,000" ("Early Modern Polish Jewry: The Rhineland Hypothesis Revisited," *Historical Methods* 40, 1 [2007]: 39–50, quotation from 49). However, it is estimated that the population of Poland in that year was 3.4 million. See *Historia Polski w liczbach*, ed. Franciszek Kubiczek, Andrzej Jezierski, et al. (Warsaw, 1993), 20. Of that population, 17 percent, or about six hundred thousand was urban (30). It is impossible to reconcile von Straten's hypothesis with these figures. The existence of huge autochthonous communities is also implied by Paul Wexler's fascinating research on the history of Yiddish, even though there is no evidence for such communities. See Paul Wexler, *Two-Tiered Relexification in Yiddish: Jews, Sorbs, Khazars, and the Kiev-Polessian Dialect* (Berlin, 2002). There is also no evidence for the theories on the Khazar origins of the East European Jews. As a matter of fact, the most recent serious study of the Khazars concludes that there never was widespread Khazar conversion. This claim, based on careful examination of the evidence by an acknowledged expert, merits careful consideration. See Moshe Gil, "The Khazars Did Not Convert to Judaism," *Zion* 75, 1 (2010): 5–14.

as "waves of migration." For the sake of simplicity, one can say that mass migration involves not only individuals and families but also larger groups of people who may share a common geographical background or identity but otherwise are not close and do not share intense mutual responsibilities with one another. "Waves of migration" refers to dramatic short-term shifts in the number of migrants. Mass migration and waves of migration should leave "fingerprints," and the presence or absence of such "fingerprints" will be very useful for the reconstruction of past developments.

Mass migration occurs under specific circumstances. When there is large-scale and life-threatening violence and flight is possible, one finds a mass exodus of the population involved.[4] This kind of population movement naturally goes in waves: when the threat is perceived. There is widespread flight. After all, no one wants to become a casualty. As time passes, the number leaving declines as fast as it went up. The longer a person lives without harm but under a threat, the easier it is to conclude that the threat is not so real. Flight is not aimless. People who flee tend to do so as family groups that include children and the elderly, and this is by nature difficult. Moreover, in the early modern period, transportation was expensive. Therefore, there were real incentives to travel as little as possible. There was also often a hope that the threat would pass and that it might be possible to return and to reclaim property and to resume previous commercial contacts. When the motive for migration is safety, the nearest point that seems secure is often the most reasonable place to stop. While this type of migration is going on, it too attracts attention and sometimes a reaction.

Migration of Jews to distant locations, like that of non-Jews, is obviously not simple. It depends to a large degree on the certainty of being able to successfully settle in the new location. This outcome could not be taken for granted with regard to potential Jewish migration to Eastern Europe in the early modern period. In addition to problems of information and adjustment that were to be expected, there was an additional factor that might be surprising. Jewish communities in Eastern Europe did not always welcome Jewish migrants. Baron noted with surprise: "Remarkably, xenophobic manifestations also appeared within the Jewish camp. At least in the latter part of the sixteenth century, when most of the immigrants had developed their own vested interests and other characteristics of a settled population,

---

[4] We should note that one type of mass migration is not a form of flight: when organized groups settle land. When settling the land, the presence of familiar people nearby can be of great help, and it is certainly not a hindrance. Indeed, much of the *Ostsiedlung* was made up of organized groups of peasants. However, Jews were not agriculturists, and organized migration to an urban environment offers few advantages. As a result, it is not common. Therefore, if there was mass migration of Jews, it would have been migration in response to danger.

6. Violence and the Migration of Ashkenazi Jews to Eastern Europe

some leaders began looking askance at the arrival of competing newcomers, whether from abroad or from other parts of Poland and Lithuania." He cited, among other sources, a resolution adopted by the Lithuanian Jewish Council in 1623: "No [Jew] from another country shall be allowed to establish a residence in any Lithuanian province without the knowledge and consent of the [Jewish] head of the province."[5] This right to limit migration was already formally recognized in 1532, although it reflected attitudes that had long been prevalent in Jewish communities.[6] This attitude certainly would not have encouraged Jews who felt threatened to flee to Poland.

One widely held view links early modern Jewish migration to Eastern Europe with non-Jewish migration. Such a connection would have made the long-distance move to Eastern Europe less risky because Jewish migration would have been part of an organized movement. Indeed, in the twelfth and early thirteenth centuries, there was large-scale migration of non-Jewish Western Europeans, mainly but not only German speakers, to Eastern Europe. This migration is known as *Ostsiedlung* or "Settlement of the East," and it had a major impact on the development of urban centers in Poland. It is a commonplace that in many early modern Polish cities, such as Kraków, the lingua franca was German and much of the town culture showed very strong German influence. The root cause of the *Ostsiedlung* was population pressures in Western and Central Europe. The peasant population grew in the Middle Ages; and after peasants had utilized all the potential lands in their vicinity, land hunger developed. There were many unfarmed lands in Eastern Europe; and Polish kings welcomed enterprising organizers who put together groups of peasants to establish villages in Eastern Europe. At the same time, cities were growing in the German-speaking lands, but not fast enough to provide occupations for all who grew up in them or wanted to live in them. For urban dwellers, the growing Polish cities offered employment and economic potential. Hence eastward migration appealed to urban populations as well.

The peasant migration was organized and structured. Peasants did not have easy access to information about foreign lands, and their limited financial resources made migration daunting for them without some organization. The dynamics of urban migration seem to have been different. Town dwellers made individual decisions to move. In any case, the numbers of urban migrants were limited. Piskorski writes: "The question of the number of settlers, especially German ones, who took part in the eastward migration

---

[5] Baron, *Social and Religious History*, 3:11–12. On this topic, see also Louis Rabinowitz, *Herem Hayishub* (London, 1945).
[6] Baron, *Social and Religious History*, 3:12–13. Worries about competition and competitors expressed by Jews and non-Jews suggest that we should be cautious about interpreting opposition to Jewish settlement as simply an issue of anti-Jewish feeling.

remains a great problem. It does not, however, appear that they existed in very great numbers, despite the traditional opinions."[7]

Some historians, notably Bernard Weinryb, regard the Jewish migration to Eastern Europe as linked to some degree to this *Ostsiedlung*.[8] Weinryb and others, however, did not try to argue that the Jewish migration was simply a subset of the general *Ostsiedlung*. The *Ostsiedlung* took place in the thirteenth and fourteenth centuries and ended with the Black Death. There is no evidence of substantial Jewish communities in Eastern Europe during this period. In addition, the massive population losses in Western and Central Europe during the plague years opened many opportunities for the surviving non-Jewish population, which no longer needed to seek opportunities in the East. It was a long time before significant non-Jewish eastward migration resumed. Nonetheless, Jews continued to migrate east after the plague years and to found new communities. Thus it appears that Jewish migration did not coincide with non-Jewish migration but instead developed later, for the most part. In light of the differences in timing, it is not possible to depict the Jewish migration as simply an element of the broader *Ostsiedlung*.[9]

Was anti-Jewish violence, then, the key factor in the Jewish migration to Eastern Europe, and could this explain the difference in timing between Jewish and non-Jewish migration? If so, what cases of violence could have stimulated flight to the Polish lands? One early event could have been the Crusades. However, there is no evidence that substantial Ashkenazi Jewish communities existed in Eastern Europe in the eleventh century. Indeed, during the Crusades, Poland's economy was not elastic enough to assimilate significant numbers of fleeing urban Jews. German Jews would not have seen Poland as a reasonable place of refuge.[10] Moreover, it was not necessary to leave an entire region to find refuge; many nearby communities offered potential solutions.

Anti-Jewish violence during the Black Death could theoretically have led to mass migration to the east. The fourteenth century brought appalling mass killings of Jews in the German-speaking lands. But at the height of the plague,

---

[7] Jan M. Piskorski, "The Medieval Colonization of Central Europe as a Problem of World History and Historiography," *German History* 22, 3 (2004): 323–43, quotation from 337.

[8] Bernard D. Weinryb, *The Jews of Poland* (Philadelphia, 1973), chap. 1.

[9] Adriaan Verhulst, "The Origins and Early Development of Medieval Towns in Northern Europe," *Economic History Review*, n.s., 47, 2 (1994): 362–73. Hanna Zaremska makes a similar statement in *Żydzi w średniowiecznej Europie Środkowej* (Poznan, 2005), 32. Uriel Weinreich, in "Yiddish and Colonial German in Eastern Europe: The Differential Impact of Slavic," *American Contributions to the Fourth International Congress of Slavicists* (Gravenhage, 1958), 369–421, already made this point on 408.

[10] Jits van Straten makes this point somewhat differently in "Jewish Migrations from Germany to Poland: The Rhineland Hypothesis Revisited," *Mankind Quarterly* 44, 3–4 (2004): 367–84.

6. Violence and the Migration of Ashkenazi Jews to Eastern Europe

it would have been difficult for any group to migrate great distances in large numbers and to find a secure place to settle.[11] This was certainly the case for Jews, who were widely accused of disseminating the plague. Once the violence ended, the pressure to migrate would have declined. Most expellees seem to have stayed in the region where they had lived. This fits in with what we know about migration in general.[12]

To be sure, persecution in and expulsion from of the German-speaking lands in the fourteenth and fifteenth centuries did contribute to documented Jewish migration—but to Italy![13] As one might expect, several factors influenced this choice of destination. The proximity of Italy to the German-speaking lands, the intensive transportation links and widespread knowledge about conditions in Italy, and the possibility of integrating into a dynamic economy undoubtedly influenced decisions of Jews who wanted to leave the German lands. Given the choice of Poland or Italy as a place of refuge, Italy had the clear advantage. In short, the assumed link between anti-Jewish violence and eastward migration was not likely, and it was certainly not proved.

The unstated assumption behind the theory of large-scale migration from west to east is that the disparity between the large numbers of Jews in Eastern Europe in recent years and the small medieval Jewish population requires explanation. Migration is a good explanation for this disparity but not, it turns out, an essential one. The estimates of Jewish population even for the beginning of the sixteenth century are not large. Ignacy Schiper estimated that there were 24,000 Jews in the Polish lands in 1500 (18,000 in Poland proper and 6,000 in Lithuania), while Weinryb proposed an even lower figure for this date—10,000–15,000.[14] An assumption of previous mass immigration or of autochthonous Jewish communities is not necessary to explain numbers like these. Even if there had been no Jews in Eastern Europe in 1400 (clearly not the case), and assuming no natural increase, a yearly immigration of

---

[11] It is hardly likely that the Jews could have been as mobile as the flagellants, who indeed did roam Europe.

[12] For a relevant discussion of some theories of migration, see www.csiss.org/classics/content/90.

[13] See Michael Toch, "Jewish Migrations to, within, and from medieval Germany," in *Le Migrazioni in Europa: Secc. XIII–XVIII*, ed. Simonetta Cavaciocchi (Florence, 1994). This article was reprinted in Toch's *Peasants and Jews in Medieval Germany: Studies in Cultural, Social, and Economic History* (Aldershot, UK, 2003).

[14] Ignacy Schiper, "Rozwój ludności żydowskiej na ziemiach dawnej Rzeczypospolitej," in *Żydzi w Polsce odrodzonej. Działaność społeczna, gospodarcza, oświatowa i kulturalna*, ed. Ignacy Schiper, Arjeh Tartakower, and Aleksander Hafftka, (Warsaw 1932), 1:21–36, esp. 26–27. I thank Tomasz Jankowski for bringing this to my attention. It was later cited by Maurycy Horn, "Wirtschaftliche Tätigkeit der polnischen Juden im Mittelalter unter Berücksichtigung des Siedlungswesens," in *Deutsche, Polen, Juden—ihre Beziehungen von den Anfängen bis ins 20. Jahrhundert: Beiträge zu einer Tagung*, ed. Stefi Jersch-Wenzel (Berlin, 1987), 54; and Weinryb, "Beginnings," 501.

250 would more than have sufficed to reach Schiper's estimate—though one can also not ignore the high rates of urban mortality at the time. Obviously, taking into account the population already in Eastern Europe and factoring in population growth, the yearly rate of migrants could have been substantially lower. These figures suggest that there was no mass immigration before 1500.[15]

How, then, can one explain the size of the Jewish population in Eastern Europe in 1700? Gershon Hundert concluded, "By the end of the seventeenth century, Polish-Lithuanian Jews probably numbered between 300,000 and 350,000; in German lands at the same time there were certainly no more than 60,000 Jews."[16] Could this be evidence of mass migration or of a massive autochthonous population?

In fact, there is a simpler explanation: population growth is exponential and not arithmetical. Population growth is like interest on a loan. Children join the population and have children of their own, just as one pays interest on a loan and interest on the interest. If a growth rate is positive, the number of children born every year constantly rises. The yearly growth rate necessary for a population to grow from ten thousand to three hundred thousand in two centuries is only 1.7 percent. That is, to reach this figure, a group of one hundred Jews would need about two more births per year than deaths. A larger starting point of twenty-five thousand would require an even lower growth rate—1.2 percent. Although high, these rates are certainly within reason.[17]

The general Polish population apparently had a yearly growth rate of 0.7 percent during this period, but growth rates among Jews could well have exceeded the Polish rate, not least because of lower child mortality among

---

[15] As Toch put it in "Jewish Migrations": "Disregarding the manifold myths on the origins of Polish Jewry, we can safely assume that its establishment was in the main a product of the late medieval migrations, internal and external, of German Jews . . . In the 15th and even more so in the 16th century this movement grew in terms of the numbers of people involved and of communities founded. Against 9 localities in the 14th century, about 60 towns were settled in the 15th century and about 200 localities during the 16th century. This eastern European population, numbering by the end of the period about ten thousand, was to become the social and cultural hub of early modern Ashkenazic Jewry and by far the most important part of the Jewish people of modern times" (647). Again, this was not an emigration that uprooted whole communities but instead a selective process in which the rich and energetic branched out and most of the poor probably remained behind.

[16] Gershon Hundert, "Comparative Perspectives on Economy and Society: The Jews of the Polish Commonwealth—a Comment," in *In and Out of the Ghetto: Jewish–Gentile Relations in Late Medieval and Early Modern Germany*, ed. R. Po-chia Hsia and Hartmut Lehmann (Cambridge, 1995), 103.

[17] This is not identical but similar to the findings of Sergio della Pergola, in his classic article: "Some Fundamentals of Jewish Demographic History," *Papers in Jewish Demography 1997* (Jerusalem, 2001), 11–33, esp. 22–23; and Joseph Jagur-Grodzinski, "Origins of Ashkenazic Jewry: Natural Growth vs. Immigration," *Papers in Jewish Demography 11 (1993)* (Jerusalem, 1997), 82.

6. Violence and the Migration of Ashkenazi Jews to Eastern Europe

Jews, extended breast-feeding among Jews, higher rates of nuptiality, and higher rates of remarriage. Poles were mainly agriculturalists, and peasants typically had lower standards of infant care than urban families.[18] This point was made as early as the seventeenth century.[19] When population dynamics are taken into account, the large Jewish population in modern Eastern Europe is easily explainable.[20]

There are documented cases in non-Jewish societies of such rapid growth. The Afrikaners in South Africa descend from a group of about two thousand settlers who arrived in the late seventeenth century. Today, approximately thirteen generations later, there are about three million Afrikaners.[21] The French-speaking population of Quebec, which today numbers about 6.5 million, is descended from five thousand or so immigrants who came to

---

[18] I am not convinced by the claims made by Jits van Straten and Harmen Snel in "The Jewish 'Demographic Miracle' in Nineteenth-Century Europe: Fact or Fiction?" *Historical Methods* 39, 3 (2006): 123–31. The authors deal well with numbers but not sufficiently with the historical context. Their article "Infant Mortality and Nefalim in Amsterdam," *Historical Methods* 39, 2 (2006): 73–81, is not relevant, since it deals with Western Europe. It is not clear why the authors did not relate to Frans Van Poppel, Jona Schellekens, and Aart Liefbroer, "Religious Differentials in Infant and Child Mortality in the Netherlands, 1855–1912," *Population Studies* 56 (2002): 277–89. I hope to return to the topic of differential mortality in the future. Jona Schellekens pointed out to me in a personal letter: "If Jewish women in eighteenth-century Eastern Europe on average married two to three years earlier than their non-Jewish neighbors, as suggested by the data from Galicia and Kurland, then Jewish fertility could have been about one birth higher. If fertility among Jewish women was 3 girls per woman instead of 2.5 and if life expectancy at birth among Jews was 37.5 years rather than 35, that is 700 girls out of 1,000 reached their fifth birthday instead of only 670, then Coale and Demeny (1966) predict an annual growth rate of 1.9 percent instead of 1.0 percent."

[19] Sebastian Miczynski wrote: "W lat dwunastu sie zenia, na wojnie nie gina, od powietrza nie umieraja, wiec sie namnozyli" (They marry at the age of twelve, they don't die in war, they don't die from the plague, so they've multiplied). Cited in Schiper, "Rozwój ludnosci żydowskiej na ziemiach dawnej Rzeczypospolitej," 1: 31.

[20] The defense taxes Jews paid rose from about six thousand złoty in 1569 to 180,000 złoty at the end of the seventeenth century. While certainly no proof, this increase suggests a period of massive population growth—even though there is little reason to believe in mass migration from the West in this period. On the contrary, the timing would favor natural growth as the deciding factor. See Maurycy Horn, "Świadczenia Żydów na rzecz obronności Polski (w XVI i XVII w.)," *Biuletyn Żydowskiego Instytutu Historycznego* 98 (1976): 5. At the same time, he mentioned, in "Żydzi ziemi sanockiej do 1650 r.," *Biuletyn Żydowskiego Instytutu Historycznego* 74 (1970): 5, that persecuted Jews from the West settled in Poland in the mid-sixteenth century, even though he cites no evidence of persecution. Here too it seems that he was repeating the conventional wisdom.

[21] Johannes Lodewikus Roos, Herman Walter Pretorius, and Maria Karayiorgou, "Clinical Characteristics of an Afrikaner Founder Population Recruited for a Schizophrenia Genetic Study," *Annals of the New York Academy of Sciences*, 1151, special issue "The Year in Human and Medical Genetics" (2009): 85–101. The discussion of population history is on 86.

North America in the seventeenth century.[22] These numbers do not *prove* that the Jewish population grew at a similar rate. They show only that such growth is possible. As a result, the possibility of rapid population growth by Jews in Eastern Europe cannot be ruled out. I would also note that in the German lands, the number of Jewish communities rose from ninety around 1238 to over one thousand in 1350! Although the exact number of Jews in the German lands remains unknown, it is clear that the main cause for the rise in numbers in this period was natural population growth.[23] What requires explanation is not why the Jewish population in Eastern Europe grew but why the Jewish population in Central Europe did not continue to grow at the same rate.[24]

But even if migration was limited, the migrants had to come from somewhere and for a reason. The evidence suggests that most migrants to Eastern Europe traveled short distances, which in the present context means that they came mainly from Bohemia, Moravia, and Silesia,[25] as well as the eastern German lands.[26] According to estimates, about three thousand Jews lived in the Czech lands in the mid-sixteenth century, one thousand of them in Prague.[27] These numbers mark the upper limit as to how many migrants could have come from this particular community. The Jewish population of

---

[22] Massimo Livi Bacci, *A Concise History of World Population*, 3d ed. (Malden, 2001), 48–52. For greater detail and documentation, see Charles R. Scriver, "Human Genetics: Lessons from Quebec Populations," *Annual Review of Genomics and Human Genetics*, no 2 (2001): 69–101. See also Hubert Charbonneau, "Essai sur l'évolution démographique du Québec de 1534 à 2034," *Cahiers québécois de démographie*, 13, 1 (1984): 5–21. Charbonneau found that in 1684–1733 the growth rate of the French-speaking population in Quebec was 2.5 percent! (17).

[23] See the editor's introduction on xxiii to Zvi Avneri, *Germania Judaica* (Tübingen, 1968), 2: xxiii.

[24] The lack of awareness of the power of exponential population growth lies at the root of Cherie Woodworth's discussion of the possibility of a large Jewish population in Eastern Europe before the Ashkenazi migration. See her review of Max Weinreich's *History of the Yiddish Language*: "Where Did the East European Jews Come From? An Explosive Debate Erupts from Old Footnotes," *Kritika: Explorations in Russian and Eurasian History* 11, 1 (2010): 107–25. Taking the math into account makes it possible to defuse the explosives. Jona Schellekens wrote me in a private letter, "Age at first marriage, however, was a major proximate determinant of fertility." He discusses this point in his study of age at first marriage among Jews in Amsterdam ("Determinants of Age at First Marriage among Jews in Amsterdam, 1625–1724," *Journal of Family History* 24 [1999]: 148–64). He added, "in Amsterdam there is some evidence for early marriage in the seventeenth century, but by the middle of the eighteenth century age at first marriage among Ashkenazim had reached levels common among non-Jewish populations in Western Europe."

[25] Many family names suggest German origin, but the use of the name of a specific city as part of the family name of an individual suggests that the origin was rare enough to be noteworthy.

[26] See the important monograph of Jürgen Bürstenbinder, *Judenschutz und Eigennutz: Auseinandersetzungen um die Juden an der Ostgrenze des Römisch-Deutschen Reiches im 13. und 14. Jahrhundert* (Saarbrücken, 2010).

[27] Tomáš Pěkný, *Historie Židů v Čechách a na Moravě*, 2d ed. (Prague, 2001), 641.

Prague and in the Czech lands grew in the sixteenth and seventeenth centuries. Therefore, only a small minority of the population could have migrated to the east. This would fit a pattern of individual or family migration but not large group migration.[28] However, this would have been enough.

A variety of evidence supports the view that Jewish migration to the east involved small groups of people traveling short distances. Patterns of regional customs among East European Jewry offer one set of indications. The Yiddish-speaking Jews of Europe in the late medieval period could be divided into regions by their religious customs, or *minhag*. The Rhineland *minhag* was distinct from the *minhag* of the Danube region (now Austria), Bohemia, and Moravia. The East European *minhag* that developed over time was generally closer to the Austrian *minhag* than to the Rhineland *minhag*.[29] This fits the theory that most eastward migrants came from Austria, Bohemia, or Moravia.

No region or town in Eastern Europe preserved the customs of a specific Jewish community in the German-speaking lands, as would have been possible had there been a mass influx of Jews from a specific German region or community. Indeed, there are documented cases that demonstrate that Jews who migrated to the east from other regions could preserve their identity. The Sephardic community of Zamość, founded in the mid-sixteenth century, maintained its identity for over a century.[30] Majer Bałaban mentions a synagogue conflict in Kraków in the early sixteenth century between newly arrived Czech Jews and local Jews.[31] The Czech Jews actually organized their own synagogue and maintained their identity. Other groups of migrants from

---

[28] We may be able to see a reflection of this situation in Israel Ta Shma's description of Rabbi Judah Ha Hasid's relations with students of his who had migrated eastward. This case involved German Jews, but there is no reason to think that it was exceptional. The migration of these students resulted from personal calculations as to the advantages and disadvantages of migration made by individuals who tried to maintain contact with their home environment after they moved. It was not mass migration by groups. See Israel Ta-Shma, "On the History of the Jews in Twelfth- and Thirteenth-Century Poland," *Polin*, no. 10 (1997): 287–317.

[29] Eric Yitzchak Zimmer, *Olam Keminhago Holekh* (Society and Its Customs), (Hebrew) (Jerusalem, 1996). Daniel Goldschmidt noted, in the introduction to the High Holiday Prayer Book that he edited (*Makhzor leYamim Noraim* [Jerusalem, 1970], 14 n. 8), the existence of differing western and eastern versions of the prayer book, with the customs of the medieval Jewish communities of Nuremburg, Rothenburg, and Regensburg being identical with the eastern version. The economic and personal ties between the community of Regensburg and Polish Jewry are well documented. See Ta Shma, "On the History of the Jews." Nuremburg had exceptionally strong economic ties with Poland in the early modern period (F. W. Carter, *Trade and Urban Development in Poland* [Cambridge, 1994], 163). It and Regensburg were on the trade route from Prague to Venice. Rothenburg lay along the trade route from Prague to Bruges and Cologne. Trade seems to have had more impact than expulsions did.

[30] Jakub Szacki, "Sfardim in Zamoszcz," *YIVO Bletter* 35 (New York, 1951): 119–20.

[31] Majer Bałaban, *Dzieje Żydów w Krakowie i na Kazimierzu (1304–1868)* (Kraków, 1912), 1:83. See also 1:87 n. 5.

a specific community in the German-speaking lands could have done the same—but there is no evidence that they did.

The easiest explanation for this is that, in general, migrants did not travel in groups and that there were never large groups of Jewish migrants from the German-speaking lands. In other words, the case of the Czech Jews in Kraków was an exception. Elchanan Reiner pointed out that one of the key innovations of Rabbi Moses Isserles, the Kraków rabbi who integrated the Ashkenazic halachic tradition into the Shulchan Aruch, was his undermining of the significance of communal customs. In the Jewish communities of the German-speaking lands, community traditions had long been more authoritative than textual sources. Elchanan Reiner, who analyzed Isserles's work, saw it as indicating that Polish Jewry was a society of immigrants and not of communities who immigrated as a group.[32]

The distinctive dialect of Yiddish spoken in Eastern Europe can also shed light on the origins of East European Jews. Already in the early modern period, in the sixteenth century if not earlier, East European Jews spoke a type of Yiddish that was clearly distinguished from western Yiddish. The geographic spread of eastern Yiddish has been mapped for the modern period. The border between east and west runs from the Baltic to the west of Poznan, down to the east of Wrocław and the west of Kraków, and south. Western Yiddish was spoken in what is today Germany, the Czech Republic, Slovakia, and Hungary.[33] The ubiquity of Yiddish speech among East European Jewry supports the hypothesis that Yiddish-speaking migrants to Eastern Europe played a central role in the formation of East European Jewry.[34] At the same time, the absence of significant numbers of loan words from Turkic languages

---

[32] Reiner did not explicitly claim that Jews who moved to Poland came from many locales and not as groups from specific communities, but this is the best explanation for the situation he described. See Elchanan Reiner, "On the Roots of the Urban Jewish Community in Poland in the Early Modern Period," *Gal-Ed* 20 (2006):13–37 (in Hebrew). The reference to a community of immigrants is on 33.

[33] See *The Language and Culture Atlas of Ashkenazic Jewry* (Tübingen and New York, three volumes so far); and the fundamental article by Steven M. Lowenstein, "The Shifting Boundary between Eastern and Western Jewry," *Jewish Social Studies* 4, 1 (1997): 60–78. This eastern Yiddish can be further divided into three main subdialects that are commonly termed northeastern, southeastern, and central Yiddish. A good understanding of how these dialects emerged would illuminate the migration history of the Jews.

[34] As far as we know, the Jews who lived in Eastern Europe before the arrival of Ashkenazi Jews came from Byzantium. The absence of loan words of Byzantine origin does not support the thesis that this was a large Jewish source population in Eastern Europe of non-Ashkenazi origin. The same can be said for an absence of words that would suggest a Khazar origin. The possibility that there was a large population of converts is interesting, but there is no evidence for this.

is one more piece of evidence against the theory that East European Jews were to a significant degree descendants of Khazars or Crimean Jewish populations.[35]

Interestingly, there was one Jewish group that preserved a Turkic language in Eastern Europe. The East European Karaites, who were unquestionably of Crimean origin, were able to preserve their language until the twentieth century. This indicates that language preservation was possible.

The question of the source or sources of eastern Yiddish has not been resolved. Nor is the geographical background of the various subdialects of eastern Yiddish clear. Some of the best minds in Yiddish linguistics have tried to identify the region where Yiddish originated, but a clear answer has eluded them.[36] If we could identify the source region, we would have to consider the possibility that most Jewish migrants came from this region. Robert King claimed that "nothing in any dialect of Yiddish points back to Alemannic (Switzerland and Southwestern Germany), Alsatian, Rhine Franconian, or Moselle Franconian. Nor is there a trace of Low German influence on Yiddish."[37] One of the more interesting proposals comes from Steffen Krogh, who suggests that Yiddish was not based on a specific regional dialect. Instead, the origins of Yiddish should be sought in the language spoken by non-Jewish German speakers in Eastern Europe.[38] This explanation suggests that individual Jews adopted the local language after they migrated. Had individuals come as a group, they would have been far more likely to preserve their home dialect. Thus, the absence of a clear geographic source for eastern Yiddish does not fit well with the theory of mass migration or flight. Cyril

---

[35] For a careful linguistic and onomastic study that comes to this conclusion, see Aleksandr Beider, "Iazik, imena i familii evreev Vostochnoi Evropy," in *Khazary: Mif i real'nost'*, ed. E. Nosenko-Shtein F. and V. Petrukhin (Moscow, 2010), 350–73. Paul Wexler presents an earlier, dissenting opinion in "Yiddish Evidence for the Khazar Component in the Ashkenazic Ethnogenesis," in *The World of the Khazars—New Perspectives: Selected Papers from the Jerusalem 1999 International Khazar Colloquium Hosted by the Ben Zvi Institute*, ed. Peter B. Golden, Haggai Ben-Shammai, and András Róna-Tas (Leiden, 2007), 387–98. Read in isolation, it is very convincing. However, I cannot convincingly integrate it into what is known from other sources. I hope to return to the question of the Khazars in a future study.

[36] Alexander Beider, "The Birth of Yiddish and the Paradigm of the Rhenish Origin of Ashkenazic Jews," *Revue des études juives* 163, 1–2 (2004): 193–244.

[37] Robert D. King, "Migration and Linguistics as Illustrated by Yiddish," in *Trends in Linguistics*, ed. Edgar Polome and Werner Winter (Berlin, 1992), 426.

[38] Steffen Krogh, *Das Ostjiddische im Sprachkontakt: Deutsch im Spannungsfeld zwischen Semitisch und Slavisch* (Tübingen, 2001). See also Hans Blosen, "Teilweise unorthodoxe Überlegungen zu einigen Problemen des Jiddischen," in *Sandbjerg 85: Dem Andenken von Heinrich Bach gewidmet*, ed. Friedhalm Debus and Ernst Dittmer (Neumünster, 1986), 161–87; and Blosen, "Jiddisch als deutscher Dialekt," *Augias* 31 (1988): 23–43. These interesting articles merit serious academic discussion. Eckhard Eggers, in his recent *Sprachwandel und Sprachmischung im Jiddischen* (Frankfurt am Main, 1998), provides strong evidence for links between early East European Yiddish and Czech. See esp. 81–177.

Aslanov regards eastern Yiddish as a koiné language, not a language that grew out of a specific German or Yiddish dialect.[39] This also fits a picture of many individual migrants but not a situation where cohesive groups migrated as a unit.

Genetic data, too, point to a small founder population for East European Jewry, not masses of migrants. Some of the genetic characteristics of East European Ashkenazi Jews may indicate that there was a population "bottleneck" in the past.[40] One study found that almost half of the female Ashkenazic population appears to be descended from just four women! It would be foolhardy to draw conclusions on the basis of genetic evidence alone, but here the information supports other types of data. Unfortunately for our purposes, the current state of genetic knowledge does not make it possible to determine the size of the population at the time of the "bottleneck or the precise date it took place."[41]

Onomastics, or the study of names, also supports the view that the number of Jewish migrants to Eastern Europe was not large. The work of Alexander Beider has transformed the field of East European Jewish onomastics, providing a new body of source materials with which to examine migration patterns. Beider found that "until the mid-sixteenth century, in Czech provinces there

---

[39] Siril Aslanov, "Izmenenie iazykovoi identichnosti evreev Vostochnoi Evropy: k voprosu o formirovanii vostochnogo idisha," in *Istoriia evreiskogo naroda v Rossii*, ed. Kulik, 398–416. See also Dan Shapira, "Yiddish-German, Slavic, or Oriental?" *Karadeniz Araştırmaları* (Journal of Black Sea Studies) 6, 24 (2010): 127–40.

[40] For a general discussion of genetics and the Jews, see David Goldstein, *Jacob's Legacy: A Genetic View of Jewish History* (New Haven, 2008). This fascinating book raises many relevant points. For example, Goldstein points out genetic differences between Jews and Sorbs (67–69) that contradict the theory that East European Ashkenazim are largely descendants of Sorbs. None of the genetic studies have found indications of strong genetic linkages between East European Jews and their neighbors. I should note that the existence of a bottleneck in the past is not beyond question. See Gregory Cochran, Jason Hardy, and Henry Harpending, "Natural History of Ashkenazi Intelligence," *Journal of Biosocial Science* 38, 5 (2006): 659–93, for a contrary opinion.

Two of the most important recent studies on Ashkenazi Jewish genetics are Gil Atzmon et al., "Abraham's Children in the Genome Era: Major Jewish Diaspora Populations Comprise Distinct Genetic Clusters with Shared Middle Eastern Ancestry," *American Journal of Human Genetics* 86, 6 (2010): 850–59; and Doron Behar et al., "The Genome-Wide Structure of the Jewish People," *Nature* 466 (2010): 238–42. These articles refer to other important studies carried out in previous years.

A recent eighteen-page study that would seem to be totally devoted to our topic is Avshalom Zoossmann-Diskin, "The Origin of Eastern European Jews Revealed by Autosomal, Sex Chromosomal, and mtDNA Polymorphisms," *Biology Direct* **5 (2010)**: 57. However, the article actually deals with the general ethnogenesis of Ashkenazi Jewry and questions the view that Jewish groups in various regions were related. He does not question the view that East European Jewry descended from migrants from the West (see esp. 6).

[41] Doron Behar in an e-mail to the author on 14 December 2009.

are no occurrences of names popular in Rhineland ... [T]his factor indicates that Rhenish immigrants were rare in Czech lands... On the other hand, migrants from German-speaking provinces neighboring Bohemia-Moravia—namely Franconia, Bavaria, and Austria—were numerous."[42] He went on: "direct migration of Jews from Rhineland to West Canaan [the Czech lands—S.S.] was rare. The routing between the two countries mainly possessed an intermediary stage through Franconia or Bavaria."

These onomastic data support the view that most migration occurred over short distances. Moreover, if few German Jews migrated directly to the Czech lands, it is highly unlikely that they traveled even farther to Eastern Europe. Beider reached a similar conclusion regarding Silesia: "Jewish names in that Slavo-German state were similar to those used in Bohemia-Moravia." He also noted, "[i]n Silesia there are numerous Semitic names absent or extremely rare in Germany and completely absent in available mediaeval sources for Bohemia-Moravia," and suggested that these may reflect the presence of descendants of older Oriental communities in this region.

Beider concluded that the name corpus of Polish and Silesian Jews was very similar: "we can assert that the arrival in Poland of Jews from Bohemia-Moravia, southeastern German (certainly Bavaria and most likely Franconia, too), Austria, and East Germany is without question. On the other hand, we cannot say with certainty that there were direct migrations from Rhineland. Several common Rhenish Jewish names such as Adelheit, Jutta, Gottschalk, and Gutheil never reached Poland, and Gumprecht was rare in Poland."[43] With regard to Lithuania, the names of Jews indicate that "[t]he Ashkenazi Jews who came to Lithuania during the 15th–17th centuries were of heterogeneous origin."[44] This suggests that they were not refugees from violence, hence probably not mass migrants. Had there been a need to flee violence, it would be difficult to understand why only a few chose to migrate.

Onomastic evidence has its limits. First-generation immigrants can give their children local names, and veteran residents can adopt the names of respected new immigrants. However, naming is often traditional. When

---

[42] Alexander Beider, *A Dictionary of Ashkenazic Given Names: Their Origins, Structure, Pronunciation, and Migrations* (Bergenfield, NJ, 2001). The references in this paragraph are from 174–76.

[43] Ibid., 185. He also wrote about "massive arrival of Yiddish-speaking immigrants from Bohemia-Moravia ... as well as from several other areas as Austria, Bavaria, and Silesia" and added, "During the following centuries, Polish communities entered a period of stability and, similarly, the corpus of their individual names remained stable" (188). However, he did not bring any evidence for the claim about mass migration. Here it seems to be "conventional wisdom" but not a conclusion based on onomastic evidence—in distinction to his other arguments.

[44] Ibid., 204.

onomastic data parallel other sources, it strengthens the view that the analysis is based on reality.

Although the sources contain no traces of evidence for mass migration of Jews to Eastern Europe in the early modern or later periods, they do refer to migration of a different nature. Baron cites two cases from the early sixteenth century.[45] One deals with the migration of Abraham of Bohemia to Poland under the protection of Sigismund I, and the other with Sigismund I's intervention on behalf of a family from Litomerice who were about to migrate to Poland. In both cases, the right to migrate was not taken for granted, and the migrants traveled in family groups, not as part of a mass migration. The existence of two individual cases does not prove the absence of large-scale migration. In the same way, cases of expulsion of communities prove little. Bałaban listed many Bohemian Jewish communities that were expelled from their homes.[46] The fact of expulsion, however, did not mean that those expelled traveled east. Even more important, most of these communities were small. The fewer the migrants, the more likely they were to find settlement alternatives close by. The privileges given to Jewish communities in Eastern Europe do not refer to group migration.[47]

Given the absence of proof that mass migration took place and strong evidence that it did not occur, it seems both prudent and reasonable to assume that individual migrants and their descendants made up the core group of East European Jewry. It is difficult to pinpoint when this movement began and how quickly it developed. However, we can ask at what point did East European Jewry crystallize as a distinct group—or, in other words, when did immigration decline and allow for the development of a distinct identity?

---

[45] Salo Baron, *A Social and Religious History of the Jews*, 2d ed., vol. 16 (New York, 1976), 5. Baron used sources cited by Mathias Bersohn, *Dyplomataryusz dotyczący Żydów w dawnej Polsce na źródłach archiwalnych osnuty (1388–1782)* (Warsaw, 1910). Baron notes that in one document, the statement is made that the Jews of Bohemia "were on the point of departing for Poland." The text reads: "Król Zydmunt zaleca manifestem Włazydsławowi Sterbergk, kanclerzowi Królestwa Czeskiego, aby dobra żydów w temże państwie znajdujące się, uważane były za zostające pod opieką króla i przeto, aby nie czynioną im była żadna krzywda w używaniu tychże dóbr, w przekazywaniu ich swym sukcesorom i w zarządzaniu niemi oddając wszystkich żydów pod prawa, innym poddanym czeskim służące." Baron's knowledge of Polish was certainly much better than mine, but I did not find a reference to the upcoming departure of Bohemian Jewry in this text. Perhaps he was thinking of another text, but I could not find one.

[46] See Baron, *Social and Religious History*, 16:317 n. 2 for the reference.

[47] The classic study on privileges is Jacob Goldberg, *Jewish Privileges in the Polish Commonwealth*, 3 vols. (Jerusalem, 1985–2001). On the first privilege, see Zofia Kowalska, "Die großpolnischen und schlesischen Judenschutzbriefe des 13. Jahrhunderts im Verhältnis zu dem Privilegien Kaiser Friedrichs II. (1238) und Herzog Friedrichs II. von Österreich (1244)," *Zeitschrift für Ostmitteleuropa-Forschung* 47 (1998): 1–20. I was not able to obtain copies of her other articles on early East European Jewry.

6. Violence and the Migration of Ashkenazi Jews to Eastern Europe

The split between western and eastern Yiddish provides some evidence for developing group identity. In 1609, Johann Buxtorf the Elder noted the existence of western and eastern Yiddish.[48] The division into two dialects must have started at least a century earlier, because crystallization of a dialect takes time. Indeed, Buxtorf saw eastern Yiddish as a reality that was taken for granted, not an innovation. Isolation is conducive to the formation of dialects. If the Jewish population of Eastern Europe had been in a state of flux in his time, due to an influx of migrants from the German or Czech lands to Poland, this would probably have delayed the development of a distinctive eastern dialect.

The assumption that there were low levels of migration already in the sixteenth century fits what we know about the conflict in Kraków between a distinct group of Jewish migrants from Bohemia and a self-aware local community took place in the early sixteenth century. It also fits evidence from liturgical practice. By the early sixteenth century, printed prayer books carried a statement on the title page that they were according to the Polish rite.[49] It seems that the bulk of the migration was completed by the mid-fifteenth century—if not earlier.[50] During this time, the Czech Jewish community continued to grow despite the Hussite wars and the expulsions of Jews from many cities. While most of those expelled from one town apparently relocated to neighboring towns, some Czech Jews may have migrated at this time to the Polish lands, and if so, in some of these cases, fear of violence may still have motivated individual decisions to leave.[51] However, there is no clear evidence

---

[48] Dovid Katz, "Origins of Yiddish Dialectology," in *Dialects of the Yiddish Language: Papers from the Second Annual Oxford Winter Symposium in Yiddish Language and Literature,* ed. Katz (Oxford, 1988), 43.

[49] The Bodleian library has a holiday prayer book printed in Prague in 1533 or earlier. See *Machsor ex ritu Polonorum Pragae* (1533), cited in David ben Abraham Oppenheim et al., *Collectio Davidis* (Hamburg, 1826), 157. The National Library of Israel has a holiday prayer book according to the Polish rite printed in Prague in 1519.

[50] This corresponds in many respects to the views of Jaroslav Miller, *Urban Societies in East-Central Europe, 1500–1700* (Aldershot, UK, 2007), 90–91. Miller noted that, in Bohemia, many Jewish communities underwent "removal" (expulsion) between 1450 and 1550. However, he adds, "[w]hile in the 15th century the Polish Jews still comprised a marginal group of inhabitants, the extensive immigration waves from the Bohemian lands, Germany, and Western Europe sparked the unprecedented growth of the Jewish population in Poland," whereas we would suggest that it was not waves but simply uninterrupted population growth. Much of the history of Yiddish is still unclear. The standard work is Max Weinreich's *History of the Yiddish Language,* which has been published in a complete translation by Yale University Press (2008). In addition to other works cited here, see also Dov-Ber Kerler, *The Origins of Modern Literary Yiddish* (Oxford, 1999). He discusses dialects in the introduction.

[51] I am grateful to Dr. Mark Tolts for reminding me of this.

for this view. Migration did not stop in the fifteenth century, but the bulk of migration was probably over by then.[52]

The growth in Jewish settlement in the fifteenth and sixteenth centuries in Eastern Europe can easily be seen as the product of migration generated by population pressures caused by natural population growth in nearby regions. There is indirect evidence for this point. Distance migrants tend to gravitate to the largest communities, since these are the ones they have heard about while still in their place of origin. Migration to secondary communities is typical of short-distance migration by individuals who are already quite familiar with local conditions. The growth in Jewish settlement in the Polish-Lithuanian lands at this time seems to have focused on settlement in mid-sized communities rather than the largest communities. The conclusion is clear. The migrants were already familiar with the region, which means that they lived nearby.

We can now draw some conclusions about the role of anti-Jewish violence in migration to Eastern Europe. Anti-Jewish feeling was certainly prevalent in the late medieval and early modern periods, but it is important to distinguish between presence and a causal relationship. As we have seen, there is no real evidence that violence was the impetus for mass migration either from the German or from the Czech lands.[53] There is a much simpler and convincing explanation for the formation of East European Jewry. The Jewish population in the Czech lands was growing in the early modern period because of natural fertility, but there was no parallel growth in production and means of income. Overpopulation in the general population in Western Europe and in the German lands before the mid-fourteenth century had led to the *Ostsiedlung*. Only the immense population losses of the Black Death put a halt to this movement. The same pressures existed among Jews.

Moreover, the Black Death may have affected the Czech lands and Eastern Europe much less than the German lands. As Philip Ziegler put it, "certain

---

[52] Increased documentation sometimes indicates better sources but not necessarily an increase in the number of cases. Whether that was true here is a moot point.

[53] There is one report of migration in 1098 from Prague in the wake of anti-Jewish violence. The text has been widely quoted as referring to large-scale flight. This apparently was not the case. See Jits van Straten, "Cosmas of Prague and the Western Migration of Jews to Poland," *Zutot*, no. 4 [2004] (2007): 57–63.

areas escaped lightly: Bohemia; large parts of Poland etc.,"[54] although there are dissenting opinions.[55] Without the population losses of the Black Death, conditions in the Czech lands should have led to population pressures that promoted emigration. The same demographic and economic pressures that contributed to Jewish migration may have also stimulated anti-Jewish behavior, but this question is outside the scope of this chapter.

The pattern of individual migration we found is exactly the type of response to population pressures that one would have anticipated. Economic and demographic pressures force many individual decisions but not necessarily a group decision. Violence is neither the simplest nor a necessary explanation for the migration. Instead, the data point to indisputable demographic and economic factors as sufficient to explain this phenomenon. Although there is no absolute proof, a variety of factors indicate that East European Jewry grew out of the migration of individuals concerned mainly with solutions to economic and demographic problems. Anti-Jewish feeling was present, but it was not the central factor.

The reliance on hatred of Jews as an explanatory argument in the study of Jewish history lies deep within the consciousness of many Jews. David Engel has pointed out how prevalent the self-awareness of Polish Jewry is in the historical study of Polish Jewry.[56] As he puts it, "narratives of unique righteousness, maintained even in the face of unique suffering, have consistently lain at the heart of how historians of the Poles and the Jews have taught their respective communities to see themselves, not in relation to one another but absolutely."

Some Poles also manifest awareness of anti-Jewish sentiments. Engel cites Stanisław Kutrzeba, who described Poland as offering the Jews a "secure and beneficent oasis" during the medieval period when elsewhere they were humiliated, beaten, and expelled. The self-perception of tolerance rests on an assumption that such behavior was exceptional and its absence significant. In the case of migration to Poland, and to Eastern Europe in general, it seems that it was the desire of many Jews for a better life—and the enlightened self-interest of a host population that gained from the expansion of economic ties and activities—that led to the establishment of the largest Jewish community

---

[54] Philip Ziegler, *The Black Death* (Harmondsworth, UK, 1969), 118.
[55] See Ole J. Benedictow, *The Black Death, 1346–1353: The Complete History* (Woodbridge, 2004), 216–26. He raises questions about the immunity to the Black Death in these regions. For a different view, see Ken Lastufka, "Bohemia during the Medieval Black Death: A Pocket of Immunity," *East European Quarterly* 19 (1985): 275–80. This article was not mentioned by Benedictow.
[56] David Engel, "On Reconciling the Histories of Two Chosen Peoples," *American Historical Review* 114, 4 (2009): 914–29, quotations from 925 and 918.

in the world. The interpretation that violence lay behind this is a projection of the observers' understanding of the past—but not of what was there.

7. Uses and Abuses

"Pogrom" in the Anglo-American Imagination, 1881–1919

Sam Johnson

> The disposition of the St. Paul small boy to pogrom the public school janitors is most reprehensible and should be curbed with a slat before it goes too far.
>
> —*St. Paul Globe (MN), 25 September 1903*
>
> *A Pianoforte Pogrom*
> A picturesque way of removing surplus stock has been adopted by Messrs. Allan, pianoforte dealers, of Melbourne [Australia]. Recently, fifty-one obsolete pianofortes were borne through the streets to the strains of "Auld Lang Syne," heaped in a pile, soaked in kerosene, and—cremated!
>
> —*Musical Times (London, UK), 1 June 1914*

Terminology has long been a challenging matter for historians of the East European Jewish experience, especially in their encounters with the popular and even the scholarly imagination without the field. Several terms often present more problems of interpretation than they solve. For instance, Pale of Settlement usually prompts confusion, since its boundaries are delineated incorrectly and the Kingdom of Poland is categorized within its legislative remit. Jewish emigration from the Russian and Habsburg empires, or at least the supposed reasons behind it, is inextricably fused with persecution—notwithstanding the complex motivations that encouraged Jews, like other emigrants, to leave their homelands. Likewise, the question as to whether to employ antisemitism or Judeophobia when analyzing tsarism's Jewish question in the late imperial period remains a sticking point, even for historians within the field. But, of course, it is in relation to the pogrom that the most misunderstanding, not to say misappropriation, can be found. Consider, for example, the following quotation from an unquestionably important study on the international protection of Jewish minority rights in pre–World War II Europe: "What happened in Pińsk on April 5, 1919, was not literally a 'pogrom'—an organized, officially tolerated, or inspired massacre of a minority such as had occurred in Lemberg—but rather a military execution of a small suspect group of civilians."[1]

The event discussed here, the summary execution of twenty-five civilian Jews by a firing squad of Polish troops, remains a controversial component of the historical context into which the Second Republic was born.[2] In fact, at the moment these and other murders occurred, it was widely believed, especially in Western Europe, that no pogroms had actually taken place.[3] Although, from late 1918, Jewish news agencies sent out hundreds of telegrams to Western governments, newspapers, and individuals, which urged humanitarian assistance or warned of imminent attacks, this reaction was regarded as proof of yet another tiresome Jewish case of crying wolf.[4] According to one British commentator writing in a publication that openly supported Roman Dmowski and the Polish National Democratic Party, pogroms were "affairs of the Black Ages and utterly alien to the spirit of the new and freedom-loving nation [i.e., Poland]."[5] So, on that non-negotiable basis, they simply could not have happened.

---

[1] Carole Fink, *Defending the Rights of Others: The Great Powers, the Jews, and International Minority Protection, 1878–1938* (Cambridge, 2004), 185.

[2] For the historiography dealing with the Polish pogroms of the immediate post–World War I period, see Leszek Tomaszewski, "Pińsk, Saturday 5 April 1919," *Polin* 1 (1986): 227–51; Józef Lewandowski, "History and Myth: Pińsk, April 1919," *Polin* 2 (1987): 50–72; William Hagen, "Murder in the East: German-Jewish Liberal Reactions to the Anti-Jewish Violence in Poland and Other East European Lands, 1918–1920," *Central European History* 34, 1 (2001): 1–30; William Hagen, "The Moral Economy of Popular Violence: The Pogrom in Lwów, November 1918," in *Antisemitism and Its Opponents in Modern Poland,* ed. Robert Blobaum (Ithaca, NY, 2005), 124–47; and Przemysław Różański, "Wilno, 19–21 kwietnia 1919 roku," *Jewish History Quarterly,* 1 (2006): 13–34.

[3] A number of Western investigations were undertaken in 1919 to ascertain whether pogroms had taken place in Poland, including those by the president of the Board of Deputies of British Jews, Stuart Samuel; Israel Cohen on behalf of the Central Zionist Organization; and Henry Morgenthau, under the auspices of the American Jewish Committee. See Israel Cohen, *A Report on the Pogroms in Poland* (London, April 1919); Stuart M. Samuel, "Report on Mission to Poland, 1 July 1920," *Papers by Command,* 51: 1121 (Parliamentary Command Paper, no. 674, London, 1920).

[4] The archive of the Board of Deputies of British Jews, London Metropolitan Archive, London, UK, contains numerous telegrams appealing for aid and attention. See files ACC3121/C11/2/13; ACC3121/C11/4/2; ACC3121/C11/12/56; and ACC3121/C11/12/60–66.

[5] *New Poland* [London—hereafter, L], 5 October 1919, 18. For further discussion of the British response to the pogroms in the post–World War I period, see my monograph, *Pogroms, Peasants, Jews: Britain and Eastern Europe's "Jewish Question," 1867–1925* (London, 2011), chap. 6.

What was more, it was said, surely it was not coincidental that these supposed pogroms were happening at a time when Jewish allegiances to the new Poland appeared dubious indeed. But, most crucially, since there was virtually no Polish government in many places of Jewish residence, it was believed that pogroms could simply not happen. After all, was it not necessary for the authorities to order, organize, or tacitly legitimize any collective act of violence, plunder, and punishment directed toward the Jews? In short, if there were no authorities, there could be no pogroms. In this aspect, therefore, Carole Fink's assertion—that events in Pińsk in April 1919 cannot technically be deemed a real pogrom—ties in with the long-established myth that pogroms must, by definition, be orchestrated from on high. In other words, without the coercion of the powers that be, whether in the Polish Second Republic, tsarist Russia, or elsewhere, everyday folk, in or out of uniform, did not seek to attack their Jewish neighbors—unless officially sanctioned to do so.

The role of the authorities—whether as soldiers, local officials, or government ministers, as perpetrators and, sometimes, complicit and passive bystanders—lies at the heart of the most widely accepted understanding of the term "pogrom." Undoubtedly, the founding fathers of East European Jewish historiography contributed to this interpretation. Simon Dubnow, for instance, referred to a tsarist "pogrom policy"; and Elias Tcherikower, though primarily concerned with the violence of a later period, similarly viewed the pogrom as a top-down process.[6] Salo W. Baron, who eschewed the "lachrymose conception" of Jewish history embraced by both Dubnow and Tcherikower, nevertheless upheld the conspiratorial theory of the pogroms.[7] The consolidation of this definition, however, occurred outside the field. Although, for example, the *Oxford English Dictionary* has recently revised its findings as to the first usage of "pogrom" in the English language (upward from 1882 to 1891), it continues to maintain the following two definitions:

1. In Russia, Poland, and some other East European countries in the late nineteenth and early twentieth centuries: an organized massacre aimed at the destruction or annihilation of a body or class of people, *esp.* one conducted against Jewish people. Now *hist.*

---

[6] See S. M. Dubnow, *History of the Jews in Russia and Poland: From the Earliest Times until the Present Day*, 2 vols. (Philadelphia, 1918); for an analysis of Tcherikower's approach, see Joshua Karlip, "Between Martyrology and Historiography: Elias Tcherikower and the Making of a Pogrom Historian," *East European Jewish Affairs* 38, 3 (2008): 257–80.

[7] See Salo W. Baron, *The Russian Jew under Tsars and Soviets* (New York, 1964); and David Engel, "Crisis and Lachrymosity: On Salo Baron, Neobaronianism, and the Study of Modern European Jewish History," *Jewish History* 20, 3/4 (2006): 243–64.

2. An organized, officially tolerated, attack on any community or group. Also *fig.*[8]

For contemporary commentators following events in Eastern Europe from the late nineteenth century onward, Jewish popular memory, and many historians outside the field of East European Jewish studies, the key components within these definitions are "organized" and "officially tolerated."

In essence, such an interpretation imagines that this type of massacre or attack, the pogrom, requires planning and careful arrangement: it does not occur on the spur of the moment. The first *OED* definition does not, of course, insist on the role of the authorities in the instigation of the pogrom, but the second certainly does. It is this latter, somewhat flexible definition that has enabled scholars to apply the term in a variety of national, ethnic, religious, and social contexts. According to one historian, for example, the "first antisemitic pogrom" occurred in 146 BCE in Alexandria and was instigated by the Egyptian king, Ptolemy Physcon.[9] In the modern period, we have become accustomed to hearing Germany's 1938 *Reichskristallnacht* described as the "November pogrom," where the role of the Nazi authorities, both above and below, as bloody provocateurs and executioners is indisputable.[10] Contemporary commentators went a step further than this, however, and referred to the entire Jewish experience in the Nazi Germany of the 1930s as a "cold pogrom."[11]

As the second *OED* definition concedes, the victims of a pogrom need not be Jews. "Pogrom" has, therefore, been used to explicate various ethnic or religious riots in, for example, 1917 East St. Louis, Illinois, Northern Ireland in the 1930s, and twenty-first-century India.[12] A year before the beginning of World War I, a British journalist reported on the circumstances of a recent

---

[8] http://dictionary.oed.com/cgi/display/50182486?keytype=ref&ijkey=1PSarDK4HM3SU (accessed 10 October 2009). The reference from 1891 is from George Kennan, *Siberia and the Exile System* (London, 1891), 236. While this appears to have been the first use of the term in the English language (and my own research found no earlier appearance), it was utilized by the United States' leading Russian expert, who was more subject than most commentators to Russian linguistic and cultural influences. His embrace of the term is an indication of the degree to which "pogrom" had, by this stage, been absorbed into everyday usage in the Russian language, rather than English.

[9] Lawrence H. Schiffman, *Texts and Traditions: A Source Reader for the Study of Second Temple and Rabbinic Judaism* (New York, 1998), 182.

[10] For example, Marion A. Kaplan, *Between Dignity and Despair: Jewish Life in Nazi Germany* (Oxford, 1998), 119ff.

[11] George T. Walmer, "Germany's Fury: The Old Roots of the New German Nationalism," *Sewanee Review* 42, 1 (1934): 37.

[12] Charles L. Lumpkins, *American Pogrom: The East St. Louis Race Riot and Black Politics* (Athens, OH, 2008); "Northman," "Present Position of Catholics in Northern Ireland," *Studies: An Irish Quarterly Review* 25: 100 (December 1936), 591; Rupal Oza, "The Geography of Hindu

outbreak of violence in quite different circumstances, in the southwest English city of Bristol:

The Bristol Pogrom

> The Bristol police must either be the least efficient or the worst-principled force in the kingdom. They are allowing a students' pogrom against the suffragists to go under their very noses. On Thursday, some suffragists [sic—the author meant Suffragettes, who were more militant] burnt down the University Sports' Pavilion, and on Friday, the students in revenge ransacked a shop kept by suffragists. They were not presumably, the same suffragists who burnt the pavilion, or they would have been under arrest; but even if there was real grounds for suspicion, it would make no difference. Lynch-law is not one of the recognised institutions of the country. But the sequel is even worse. On the following day, the suffragists reoccupied their shop, and 300 students came down in force and repeated the misconduct of the previous day. They tore down the boarding, drove off the women occupying the premises, and broke everything in them that was breakable. The police, we are told, were powerless to stop the disturbance, and no arrests were made. This is lynch-law under police supervision—a refinement of lawlessness hitherto unknown outside Russia. We make every allowance for the unbalancing effect of the suffragist crime in some minds, but the whole story remains a disgrace to the Bristol police. The worst criminal in the land has a right to protection from the mob, and the suffragists who kept this shop were not only not criminals, but were doing nothing that they had not a perfect right to do.[13]

Evidently, there are no Jews in this story. Instead, the victims were suffragettes—not an ethnic or religious group at all—the perpetrators were the three hundred students, and the facilitators the local constabulary.[14] Ultimately, it

---

Right-Wing Violence in India," in *Violent Geographies: Fear, Terror and Political Violence*, ed. Derek Gregory and Allan Pred (Oxford, 2007), 153–75.

[13] *Manchester Guardian*, 27 October 1913, 8; a similar protest appeared in the local press, though it did not use the term "pogrom," see Rev. Arthur E. Girdle-Tone to the *Bristol Evening News*, 28 October 1913, 4.

[14] It is little wonder that the *Manchester Guardian* reached for the descriptive power of "pogrom"—which was evidently used for its shock value—when discussing the student attacks on the suffragettes' shop. The first attack was recorded in the *Bristol Evening News*, 25 October 1913, 4, as follows: "Leaving the University at five o'clock, a body of students estimated at between three and five hundred dashed down [to the Suffragettes' shop] and many being armed with bricks the plate-glass front was smashed to atoms in a moment. Entrance being easy, a few of them had the contents of a shop into the street at once, while two or three, rushing upstairs, broke the large glass windows there, and with hatchets hacked the furniture to pieces. Within

was the Bristol police, the supposed guardians of civil order, who were most at fault. They had, it appeared, wholly shirked their duties and allowed the violence to occur under their very noses, just as the authorities had apparently done on so many occasions in tsarist Russia.

In our own time, it is evident that outwith the field of East European Jewish historiography, the term "pogrom" maintains the same associations it did over a century ago. And this is in spite of the meticulous scholarly research on the topic over the last forty years by scholars such as Hans Rogger, Michael Aronson, and Heinz Dietrich-Löwe.[15] John Klier devoted something like thirty years to the subject and, in many ways, made it entirely his own. In his final monograph, *Russians, Jews, and the Pogroms of 1881–1882*, a monumental study of the 1881–1882 pogroms, for which I was privileged to act as a "friendly reader," he stressed that the origins and motivations that lay behind the pogroms were inherently associated with the changing nature of late imperial Russian society. Like Aronson, Rogger, and others before him, Klier demonstrated that "Russian officials neither desired, encouraged, or tolerated pogroms," and rather than existing as proof of autocracy's anachronisms, the anti-Jewish violence of the late nineteenth century was a product and expression of modernity's unrelenting advances in the Russian Empire.[16]

In particular, Klier showed that pogroms were born out of the widespread social and economic insecurity that dogged the Russian Empire in the wake of Alexander II's Great Reforms, and that Jews, long regarded as "ethnic strangers," were often associated with the negative aspects of this change. Interethnic violence, whether verbal or physical, was nothing new in tsarist Russia. Indeed, Klier extensively explored what he described as the "dialogue of violence" that had for decades marked Jewish and non-Jewish interactions

---

three minutes of the onslaught and the flying bricks, the contents of the shop and office were in the street, being scattered about and broken into fragments by many willing hands . . . The din was terrific, and a large crowd promptly collected. While the first party attacked the shop, a second body dragged down . . . a huge basket, or crate, filled with shavings and other flammable material, [which] burst into flames so fierce that it was taken no nearer the Suffragettes' headquarters, and the pieces of furniture which were ejected from the premises were brought to the fire and burned. The greatest excitement prevailed, and many of the onlookers encouraged the young men in their work of destruction." There is no mention of the police in this report, either as passive onlookers or interveners.

[15] See, for example, Hans Rogger, *Jewish Policies and Right-Wing Politics in Imperial Russia* (London, 1986); I. Michael Aronson, *Troubled Waters: The Origins of the 1881 Anti-Jewish Pogroms in Russia* (Pittsburgh, 1990); and Heinz-Dietrich Löwe, "Pogroms in Russia: Explanations, Comparisons, Suggestions," *Jewish Social Studies* 11, 1 (2004): 16–23.

[16] John Doyle Klier and Shlomo Lambroza, eds., *Pogroms: Anti-Jewish Violence in Modern Russian History* (Cambridge, 1992); John Doyle Klier, *Russians, Jews, and the Pogroms of 1881–1882* (Cambridge, 2011), 384. As ever, more than a little of this study owes a debt to John and his generous, warm, enthusiastic spirit.

in the Pale of Settlement and elsewhere.[17] In relation to 1881–1882, he showed that the bipolarity, which had always existed between Jews and non-Jews, was, given the significance of economic and other pressures, accentuated; the violence of those years therefore focused on all Jews as the target.[18] Rather than assuming that the *pogromshchiki* were peasants, as so many contemporary commentators did, Klier's investigations showed that pogroms were essentially urban phenomena and spread in waves as a consequence of modern means of communication—the railways, the telegraph, and mass media. It was the prejudices, frustrations, and furies of the modern town and city that wreaked havoc in 1881–1882, not the resentments of the peasantry. It did not follow, however, that Klier entirely absolved the tsarist regime from responsibility in 1881–1882. He argued that the "true failure of Russian statesmen lay not in preventing pogroms, but in failing to understand them."[19] The latter notion can be similarly applied to the limited understanding demonstrated by interpretations of pogroms outside the field of East European Jewish studies, which fail to move beyond simplistic assumptions rooted in popular mythology.

The aim of the present chapter is to consider the process by which the term "pogrom" was absorbed into the English language in both Britain and the United States. It looks at the manner in which the word acquired specific meanings, as well as the parameters and significance of those meanings against the backdrop of wider reportage on Eastern European Jewish life. It begins with an important contextualization, an examination of how the pogroms of 1881–1882 were received in the British and American press, then looks at the vitally significant role played by the pogroms that occurred in the Russian Empire during the first decade of the twentieth century.

The Backdrop: Pogroms and Expulsions, 1881–1891

It is often assumed that "pogrom" was the first Russian word embraced by the English language and that this happened as a consequence of Western reportage of the 1881–1882 pogroms.[20] This is a myth. In fact, it was not until

---

[17] John D. Klier, "Christians and Jews and the 'Dialogue of Violence' in Late Imperial Russia," in *Religious Violence between Christians and Jews: Medieval Roots, Modern Perspectives*, ed. Anna Sapir Abulafia (London, 2002), 157–70.
[18] Klier, *Russians, Jews, and the Pogroms of 1881–1882*, 80.
[19] Ibid, 88.
[20] Although this is largely speculation, the first Russian words to be absorbed into English were probably "tsar" (not actually "proper" Russian, since it is a corruption of caesar), "steppe," and "Cossack"—also not technically a Russian word, though in the West European imagination,

over twenty years later, in the six months following the 1903 Kishinev pogrom, that British and American newspapers found a regular purpose for the term. Evidently, the daily and weekly press, which, by the turn of the twentieth century, had burgeoned at an enormous rate on both sides of the Atlantic, is a useful gauge of intercultural linguistic transference. Given the presence of foreign correspondents in the tsarist empire, the growth in influence of telegraphic news agencies, such as the Associated Press and Reuters, it was in newspaper columns that new foreign words and phrases were most likely to appear. How, therefore, in the absence of the term "pogrom," were the events of 1881–1882 described and discussed in the Anglo-American press, and what was their impact on the manner in which the tsarist regime's Jewish policy was imagined in this period?

It took less than a week for news of the first pogrom, which took place on 27 April 1881, in Elisavetgrad, Kherson province, to reach the columns of the British and American press, though it was the former that devoted the most copy to this and subsequent outbreaks of violence in 1881.[21] Given the closer geographical proximity of British correspondents to the Russian Empire, as well as a long-established popular concern for any domestic problem encountered by the tsar and whether it might have an impact on the international arena, it was inevitable that the British press would cover the troubles in the empire's southern provinces more intensively. Furthermore, the assassination attempt in July 1881 on U.S. President James Garfield, who eventually died from his wounds, meant that the U.S. press focused on matters closer to home.

Throughout 1881–1882, Anglo-American reportage used a number of expressions to describe the pogroms, including "riots," "outrages" (usually a euphemism for rape), "atrocities," "disturbances," "excesses," and, mirroring the tsarist regime's own terminology, "disorders" (*besporiadki*).[22] The earliest explanations, following Elisavetgrad, deemed the pogroms a foreign importation, especially from imperial Germany, which had recently witnessed the deliberate burning down of a synagogue in Neustettin, Pomerania.[23] Subsequently, other reasons were proffered, including nihilist infiltration, allegedly conducted among the gullible peasantry to unsettle the regime—a

---

this and other terms were assumed to be Russian. According to the *OED*, the first recorded use of these words in English were in 1551, 1671, and 1598, respectively, predating "pogrom" by several centuries.

[21] All dates given here are in the Gregorian calendar.

[22] For example, *Morning Post* [L], 3 May 1881, 5; and *Daily News* [L], 11 May 1881, 5.

[23] *Sacramento Daily Record*, 16 May 1881, 2; *Daily News* [L], 23 May 1881, 5; *The Graphic* [L], 28 May 1881, 514; *Jewish World* [L], 6 May 1881, 4–5. This connection was widely assumed in 1881. See John D. Klier, "Russian Judeophobes and German Antisemites: Strangers and Brothers," *Jahrbucher für Geschichte Osteuropas* 37, 4 (1989): 524–40.

7. Uses and Abuses

notion that, not by coincidence, conformed with tsarism's own prognosis.[24] The role of the ordinarily passive, stupid, vodka-sodden peasant formed the next line of inquiry, and of especial concern was his economic link to the Jew.[25] In the British press, the exploitative qualities of the Jewish moneylender were indicated as the reason for peasant animosity. According to one newspaper, the Russian peasantry looked "upon the Jew as the vampire that sucks their life-blood," an image not without broad appeal in the British context.[26]

As to the role of the regime, a theme the U.S. press did not examine throughout 1881, from a British perspective, there appeared to have been instances when the local police force had been reluctant to act against the *pogromshchiki*.[27] But there was certainly not, in the first year of the disturbances, a universal belief in a Petersburg-inspired conspiracy against the Jews. Indeed, many newspapers noted the presence of troops in various towns and cities and, in mid-1881, reported on a number of *pogromshchiki* trials and the guilty sentences that were handed down.[28] There was a single exception: the London-based popular Jewish weekly, the *Jewish World*, which, in mid-June 1881, sent its own special correspondent to investigate the disturbances in the Russian Empire's southern provinces. This journalist, who filed a weekly column from late June until November 1881, categorically asserted that the violence was "pre-arranged."[29] This perspective did not assume wider significance, however, until early 1882, following the Warsaw pogrom of Christmas 1881.

The attack in the Polish capital was, without question, the most momentous pogrom from the perspective of the Anglo-American press, not least because in both London and New York City, it inspired the convening of well-publicized protest meetings, which were to have international ramifications.[30] Yet the very fact of a pogrom in Congress Poland, many hundreds of miles from the

---

[24] *The Graphic* [L], 14 May 1881, 474; *St. James's Gazette* [L], 17May 1881, 6; *Morning Post* [L], 26May 1881, 4. For discussion of the regime's response, see Klier, *Russians, Jews, and the Pogroms of 1881–1882*.

[25] *Omaha Daily Bee* [NE], 27 September 1881, 4; *The Graphic* [L], 28 May 1881, 514.

[26] *The Scotsman* [Edinburgh], 14 May 1881, 8.

[27] Most of the American coverage of Russian-Jewish affairs in 1881 was related to emigration, especially arrivals in the United States. See *New York Times*, 28 September 1881, 3.

[28] *Evening Standard* [L], 2 June 1881, 5; *Morning Post* [L], 3 June 1881, 5; *Daily News* [L], 8 June 1881, 5.

[29] *Jewish World* [L], 15 July 1881, 5–6. In all probability, the journalist was Meier Bankanovich, who was identified in other newspapers, such as *The Scotsman* [Edinburgh], 6 January 1882, 6.

[30] London's meeting was held on 1 February 1882 in the Mansion House and attended by the leading philanthropist of the day, Lord Shaftesbury, as well as various political and religious leaders. See *Morning Post* [L], 2 February 1882, 4; *Evening Standard* [L], 2 February 1882, 4; *Jewish World* [L], 3 February 1882, 4–5; and *New York Times*, 2 February 1882, 3. In New York, a meeting was held in Chickering Hall, Manhattan (it no longer exists, but was on Fifth Avenue, near Union Square) the day after the London event, an indication of the degree to

155

established epicenter of the bloodshed and chaos in the south, prompted a reassessment of the pogroms' causes. Instrumental in this matter were two articles in the London *Times* penned by Joseph Jacobs, a Jewish historian and author who was also involved in the recently convened British philanthropic organization for Russian Jews, the Russo-Jewish Committee. These pieces were undoubtedly influenced by the numerous articles authored by the *Jewish World*'s special correspondent: Jacobs had not visited the tsarist empire, had no direct facility to garner his own evidence about the pogroms and so relied on his connections in London. Not by coincidence, Jacobs's articles contained the same stories that appeared in the *Jewish World*. He described, for instance, children being "dashed to death, or roasted alive in their own homes," the raping of thirty women in Elisavetgrad alone, and the "razing of whole streets inhabited by Jews."[31] Like those in the *Jewish World*, Jacobs's accounts were exaggerated, but since they appeared in the *Times*, their impact was bound to be considerable. Indeed, in less than two weeks, these articles and their "trustworthy facts" found their way into the *New York Times* and other U.S. newspapers.[32]

The consequences of the heightened reportage following the Warsaw pogrom were twofold. First, the manner in which the pogroms were depicted grew ever more lurid. In the *New York Times*, a retrospective analysis of the Odessa pogrom, which had occurred on 15 May 1881, described the pouring of petroleum "on a man's head [which was] set on fire, the man died in agony. Subsequently many children were mercilessly killed."[33] As with so many reports, this was an exaggeration.[34] Nevertheless, as would happen during future pogroms, by early 1882, newspaper coverage more than willingly strayed into the realms of sensationalism. The second consequence of events in Warsaw was the almost universal acceptance of the belief that the pogroms were deliberately coordinated by the regime in St. Petersburg. The *New*

---

which Anglo-American reportage and response were interlinked at this point. See *New York Times*, 2 February 1882, 4.

[31] *The Times*, 11 January 1882, 4; see also the editorial in this issue, 9; the second article, appeared on 13 January 1882, 4. These articles were soon published as a pamphlet: *Russian Atrocities, 1881: Supplementary Statement Issued by the Russo-Jewish Committee* (London, 1882). For comparable accounts in the *Jewish World*, see 15 June 1881, 4–5; 5 August 1881, 5–6; 26 August 1881, 5–6; 9 September 1881, 5–6; 16 October 1881, 5–6; and 23 October 1881, 5–6.

[32] *New York Times*, 28 January 1882, 3; *The Globe* [MN], 29 January 1882, 4; *Sacramento Daily Record*, 1 February 1882, 2; *Omaha Daily Bee* [NE], 6 February 1882, 1; *Salt Lake Herald*, 9 February 1882, 4.

[33] *New York Times*, 17 February 1882, 3.

[34] As John Klier demonstrated, the total deaths for all pogroms occurring in 1881 and 1882 numbered around fifty, of whom about half were Jews. See Klier, *Russians, Jews and the Pogroms of 1881–1882*, 84; and his entry on pogroms in *The YIVO Encyclopedia of the Jews in Eastern Europe* (New Haven, 2005).

York Times, for instance, wrote about the "Russian war on the Jews" and the extent to which local police and soldiers appeared to participate willingly in the violence.[35] In the same vein, British newspapers rang out a chorus of disapproval, asserting that the violence had been "instigated by the state."[36] According to the influential weekly the *Spectator*, the "guilt of the Russian government in this business is very great."[37]

Yet in 1881–1882, Western observers and commentators did not require the word "pogrom" to indict the tsarist government for its role in instigating or permitting violence to occur on its watch. After all, even if the regime had not played a direct hand in the attacks, it was believed that it still had something to gain by not interfering in the rioting. In the view of one journalist, the government was afraid to halt the violence, lest the *pogromshchiki* switch targets and vent their anger on the regime. The Jews, therefore, served a useful purpose as the "nearest irritating object" for a population riddled with political and economic resentments, a not entirely ill-informed diagnosis.[38] But in 1881–1882, there was no need for the word "pogrom." An explanation for the anti-Jewish violence was easily found, and a decade later, this perspective was further emphasized by the actions of the tsarist government in expelling Jews from various cities in the interior of the empire and sending them to the Pale of Settlement.

The expulsions of 1890–1891 had the same impact as the pogroms, only it was a more straightforward matter to assign blame. After all, the expulsions were administered by both government statute and officials; the regime's Jewish policy was transparently obvious, and it needed no journalist on special assignment to unravel the regime's motivations.[39] Thus the pieces of the puzzle were already in place long before "pogrom" came into Anglo-American usage. The way these pieces were assembled into the picture of a government conspiracy against the Jews had nothing to do with there being a specific Russian word attributable to this policy. No, it was the well-established perspectives of the regime that guaranteed this, not the word itself. It was the

---

[35] *New York Times*, 18 February 1882, 4.
[36] *Birmingham Daily Mail* [UK], 25 January 1882, 2.
[37] *The Spectator* [L], 14 January 1882, 43.
[38] *New York Times*, 12 March 1882, 4.
[39] For examples of coverage of the expulsions, see *Birmingham Daily Post* [UK], 16 July 1890, 8; "The Tsar and the Jews," *Blackwood's Edinburgh Magazine* (October 1890): 441–52; *The Spectator* [L], 2 May 1891, 619–20; *The Times*, 8 May 1891, 9; *Hampshire Telegraph* [UK], 9 May 1891, 2; *Pall Mall Gazette* [L], 23 May 1891, 6; *Glasgow Herald* [UK], 28 May 1891, 6; *Sacramento Daily Record*, 1 August 1890, 2; the *Climax* [KY], 3 December 1890, 1; *Salt Lake Herald*, 24 April 1891, 4; *Morning Call* [CA], 6 May 1891, 1; *New York Times*, 1 June 1891, 1, and 7 December 1891, 1. The last article, by Harold Frederic, included a list of names of Jews expelled from Moscow.

manner in which Anglo-American journalists accumulated evidence specific to the story they wished to tell, the image of the regime they wished to cast and imprint onto the Western imagination.

Kishinev and After: A National Institution

The Kishinev pogrom has been deemed a "turning point" by scholars of the modern Jewish experience.[40] In the first place, the violence itself, which occurred over two days in April 1903, greatly overshadowed previous incidents of anti-Jewish hostility in the tsarist empire, with around fifty deaths in total, mostly Jews.[41] Additionally, Kishinev's immediate impact was more noticeable than that of the 1881-1882 pogroms. For example, advances in printing and photographic technology made this pogrom the first to enter the world's consciousness in visual terms. Hitherto, descriptions of pogroms had been accompanied with sketches, cartoons, and caricatures. But within weeks of Kishinev, photographs were published that showed bloodied corpses laid out in an improvised mortuary, the devastation of vandalized buildings, and pavements strewn with broken furniture and glass.[42] The world mobilized in shared repugnance at these events and, in the United States in particular, called for the financial ostracization of the tsarist regime, an action promoted by the banker and philanthropist Jacob Schiff.[43]

The reportage of Kishinev followed familiar lines, though with even greater intensity than in 1881-1882. The pogrom's brutality was minutely analyzed and some grisly detail recorded. There were references to disemboweled corpses stuffed with feathers. Other cadavers were mutilated, their eyes gouged out and ears chopped off.[44] Another victim had nails driven into his temples.[45] Yet more were "literally slaughtered and hung up in the butchers'

---

[40] Monty Noam Penkower, "The Kishinev Pogrom of 1903: A Turning Point in Jewish History," *Modern Judaism* 24, 3 (2004): 187.

[41] Edward H. Judge, *Easter in Kishinev: Anatomy of a Pogrom* (New York, 1992), 72-75.

[42] *Jewish Chronicle* [L], 29 May 1903, 10-11; photographs taken by the journalist Michael Davitt were reproduced on 26 June 1903, 8-9. Davitt, a former Irish member of Parliament, was one of the first Western observers to arrive in Kishinev, a couple of months after the pogrom. He published a book, *Within the Pale: The True Story of the Antisemitic Persecution in Russia* (London, 1903), which reiterated the notion that the pogrom was officially inspired.

[43] For a discussion of the American response to Kishinev, see P. E. Schoenberg, "The American Reaction to the Kishinev Pogrom of 1903," *American Jewish Historical Quarterly* 63, 3 (1974): 262-83. For a contemporary response, see Cyrus Adler, *The Voice of America on Kishinev* (Philadelphia, 1904).

[44] *Jewish Chronicle* [L], 22 May 1903, 7.

[45] Ibid., 15 May 1903, 9.

shops," and "women were hung up by their hair to trees, human heads were stuck on poles."[46] This was all accompanied by the reek of paraffin that hung in the air after many fires had been deliberately set.[47] Undoubtedly, what happened in Kishinev deeply shocked Anglo-American newspaper staffs and readers. But even though Kishinev continues to this day to be considered the most notorious and heinous outbreak of anti-Jewish violence in the tsarist empire—synonymous, in fact, with pogrom—Anglo-American newspapers still did not use the term "pogrom" in their descriptions.[48] Instead, they continued to rely on "outrages," "crimes," "disorders," and the like.

In fact, not until after the pogrom in Gomel, Minsk province, on 9 September 1903 did the word finally enter the vocabulary of the Anglo-American press. In Britain, it debuted in the *Manchester Guardian* and the *Jewish Chronicle*, while in the United States, it made a simultaneous appearance on 24 September 1903, courtesy of an Associated Press report wired across the world, in the *Alexandria Gazette, St. Paul Globe, Bourbon News, New York World,* and *San Francisco Call*.[49] Remarkably, two days later, the word was used in a non-Russian, "humorous" context to describe the activities of a schoolboy in St. Paul, Minnesota (see the first epigraph). By December 1903, the increasing familiarity of the word sparked enough interest to warrant a full analysis and explanation, helpfully provided by the London *Times*. It is worth citing in its entirety, since it represents the first effort in the Anglo-American press to interpret "pogrom" and its meanings:

> It is perhaps because the word pogrom is not understood in Western Europe that the occurrences at Kishinev and Gomel were described as massacres. There is an important distinction, for the *pogrom* is a national institution, and it was not a massacre in the ordinary sense of the term, but a *pogrom* that took place in the towns. The word grom means thunder and the word *pogrom* implies a desire to shatter or destroy as a thunderstorm

---

[46] Ibid., 22 May 1903, 7; *Daily Mail* [L], 2 May 1903, 2.
[47] *Daily Telegraph* [L], 12 May 1903, 10.
[48] In the reportage of the pogrom that covers the period April–June 1903, I have located just one instance of "pogrom," and not by a newspaper correspondent. A letter from Nathan Bernstein, a Kishinev inhabitant and cousin of a Russian Jew resident in Washington DC, appeared in the *Washington Times* on 14 June 1903, 6; "Dear cousin, how shall I begin my writing to you. My head is still turning from the storm and torture of the 'pogrom' we have endured." No explanation of the term is given. A few weeks later, the translator of this letter, Rabbi Julius Loeb, sent a letter to the same newspaper, using the term "pogrom," in which he urged the world to act; again, there was no editorial or comment on the word itself (*Washington Times*, 12 July 1903, 6).
[49] *Manchester Guardian*, 25 September 1903, 5; *Jewish Chronicle* [L], 2 October 1903, 10, 15; *Alexandria Gazette* [VA], 24 September 1903, 3; *St. Paul Globe*, 24 September 1903, 1; *Bourbon News* [KY], 24 September 1903, 3; *New York World*, 24 September 1903, 3; *San Francisco Call,* 24 September 1903: 9.

destroys. A mob assembled for purposes of devastation does not, however, constitute a *pogrom* unless it follows certain well-established and characteristic rules. Thus, until now, *pogroms* have only been directed against Jews, though the system could be extended to other sections of the population. The *pogrom* was first instituted after the assassination of Alexander II, in 1881, when antisemitism and reaction flourished under General Ignatiev [minister of the interior]. The *pogrom* was encouraged as a means of terrorising the Jews.

The method is as follows: - first there is a period of incubation. Hints are received "from above" by the local police that it would be well to give the Jews a lesson. It will then so happen that some three or four months before Easter a propaganda is commenced in dram shops, cheap restaurants, and other places of popular resort. Rumours are circulated that the Jews are exploiting the people, that they are enriching themselves, that they have killed for ritual purposes a Christian child. Then, when Easter comes, the smallest incident suffices for a *pogrom*. At Kishinev it was a squabble with a Jew who was managing a merry-go-round; at Gomel it was a dispute with a woman selling herrings. The first manifestation of a *pogrom* is made by small boys. They march around the town shouting, throwing stones, and smashing windows of houses inhabited by Jews. If the *pogrom* has commenced spontaneously or its occurrence is not considered desirable by the authorities, the police arrest some of the small boys, give them a flogging in a public square, and there the matter ends. But if on the morrow it is ascertained that no boys have been flogged, a mob of adults gathers, and matters become more serious. The houses of the Jews are entered, though as a rule, no one is hurt, and only the furniture is smashed. But, above all, the great feature of a *pogrom* is the bringing of bedding to the windows and discharging the feathers it contains into the street below. The Jews are very great consumers of poultry, and they carefully keep their feathers. Thus, feather beds become a mark of social distinction and indicate the wealth of a family. To slit open a feather quilt cuts at once at the pride and purse of the Jew. The scattering of the feathers also greatly amuses the crowd, and it is considered a fine sport. The police stand aside, only interfering should the Jews resist; then they separate the contending parties.

On the morning of the third day the Governor or the local authorities issues proclamations, professing to be very grieved at what has occurred and forbidding the people to assemble in the streets. Perhaps two or three muzhiks are arrested and publicly flogged. Here the *pogrom* generally terminates, and such *pogroms* have now taken place off and on for more than 20 years, that they fail to cause any particular concern unless they are allowed to continue for the third day. By that time the criminal instincts have developed, and the professional criminal ceases to fear the police. Then it is that men are murdered and women violated. A *pogrom* is, therefore, a five-act drama. First there is the propaganda; secondly, some squabble that provides the pretext; thirdly, little boys go forth and see if the authorities are willing, and if they are not punished for smashing the windows, then the fourth act begins and the mob breaks the furniture and scatters the feathers of the bedding. Finally, at the fifth act, the lowest passions finding themselves unrestrained, rape and murder terminate the drama. But from the very first pebble thrown by a small boy to the last murder committed, all is absolutely under the control of the Government.[50]

Here, at last, was a special Russian term that expressed the extraordinary actions perpetrated by the tsarist regime and its subjects against Jews, a phenomenon unique to the Russian Empire. Nevertheless, apart from the word itself, there was nothing new in this description of how anti-Jewish violence panned out in the tsar's lands. Every component—from the small boys, the ancient religious accusations, the notion of "teaching the Jews a lesson," the choking mass of feathers pervading the atmosphere, the reluctance of the police to become involved, and, above all, the degree to which the violence occurred in stages, and was, in fact, planned—played an essential part in the long-established narrative that dated back to 1881–1882.

All these details contributed to the habitual exoticization of the Russian experience, particularly in relation to the tsarist regime's Jewish policy. Even the explanation of the term "pogrom," which connected it to thunder, suggested a sense of cultural and linguistic otherness. After all, was there not something picturesque, even if the consequences were devastating, in equating a riot with a natural, meteorological phenomenon? In the Russian, the origins/inspirations behind the word more than hint at the involvement of a vengeful god (*porazhaet gromom*—striking a sinner with thunder), although no Anglo-American commentator explored such connotations (notwithstanding the well-known thunderbolts of the Greek and Norse gods, Zeus and Thor).[51] Instead, the word was a source of fascination, since it clearly

---

[50] *The Times*, 7 December 1903: 10; it was reproduced in full in *Jewish Chronicle* [L], 11 December 1903, 14.
[51] My thanks to my good friend and colleague, Alexander Ivanov, at the European University in St. Petersburg for his advice on the linguistic origins and understandings of pogrom in Russian.

indicated and reaffirmed that there was a singular policy orchestrated against the Jews in the Russian Empire, that the pogrom was a "national institution."

Tsarism's Final Decade

The acquisition of the word "pogrom" in the English language on both sides of the Atlantic was not wasted in the years following Kishinev and Gomel, since imperial Russia's national institution was hardly on the wane. The years running concurrent with the 1905 revolution witnessed an unprecedented escalation in anti-Jewish violence throughout the tsarist empire and, among many places, Chernigov province in the south, Congress Poland, the cities of Kiev, Odessa, and Vilna, all experienced tragic outbreaks. Historians assert that around six hundred fifty pogroms occurred between October 1905 and September 1906, with the estimate of those who were killed standing at a staggering three thousand.[52] These events consolidated the full absorption of "pogrom" into the English language, especially the three most serious attacks, in terms of the loss of life, in Odessa (30 October 1905), Białystok (13 June 1906), and Siedlce (10 September 1906)—over two decades, or a generation, after the time when it has long been generally assumed that the word gripped the Western imagination.

The reportage following these events continually stressed the elements essential to a pogrom as cited in the December 1903 *Times* definition. Reporting on the Odessa pogrom, for instance, the London *Jewish Chronicle* described the distribution of antisemitic propaganda and the bands of "cutthroats," "ruffians," Cossacks, and policemen that controlled the city. These officials, and those who operated according to their commands, laid waste to property and butchered people in horrifying ways—drenching the elderly with petroleum and burning them alive, for instance. Undoubtedly, the entire massacre was believed to have been "prearranged"; and although many local elements were culpable, the controlling influence was in St. Petersburg.[53] Similar sentiments about the culpability of the regime were expressed in the U.S. press in relation to the Białystok pogrom. The *Deseret Evening News* in Salt Lake City, for instance, described "evidence of a general, deliberate plan."[54]

---

[52] All these statistics are taken from Shlomo Lambroza, "The Pogroms of 1903–1906," in *Pogroms: Anti-Jewish Violence in Modern Russian History*, 228–31.

[53] *Jewish Chronicle* [L], 10 November 1905, 9–14; an important article was anonymously written about the Odessa pogrom by two leading British historians of Russia, Bernard Pares and Maurice Baring, who concluded the pogrom was "a weapon of reaction." See their "The Russian Government and the Massacres," *Quarterly Review* 205 (July/August 1906): 594.

[54] *Deseret Evening News*, 4 July 1906, 1; *Los Angeles Herald*, 4 July 1906, 2; *New York Daily Tribune*, 10 July 1906, 7.

As for the massacre in Siedlce, the *Los Angeles Herald* revealed in graphic detail how the streets of the town ran "red with blood": "the outbreak at Siedlce apparently was prepared beforehand. Bands of strangers, ostensibly soldiers on furlough, took a most active part with the soldiery. At one stage of the fighting the Jews succeeded in driving the soldiers back."[55]

This particular piece was taken from an Associated Press dispatch, which, in turn, was drawn from an account in Berlin's well-known newspaper *Voßische Zeitung*. This indication of the interconnectedness of the world's press by this stage also illustrated the extent to which the pogrom myth was universally embraced, not only in Britain and the United States but throughout Western Europe too.

A sign of the universal acceptance of the "pogrom-as-a-policy" narrative was the degree to which, by 1907, the term and its associations moved beyond and out of the newspaper column to realms perhaps more intellectually legitimate. For instance, in 1907, a book authored by the Russian activist E. P. Semenov was translated into English and prefaced by a leading figure in the Anglo-Jewish establishment, Lucien Wolf. Wolf assigned responsibility for the pogroms in uncompromising tones: "the political advisers of the Tsar deliberately and systematically use massacre as an instrument of government, and this not in times of armed conflict with the people or a section of the people, but as a normal expedient for assuring the stability of the Autocratic system!"[56]

The next year, a second relevant publication emerged from within the Russian Empire, this time by the former governor of Bessarabia S. D. Urusov. In *Memoirs of a Russian Governor*, Anglo-American readers now had proof from, as it were, the horse's mouth of a high-level conspiracy in St. Petersburg aimed at fomenting pogroms.[57] This analysis was further consolidated with the publication in 1910, under the auspices of the Central Zionist Organization, of the two-volume *Die Judenpogrome in Russland*.[58] Pseudonymously authored by a Russian Jew, Leo Motzkin, who had witnessed the 1881 Kiev pogrom as a teenager, this was a detailed overview of all the pogroms in the Russian Empire from 1881 onward. Although not translated into English, it "came

---

[55] *Los Angeles Herald*, 11 September 1906, 2.
[56] E. P. Semenov, *The Russian Government and the Massacres: A Page of the Russian Counter-Revolution* (London, 1907), xi.
[57] S. D. Urusov, *Memoirs of a Russian Governor* (New York, 1908). For a review, see *New York Sun*, 9 February 1908, 2. Paul Nathans, a leading figure of the German-Jewish community, was instrumental in securing the rights to publish the book in English and German; see the correspondence between him and David Gintsburg in the Gintsburg Archive, Russian National Library, St. Petersburg, Russian Federation, f. 183, d. 1394.
[58] *Die Judenpogrome in Russland*, 2 vols. (Cologne, 1910).

to serve primarily as a convenient reference work, a compilation of all the despicable episodes of tsarist anti-Jewish politics in action."[59]

Elsewhere, in the literary world, a story written by the celebrated British satirist H. H. Munro, otherwise known as Saki, recorded an ironic take on the pogrom phenomenon. The setting of the story was a country house in a small English village, where Munro's eponymous, mischievous hero, Clovis, inveigles himself into the home of an unsuspecting victim, a Mr. Huddle. Clovis has previously overheard a friend of Mr. Huddle advise him against his sedentary and predictable lifestyle and urge him to take an "unrest-cure" to enliven his somewhat staid existence. Disguised as a Prince Stanislaus (a suitably Slavonic name), Clovis counsels the unsuspecting Huddle:

> "Tonight is going to be a great night in the history of Christendom," said Clovis. "We are going to massacre every Jew in the neighbourhood."
>
> "To massacre the Jews!" said Huddle indignantly. "Do you mean there is to be a general rising against them?"
>
> "No, it's the Bishop's own idea. He's in there [the house's library] arranging all the details now."
>
> "But—the Bishop is such a tolerant, humane man."
>
> "That is precisely what will heighten the effect of his action. The sensation will be enormous."
>
> That at least Huddle could believe.
>
> "He will be hanged!" he exclaimed with conviction.
>
> "A motor is waiting to carry him to the coast, where a steam yacht is in readiness."
>
> "But there aren't thirty Jews in the whole neighbourhood," protested Huddle, whose brain, under the repeated shocks of the day, was operating with the uncertainty of a telegraph wire during earthquake disturbances.
>
> "We have twenty-six on our list," said Clovis, referring to a bundle of notes. "We shall be able to deal with them all the more thoroughly."

---

[59] Klier, *Russians, Jews, and the Pogroms of 1881–1882*, 412.

7. Uses and Abuses

"Do you mean to tell me that you are meditating violence against a man like Sir Leon Birberry," stammered Huddle; "he's one of the most respected men in the country."

"He's down on our list," said Clovis carelessly; "after all, we've got men we can trust to do our job, so we shan't have to rely on local assistance. And we've got some Boy-scouts helping us as auxiliaries."

"Boy-scouts!"

"Yes; when they understood there was a real killing to be done they were even keener than the men."

"This thing will be a blot on the Twentieth Century!"

"And your house will be the blotting-pad. Have your realized that half of the papers of Europe and the United States will publish pictures of it? By the way, I've sent some photographs of you and your sister, that I found in the library, to Matin and Die Woche; I hope you don't mind. Also a sketch of the staircase; most of the killing will be done on the staircase."

The emotions that were surging in J. P. Huddle's brain were almost too intense to be disclosed in speech, but he managed to gasp out: "There aren't any Jews in this house."

"Not at present," said Clovis.[60]

Evidently, the term "pogrom" is not used in the extract, nor in the remainder of the story, which therefore unwittingly references the style of reportage during 1881 and 1882. All the same, the parameters and inferences of Saki's story would have been obvious to his readers. For a start, the massacre was meticulously planned (even to the extent of an escape route for the perpetrators). It was the work of a key local establishment figure, the bishop, supported by a faintly militarist cohort of bloodthirsty Boy Scouts (an unnervingly convincing suggestion). There was even a list of Jews to be targeted, an appointed place of execution, and a press already primed to create the "sensation" so urgently desired by the bishop.

Clearly, one cannot but help sense the twentieth century casting its grim shadow over what was intended to be wholly ironic and focused on the abhorrence of Mr. Huddle, rather than any brutal massacre envisaged by

---

[60] Saki, "The Unrest-Cure," in *The Chronicles of Clovis* (London, 1948), 43–44.

the bogus Prince Stanislaus. The hint at press sensationalism, though, surely retains relevant humorous intent even in the twenty-first century. Nonetheless, it is the absence of "pogrom," given the degree to which the word had been absorbed into the English language by this point (1911), that is of particular interest, not least as Munro had been a reporter for the London-based *Morning Post* during the 1905 Russian revolution. Why, when so many of the facets of the established definition of the word were present in Munro's story, was "pogrom" not used? The explanation is, perhaps, simple. After all, not only was "pogrom" a Russian word, but pogroms were also an exclusively Russian phenomenon. They were not, and never would be, a part of the British social and political landscape—even in a case of (fictional) anti-Jewish violence.

8. Look! Up There in the Sky: It's a Vulture, It's a Bat ... It's a Jew

Reflections on Antisemitism in Late Imperial Russia, 1906–1914

Robert Weinberg

This chapter explores what visual depictions of Jews in the extreme rightwing press in late imperial Russia reveal about the nature of antisemitism. Given the explosive nature of antisemitism during times of political crisis, notably the waves of popular violence that targeted Jews during the pogroms in 1881–1882 after the assassination of Tsar Alexander II and in 1905–1906 after the near toppling of the autocracy, attitudes and behavior concerning Jews were an integral part of the social and political landscape of Russia on the eve of World War I. While anti-Jewish thoughts and actions were not the preserve of political conservatives and cut across the political and social spectrums, antisemitism occupied a particularly prominent place in the hearts and minds of rightwing extremists and reactionaries who rejected policies of the autocracy designed to accommodate the forces of reform. Indeed, resistance to political liberalization found sustenance in a worldview that saw Jews as the source of *all* the difficulties encountered by Tsar Nicholas II and his ministers to prop up existing social and political structures. Moreover, this illiberal state of mind accused Jews of subverting the Orthodox Christian basis of Russian society and exploiting the long-suffering *narod*.

Historians tend to distinguish between traditional antisemitism rooted in the Jews' rejection of Jesus Christ's divinity (or anti-Judaism) and its modern variant, which tends to be motivated by developments spurred by industrial capitalism, the French Revolution, the rise of the nation-state, and the granting of civil and political rights to Jews in the eighteenth and nineteenth centuries. In the nineteenth century, the theological motivation for much of medieval and early modern European Jew-hatred tended to be

---

Thanks to Eugene Avrutin, Laurie Bernstein, Bruce Grant, Joan Neuberger, and the anonymous reader for the press for their comments and suggestions.

supplanted by an antisemitism representing a backlash to the ideologies of liberalism and socialism. One other development also contributed to the emergence of modern antisemitism as a political ideology: the appearance of a racialist discourse that redefined the distinctive characteristics of Jews from those deriving from religious affiliation to traits purportedly embedded in their biological makeup.

From the traditional antisemitic perspective, Jews who embraced Christ as their savior generally shed their Jewishness and became part of the universal Christian community, though recent scholarship on the Spanish Inquisition indicates that Jews, including those who converted to Christianity, were believed to possess an ineffable Jewish quality that could not be erased.[1] Modern antisemites, on the contrary, downplayed religion as the defining feature of Jews and rejected the partial integration of emancipated Jews into post-1789 politics and society. To be sure, many modern antisemites traced what they deemed problematic Jewish behavior to the Talmud, the compendium of rabbinic discussions and interpretations of ethics, law, rituals, and customs contained in the Hebrew scriptures. But unlike their earlier counterparts, they did not believe that conversion would alter the nature of the Jews' character. Indeed, in its radical formulation epitomized by Nazism, modern antisemitism reasoned that Jewishness was racially determined and indelibly branded on Jews regardless of religious confession.[2]

However, this dichotomization of antisemitism into mutable and cultural versus immutable and biological phenomena that correspond, respectively, to medieval and modern forms of antisemitism is not as clear-cut as historians posit and needs qualification whether we look at late imperial Russia or early twentieth-century Europe. In her analysis of French antisemitism at the turn of the twentieth century, Vicki Caron collapses the distinction between the anti-Judaism of medieval Europeans and the anti-Jewish ideology and behavior of those living in the modern era, challenging the view that the theological hatred of Jews was fundamentally different from the secular antisemitism of the late nineteenth century.[3] In Russia, too, antisemitism rooted in both

---

[1] Benzion Netanyahu, *The Origins of the Inquisition in Fifteenth-Century Spain* (New York, 1995). The folklorist Alan Dundes notes that baptism was not always seen as sufficient to change a "Jew into a Christian" ("Why Is the Jew 'Dirty'? A Psychoanalytic Study of Anti-Semitic Folklore," in *From Game to War and Other Psychoanalytic Essays on Folklore*, ed. Dundes [Lexington, 1997], 96).

[2] The literature on antisemitism is enormous. For general treatments, see Albert Lindemann, *Esau's Tears: Modern Anti-Semitism and the Rise of the Jews* (Cambridge, 1997), Marvin Perry and Frederick Schwartz, *Anti-Semitism: Myth and Hate from Antiquity to the Present* (New York, 2002), and Robert Wistrich, *Anti-Semitism: The Longest Hatred* (London, 1991).

[3] Vicki Caron, "Catholic Political Mobilization and Antisemitic Violence in Fin-de-Siècle France: The Case of the Union Nationale," *Journal of Modern History* 81, 2 (2009): 309.

8. Look! Up There in the Sky: It's a Vulture, It's a Bat... It's a Jew

theological prejudices and sociopolitical circumstances coexisted on the eve of World War I. Most tellingly, the prosecution of Mendel Beilis, a Kievan Jew arrested in 1911 for the ritual murder of a Christian youth, rested on the government's assertion, supported by the testimony of purported expert witnesses, including a Catholic priest, that the defendant needed the victim's blood for religious purposes. The Beilis affair became one of the most publicized instances of the notorious "blood libel"—the spurious accusation, which emerged in mid-twelfth-century England, that Jews engaged in the ritual slaughter of Christian youths in order to obtain blood for a variety of religious rituals and practices.[4]

One is tempted to say that the two kinds of antisemitism borrowed from each other, fueling the intensity of both phenomena as illiberal forces that challenged efforts to emancipate Jews and make them citizens with full legal and political rights. Antisemites engaged in fuzzy logic and argumentation and had difficulty distinguishing between theologically and politically motivated antisemitism.[5] Antisemitism in late imperial Russia was, at times, an admixture of religious and secular concerns, which made for a volatile situation, particularly during times of political crisis.

Nevertheless, the racialism that had begun to characterize antisemitic discourse and politics in Central Europe by the 1880s made its appearance in Russia by the turn of the twentieth century, particularly among the extreme rightwing. If, as the historian John Klier asserted, Russian antisemites in the 1880s had not yet embraced a view of Jews possessing immutable biological characteristics, then a mere two decades later, some corners of Russian antisemitism were rife with images and ideas that resembled those circulating in Western and Central Europe.[6] A brand of antisemitism had emerged by the early twentieth century in Russia that clearly distinguished it from the

---

[4] For an overview of the Beilis affair, see Hans Rogger, "The Beilis Case: Anti-Semitism and Politics in the Reign of Nicholas II," *Slavic Review* 25, 4 (1966): 615–29; Maurice Samuel, *Blood Accusation: The Strange History of the Beilis Case* (New York, 1966); and A. S. Tager, *Tsarskaia Rossiia i delo Beilisa. K istorii antisemitizma* (Moscow, 1933). The trial transcript can be found in *Delo Beilisa: Stenograficheskii otchet* (Kiev, 1914). A useful overview of the "blood libel" can be found in Helmut Walser Smith, *The Butcher's Tale: Murder and Anti-Semitism in a German Town* (New York, 2002), 91–133.

[5] Consider the accusation that the Jews' adherence to the Talmud explained their clannishness and efforts to exploit gentiles in the realm of economics and politics. The Talmud is after all a religious text that has plenty to say about how Jews should comport themselves in everyday life. Yet when antisemits in 1900 ranted about the Talmud as the source of Jewish evil, they were clearly condemning certain secular behaviors they associated with Jews due to ignorance and a willful misreading of a religious text.

[6] Klier referred to Russian antisemitism during the second half of the nineteenth century as "Judeophobia" to distinguish it from the phenomenon in Central Europe, which was embracing "a racial element," and to stress the emphasis on "religious fanaticism" placed by Russian

anti-Judaism variant and shared much in common with the kind of racialist antisemitism expressed by others on the continent such as Arthur de Gobineau.

The reason for the appearance of a racialist discourse among Russian antisemites is unclear. The emergence of academic disciplines, such as ethnography, physical anthropology, criminology, and biology that viewed the empire's minorities through the lens of race, was one factor. Race science found a welcome home among Russia's medical and scientific community as elsewhere on the continent. Another factor was the development of a commercial print culture that led to the greater circulation of ideas and news between Russia and Europe. Xenophobic and antisemitic writers in Russia drew freely from books published in Western and Central Europe. Moreover, the war with Japan in 1904 and 1905 raised Russians' awareness of racial differences; and the revolutionary unrest of 1905 led to a weakening of censorship, which allowed antisemites to print articles and drawings that relied on racist stereotypes and images of Jews and other minorities.

Eugene Avrutin has noted that the tsarist regime on the eve of World War I fostered awareness of "ethno-cultural differences based on religion, customs, and ancestry" that many saw as "ultimately unbridgeable." According to Avrutin, Jews who converted to Russian Orthodoxy found it very difficult to jettison what had become in the minds of many antisemites an "innate Jewishness."[7] For them, Judaism no longer served as the critical feature that defined Jews.[8] Tsarist officials tended not to categorize the empire's diverse population according to race as we today tend to understand the concept—that is, in terms of skin color, which is seen as permanent and generally constitutes a critical aspect of a person's self-identity and of how the state and society classify people. Instead, the notion of race in late imperial Russia was "more ambiguous," in Avrutin's words.[9] Drawing on the work of George Fredrickson, Avrutin notes that ethnicity and race are not "two distinct phenomena" when Jews in tsarist Russia are the object of study. The study of race for late imperial academics—particularly ethnographers, scientists, and physicians—had little to do with skin color. Rather, culture, heritage, language, customs, and religion—what we would term the components of ethnicity or nationality—were the elements that composed a racialized perception of Russian Jews and served to distinguish imperial subjects from one another. Influenced

---

antisemites. See John D. Klier, "German Anti-Semitism and Russian Judeophobia in the 1880's: Brothers and Strangers," *Jahrbücher für Geschichte Osteuropas* 37, 4 (1989): 524–40.

[7] Eugene Avrutin, "Racial Categories and the Politics of (Jewish) Difference in Late Imperial Russia," *Kritika: Explorations in Russian and Eurasian History* 8, 1 (2007): 16 and 18.

[8] But keeping in mind the Beilis case, we should not overlook the persistence of religious motivations behind antisemitism at the turn of the twentieth century and beyond.

[9] Avrutin, "Racial Categories," 15.

by ideas percolating elsewhere in Europe, Russian intellectuals and policy makers began to view the nature and characteristics of Jews (as well as other minorities) as indelible. Ascribing permanence to what was deemed to be the cultural, national, physiognomic, and biological traits of Jews highlighted efforts to categorize the population by race, albeit one divorced from the color of one's skin.

Examination of visual representations of Jews in rightwing, antisemitic newspapers in the Russian Empire that emerged after the 1905 revolution reveals the inroads made by racialist ideas. In particular, depictions of Jews with quintessential physical stereotypes (hooked noses, thick lips, big ears, swarthy complexions, greasy hair, scraggly beards, and body odor) that had been part of Christian Europe's cultural landscape since the late Middle Ages, illustrate the extent to which Jews had become marked with features that stemmed from an irredeemable physiognomic and biological makeup. The ethnicization (or racialization) of Jews branded them with certain physical features that made them the quintessential outsider with little or no chance of fitting in. While government officials and mainstream conservative thinkers and activists still believed in the capacity of Jews to assimilate into mainstream Russian culture and society, particularly through Russification and conversion, the extreme political right, including some writers for conservative newspapers, had begun to characterize Jewishness as an identity that was a fixed and unalterable consequence of the Jews' biological makeup.[10] For the extreme political right in Russia, conversion would not change the Jews' essential and fundamental characteristics as a group intent on subverting the existing social and political order and establishing Jewish dominion over the world.

Depictions of Jews as "grotesque and full of malice" had a rich pedigree in medieval Latin Christianity.[11] By the fifteenth century, a physical stereotype of the Jewish male had taken shape, characterized by a large bent nose, thick protruding lips, eyes with heavy lids, a scraggly beard and facial hair, horns, and other physiognomic traits that were similar to those attributed to the devil. From the medieval Christian's perspective, the Jews' steadfast refusal to embrace Christianity and complicity in the killing of Christ were evidence of their associations with the devil, something rooted in their unswerving adherence to Judaism. By the late Middle Ages, Jews had come to epitomize

---

[10] See Eli Weinerman, "Racism, Racial Prejudice, and Jews in Late Imperial Russia," *Ethnic and Racial Studies* 17, 3 (1994): 442–95, on the resistance of Russian conservatives and government officials to embrace racial or biological antisemitism.

[11] Eric Zafran, "The Iconography of Anti-Semitism: A Study of the Representations of the Jews in the Visual Arts of Europe, 1400–1600" (Ph.D. diss., New York University, 1973), 20. The classic treatment of this theme is Joshua Trachtenberg, *The Devil and the Jews: The Medieval Conception of the Jew and Its Relation to Modern Anti-Semitism* (New Haven, 1943).

moral failing and sinful behavior and, as the devil's closest associates, were seen as demonic and portrayed as bestial. Still, once Jews accepted Christ as their savior, their evil ways supposedly ceased.

However, recent scholarship has challenged the standard view that premodern antisemitism ensured Jews' redemption through conversion. Not all medieval Latin Christians were sure that Jews who forsook their religion were guaranteed salvation, notwithstanding active efforts to baptize Jews. In the words of Debra Higgs Strickland, "converted Jews were not readily accepted into Christian society; rather the suspicion that 'once a Jew, always a Jew' seems to have prevailed."[12] Jonathan Elkun recently pointed out that the "immutable quality" of Jewish identity had begun to characterize Christian perceptions of Jews by the twelfth century. According to Elkun, Jews supposedly possessed distinctive physical features that stemmed from Judaism. Yet he cautioned against imposing modern categories, ideas, and vocabulary on the Europe of nearly a millennium ago and rejected the notion that Latin Christians ascribed a "biological distinctiveness" to Jews that distinguished them from gentiles.[13] The boundaries posited by many historians between medieval and modern forms of antisemitism are more porous than once believed.

Interestingly, this representation of Jews cannot be found in Byzantine art and Orthodox Christianity, which lacked the demeaning stereotypes of Jews and "differed completely from Western art in its treatment of the Jew."[14] Indeed, the association between Jews and the devil is not present in Byzantine iconography. As John Klier stressed, traditional Russian Orthodox antisemitism lacked "the fear of the Talmud, the easy equation of Jews with the devil and satanic forces, or belief in a conspiracy to annihilate Christian Europe."[15] Moreover, in Klier's words:

> The murderous frenzy of the Crusades never communicated itself to Kievan Rus'. There was no Russian equivalent to the Western European and Polish charge that the Jews poisoned wells and spread the plague ... Russia lacked the popular identification of the Jews with the Devil, which became a significant cultural phenomenon in the West. There were no Russian equivalents

---

[12] See the chapter "Christians Imagine Jews" in Debra Higgs Strickland, *Saracens, Demons, and Jew: Making Monsters in Medieval Art* (Princeton, NJ, 2003), 144.
[13] Jonathan Elukin, "From Jew to Christian? Conversion and Immutability in Medieval Europe," in *Varieties of Religious Conversion in the Middle Ages*, ed. James Muldoon (Gainesville, FL, 1997), 171–89.
[14] Elizabeth Revel-Neher, *The Image of the Jew in Byzantine Art* (Oxford, 1992), 107–8.
[15] John D. Klier, "Traditional Russian Religious Anti-Semitism," *Jewish Quarterly* 174 (Summer 1999): 29–34.

of the anti-Jewish stereotypes which appeared in the medieval miracle plays, or in Church art and architecture.[16]

This absence of a link between Jews and evil is important for any discussion of Russian antisemitism since Russian Orthodoxy was an offshoot of Orthodox Christianity and thus more closely associated with Byzantine traditions than with the church of Latin Europe. So how can we explain the presence of visual anti-Jewish stereotypes in Russian culture and politics many centuries later?

First, it bears keeping in mind that the lack of anti-Jewish visual representations did not mean that the Russian Orthodox Church during the first several centuries of its existence (from the tenth through the fourteenth centuries) did not share the suspicion of Judaism and Jews exhibited elsewhere in Europe. To be sure, the views of Saint John Chrysostom, the fourth-century theologian whose homilies are viewed by many as one of the fundamental texts of antisemitism, first took root in Byzantine society and, when it emerged in the tenth century, the Russian Orthodox Church. But the fact that Chrysostom was railing against Judaizers, not Jews per se but Christians who observed both Jewish and Christian traditions, attended synagogue and church, and encouraged other Christians to do the same, may or may not absolve him of personally hating Jews. It is critical to point out that Russian church and political leaders focused on the perceived threat of proselytism by Jews and were, for the most part, impervious to the views and attitudes displayed in the Latin West. Still, Chrysostom's ideas undoubtedly helped foster intolerance of Jews and their religion among Orthodox Christians for many centuries to come. Thus by the second half of the sixteenth century, Tsar Ivan IV (Ivan the Terrible) decreed that Jews were forbidden to live in Russia or even conduct business in Russia on a temporary basis.[17]

Second, Russian Orthodoxy may have been the offspring of the Byzantine church, but this did not mean the Russian church was cut off from contact with and influence from churches in the Latin West. By the sixteenth and seventeenth centuries, the Russian church had picked up elements of the Latin rite, a state of affairs that prompted church officials under the direction of Patriarch Nikon in the mid-seventeenth century to purge Russian Orthodoxy of offending accretions and led to the formation of the Old Believer schismatic sects that rejected Nikon's reforms. In addition, by the time Peter the Great assumed the throne at the end of the seventeenth century, intellectual and cultural currents from Latin Europe had been circulating inside Russia for

---

[16] John Doyle Klier, *Russia Gathers Her Jews: The Origins of the "Jewish Question" in Russia, 1772–1825* (DeKalb, IL, 1986), 23–24.
[17] Robert Wilken, *John Chrysostom and the Jews: Rhetoric and Reality in the Late 4th Century* (Berkeley, CA, 1983) and Klier, *Russia Gathers Her Jews*, 24–25.

many decades. It is reasonable to believe that the anti-Jewish culture of church, state, and society in the Latin West gradually came to influence the inhabitants of Russia, who already possessed a religious predisposition against Jews and Judaism.

Nevertheless, it was not until Russia incorporated a large swath of the Polish-Lithuanian Commonwealth under Catherine the Great in the late eighteenth century that anti-Jewish ideas and values, especially those concerning Jews as economically and socially suspect and dangerous, displaced the fear of apostasy as the motivating factor in Russia's desire to maintain its insularity from Jews. Catherine's territorial acquisitiveness made hundreds of thousands of Jews subjects of the Russian crown and sparked the emergence of a "Jewish Question," since the preexisting relations between Jews and their Catholic neighbors in the Polish-Lithuanian Commonwealth had been inherited by the Russian Empire and demanded the attention of tsarist officials. Catherine's reign marked the beginning of a concerted effort by tsarist officials to protect the *narod* from the perceived machinations of Jews and to render Jews in the Russian Empire less able (and less willing) to exploit their non-Jewish neighbors through a two-pronged policy of segregation and acculturation/integration that tended to work at cross-purposes. It was also during the latter half of the eighteenth century that the blood libel made its appearance in Russia, precisely at the time it took control of territory where the libel was alive and well. By the middle of the nineteenth century, the blood libel captured the imagination of Russia's Orthodox populace.[18] Given the greater circulation of ideas and attitudes between Russia and its neighbors to the West, it stands to reason that the visual association of Jews with the devil also began to percolate in the minds of Russians at this time, thereby accounting for the dissemination of antisemitic iconography that had been previously limited to Catholic and Protestant Europe. In the century after the partitioning of Poland, antisemitism acquired a mass dimension, becoming rooted in the thinking of government officials and in the popular imagination as a result of the circulation of anti-Jewish beliefs and sentiments. By the twentieth century, the exchange of cultural, political, and intellectual patterns of thought between imperial Russia and the rest of Europe ensured that antisemites throughout the continent could draw upon many of the same tropes, representations, and arguments.

Several developments explain the spread of antisemitism in Russia in the nineteenth century, particularly in the half-century after the emancipation of

---

[18] As John Klier noted, "Before the partitions of Poland, the Russian state proved insensitive to the Blood Libel" ("The Origins of the 'Blood Libel' in Russia," *Newsletter of the Study Group on Eighteenth-Century Russia* 14 [1986], 16).

8. Look! Up There in the Sky: It's a Vulture, It's a Bat ... It's a Jew

the serfs in 1861. First, the postreform era witnessed the public articulation and discussion of the "Jewish Question" in newspapers and journals, which proliferated during these decades and sought to make sense of the impact of the Great Reforms on the peasantry and the role of the Jews in Russia's society and economy.[19] In addition, the emergence of a revolutionary movement and the quickening pace of the country's modernization as evidenced by urbanization, industrialization, and appearance of a nascent civil society prompted a backlash by conservative forces that, in the words of Heinz-Dietrich Löwe, used antisemitism as an "ideology of a pre-modern way of life."[20]

An examination of rightwing depictions of Jews illustrates the extent to which attitudes toward Jews in late imperial Russia resembled ideas and values elsewhere in Europe. The following discussion focuses on the visual representation of Jews as inhuman and bestial—specifically as vultures, bats, locusts, and other pesky insects—and gives an opportunity to reflect on the nature of antisemitism in the decade or so before World War I. The mixing of diverse motifs of antisemitism derived from the supposed religious, behavioral, and innate characteristics of Jews made for an especially volatile and combustible situation given the enormous social, economic, and political strains confronting Russia at this time. Given the persistence of a religious worldview, the overwhelmingly agrarian nature of society, and the relatively low rate of literacy, it comes as no surprise that antisemitism stemming from religious prejudices would continue to find a receptive audience in Russia. At the same time, however, Russia's pursuit of industrialization, rapid urban growth, cultural Westernization, the strengthening of civil society, and the emergence of liberal and socialist political movements ensured that antisemitism, as a reaction to the principles of 1789 and the impact of modernization, would develop along with other, older attitudes that demonized Jews. The experiences of Jews in late imperial Russia suggest that suspicion and hostility on the part of gentiles and government need not stem from centuries-long, firsthand contact and experience. Rather, long-standing religious prejudices and socioeconomic and political tensions specific to the late nineteenth and early twentieth centuries were sufficient to foster an atmosphere of hate when tsarist governments found themselves host to some five million Jews by 1900.

---

[19] John Doyle Klier, *Imperial Russia's Jewish Question, 1855–1881* (Cambridge, 1995).
[20] Heinz-Dietrich Löwe, *The Tsars and the Jews: Reform, Reaction, and Anti-Semitism in Imperial Russia, 1772–1917* (Chur, Switzerland, 1993), 422.

The drawings analyzed here appeared in two newspapers from the post-1905 era: *Veche* (Town Assembly), published in Moscow between 1905 and 1909; and *Znamia* (Banner), which came out in Odessa during the first half of 1914.[21] They were two out of dozens of archconservative publications that appeared in the aftermath of 1905; but unlike many other rightwing newspapers and journals, *Veche* and *Znamia* expended the time and money to include political cartoons. Published by the extreme right wing (known as the Black Hundreds in popular parlance and organized in several political parties, the most notable being the Union of the Russian People), these newspapers promoted a strident form of nationalism and antisemitism that appealed to members of the Black Hundreds. Moreover, given the political significance of the political Right in these years, the newspapers published by the Black Hundreds would have circulated beyond the official membership and found a welcome among sympathizers and other like-minded thinkers. Although it is difficult to ascertain the composition of the readership of these newspapers, the Black Hundreds drew their membership from a cross-section of society, namely Orthodox Christian students and clergy, peasants, shopkeepers, artisans and factory workers, professionals, merchants, gentry's landowners, policemen, and day laborers.[22] The spread of literacy during the latter part of the nineteenth century meant that increasing numbers of Russians of all social and economic backgrounds in not only towns and cities but also villages took up reading newspapers as a source of information and entertainment.[23]

According to the Black Hundreds, Jews were leaders of a vast conspiracy to undermine the autocracy and responsible for all the ills besetting Russia: the economic exploitation of Russian peasants; the stranglehold exerted by Jewish capitalists on the internal and external affairs of the government; and the revolutionary efforts to subvert Russian culture and society. Steadfastly devoted to Tsar Nicholas II and autocracy, the extreme Right worked to push back the political reforms of 1905. The Black Hundreds asserted that Jews were manipulating the fledgling parliamentary system by controlling the actions of all but the most conservative non-Jewish politicians and activists.

---

[21] *Veche* refers to the town assembly or meeting that existed in Kievan Rus and Novgorod prior to the unification of Russia under Muscovy in the fourteenth and fifteenth centuries. It is curious that a newspaper that stridently supported the autocracy was named after an institution that impeded the growth of tsarist power.

[22] Don Rawson, *Russian Rightists and the Revolution of 1905* (Cambridge, 1995), 62–63.

[23] See Jeffrey Brooks, *When Russia Learned to Read* (Princeton, NJ, 1985); and Louise McReynolds, *The News under Russia's Old Regime* (Princeton, NJ, 1991).

8. Look! Up There in the Sky: It's a Vulture, It's a Bat ... It's a Jew

From the perspective of the Black Hundreds, Jews threatened the very fabric of late imperial Russian society, culture, and politics.[24]

Veche and *Znamia*, along with other Black Hundreds' publications, provided a political education of sorts for their readers and framed post-1905 political developments from the perspective of the extreme Right. Indeed, *Znamia* announced that it spoke for the *narod*—that is, Orthodox Christian peasants and workers—when it proclaimed on its masthead that it "takes upon itself the defense of all Russians who suffer from the oppression, concern, and deceit of the Kikes."[25] For the most part, the messages in the drawings in these publications tended to be transparent and easily grasped; but at times, readers needed to be familiar with current political affairs in order to understand what the artist was trying to convey, particularly when only a short caption accompanied the drawing. Visual representations, just like written texts, are open to multiple readings and interpretations, especially when they draw on the diverse values, attitudes, beliefs, and experiences of the readership. A person views and understands texts in a manner that reflects his or her specific life experiences. Moreover, difficult as it is to ascertain how readers may have interpreted a political cartoon, it is also challenging to establish with certainty the intended message of the artist.[26] Visual artists do not and cannot control how viewers will apprehend drawings, and they do not always intend for their work to be transparent, even to the informed eye. To be sure, a political cartoonist does not want to draw images that are too complex and contain obscure allusions. Yet symbols are politically effective when their meanings are ambiguous. As the anthropologist Katherine Verdery noted, it is the very ambiguity of symbols that helps to mobilize groups of people politically.[27]

---

[24] On the Black Hundreds, see Jacob Langer, "Corruption and the Counterrevolution: The Rise and Fall of the Black Hundred" (Ph.D. diss., Duke University, 2007); Hans Rogger, "The Formation of the Russian Right: 1900–1906," and "Was There a Russian Fascism? The Union of the Russian People," in his *Jewish Politics and Rightwing Politics in Imperial Russia* (Berkeley, CA, 1986), 188–201 and 212–32; Vladimir Osipovich Levitskii, "Pravye partii," in *Obshchestvennoe dvizhenie v Rossii v nachale XX-go veka*," ed. Lev Martov, Petr P. Maslov, and Aleksandr Nikolaevich Potresov, vol. 3, book 5 (St. Petersburg, 1914), 347–469; Rawson, *Russian Rightists and the Revolution of 1905*; Sergei Aleksandrovich Stepanov, *Chernaia sotnia v Rossii (1905–1914 gg.)* (Moscow, 1992); Iurii Il'ich Kir'ianov, ed., *Pravye partii, 1905–1917: Dokumenty i materialy*, 2 vols. (Moscow, 1998).

[25] By 1900, *zhid* (pl. *zhidy*), one Russian word for "Jew" had acquired a negative connotation, similar to "Kike" or "Yid" in English. See John D. Klier, "*Zhid*: Biography of a Russian Epithet," *Slavonic and East European Review* 60, 1 (1982): 1–15.

[26] Victoria Bonnell noted that political art is open to diverse interpretations as viewers respond based on the "cultural repertoires" available to them. See her *Iconography of Power: Soviet Posters under Lenin and Stalin* (Berkeley, CA, 1997), 14 and 83.

[27] Katherine Verdery, "Whither 'Nation' and 'Nationalism'?" *Daedalus* 122, 3 (1993): 36–46.

Figure 8-1 appeared at the end of 1906 and revealed the Black Hundreds' concern that Jews might exercise undue influence on the peasantry. In other issues of *Veche*, Jews were depicted as manipulating peasant discontent into insurrection. Figure 8-1 shows a horde of what appears to be locusts with stereotypical male Jewish faces zeroing in on a group of peasants engaged in conversation. The locusts' front legs hold pieces of paper that, according to the caption, are political manifestos and proclamations. The caption states that "The Kike Locust in the Countryside Has Already Begun Its Activities before Elections to the State Duma," a not very subtle reference to efforts by Jewish politicians to influence male peasants, a group enfranchised by a 1906 law establishing the State Duma, or parliament. When drawing up the suffrage legislation, the regime placed its faith in what it believed were the conservative proclivities of the peasants, particularly the relatively well-to-do ones, to resist the overtures of liberals, radicals, and other antigovernment forces. This may explain why the village, despite its dirt road, appears to be, if not prosperous, then at least certainly not destitute and impoverished. Similarly, the peasants, while dressed in typical peasant garb, do not appear to be down-and-out and in dire economic straits. The Black Hundreds evidently feared that politically active male Jews who had secured the right to vote and hold office in the Duma, along with males from other national minorities, would entice those peasants, on whom the regime believed it could rely, to vote for liberal and radical Duma candidates. To be sure, Jews and Jewish political parties were not the only ones seeking the peasant vote. The 1905 revolution unleashed a flurry of mobilization across the entire political spectrum that affected all social, ethnic, and religious groups, but the Black Hundreds viewed the involvement of Jews in the electoral process as particularly dangerous for the well-being of Russia.

8. Look! Up There in the Sky: It's a Vulture, It's a Bat... It's a Jew

Жидовская саранча въ деревнѣ уже начала свои дѣйствія передъ выборами въ Государственную Думу.

FIGURE 8-1. *Veche*, 24 December 1906. "The Kike Locust in the Countryside Has Already Begun Its Activities before Elections to the State Duma"

Figure 8-2, from early 1907, depicts a bat with "Anarchy" inscribed on the underside of its outspread wings and a head possessing stereotypical features of a Jewish man. The bat is about to land near a buxom woman representing "Mother Russia" who, reposed in a seductive manner, is waking from a fitful sleep marked perhaps by a disturbing dream. The caption reads "A Grim Dream, but Waking Up Will Be Sweet": evidently the autocracy had been caught off-guard (literally napping), which explains the spread of anarchy and unrest under the direction of Jews, and is now waking up from a bad dream. Naturally, the reforms stemming from the 1905 revolution were very much real and no mere dream. Fortunately for Russia, a *bogatyr* (medieval Russian warrior from folk tales) with the words "Union of the Russian People" emblazoned on his sword is about to smite the bat. As Helena Goscilo has written, the *bogatyr* is a "protector of national borders and Orthodox Christianity" who is an "emblem of indomitable strength and invincibility." Moreover, the virile *bogatyr* complemented representations of the genuine Russian woman who was depicted as fertile and dependent on the man for

179

protection.[28] In other words, the extreme Right is coming to the defense of the autocracy, which had failed to protect itself. The imagery of the predatory Jew, which appeared in other issues of *Veche* as well as in other rightwing publications, underscored the Black Hundreds' belief that Jews intended to subvert the imperial order: Mother Russia herself was in danger of falling victim to alien forces.

The evident sexual imagery reflected a turn-of-the-century perception that Jewish men were sexual predators who threatened the virtue of non-Jewish women. Moreover, Jews in general were regarded as engaging in a conspiracy to sap the vitality and health of the Russian populace. No doubt the public discussion of the purported role of Jews in the white slave trade bolstered the suspicion that Jews were behind the social, cultural, and political disorder many intellectuals believed characterized Russia in the post-1905 environment.[29]

FIGURE 8-2. *Veche*, 28 January 1907. "A Grim Dream, but Waking Up Will Be Sweet"

---

[28] Helena Goscilo, "Viktor Vasnetsov's *Bogatyrs*: Mythic Heroes and Sacrosanct Borders Go to Market," in *Picturing Russia: Explorations in Visual Culture*, ed. Valerie Kivelson and Joan Neuberger (New Haven, 2008), 248.

[29] Laura Engelstein, *The Keys to Happiness: Sex and the Search for Modernity in Fin-de-Siècle Russia* (Ithaca, NY, 1992), especially chap. 8. On the accusation that Jews controlled the international trade in prostitutes, see Edward Bristow, *Prostitution and Prejudice: The Jewish Fight against White Slavery, 1870–1939* (Oxford, 1982).

8. Look! Up There in the Sky: It's a Vulture, It's a Bat . . . It's a Jew

The depiction of the Jew as a bat raises questions about viewing Russian society and culture of the early twentieth century through our eyes one hundred years later. The association of bats with vampires who prey on unsuspecting women in order to suck their blood may seem obvious to today's viewers of the drawing, but we would be wrong to conclude that Russians in 1907 "read" it in similar terms. While the lore about Dracula and vampirism, including the ability of vampires to change into an animal, was well established in Russia by 1900, the association of vampires with bats gained currency only after the publication of Bram Stoker's *Dracula* in 1897. In addition, knowledge of vampire bats, which live only in Latin America and lick rather than suck blood, was not widespread in Europe in the nineteenth century. Stoker was the first to conjure up the image of vampires morphing into bats, and vampires in Russian folklore were not of the blood-sucking variety.[30] According to Slavic folk traditions, vampires could transform themselves into a whole range of animals, including cats, dogs, rats, birds, frogs, and even flies. But bats were not among them.[31] Nor did Russians necessarily view bats in a negative light. According to Russian folk traditions and customs, bats' wings possessed magical qualities, and "a dried bat worn at the breast was a good-luck charm."[32]

Consequently, it is unlikely that Russian readers of *Veche* in 1907 would have associated the Jewish bat with a vampire about to suck the life out of helpless Mother Russia. Even though Stoker's *Dracula* appeared in Russian as early as 1902, it is unlikely that the novel was on the bestseller list of the Russian public. Of course, the cartoonist may have been familiar with Stoker's version of the Dracula story, perhaps having gained knowledge of it through firsthand exposure or as the result of conversations with others who knew the novel. But even if that were the case, the artist could not assume that readers of *Veche* would have drawn the connection between blood-sucking bats and vampires.

It may not be important that a typical Ivan or Katia looking at the drawing of a bat with the head of a Jew did not associate bats with vampires. Even in the absence of the vampire legend, people tend to frighten easily when they encounter bats, and so it is not surprising that the Black Hundreds'

---

[30] Felix Oinas, a preeminent authority on Russian folklore, wrote that vampires "appear among the Slavs as bats." However, I am skeptical of the statement's accuracy because the source Oinas quoted does not substantiate his assertion. See Felix Oinas, "East European Vampires," in his *Essays on Russian Folklore and Mythology* (Columbus, OH, 1984), 112.

[31] Paul Barber, *Vampires, Burial, and Death: Folklore and Reality* (New Haven, 1988), 33; Wayne Barrett and Flavia Idriceanu, *Legends of Blood: The Vampire in History and Myth* (Westport, CT, 2006), 97–99; Gary McCracken, "Bats and Vampires," *Bats* 11, 3 (1993), 13–15; Elizabeth Miller, "Bats, Vampires, and Dracula," *Newsletter of the Florida Bat Conservation Center* (Fall 1998).

[32] W. F. Ryan, *The Bathhouse at Midnight: Magic in Russia* (University Park, PA, 1999), 253 and 283.

cartoonists drew on this fear. In addition, the notion of Jews as "bloodsuckers" was common currency a century ago, regardless of whether or not Russians associated bats with vampirism, in both the literal and figurative senses of the word. Russians tended to associate Jews with moneymaking and felt justified labeling them "bloodsuckers" because of their purported exploitation of non-Jews. Indeed, the supposed economic exploitation of gentiles by Jews was at the heart of the autocracy's discriminatory policies toward Jews in the nineteenth century. Fear of Jewish merchants, tavern keepers, and arendators prompted the decision by Catherine the Great to impose residency restrictions after an initial period of toleration. Furthermore, the blood libel was accepted as real by many people living in late imperial Russia who had no difficulty believing Jews were intent on sucking dry the spiritual and cultural essence of Russian society and culture. Jews supposedly made the host bleed as a way to mock the suffering of Jesus. The prosecution's case against Beilis rested on the unsubstantiated assertion that the victim was killed in such a manner as to maximize the loss of blood, essentially reiterating the canard expressed in 1911 by a journalist who wrote that "the aim of the Jews is not only to pervert the Russian people to the marrow of their bones, both physically and spiritually."[33] We may not be able to determine why the artist of Figure 8-2 depicted the Jew as a bat, but we can be confident in our belief that readers of the Black Hundreds' press associated Jews with draining Russia of its life forces.

The association of Jews with monsters remained alive throughout the nearly ten years between the disturbances of 1905–1906 and the outbreak of world war in 1914. Jumping ahead to the eve of World War I, the cover of the 1 April 1914 issue of *Znamia* (Figure 8-3) displayed a creature called "Kikeosaurus," which possessed a Jewish male's head with fangs, hooked nose, big ears, scraggly beard, and skull cap. The head was attached to a lizardlike body that had the heads of several male Jews sticking out of its torso and a set of webbed feet and claws that allowed the creature to scutter about.

---

[33] Engelstein, *Keys to Happiness*, 305.

8. Look! Up There in the Sky: It's a Vulture, It's a Bat... It's a Jew

FIGURE 8-3. *Znamia*, 1 April 1914. "The Antedeluvian Beast—The Kikosaurus"

The final drawing (Figure 8-4) appeared in mid-July 1914, less than a week before *Znamia* stopped publishing because of the heightened tensions between Russia and Austria. Captioned "Who Is He?" the drawing depicts a tall, thin Jew with the nose of an anteater leaning over a passing steam engine and looking as if he is ready to vacuum up the countryside. The development of the railway system helped create a national market and fostered the penetration of urban Russia into rural areas, particularly by Jews who took advantage of Russia's modernization to gain a foothold in agrarian Russia. Figure 8-4 is clearly a barb at the supposed inroads made by Jewish investors in acquiring land from peasants and landlords who could not meet their mortgage payments and other financial burdens, such as taxes. While gentile merchants and professionals may have taken advantage of tax arrears and defaults on mortgages to buy land for country homes and speculation, the Russian gentry and peasantry, not Jews, constituted the majority of those who bought land on the eve of World War I.[34] The fact that Jews could not legally own land evidently did not deter the political Right from associating Jews with land speculation and probably grew out of fears that outsiders from the city were insinuating themselves in the countryside to the detriment of gentry and peasant alike.

---

[34] Seymour Becker, *Nobility and Privilege in Late Imperial Russia* (DeKalb, IL, 1985), 35.

FIGURE 8-4. *Znamia*, 15 July 1914. "Who Is He?"

Finally, what are we to make of the larger-than-life nose? In Freudian terms, the length and girth of a man's nose, or his fingers for that matter, corresponded to the size of his penis. By giving him a long, curved, and pointed nose the artist implicitly endowed him with an oversized penis, transforming a Jewish man into a predatory male who posed a threat to all gentiles, men through economic exploitation and women through sexual aggressiveness. But as some scholars have concluded, the depiction of a Jewish man with a hooked and misshapen nose represented the Jewish man's circumcised penis, which rendered him less than virile, if not impotent, regardless of the length and girth of his member. In the words of Sander Gilman, "The specific shape of the Jews' nose indicated the damaged nature, the shortened form, of his penis. The traditional positive association between the size of the nose and that of the male genitalia and this reversal was made a pathological sign."[35] Hence the cartoon is polyvalent and allows for multiple readings and interpretations, thereby making it difficult to know with exactitude not only the intent of the artist but also the readership's reception of the drawing.

---

[35] Sander Gilman, *The Jews' Body* (New York, 1991), 189.

8. Look! Up There in the Sky: It's a Vulture, It's a Bat... It's a Jew

Depictions of Jews in the Black Hundreds' press shared striking similarities with rightwing publications in France during the Dreyfus Affair in the decade before 1905. The novelist Comtesse Sibylle Martel de Janville, for example, illustrated her story from 1896 in the satirical journal *La Rire* with a depiction of Algerian Jews as locusts.[36] Likewise, the "Kikeosaurus" in Figure 8-3 is reminiscent of the portrayal of Dreyfus as the Hydra in V. Lenepveu's *The Traitor* (1900), one of fifty-one posters that portrayed Dreyfusards and Jews as part-human, part-animal, between 1899 and 1900.[37] In addition, Théodore Garnier, a priest active in the anti-Dreyfus campaign, "referred to Jews... as 'vampires and parasites' who had 'poisoned' true Frenchmen and 'sucked' the lifeblood out of the French body."[38] The rhetoric and imagery of French antisemites were in lockstep with those of the Black Hundreds; and in the absence of clear linguistic or thematic content, an observer would have difficulty distinguishing portrayal of Jews in anti-Dreyfus and Black Hundreds' publications. Clearly, this similarity underscores the transnational quality of antisemitic ideology, which had little difficulty crossing porous geographic, cultural, and political boundaries. If, as we have noted earlier, Russian antisemites rejected the injection of racialist discourse in the 1880s, then the embrace of imagery and ideas similar to those found elsewhere in Europe in the decade prior to 1914 indicates the vibrant circulation of ideas across the continent.[39] Moreover, the role played by political system is correspondingly less important since Black Hundreds operated in an autocratic polity and French antisemites in a parliamentary one.

Antisemitic publications throughout Europe at this time drew on the convention of poking fun at public personages by giving them animal characteristics. Moreover, demonic and nonhuman representations of Jews were common currency in the cultures of Europe, Russia, and the United

---

[36] Norman Kleeblatt, ed., *The Dreyfus Affair: Art, Truth, and Justice* (Berkeley, CA, 1987), 154, plate 3.

[37] Ibid., 246, plate 171.

[38] Caron, "Catholic Political Mobilization," 319.

[39] On the association of the Jew and Satan in the United States, see Robert Rockaway and Arnon Gutfeld, "Demonic Images of the Jew in the Nineteenth-Century United States," *American Jewish History* 89, 4 (2002): 355–81. On the association in Russia, see the cover of *Knut* (Knout), no. 2 (1908), where a devil with stereotypical Jewish facial features welcomes newly arrived denizens of hell. Moreover, these visual depictions of Jews crossed the divide of 1917 throughout Europe, including the Soviet Union. One noteworthy example from post-1917 Russia is a color poster depicting a bestial Leon Trotsky with red skin and oversized hands, feet, and forearms commanding the fledgling Soviet government. The poster is entitled "Peace and Freedom in the Soviet of Deputies."

185

States. Yet the portrayal of Jews as creatures that combined human and animal physiognomies went beyond the conventional use of animal traits for political satire. When a gentile politician was the target of a cartoonist, the negative traits applied to that specific individual and were not generalized to all gentiles. To be sure, certain prominent Jews were singled out as the target of the right wing's opprobrium; but for the most part, Jews as a group shared the physical, behavioral, and attitudinal traits with which the Black Hundreds branded them. The drawings in *Veche* and *Znamia* targeted all Jews, not just certain individual ones, and prompted viewers to regard all Jews as alien, beastly, and inhuman. While antisemitism in late imperial Russia still possessed aspects that stemmed from timeworn religious prejudices, other concerns associated with Russia's ambiguous relationship with modernity also characterized antisemitic ideas. Much like elsewhere on the continent, concerns and anxieties about the changing social, economic, cultural, and political landscape fostered political movements that focused on Jews as the source of Russia's troubles. Furthermore, Jewishness as an identity, both in Russia and in the rest of Europe, was beginning to be uncoupled from religious observance and to be perceived as a permanent and integral aspect of Jews. Antisemitism in Russia on the eve of World War I may have stemmed from a mix of motives—some centuries old, others of relatively recent vintage—but there was a growing perception among some antisemites that Jews were indelibly marked by intrinsic features and traits that were essential elements of their being. By 1914, Russia more closely resembled Western and Central Europe in terms of social, economic, and political developments, but this convergence of Russia with the rest of Europe meant that the forces of antisemitism in Russia and on the continent were also beginning to share a common racialist basis.

9. Shots in the Back

On the Origin of the Anti-Jewish Pogroms of 1918–1921

Oleg Budnitskii

The pogroms of the Russian Civil War period (1918–1921) were the most serious outbreak of anti-Jewish violence in Eastern Europe between the Khmelnytsky Uprising of 1648 and the Holocaust. In 1918–1921, in the Ukraine alone, there were over 1,500 pogroms and "excesses" in about 1,300 localities. According to various estimates, from fifty to sixty thousand to two hundred thousand Jews were killed or mortally wounded. Another two hundred thousand were injured and mutilated. Many thousands of women were raped. About fifty thousand women were widowed, and three hundred thousand children orphaned.[1] The information on the pogroms and their victims was collected more or less systematically from May 1919 on,[2] but the precise number of casualties will never be known.

Given the pogroms' unprecedented scope and cruelty, it is understandable that witnesses at the time and later historians have sought to understand the motivation of the perpetrators. The following motives were the most favored:

---

[1] Salo Baron calculated that the number of victims "easily" exceeded fifty thousand (*The Russian Jew under Tsars and Soviets*, 2d ed. [New York, 1975], 184); Nora Levin gives the number of fifty to sixty thousand (*The Jews in the Soviet Union since 1917* [New York, 1988], 1:49); S. Ettinger cites seventy-five thousand (H. H. Ben-Sasson, ed., *A History of the Jewish People* [Cambridge, MA, 1976], 954). N. Gergel, "The Pogroms in the Ukraine in 1918–21," *YIVO Annual of Jewish Social Science* 6 (1951), 251; and S. Gusev-Orenburgskii in his *Kniga o evreiskikh pogromakh na Ukraine v 1919 g.* (Petrograd, n. d.), 14, speak about one hundred thousand fatalities. Finally, the number of two hundred thousand victims is cited in Iurii Larin, *Evrei i antisemitizm v SSSR* (Moscow and Leningrad, 1929), 55. See also Richard Pipes, *Russia under the Bolshevik Regime* (New York, 1995), 112; "Pogromy," *Kratkaia evreiskaia entsiklopediia* 6 (Jerusalem, 1992), 569–75; and "Ukraina," ibid., 8:1226. Gergel considered that the figure of fifty to sixty thousand Jewish dead due to pogroms could be documented, but he noted that, considering the lack of precise data, the actual number could well be twice that figure. The author of a recent study on the "Jewish question" in the Ukraine accepts the relatively lower figures for those who were killed or perished from pogroms (Henry Abramson, *A Prayer for the Government: Ukrainians and Jews in Revolutionary Times, 1917–1920* [Cambridge, MA, 1999], 110).

[2] David Roskies, *Against the Apocalypse: Responses to Catastrophe in Modern Jewish Culture* (Cambridge, MA, 1984), 138–40.

retribution for Jewish participation in Bolshevism and the "destruction of Russia"; well-established economic antagonism, aggravated by war and revolution; a criminal desire to plunder and rob; and, on a more specific level, the "incorrect" voting of the Jewish parties in the Ukrainian Rada on the issue of Ukraine's independence. A recurrent motif was the claim that shots were fired at retreating troops from the windows of the Jewish apartments and houses. This theme is the focus of this chapter.

For the most part, these diverse and contradictory explanations represent an effort to rationalize the irrational. There is something clearly amiss in the syllogism that if Trotsky heads the Red Army, then it is necessary to chop off the arms of a shoemaker from some shtetl, to rape his wife, and to smash in the head of his child. Likewise, if the Jewish socialist parties vote "wrongly" in the Rada, how does blame extend to the voters for religious parties or, as was mostly the case, the apolitical majority who had no interest in politics and did not bother to vote at all? If some Jews want to prove their loyalty by fighting in the ranks of the Whites against the Bolsheviks, why are qualified candidates denied officer rank, in a sort of reverse political correctness? Why, if the Jews are responsible for Bolshevism, do members of the nascent Red Army engage in pogroms at the slightest loosening of discipline?

In the 1920s and 1930s, historians sought to explain pogroms carried out by the Whites by emphasizing that they were monarchists and "counterrevolutionaries." Such a characterization of the White movement itself is very dubious,[3] but even if it were true, the conservatism or monarchism of individual political or military leaders need not necessarily lead them to espouse anti-Jewish violence. The followers of the Ukrainian leader Simon Vasil'evich Petliura declared themselves republicans and socialists, but their troops in the field carried out some of the most ghastly pogroms. Clearly the nature of the pogroms of 1918–1920 is best understood by viewing them in both a short- *and* a long-term perspective.

The scholar Joseph Schechtman, a contemporary of the events he was investigating, was one of the first to insist that "the Jewish pogroms of the Volunteer Army period were of a *purely military nature*... They were promulgated exclusively by the *regular regiments of the Volunteer Army*."[4] In my opinion, a general characterization of the pogroms as an essentially military phenomenon can be made of nearly all the pogroms of the Civil War, whether carried out by the troops of the Directory, the Red Army, the followers of Nikifor Aleksandrovich Grigor'ev, the brigades of Stanislav Nikodimovich

---

[3] See Oleg Budnitskii, "Jews, Pogroms, and the White Movement: A Historiographical Critique," *Kritika: Explorations in Russian and Eurasian History* 2, 4 (2001): 751–72.

[4] Joseph B. Schechtman, *Pogromy Dobrovol'cheskoi armii na Ukraine (k istorii antisemitizma na Ukraine v 1919–1920 gg.)* (Berlin, 1932), 153.

Bulak-Balakhovich, or miscellaneous armed bands. The term "pogrom" itself is not quite fit to describe the anti-Jewish violence of the Civil War era. In the "classic" definition, pogroms are seen as more or less spontaneous outbreaks of violence against the Jews carried out by civilian groups. Despite the subsequent identification of "Cossacks" and pogroms, in prerevolutionary Russia, the role of the military was the *suppression* of pogroms.[5] In the Civil War period, the civilian population, almost invariably peasants, joined in the looting only after it had been initiated by armed troops.

It is important to note that a considerable percentage, if not the majority, of the combatants in the Russian Civil War who had served in the Imperial Russian Army were veterans of World War I.[6] Recall that about fifteen million persons were recruited into the Russian military during the war. Consequently, two factors must be kept in mind when considering the "military" aspect of the Civil War pogroms. The first is the general attitude toward the Jews of the leaders of the Russian army in the prewar period. The second is the experience of the Russian army and the Jews during the war itself.

The author of a relatively recently published study of the Jews in the Russian army, Yohanan Mironovich Petrovsky-Shtern, writes, the "Russian army has attained a reputation of an unequivocally antisemitic, if not the most antisemitic, institution in prerevolutionary Russia." According to the author, however, the "widely-held opinion, accepted at face value by the Russian and Jewish historians, requires a decisive revision."[7] In my opinion, on the contrary, the evidence of Petrovsky-Shtern's own research undermines his "revisionist" conclusions.[8]

---

[5] I. Michael Aronson, "The Anti-Jewish Pogroms in Russia in 1881," in *Pogroms: Anti-Jewish Violence in Modern Russian History*, ed. John Doyle Klier and Shlomo Lambroza (Cambridge, 1992), 55; Shlomo Lambroza, "The Pogroms of 1903–1906," in *Pogroms*, 209, 217; at the same time, as Shlomo Lambroza noted, "the action of troops and police usually depended upon the conviction of their superior officers. At times troops and police halted pogroms, at other time they joined in the looting and murdering" ("Pogroms of 1903–1906," 218).

[6] As is generally known, the White movement was a movement of army men. Almost all White officers took part in World War I. So did those of the Red Army, which had seventy to seventy-five thousand former officers of tsarist and provisional government armies. These officers accounted for the vast majority of middle and supreme command (A. G. Kavtaradze, *Voennye spetsialisty na sluzhbe Respubliki sovetov, 1917–1920* (Moscow, 1988), 210, 214). It is not surprising that the most famous atamans of the Civil War, who excelled all others in exterminating Jews, were low-ranking officers of the Imperial Russian Army: Grigor'ev, Zeleny (real name—Daniil Ilyich Terpilo), Ivan Semesenko, Il'ko Timofeevich Struck, Ivan Galaka (real name—Ivan Alexeevich Vasil'chikov) and others. Some of them, like Grigor'ev and Galaka, served for some period of time in the Red Army.

[7] Y. Petrovskii-Shtern [Yohanan Petrovsky-Stern], *Evrei v russkoi armii, 1827–1914* (Moscow, 2003), 298.

[8] See ibid., 297, 344–51; O. V. Budnitskii, *Rossiiskie evrei mezhdu krasnymi i belymi* (Moscow, 2005), 158–64; and Dzh. [John] D. Klier, "Kazaki i pogromy," in *Mirovoi krizis*

Jews were constantly under suspicion in the army. They were suspected of the absence of patriotism, connivance with their coreligionists, negligent service. The Jews and Catholics (i.e., Poles) were not allowed to occupy positions as scribes, telegraphists, draftsmen, conductors, machinists, millers, gunsmiths, and examiners of military warehouses; and they were not drafted into engineering corps, pharmacy and veterinary attendants, or as doctors and their assistants in the western military regions and fortress garrisons.[9] It is not hard to notice that the Jews were viewed as potential traitors, saboteurs, and swindlers. They were barred from positions that involved access to material valuables, military equipment, and classified information. There was serious discussion within the army of ending the military recruitment of Jews as a justification for denying them full civil rights.[10]

At the outbreak of World War I, the whole Jewish population was placed under suspicion by the High Command. The Jews were a priori considered disloyal, predisposed to betrayal and espionage for the enemy. The spy mania reached a truly pathological scale. Accusations spread that Jews "communicate with the enemy by means of subterranean telephones and airplanes and provide them with gold and provisions." According to one version, the Jews tied gold to goose feathers, and the birds carried it to the enemy; according to another avian theory, poultry was stuffed with gold, then shipped off to Germany. In Bereznitsy (Volynia province), a priest informed his parishioners that the Jews were spies and that a telephone had been found in a cow's belly that they had fashioned to communicate with the enemy.[11] The authorities received denunciations from informants that the Jews were sending dispatches to Germany "in the eggs of hens of valuable kinds" or that the Jews of Vilna were using "cellars and slums" to store pans for use in smelting artillery shells for the enemy.[12] The Jews were purportedly trying to transfer a million and a half rubles in gold to the Germans, having hidden them in a coffin; a Jewish miller allegedly contacted the Austrians by means of a telephone installed in his cellar; others cut Russian telephone wires or connected them to the Austrian ones; the Jews used fires and light signals to transmit information to

---

1914–1920 godov i sud'ba vostochnoevropeiskogo evreistva, ed. O. V. Budnitskii et al. (Moscow, 2005), 53.

[9] Petrovskii-Shtern, *Evrei*, 321–22, 324.

[10] A. Litvin, ed., "Generaly i evrei," *Vestnik evreiskogo universiteta* 4, 22 (2000): 273–85; Joshua A. Sanborn, *Drafting the Russian Nation: Military Conscription, Total War, and Mass Politics, 1905–1925* (DeKalb, IL, 2003), 118–19; and Klier, "Kazaki i pogromy," 53.

[11] "Iz 'chernoi knigi' rossiiskogo evreistva: Materialy dlia istorii voiny 1914–1915 g.," *Evreiskaia starina*, no. 10 (1918): 269.

[12] S. Nelipovich, "V poiskakh vnutrennego vraga: Deportatsionnaia politika Rossii," in *Pervaia mirovaia voina i uchastie v nei Rossii (1914–1918): Materialy nauchnoi konferentsii* (Moscow, 1997), 61.

the enemy; they signaled from windows of their own houses, from trees and rooftops, disclosing to the enemy the positions of Russian troops; the Jews made plans to organize a mutiny in Kronshtadt and tried to deliver the plan of the mutiny to the Germans in Danzig, having thrown a sealed bottle with a message into the sea. The fantastical charges were boundless.[13] In Petrograd, the choral synagogue and the apartment of its chairman of the board, Mark Abramovich Varshavskii, were searched. Spy hunters were looking for an "apparatus to communicate with the enemy via wireless telegraph."[14]

The policy of persecuting Jews reflected more than the well-documented personal antisemitism of the army's commander in chief, Grand Duke Nikolai Nikolaevich, and especially his chief of staff, General Nikolai Nikolaevich Yanushkevich.[15] This policy was stipulated by the theory of military statistics; the officers were inundated with information on the harmful and suspicious elements within the population while in military schools and academies.[16] Theory substantiated the prejudices that most Orthodox Russians had imbibed since their early childhood. The Jews were adherents of a different faith that rejected Christ; they were exploiters who did not plow and did not sow but managed to extract profit as if from the air itself; they were troublemakers who undermined the power of the tsar and the very foundations of Russian life. They were the embodiment of the alien and the hostile.[17]

In the Pale of Settlement, where most of the draftees had never been before, this last element especially caught the eye. The Jews spoke a different language, they dressed strangely, their customs were bizarre and suspicious. They easily fit the role of those who could be held respon-

---

[13] S. Ansky, *The Enemy at His Pleasure: A Journey through the Jewish Pale of Settlement during World War I* (New York, 2003), 3-4. Henceforth, the book of S. A. An-sky (alias Shlomo-Zainvl Rapoport), *The Destruction of Galicia*, published posthumously in Yiddish as *Khurbn Galitsye* (Vilna, 1921), is cited from the English translation. We also used fragments of the original Russian manuscript of *Khurbn Galitsye* located at the Vernadsky Ukrainian Academic Library in Kiev. Irina Sergeeva and Victoria Mochalova kindly presented a copy of An-sky's manuscript to me.

[14] D. A. El'iashevich, *Pravitel'stvennaia politika i evreiskaia pechat' v Rossii 1797-1917: Ocherki istorii tsenzury* (St. Petersburg and Jerusalem, 1999), 500; S. Dubnov, *Kniga zhizni* (St. Petersburg, 1998), 348.

[15] Klier, "Kazaki i pogromy," 53-55; Semen Goldin, "Russkoe komandovanie i evrei vo vremia Pervoi mirovoi voiny: prichiny formirovaniia negativnogo stereotipa," in *Mirovoi krisis 1914-1920 godov*, 29-46.

[16] Peter Holquist, "To Count, to Extract, and to Exterminate: Population Statistics and Population Politics in Late Imperial and Soviet Russia," in *A State of Nations: Empire and Nation-Making in the Age of Lenin and Stalin*, ed. Ronald Grigor Suny and Terry Martin (Oxford, 2001), 115.

[17] On antisemitism in Russia in the late nineteenth and early twentieth centuries, see Budnitskii, *Rossiiskie evrei mezhdu krasnymi i belymi*, 37-41.

sible for both military failures and economic troubles. At the same time, they were absolutely vulnerable. The commanders justified setbacks by citing Jewish "betrayal" and sanctioned violence toward the Jews. The limits of this violence were determined individually in each specific case.

Anti-Jewish violence proliferated from the very first days of World War I, breaking out from *below*, even *before* official sanctions from the military authorities. The period of mobilization, when the troops were concentrated at railway junctions, was marked with a series of attacks on Jews.[18] Attacks occurred later as well, as in August 1915, when the Kherson governor reported "insignificant" disturbances as the reservists were being drafted. This classification included beatings administered by draftees to "Jewish passers-by," the "causing" of two light knife wounds to the Jew Warshavsky, and the stoning of windows in houses that belonged to Jews.[19] To be sure, these were merely trifles compared to the things that were unfolding along the front at the same time.

The Russian High Command ordered mass deportations of Jews from the front line as preventive measures against Jewish espionage and treason. About 250,000 people were deported, and another 350,000 fled to the interior of the country to escape the advancing Germans.[20] Not only Jews were deported. The same fate was shared by Germans, Gypsies, Hungarians, and Turks.[21] The deportations went hand in hand with violence. Suspected Jewish espionage and sympathy with the enemy led to speedy courts-martial with predetermined verdicts. Typically, the problem was dealt with well before it reached a court. As one military judge informed Prince Pavel Dmitrievich Dolgorukov, he "has not had to sign a single death warrant [in cases of "Jewish espionage"— O.B.], since every regimental commander hangs those who look like spies to

---

[18] Eric Lohr, *Nationalizing the Russian Empire: The Campaign against Enemy Aliens during World War I* (Cambridge, MA, 2003), 14. The "recruitment pogrom" was a tradition dating at least to 1904. See Lambroza, "The Pogroms of 1903–1906," 213–16.

[19] D. Amanzholova, ed., *Evreiskie pogromy v Rossiiskoi imperii, 1900–1916* (Moscow, 1998), 231.

[20] According to Mordechai Altshuler's calculations, five hundred to six hundred thousand Jews were deported and evicted in the course of the war ("Russia and Her Jews: The Impact of the 1914 War," *Wiener Library Bulletin* 27, 30/31 [1973]: 14). Jonathan Frankel believes that this figure reached one million by the end of 1915 (see his edited volume *Studies in Contemporary Jewry: An Annual*, 4: *The Jews and the European Crisis, 1914–1921* [Bloomington, IN, 1988]: 6). The most recent studies on the topic are Eric Lohr, "The Russian Army and the Jews: Mass Deportation, Hostages, and Violence during World War I," *Russian Review* 60, 3 (2001): 404–19; Lohr, *Nationalizing the Russian Empire*, 137–45; Lor [Lohr], "Novye dokumenty o rossiiskoi armii i evreiakh vo vremena pervoi mirovoi voiny," *Vestnik Evreiskogo universiteta* 8, 26 (2003): 245–68; and G. Z. Ioffe, "Vyselenie evreev iz prifrontovoi polosy v 1915 gody," *Voprosy istorii*, no. 9 (2001): 85–96.

[21] Nelipovich, "V poiskakh vnutrennego vraga," 59; Lohr, *Nationalizing the Russian Empire*, 121–37, 150–54.

them without the services of the court."[22] According to German sources, over one hundred Jews were executed for suspected espionage in the first weeks of the war.[23] It is quite probable that the total number of victims was much higher. According to a Red Cross worker, several dozen Jews were hanged in Ivangorod alone; but, as he recorded in his diary, "evidently, espionage still seems to flourish among them."[24]

What were the grounds for holding Jews guilty of espionage and treason? Did any factors operate here besides prejudice? It was clearly nonsensical to accuse the Jewish population in its entirety of espionage and collaboration with the enemy and to engage in the preventive deportation of hundreds of thousands of people, including women and children. But were there any real foundations for this policy, as detrimental as it was to the inner stability of the empire? One can hardly doubt the existence of enemy agents among the Jewish population, especially in the border regions. It is also a foregone conclusion that many Jews did not harbor patriotic sentiments toward their unkind Motherland. However, there is a huge distance between dislike and serving the enemy. How many people in fact traversed the distance? This is hard to estimate for at least two reasons. First, espionage suspects were frequently executed without any legal procedures. Second, data based on the indictments issued by courts-martial, which took place in the absence of any legal defense, with the defendants often incapable of speaking Russian and understanding the nature of the charges against them, are hardly indicative. When cases involving Jews were heard by proper military regimental courts with defenders, they almost inevitably ended in acquittal in the absence of any credible evidence.[25]

The deportations were often accompanied by rape, pillage, and pogroms. Looting often occurred under the guise of "requisitioning" and was de facto sanctioned from above. The Staff of the Fourth Army of the Southwestern Front responded to an inquiry about the "procedure of requisitioning in the theater of military action and in the threatened regions": "From the kikes take everything."[26]

It is revealing that the chronicle of the devastation of the Jewish population of Lithuania and Belorussia in the summer and fall of 1915 differs little from

---

[22] S"ezdy i konferentsii Konstitutsionno-demokraticheskoi partii, vol. 3, book 1 (Moscow, 2000), 146.

[23] S. Aschheim, *Brothers and Strangers: The East European Jew in German and German Jewish Consciousness, 1800–1923* (Madison, 1982), 143.

[24] N. N. Vrangel' [Wrangel], baron, *Dni skorbi: Dnevnik 1914–1915 godov* (St. Petersburg, 2001), 77. Entry of 29 October 1914.

[25] Ia. G. Frumkin, *Iz istorii russkogo evreistva. Kniga o russkom evreistve ot 1860-kh godov do revoliutsii 1917 g.* (Jerusalem, Moscow, and Minsk, 2002), 93.

[26] Nelipovich, "V poiskakh vnutrennego vraga," 60–61.

the reports on the pogroms during the Civil War. The pillage and pogroms were mostly perpetrated by the Cossacks and dragoons. In the Kovno region, fifteen localities suffered from pogroms in July 1915. The dragoons killed a Jewish miller and his son near the shtetl of Onikshty for their refusal to surrender the wife and daughter and raped the fourteen-year-old Alta Schmidt near Vol'niki.[27]

In the Vilna region, nineteen shtetls were demolished in August–September 1915. A shtetl called Smorgon' suffered the most. The Cossacks raped women in the synagogue and killed several people. Violence stopped only when the *pogromshchiki* clashed with Jewish soldiers. During the deportations, a certain Leiba Sobol' told a Cossack officer that he could not leave his sick and senile father. The officer promptly shot the old Sobol' and declared that his son was now free to leave Smorgon'. The Cossacks set houses on fire both in Smorgon' and in other places. Some Jews were burnt alive.[28]

The wave of pogroms rolled over Minsk, Volynia, and Grodno provinces. Local peasants took part in the looting of Jewish belongings, just like in Ukraine in 1919. Again, it was mostly the Cossacks who distinguished themselves. Rape was commonplace, and murder was not infrequent. In Lemeshevichi (Pinsk district) three twelve-year-old girls and an eleven-year-old were raped; in Lebedev (Vilno province), most of the rape victims were old women, including some over seventy years of age. In the village of Bereznovka (Borisov district), ten Cossacks raped a seventy-two-year-old woman. Sometimes the raped women were murdered. According to intelligence reports of the Department of Police, all the shtetls and nearly all villages where Jews resided in the western part of Borisov district (Minsk province) were pillaged in September 1915. Cossacks did most of the looting, although mounted uhlans also did their share of robbery and murder. Local peasants took the most active part in pillage and instigation of pillage. The troops imposed "contributions" and demanded under the threat of death deliveries of tobacco and cigarettes.[29]

In Grodno, the population hid in the cellars during fighting with the Germans. Cossacks roamed the city, sticking spades in the earth to find those in hiding. The narrator (Bronislava Brzhenkovskaya) was wounded by a Cossack spade. She was dragged out of the cellar and brought to an officer with the following accusation: "The kikes hide in the cellars and shoot at us." The officer gave orders that all the hiding Jews be hauled out of the cellars and killed, and his orders were followed. When it transpired that the wounded Brzhenkovskaya was Polish, she was freed.[30]

---

[27] "Iz 'chernoi knigi,'" 274–77.
[28] Ibid., 282–83.
[29] Ibid., 292–95; *Evreiskie pogromy v Rossiiskoi imperii*, 233–39.
[30] "Iz 'chernoi knigi,'" 290–91.

9. Shots in the Back

The violence that the Jews of Galicia, these "alien kikes," suffered at the hands of the Russian army far surpassed the ordeal of the Russian Jews. After the Russians invaded Galicia in August 1914, pogroms of varying degrees of destruction and cruelty occurred in Brody, Radzivilov, L'vov, Sokal, and other cities and shtetls. Again, the Cossacks were the most violent. After the establishment of a "normal" occupational regime, the violence subsided, as a rule.[31]

Descriptions of attacks on the Jewish shtetls through which the Russian army passed during the Brusilov Offensive in the spring and summer of 1916 differ little from the pogrom chronicles of 1919. In Buchach, a Jewish soldier of the Russian army witnessed a ten-year-old boy with broken arms, lying next to his mother with a smashed skull and sundered legs, a corpse of a woman raped and then beaten to death, men with smashed heads and gouged eyes, of smothered and burnt bodies.

From the shtetl of Monastyrzhisk, taken over by the Russian army for the second time, all the Jews escaped except for three insane people and one paralyzed person. The last, a man of about sixty, owned several estates. When the Cossacks first stormed into town, they told the man, "You kike, under the Austrians, you were allowed to own land, under the Russians you will eat earth." He was forced to crawl on all fours and dig his nose into the soil, prodded on by whipping. The next day, he was paralyzed.[32]

Humiliation accompanied the violence. In Buchach, soldiers tossed Torah scrolls out of twenty-three synagogues. Altogether, the author of the memoir gathered four poods (about sixty-five kilograms) of Torah scrolls in fifteen towns of Galicia and Bukovina ravaged by the Russian troops. In Monastyrzhisk, one of the synagogues was fashioned into an infirmary, while the other one was used for sewage. A Jewish cemetery was destroyed: graves were opened, marble monuments broken, and the fence around the common grave of German Jewish soldiers smashed.[33]

Wartime antisemitic propaganda effectively molded the image of an alien enemy within and without. In this way, violence against the Jewish population was de facto legalized. Anti-Jewish violence became a common and accepted undertaking for the military. The "model" of the *military pogroms* of the Civil War era was tested well in advance of the Civil War.

---

[31] Ansky, *The Enemy at His Pleasure*, 68–73, 78, 101, 138, 143–44, 158–59, 165–66, etc. See also *The Jews in the Eastern War Zone* (New York, 1916).

[32] Abba Lev, "Razgrom galitsiiskikh evreev v krovavye gody mirovoi voiny (Otryvok iz dnevnika)," *Evreiskaia letopis'* 3 (Leningrad and Moscow, 1924), 174–76. About the author of the cited memoirs, see Ansky, *The Enemy at His Pleasure*, 80–81.

[33] Abba Lev, "Razgrom galitsiiskikh evreev," 174–76.

The February Revolution of 1917 brought equality to the Jews, including the right to become officers. Attitudes toward them in the army, however, changed little.

Soon after the revolution, *Evreiskaia nedelia* (Jewish Week) proclaimed, "today's army is not an army in the typical sense. It is an army of the people, in the full sense of the word . . . The future of Russia, and we with her, are experiencing the dawn of a new, fortunate era where happiness and freedom are being reborn."[34]

This patriotic fervor would, however, soon cool. The "people's" army still bore the prejudices shared by the masses and the military in general. News of the acceptance of a large number of Jews into the officer corps resulted in the adopting of a resolution among a council of soldier's and officer's delegates of a certain regiment expressing their reluctance to *"have Jews as officers in light of their incompetence . . .* [which,] relying on the rule that no officer can be accepted to the regiment without the agreement of all officers, compelled them to warn the new Jewish officers that such promotions would not be accepted by the regiment in question."[35]

In another regiment, seventy-four Jewish soldiers were arrested under the *suspicion* of sympathizing with two deserters.[36] One of the recent Jewish graduates from the Aleksandrovskii Academy, as a result of discrimination against him on the part of his Orthodox comrades and in light of his belief that "Jewish officers will not be able to overcome the antisemitism ingrained in the soldiers," wrote a report to Alexandre Fedorovich Kerenskii requesting to be sent to the front as a common soldier.[37] Solomon Pozner, citing antisemitism in the divisions quartered in Odessa and Pskov, and noting the generally negative attitude in army circles towards Jews, claimed, "It was and so remains—antisemitism in the army."[38]

The image of the Jews as traitors and spies became firmly settled in the mind of the average citizen, and especially in the minds of the military. The archetypal act of treason, the symbolic "stab in the back," materialized in the motif of gunshots fired at retreating forces. These "shots" were variously heard by the Petliurists, by troops of the Volunteer Army, and even by the Reds. The identity of the Jewish perpetrators varied according to circumstances: they might be Bolsheviks or counterrevolutionaries, bourgeoisie or commissars.

---

[34] L. Sh—g, "Pred novoi eroi," *Evreiskaia nedelia*, no. 10–11 (14 March 1917): 5–7.
[35] O. Z., "Osoboe mnenie osobogo polka," *Evreiskaia nedelia*, no. 22 (4 June 1917): 7.
[36] "Khronika," *Evreiskaia nedelia*, no. 22 (4 June 1917): 7.
[37] *Evreiskaia nedelia*, no. 22 (4 June 1917): 30.
[38] S. Pozner, "Antisemitizm v armii," *Evreiskaia nedelia*, no. 34 (27 August 1917): 2. By the second half of May, the military censors had noticed the displeasure of the masses, who had come to believe that "German dominance" had been replaced by a "Jewish" version. Many officers believed that the Jews were planning to seize power (see M. Frenkin, *Russkaia armiia i revoliutsiia, 1917–1918* [Munich, 1978], 250).

This motif had established firm roots in the tradition of civilian pogroms. On a number of occasions during the pogroms of 1881–1882, Jews were accused of firing into crowds with revolvers. Such actions apparently broke the unwritten rule of these events that Jews were "allowed" to resist with physical force, but the use of firearms violated the rules of the game. Local authorities reported that when the use of firearms was reported, "the crowd went wild." It was on such occasions that the few Jewish fatalities of the 1881–1882 period typically occurred. Likewise, the "political pogroms" during the October Days of 1905 were often triggered by shots reportedly fired on a crowd of loyalist demonstrators.

While the main outlines of the motif remained the same, a striking innovation during the war was the feminization of the identity of the gunman—or, rather, gun-woman. Thus a shot purportedly fired at Russian troops by a Jewish girl typically triggered pogroms in Galicia during World War I. In Brody, the daughter of a local hotel owner allegedly fired at Cossacks. The troops murdered the girl and four male Jews and torched part of the city. It was later established that there had been no gunfire, and that no Cossacks were either killed or wounded. In L'vov, in response to "a shot fired by a Jewess from her window," eighteen Jews were murdered and a Jewish block of houses looted. Such "shots" served as signals for the beginning of pogroms in a dozen other places. A member of the State Duma and the organizer of a frontline medical corps, Igor' Petrovich Demidov, reported to Semen Akimovich An-sky that in each town where such incidents were reported, the "shot of the Jewess" was invariably fired from the window of the residence that housed the best shop in town.[39]

Demidov implied that the "shot in the back" was basically a pretext for robbery and looting. In my opinion, the reality may have been both simpler and more complex. The gunshot from behind is a "materialization" of treason already anticipated, and a shot fired by a woman indicates a double treachery. This is a "wandering" motif that emerges at different times under varying circumstances. One might note the widespread legends of female sharpshooters that became so widespread during the First Chechen War and even provided the storyline for a popular Russian film, *Blokpost* (The Blockhouse).[40] Equally well known were legends of the so-called "White Pantyhose," the young female snipers from the Baltic states of the former Soviet Union, who fought on the side of the Chechen separatists during the First Chechen War. No one has ever

---

[39] Ansky, *The Enemy at His Pleasure*, 68–70, 88; S. A. An-sky, "Razrushenie Galitsii" (manuscript).
[40] The plot of *The Blockhouse* centers on a Chechen girl who procures the sexual services of her sister, who had previously been "spoilt" (raped) by Russian soldiers. The soldiers pay with the hardest currency in the Caucasus—gun cartridges. The young souteneuse, who also happens to be a sniper, then uses the cartridges to kill her clients.

seen or identified any such Baltic sharpshooters in Chechnya, but this did not deter some Russian newspapers from treating their existence as proven fact.

The gunshots of Jewish snipers continued to be heard by members of various armed groups as the Great War merged into the Civil War. While staging a panicked retreat in the spring of 1918 under the blows of the German army, Red Army soldiers responsible for several pogroms in the northern districts of Chernigov province claimed that the "kikes shoot down the Red Army," that they are "all counterrevolutionaries," and that they enthusiastically welcome the Germans.[41] At the same time, an instructor of the military commissariat in Kursk by the name of Fomin reported to Moscow that members of a Jewish self-defense unit had fired at the retreating Red Army men.[42]

Not only Russians heard gunshots. In Pinsk, on 5 April 1919, Polish legionnaires arrested participants in a local meeting of Zionists, who were discussing the distribution of the aid they received from the United States. Almost all of those arrested (thirty-seven or thirty-five, according to different sources) were taken to the marketplace and machine-gunned. According to the official version, spread by the Polish Telegraph Agency, "even as the city was being taken over, gunshots rained down in the dusk on the advancing uhlans in different districts from the windows of Jewish houses." The meeting was purportedly a gathering of Bolsheviks, and the Poles had found "tremendous stores of weaponry."[43]

The soldiers of Petliura, in turn, were assured at the beginning of 1919 that the Jews "created their own special regiments, that they support the old regime and fight for the landowners, that they were firing from the windows at the rebelling people, and even scalded the insurgent masses with boiling water from their windows."[44]

While units of the volunteer army and the Bolsheviks fought over Kiev in October 1919, rumors spread among the Whites, who apparently possessed more imagination than the Ukrainian peasants who formed the backbone of Petliura's forces, that the Jews poured not only boiling water but also sulfuric acid over "our nurses." An officer "with a university badge on his lapel"

---

[41] M. Ionovich, "Na krasnom fronte," *Rassvet*, no. 18 (26 May 1918): 9.
[42] I. M. Cherikover, *Antisemitizm i pogromy na Ukraine, 1917–1918* (Berlin, 1923), 152–53; S. Agurskii, *Evreiskii rabochii v kommunisticheskom dvizhenii (1917–1921)* (Minsk, 1926), 152.
[43] "Zverstva poliakov v Pinske," *Khronika evreiskoi zhizni*, no. 16 (9 May 1919): 10–13. The "Pro-Polish" version of the event is in Norman Davies, *White Eagle, Red Star: The Polish-Soviet War, 1919-20* (London, 1972), 47–48. Murders of Jews also marked the occupation of Vilno by Polish troops in April 1919 (Davies, *White Eagle, Red Star,* 240).
[44] Iv. Nazhivin, *Zapiski o revoliutsii* (Vienna, 1921), 179, 196.

declared that the "kikes cut up our soldiers, throw boiling water and *burning* tar over the nurses, and help the Bolsheviks."[45]

Immediately after the Whites' return to Kiev, a local newspaper, *Vechernye ogni* (Evening Fires), published a list of houses and apartments from which Jews had fired at troops of the retreating volunteer army and poured sulfuric acid and boiling water over them. A special commission checked the addresses on the list and refuted the newspaper's information. It might seem that any rational evaluation would have seen the incongruous nature of these charges without the need to verify addresses: events were not unfolding in a medieval fortress, nor at the time of the Tatar Yoke. Given the circumstances, gunshots from the windows of one's *own* house could only signal the shooter's extreme foolishness, or some suicidal impulse.[46] Nonetheless, further investigations were conducted in order to establish that puffs of smoke emanating from the windows of Jewish apartments in Kiev were caused by ricocheting bullets rather than fusillades fired by the residents.

The commander of a Red Army regiment, fighting its way through the Polish-held town of Białystok at the end of August 1920, reported that he "was forced to fight more with the population of Białystok than with the Polish troops, while the Jewish population took an active part in the hostilities."[47] Most likely, this was the echo of the stereotype deeply etched onto the minds of the Russian military, regardless of the uniform they happened to wear, of Jewish "shots in the back." All the political intelligence reports arising from the Soviet-Polish War indicate that the Jewish population supported only the Reds.

Only in the bitterness of defeat and exile did some participants in the Civil War reconsider the "shots in the back" syndrome. In his memoirs, the former commander in chief of the volunteer army, General Anton Ivanovich Denikin, acknowledged that "alongside actual facts, there were simulations— to cover up violence already committed—that the notorious gunshots were often of 'Christian,' and sometimes even of mythical origin. But mutual hatred dimmed minds, any hostile action from the Jews was *objectively* possible, and the masses accepted all the accusations—whether true or false—at face value."[48]

---

[45] V. A. Poliakov, "Zhutkie dni na Ukraine," *Evreiskaia letopis'* 2 (Petrograd and Moscow, 1923): 21–23. A nurse was brought to Slobodka, where the Whites were stationed. The nurse had allegedly been showered with sulfuric acid by "zhidy." It soon transpired that she had toppled a cistern of boiling water onto herself (ibid., 32–33). But such a banality was of little interest to anyone.

[46] V. A. Poliakov, "Pytka strakhom," *Evreiskaia letopis'*, 3:61.

[47] *Pol'sko-sovetskaia voina 1919–1920 (Ranee ne opublikovannye dokumenty i materialy)*, pt. 2 (Moscow, 1994), 5–6.

[48] A. I. Denikin, *Ocherki russkoi smuty*, vols. 4–5 (Moscow, 2003), 5:538–39.

The theoretically *possible*, when the military of all sides came in contact with Jews, was often transformed into the *actual*. For example, several Petliurists encountered a Jewish tailor with two daughters, fourteen and eleven years old. Having noticed that the older daughter was carrying scissors, they accused the girls of severing telegraph wires, and promptly cut their tongues, gouged out their eyes, and murdered them.[49] White officers killed a Jewish university student and his wife "for espionage" when they found he was carrying a small address book. The student was an associate of one of the Kiev newspapers who had left the city at the time of the Bolshevik occupation. When the student and his wife hurried back to "liberated" Kiev, they encountered the volunteer army ... and their fate.[50]

The classic literary depiction of the Civil War, Isaac Emmanuilovich Babel's *Red Cavalry*, includes in the story "Berestechko" a matter-of-fact description of the Cossack way of dealing with "espionage" invariably committed by a Jew. "Right under my windows several Cossacks were executing an old Jew with a silver beard for espionage. The old man squealed and tried to break loose. Then Kudria from the machine-gun team took his head and placed it under his arm. The Jew went quiet and steadied his feet apart. Kudria took out a dagger with his right hand, and carefully slaughtered the old man, without getting any of the blood on himself."[51]

When considering the causes of anti-Jewish pogroms during the Civil War, one must not underemphasize the large number of contributing factors. There was the socioeconomic rivalry between the Jews and the local population, exacerbated by the privations of wartime. Antisemitism featured as the trump card in anti-Bolshevik propaganda and as a sincere conviction of many adversaries of Bolshevism who genuinely regarded it as the brainchild of the Jewry.[52] Cossacks in the service of the anti-Bolshevik cause—and sometimes the Bolshevik forces as well—seized the opportunity for rampage and plunder presented by the "fog of war."

---

[49] Ia. Lobach, "Ovruch-Korosten' (Iz pogromnoi epopei na Ukraine)," *Khronika evreiskoi zhizni* 6–7 (February 28, 1919): 24.

[50] V. A. Poliakov, "Zhutkie dni na Ukraine," 25.

[51] Isaak Babel', "Konarmiia," in his *Sobranie sochinenii*, 2 vols. (Moscow 2002), 1:349. The short story *Berestechko* was dated "Berestechko, August 1920." On the attitudes of the "red Cossacks" toward Jews as well as the Red Army in general, see Oleg Budnitskii, "The 'Jewish Battalions' in the Red Army," in *Revolution, Repression, and Revival: The Soviet Jewish Experience*, ed. Zvi Gitelman and Yaacov Ro'i (Lanham, MD, 2007), 15–35; and Budnitskii, "The Reds and the Jews, or the Comrades in Arms of the Military Reporter Liutov," in *The Enigma of Isaac Babel: Biography, History, Context*, ed. Gregory Freidin (Stanford, CA, 2009), 65–81.

[52] Peter Kenez, *Civil War in South Russia, 1919–1920* (Berkeley, CA, 1977), 176–77; Kenez, "Pogroms and White Ideology in the Russian Civil War," in *Pogroms*, 310–11.

9. Shots in the Back

But another factor cannot be discounted: a deeply rooted Orthodox Christian image of the Jews as a treacherous tribe that had betrayed Christ and, given a chance, was prepared to betray Russia and collude with the heathen and alien. This image of traitors was colored with additional hues during World War I. The legend of the "shot in the back" was the concrete expression of these ingrained fears and prejudices. Throughout the war years, the army was subjected to the most intense antisemitic propaganda and, for the first time, obtained a de facto license for violence specifically against Jews. It is not surprising that the seed fell on receptive soil. The Jewish pogroms of 1918–1920 were the zenith and direct continuation of the anti-Jewish violence that started in August 1914.

Translated by Eugene Budnitsky

10. Between External Persecution and National Renaissance

Simon Dubnow's Lachrymose Vision of Russian-Jewish History

Joshua M. Karlip

Over the past three decades, historians of the Russian-Jewish experience have examined the relationship of the tsarist state to its Jewish subjects in a comparative context.[1] Historians of Russian Jewry from the late nineteenth through the mid-twentieth centuries, in contrast, advanced a model of Jewish exceptionalism that understood almost all tsarist policies regarding the Jews as animated by vicious antisemitism, created to embitter the lives of Jews as much as possible. This historiographical portrayal of Russian Jewry can be traced back to Simon Markeevich Dubnov ([Dubnow], 1860–1941), the most influential Russian-Jewish historian of the first half of the twentieth century

---

I would like to thank Dr. Harriet Murav and Dr. Eugene M. Avrutin as well as the anonymous reader for their comments, which strengthened the arguments in this essay. Conversations with Dr. Steven J. Zipperstein, Dr. Israel Bartal, and Dr. Michael Brenner helped me refine this chapter's thesis. Special thanks to Dr. Hasia Diner for sharing her unpublished essay on Michael Davitt's work with me. I also thank Shimshon Ayzenberg for serving as my research assistant for this article.

[1] For an analysis of Russian policies toward the Jews as part of the attempts of successive tsarist regimes to integrate the various nationalities of the western provinces into the Russian state, see Michael Stanislawski, *Tsar Nicholas I and the Jews: The Transformation of Jewish Society in Russia, 1825–1855* (Philadelphia, 1983); John Doyle Klier, *Russia Gathers Her Jews: The Origins of the "Jewish Question" in Russia, 1772–1825* (DeKalb, IL, 1986); Klier, *Imperial Russia's Jewish Question 1855–1881* (Cambridge, 1995). For a comparative approach that posited a process of "selective integration" of Jews during the reign of Alexander II, see Benjamin Nathans, *Beyond the Pale: The Jewish Encounter with Late Imperial Russia* (Berkeley, CA, 2002). For a refutation of the myth of government conspiracy in the pogroms of 1881–82, see John Doyle Klier and Shlomo Lambroza, eds., *Pogroms: Anti-Jewish Violence in Modern Russian History* (Cambridge, 1992); and Klier, *Russians, Jews and the Pogroms of 1881–1882* (Cambridge, 2011). For an analysis of legal restriction imposed on Jews by the regimes of Alexander III and Nicholas II from the perspective of larger trends occurring within late imperial Russia, see Hans Rogger, *Jewish Policies and Right-Wing Politics in Imperial Russia* (Berkeley, CA, 1986).

10. Between External Persecution and National Renaissance

and the self-appointed founder of East European Jewish historiography.[2] Dubnow's historiographical vision was intimately linked to his ideology of diaspora nationalism, which envisioned the Jews as an extraterritorial nation deserving of national as well as personal rights in a future democratic Russian state.[3]

In this chapter, I agree with the assessment of several scholars who, over the past decade, have argued that Dubnow's historiographical view of Jewish exceptionalism under tsarist rule had its origins in the late tsarist period itself.[4] Specifically, I use this insight to explore the ways in which Dubnow connected tsarist oppression to Jewish national renaissance in both his publicistic and his scholarly writing. I argue that Dubnow, despite his protestations to the contrary, adopted what the historian Salo Baron referred to as the "lachrymose conception of Jewish history," the tendency to paint the Jewish past in black terms, from his *Wissenschaft des Judentums* predecessors.[5]

---

[2] For Dubnow's claims to be the first Russian Jew to take an interest in the Russian Jewish past, see his manifesto, S. M. Dubnov, *Ob izuchenii istorii russkikh evreev i ob uchrezhdenii istoricheskogo obschestva* (St. Petersburg, 1891). Recently, Israel Bartal argued that despite Dubnow's assertion in this manifesto that Russian Jewry lived only in the present, Hebrew writers of the East European Haskalah, such as Shmuel Yosef Fuenn and Shlomo Buber, critically analyzed such sources as grave inscriptions and archives for the reconstruction of local histories of Jewish communities. Dubnow thus continued, rather than created, a historical consciousness that envisioned the Jews as possessing "a cultural identity of an ethnic group that would replace the pre-modern religious one." Israel Bartal, "'Neither a Future, nor a Past': Simon Dubnow and his Predecessors," presented at the International Conference, *Historicizing the Jewish People: Simon Dubnow at 150* (Leipzig, 4 November 2010). Benjamin Nathans argued that it was Russian-Jewish lawyers at the end of the nineteenth century, rather than Dubnow, who truly founded Russian-language Russian Jewish historiography. See Nathans, "On Russian-Jewish Historiography," in *Historiography of Imperial Russia: The Profession and Writing of History in a Multinational State*, ed. Thomas Sanders (Armonk, NY, 1999), 397–432; and Nathans, *Beyond the Pale*, 315–20.

[3] S. M. Dubnov, *Pis'ma o starom i novom evreistve (1897–1907)*, rev. and enl. ed. (St. Petersburg, 1907). For a full Yiddish translation, see S. M. Dubnov, *Briv vegen altn un nayem yidntum*, trans. Moshe and Shaul Ferdman (Mexico City, 1959). For an abridged English translation, see Simon Dubnow, *Nationalism and History: Essays on Old and New Judaism*, ed. and trans. Koppel S. Pinson (Philadelphia, 1961).

[4] See Anke Hilbrenner, "Simon Dubnov's Master Narrative and the Construction of a Jewish Collective Memory in the Russian Empire," *Ab Imperio*, no. 4 (2003): 143–64; Jeffrey Veidlinger, "Simon Dubnow Recontextualized: The Sociological Conception of Jewish History and the Russian Intellectual Legacy," *Simon Dubnow Institute Yearbook* 3 (2004): 411–27; Simon Rabinovitch, "The Dawn of a New Diaspora: Simon Dubnov's Autonomism, from St. Petersburg to Berlin," *Leo Baeck Institute Year Book* 50 (2005): 267–88; and Rabinovitch, "Alternative to Zion: The Jewish Autonomist Movement in Late Imperial and Revolutionary Russia" (Ph.D. diss., Brandeis University, 2007).

[5] Salo Baron, "Ghetto and Emancipation: Shall We Revise the Traditional View?" *Menorah Journal* 14, 6 (1928): 515–26.

203

In his critique of *Wissenschaft des Judentums*, Dubnow had argued against its reduction of the Jewish experience to *leidensgeschichte* (the history of suffering) and of the twin axes of *lernen und leiden*, study and persecution. Dubnow similarly declared his intention to move away from the historiographical tradition of his Russian-Jewish lawyer predecessors who limited their studies to an explication of anti-Jewish tsarist legislation. Rather than writing about what others did to the Jews, Dubnow sought to write a national history that emphasized the communal, social, and political accomplishments of the Jewish people itself.[6] Yet, in reality, Dubnow's historiography did not transcend these intellectual legacies but rather incorporated them into its nationalist vision.[7] This adoption made sense given the similarities between the struggles for emancipation by late imperial Russian Jewry and its German predecessor. Both communities turned to historiography during their respective protracted struggles for emancipation.[8]

This study, moreover, furthers the recent scholarship on Dubnow's historiography by discussing the ideological reasons behind Dubnow's failure to accomplish his stated goal of writing a truly "sociological" history of Russian Jewry. In his desire to portray the history of Russian Jewry as "a living national organism," Dubnow envisioned tsarist persecution as a catalyst to national consolidation and renaissance.[9] Dubnow, therefore, combined the legacies of both German *Wissenschaft des Judentums* and the school of Russian-Jewish historiography that concentrated on anti-Jewish legislation. He refashioned

---

[6] S. M. Dubnov, *Weltgeschichte des Judischen Volkes Von seinem Uranfangen biz zur Gegenwart* (Berlin, 1928), 1:xiv–xv. For an English translation, see Simon Dubnow, "A Sociological Conception of Jewish History," *Menorah Journal* 14, 3 (1928): 257–67. For a discussion of the relationship of Dubnow's history to that of Graetz, see Frankel, "S. M. Dubnov: Historian and Ideologist," 12–17; and Robert Seltzer, "From Graetz to Dubnow: The Impact of the East European Milieu on the Writing of Jewish History," in *The Legacy of Jewish Migration: 1881 and Its Impact*, ed. David Berger (New York, 1983), 49–60. Also see Koppel S. Pinson, "Simon Dubnow: Historian and Political Philosopher," in Dubnow, *Nationalism and History*, 3–65. For a discussion of Dubnow's repudiation of the emphasis on law in Russian-Jewish historiography, see Nathans, "On Russian-Jewish Historiography," 413–19.

[7] Simon Dubnow, *History of the Jews of Russia and Poland: From the Earliest Times until the Present Day*, trans. I. Friedlaender, 3 vols. (Philadelphia, 1916, 1918, 1920).

[8] Regarding this particular point, I disagree with Hilbrenner's assessment of a radical divergence between the goals of *Wissenschaft* and Russian-Jewish scholarship. See Hilbrenner, "Simon Dubnov's Master Narrative," 144–45. For the historical context regarding the struggle for emancipation in both Russia and Germany, see Nathans, *Beyond the Pale*, 367–81; and Ismar Schorsch, "Ideology and History in the Age of Emancipation," in Heinrich Graetz, *The Structure of Jewish History and Other Essays*, trans., ed., and intro. Ismar Schorsch (New York, 1975), 1–62.

[9] Nathans has argued that Dubnow's conception of "sociological" history had little to do with the discipline of sociology but much to do with his desire to portray the Jewish people as a "living national organism" ("On Russian-Jewish Historiography," 416).

10. Between External Persecution and National Renaissance

these legacies, especially that of lachrymose historiography, for his nationalist metanarrative of crisis leading to Jewish national renaissance. In fact, Dubnow argued implicitly that *leiden* begot *lernen*, that Jewish suffering in Russia led to Jewish national renaissance. As early as the 1890s, Dubnow applied this schema to the entire Diaspora Jewish experience. Taking a page from his *Wissenschaft* predecessors, Dubnow described the leitmotif of the Diaspora Jewish experience as "to think and to suffer."[10] Contrasting the emphasis on physical might among other nations with the Jews' spirituality, he wrote of this period: "It gives heartrending expression to the spiritual strivings of a nation whose brow is resplendent with the thorny crown of martyrdom. It breathes heroism of the mind that conquers bodily pain. In a word, Jewish history is history sublimated."[11]

As Michael Brenner recently elucidated, whereas Dubnow presented *leiden*, or Jewish persecution, in the same lachrymose tone as did his German predecessor, he transformed the meaning of *lernen* from a concentration on religious texts to the emergence of a Jewish national consciousness and culture.[12]

This chapter focuses on Dubnow's publicistic and historiographic writings between 1912 and 1917 in an effort to analyze his adaptation of lachrymose historiography to the Russian context. In particular, I engage in a close reading of sections of Dubnow's *History of the Jews of Russia and Poland*, written by Dubnow between 1913 and 1916 but published between 1916 and 1920 by the Jewish Publication Society of America. Israel Friedlaender (1876–1920) commissioned this work and translated it into English. This analysis demonstrates Dubnow's metanarrative of Russian-Jewish martyrdom paving the way for national liberation. Despite the great attention paid to Dubnow's historiographical *oeuvre* in the last decade, few studies have addressed the issue of Dubnow's dramatic articulation of this narrative, particularly in the years of World War I. It was at this time when Russian Jews experienced

---

[10] S. M. Dubnow, *Jewish History: An Essay in the Philosophy of History*, trans. Israel Friedlaender (Philadelphia, 1903), 19. This essay originally appeared in German, also translated from the Russian by Israel Friedlaender. For this quotation in the original German, see S. M. Dubnow, *Die Jüdische Geschichte: Ein geschichtsphilosophischer Versuch. Autorisierte Übersetzung aus dem Russischen von J.F.* (Berlin, 1898), 8. Without an extant original Russian text, it is impossible to compare it to the German translation. Given that the translation was authorized by Dubnow, however, one can assume that it represented the meaning of the original. Friedlaender's English version from 1903 translated the German text faithfully. A 1927 English edition of the essay published by the JPS reprinted the 1903 translation without any changes.

[11] Dubnow, *Jewish History*, 21. For the German original, see Dubnow, *Die Jüdische Geschichte*, 9.

[12] Michael Brenner, "Graetz and Dubnow: A Juxtaposition," presented at the International Conference "Historicizing the Jewish People: Simon Dubnow at 150" (Leipzig, 4 November 2010).

both unprecedented suffering under the *ancien régime* and hoped for an amelioration of their political and national status at the war's end. A historical study of tsarist treatment of the Jews would inspire Dubnow's fellow Jews at home and abroad to struggle for the attainment of Jewish rights at the war's end. An emphasis on the rise of Jewish national culture in the wake of this persecution eased Dubnow's own anxieties about the possibilities of assimilation in the wake of emancipation.

In his *History of the Jews of Russia and Poland*, Dubnow repeatedly invoked the metaphor of war to describe the relationship of the tsarist government to its Jews. In this regard, Dubnow dramatically diverged from the perspective of his *Wissenschaft* predecessors, who looked to the nineteenth-century German states as potential sources for the emancipation of the Jews.[13] In contrast, Dubnow argued that what he labeled the "thirty years' war" of the tsarist government against the Jews, begun in 1881, proved that only the gradual transition of Russia into a liberal democracy could bring about Jewish emancipation in Russia. This essay thus begins with a brief analysis of Dubnow's publicistic article from 1912, the height of the era of tsarist reaction, in which he first employed this metaphor of the "thirty years' war."

The fact that this article expressed the schema of national martyrdom leading to national rebirth helps address the methodological question of the extent to which Friedlander shaped the narrative of the three-volume history through his translation. Dubnow did give Friedlaender permission to abridge and edit his work, provided that he would not alter its basic meaning.[14] The strong presence in these three volumes of Dubnow's metahistorical schema, which he had developed several years earlier, demonstrates that Friedlaender followed Dubnow's request in not altering the basic theme of the text. The chapter ends with a brief analysis of Dubnow's reaction to the February Revolution, which he understood in light of his metanarrative as the event that would lead to the transition from the darkness of tsarist oppression to the light of personal and national emancipation.

---

[13] Schorsch, "Ideology and History in the Age of Emancipation," 9–31.
[14] English translation of Dubnow to Friedlaender, 13 (26) December 1913, as quoted in Moshe Davis, "Jewry, East and West (The Correspondence of Israel Friedlaender and Simon Dubnow)," *YIVO Annual* 9 (1954): 27. Dubnow's original letter, not included in this article, was in Hebrew.

The Lachrymose Conception of Jewish History

To understand this metanarrative, we must understand the dynamics of the lachrymose conception of Jewish history. In his celebrated 1928 essay, "Ghetto and Emancipation," Baron argued that nineteenth-century German-Jewish historians adopted the lachrymose conception as a tool in their battle for Jewish emancipation.[15] David Engel recently argued that the lachrymose conception of Jewish history emerged as part of the reevaluation of the Diaspora experience that occurred in the wake of the French Revolution. Whereas the Jewish religious tradition understood the Diaspora as an unfortunate, temporary condition brought about by sin, the emancipated Jewries of West and then Central Europe came to view their present in the Diaspora as highly advantageous and permanent. By portraying the preemancipation history of the Jewish Diaspora in dark, lachrymose terms, recently emancipated French Jews could revel in their transition from slavery to freedom.[16] Nineteenth-century proponents of *Wissenschaft des Judentums* used lachrymose history both to present this reinterpretation of the Diaspora to their readers and to inspire them to struggle for emancipation.[17]

Paradoxically, it was Dubnow's ideology of diaspora nationalism that led him to embrace the lachrymose conception of Jewish history. Renée Poznanski observed that in the aftermath of the Kishinev pogrom of 1903, Dubnow moved "from a view of the Jews as a people *despite* the Diaspora to a view of the Jews as a people *because* of the Diaspora." The often dark conditions of the Diaspora, argued Dubnow, forced the Jews to develop their system of communal autonomy, which ensured their eternality as a nation.[18] Persecution thus led to national consolidation. In response to Friedlaender's criticism that Dubnow had concentrated too much on political history to the detriment of culture, Dubnow responded with his historiographical perspective that "history is essentially the development or decline of the national self in relation to the environment."[19] Only a lachrymose portrayal of the Jews' legal and social status in the tsarist empire, therefore, could lead

---

[15] Salo Baron, "Ghetto and Emancipation."
[16] David Engel, *Historians of the Jews and the Holocaust* (Stanford, CA, 2010), 28–84.
[17] Schorsch, "The Lachrymose Conception of Jewish History," in Schorsch, *From Text to Context: The Turn to History in Modern Judaism* (Boston, 1994), 376–88.
[18] Rabinovitch, "The Dawn of a New Diaspora," 281–82. For the original quotation, see Renée Poznanski, "Dubnov and the Diaspora," in *A Missionary for History: Essays in Honor of Simon Dubnov*, ed. Kristi Groberg and Avraham Greenbaum (Minneapolis, MN, 1998), 5–11. The quotation cited is on 5.
[19] Dubnow to Friedlander, 13 (26) December 1913, quoted in Davis, "Jewry, East and West," 27.

to an adequate appreciation of their heroism in forging a national culture in reaction to these conditions.

Inspiring National Renaissance during the Years of Reaction

After P. A. Stolypin's 1907 *coup d'état* ended the brief flourishing of Russian-Jewish mass politics that had occurred in the aftermath of the 1905 revolution, many Jewish political and cultural activists turned to Yiddish scholarship and cultural production.[20] Both politically and culturally, a centrist position emerged between the Jewish Labor Bund and the Zionists that presented Jewish national concerns to Russian and Yiddish readers. Representative of this centrist turn was the appearance of the highbrow Jewish nationalist but non-Zionist Russian-language journal *Evreiskii mir*, for which Dubnow served on the editorial board and published articles. The journal's transformation from a Russian-language to a Yiddish-language periodical of the same name *(Yidishe velt)* mirrored the younger diaspora nationalist intelligentsia's embrace of the Yiddishist desire to create a highbrow culture in the Jewish vernacular.[21] In the opening editorial, the editors urged cultural work and political activism as a response to tsarist reaction.[22]

In his article for this inaugural issue of *Yidishe velt*, Dubnow echoed this theme by cautioning against despair and against the Zionist interpretation of tsarist reaction as proof of the untenability of Jewish life in the Diaspora. Just as during past periods of persecution, so too in the present era were Jews demonstrating "the strong will to live of an old historical people."[23] Martyrs, no less than active heroes, had the power to save the nation.[24] Russian Jewry

---

[20] For a discussion of the emergence of Jewish mass politics in the wake of the 1905 revolution, see Jonathan Frankel, *Prophecy and Politics: Socialism, Nationalism, and the Russian Jews* (Cambridge, 1981), 133–70. For a discussion of the response of these new political parties to tsarist reaction, see Vladimir Levin, "The Jewish Socialist Parties in Russia in the Period of Reaction," in *The Revolution of 1905 and Russia's Jews*, ed. Stefani Hoffman and Ezra Mendelsohn (Philadelphia, 2008), 111–27.

[21] Joshua Karlip, "The Center That Could Not Hold: 'Afn sheydveg' and the Crisis of Diaspora Nationalism" (Ph.D. diss., Jewish Theological Seminary of America, 2006), 90–92. For an argument that links the rise of Yiddish scholarship and publicistics to the aftermath of the revolution of 1905, see Barry Trachtenberg, "The Revolutionary Origins of Yiddish Scholarship, 1903–1917," in *The Revolution of 1905 and Russia's Jews*, 174–84. For another perspective that questions this causal nexus, see Kenneth B. Moss, "A Jewish Cultural Revolution? Revolutionary and Evolutionary Dynamics in the East European Jewish Cultural Sphere, 1900–1914," in *The Revolution of 1905 and Russia's Jews*, 185–98.

[22] "Undzer veg," *Di yidishe velt*, no. 1 (1912): 3–5.

[23] Dubnov, "Nokh draysik-yorikn krig," *Di yidishe velt*, no. 1 (1912): 7.

[24] Ibid.

10. Between External Persecution and National Renaissance

reached great spiritual heights in proportion to the external oppression that it had endured. In 1911, argued Dubnow, the Jewish press had failed to mark the thirtieth anniversary of the war that the Russian government had declared against the Jews with the initiation of pogroms in 1881. Dramatically, Dubnow wrote: "The spring days of the year 1881 belong to the great national anniversaries in Jewish history, such as the spring days of the year 1096 (the Crusades), the summer days of 1492 (the Spanish Expulsion) or of 1648 (the Ukrainian massacres). From all these days were drawn tens and hundreds of years of afflictions and persecutions."[25]

At first glance, it appears jarring that a sober historian such as Dubnow would enshrine the pogroms of 1881, marked by large-scale destruction of property and terror but by little loss of life, in the pantheon of the greatest mass murders and expulsion of Jewish life in the Diaspora. Such a depiction, however, fit neatly with his historiographical assertion that spiritual and cultural renaissance often followed on the heels of Jewish catastrophe.[26] Anke Hilbrenner sought to understand Dubnow's concentration on the catastrophic as his attempt to transmute the premodern "sacral" Jewish conception of the repeating cycles of Jewish oppression into a nationalist conception of a "similarity of Jewish destinies" that forged the "'Jewish national soul.'"[27]

His portrayal of 1881 as part of a schema of suffering and renaissance, however, also demonstrates the manner in which Dubnow's historiography often merged with his political and cultural ideology. This ideological triumphalism emerged in his declaration of a polemical victory for Jewish nationalism over Russian-Jewish assimilationists and apostates:

> Have we lost the 30-year battle for our existence, which we conducted under such terrible conditions? ... No, as always in our long history, the oldest cultural nation withstood the new difficult test ... The final analysis demonstrates that in rightlessness and political slavery we remained internally free, with a burning yearning for freedom; that external humiliation awoke within us national pride; that fleeing from the Jewish camp—as often as it occurred recently—is nonetheless an exception and not a rule.[28]

---

[25] Ibid., 8.
[26] Frankel, "S. M. Dubnov," 15. As early as 1903, Dubnow compared the Kishinev pogrom to the Chmielnicki and Haidamak massacres. See Frankel, "S. M. Dubnov," 19. For the original, see Dubnov, "Istoricheskii moment," *Voskhod: Nedel'naia khronika*, no. 21 (22 May 1903): 5.
[27] Hilbrenner, "Simon Dubnov's Master Narrative," 153–55. The quotation from Dubnov comes originally from Dubnov, *Die Jüdische Geschichte*, 13. For the English translation, which agrees with that of Hilbrenner, see Dubnow, *Jewish History*, 28.
[28] Dubnov, "Nokh draysik-yorikn krig," 10.

Russian Jewry had reacted to the events of 1881–1882 by producing a new intelligentsia that had created a national Jewish politics and culture. Even emigration from Russia led to national renewal through the creation of two new Jewish centers, the United States and Palestine.[29] Dubnow urged his readers that they must continue the national struggle. In his words: "Let us further conduct the difficult historical war—the most beautiful and holiest that an oppressed nation can conduct. If we now lack the strength of heroes, let us go into the ancient battle with that fire of martyrs, of the tortured, the persecuted, which lies very deep in the Jewish soul, which only must be uncovered in order to be transformed into a powerful, moving, and enlivening power."[30]

Unlike German-Jewish historians, Dubnow engaged in a process of enshrining recent and contemporary, rather than distant, events into the pantheon of Jewish martyrdom. By arguing that Russian Jewry had reacted to its suffering through national renaissance, he pointed toward what he viewed as the ready-made antidote to the assimilatory excesses that had resulted from West European Jewish emancipation. Russian Jewry, purified in the crucible of tsarist suffering, would react to its eventual political liberation not through assimilation but rather through national cohesion. This dual usage of the image of the Russian-Jewish martyr as both progenitor of emancipation and representative of preemancipatory Jewish national solidarity fit well with Dubnow's own ambivalence about the legacy of Jewish emancipation. It equally matched his conception of Jewish national autonomy as the Hegelian synthesis between premodern Jewish separateness and Jewish emancipation.[31]

Israel Friedlaender, the JPS, the Great War, and the Commissioning of Dubnow's *History*

It was Israel Friedlaender who commissioned the publication of Dubnow's three-volume history for the Jewish Publication Society of America (JPS). Proposing in 1906 that the JPS translate and publish Dubnow's multivolume *History of the Jews*, Friedlaender was satisfied several years later when the

---

[29] Ibid., 9–10.
[30] Ibid., 11–12.
[31] See Dubnov, *Pis'ma o starom i novom evreistve*, 74–112. I owe much of this insight regarding the conflicted dual role of the Russian-Jewish "martyr" in works of Russian-Jewish historiography to Olga Litvak's analysis of late tsarist historiographical and fictional accounts of Jewish conscription during the reign of Nicholas I. See Olga Litvak, *Conscription and the Search for Modern Russian Jewry* (Bloomington, IN, 2006), 171–203.

10. Between External Persecution and National Renaissance

publication society expressed an interest in the much shorter project of a history of the Jews in Russia and Poland. Friedlaender wrote to Dubnow in 1910, arguing that the publication committee believed that the presentation of this work in English "will have a great and beneficial effect upon the standing of the Russian Jews in America."[32]

The commissioning of this project represented a confluence of interest between Friedlaender and the leaders of the JPS. Born in the Ukraine and educated in Germany, Friedlaender believed that American Jewry could emerge as a major center of Jewish culture only if it benefited from the fructifying influence of Russian-Jewish culture. It was this desire to create a synthesis between east and west that led Friedlaender to initiate correspondences with both Dubnow and Ahad Ha'am, and to sacrifice his scholarship in order to translate their works into German and English.[33] For over twenty years, Dubnow and Friedlaender enjoyed a long-distance relationship, first as mentor/student and then as colleagues. As early as 1898, Friedlaender had translated Dubnow's seminal essay on the philosophy of Jewish history into German.[34]

The leaders of the JPS, in the meantime, had their own political goals in publishing Dubnow's work. This publication society had sought to highlight the catastrophic aspects of Russian-Jewish history since its 1903 publication of Michael Davitt's *Within the Pale: The True Story of Anti-Semitic Persecutions in Russia*. This work served as this Irish nationalist journalist's reportage of the Kishinev pogrom. Hasia Diner argued that the powers behind the JPS, such as the American-Jewish leaders Jacob Schiff and Cyrus Adler, commissioned the publication of Davitt's work because of their political goal of preventing the United States from closing its doors to Russian-Jewish immigrants by presenting them as victims of religious and political persecution.[35] The same American-Jewish leaders in the JPS no doubt interested themselves in Friedlaender's proposal of a translation of Dubnow's *History of the Jews of Russia and Poland* for similar reasons.

---

[32] Davis, "Jewry, East and West," 14–15. For the quotation from Friedlaender's letter, see Friedlaender to Dubnow, 6 December 1910, quoted in Davis, "Jewry, East and West," 19.
[33] Ibid., 9–12.
[34] For Dubnow's description of his relationship with Friedlaender, see S. M. Dubnov, *Kniga zhizni: Vospominaniia i razmyshleniia. Materialy dlia istorii moego vremeni* (Riga, 1934–40). See 1:339–40, 413; 2:2, 29, 118, 172, 184, 310, 316, 320–21, 323, 355. Also see Dubnow's obituary of Friedlaender, "Israel Friedlaender, pamiati rodnoi dushi," *Evreiskii vestnik* (1922): 1.
[35] Hasia Diner, "Michael Davitt: Irish Nationalism, the Pogroms, and American Jewry," unpublished paper. I would like to thank Dr. Steven Zipperstein for bringing Diner's work on this subject to my attention and for pointing out to me the JPS's continued interest in the catastrophic aspects of Russian-Jewish history.

Initially, neither Friedlaender nor Dubnow shared the JPS leaders' political goal. It was Friedlaender's cultural goal, which Dubnow described as "connect[ing] the American branch of Jewry, which is continually developing and occupying an important place in the future of our people, to its ancient root in the east of Europe" that attracted Dubnow to the project.[36] Regarding the content of that cultural history, Friedlaender and Dubnow differed. Responding to Friedlaender's critique that Dubnow's work dealt with the history of anti-Jewish legislation to the exclusion of cultural history, Dubnow argued that a history of a people, as opposed to literary history, necessitated a discussion of how it responded to its environment.[37] Here, Dubnow hinted at his schema of political repression leading to national renaissance. He made this causal nexus between external politics and Jewish culture explicit in a revealing statement:

> As to the political side, to which you consider excessive space has been given, I ought to explain that it has been done with a special purpose, a scientific purpose, of course; by no means a political purpose. In my opinion Russia has a special mission as Spain had in her day. Russia originated the political inquisition, as Spain originated the religious inquisition, and this peculiar mission engraved its mark on the life of Israel in the northern country. I endeavor to describe this influence in our history as a historical type of a special kind.[38]

Dubnow also made clear to Friedlaender that this "influence ... of a special kind" manifested itself in the emergence of secular nationalist culture among Russian Jews rather than in the "static" aspects of religious life that interested Friedlaender. In contrast to Friedlaender the theologian, Dubnow, the architect of secular Jewish identity, envisioned the history of "Rabbinism and Hassidism" in nineteenth-century Eastern Europe as one of "sterility and decline." By seeking to concentrate on the "dynamic" rather than the "static," Dubnow in reality was arguing that external tsarist repression had led to the emergence of secular Jewish national culture.[39]

The outbreak of World War I occurred in the midst of Dubnow's and Friedlaender's collaborative effort. During the war, Russian Jews looked to American Jewry in the hope that it could represent their plight to the U.S.

---

[36] Dubnow to Friedlaender, 26 December 1910, as quoted in Davis, "Jewry, East and West," 20. This article wrongly provides the date of 1901, rather than 1910, for the writing of this letter. Given that Dubnow wrote this letter as a reply to Friedlaender's letter dated 6 December 1910, the date of 1901 rather than 1910 is clearly a typographical error.

[37] Dubnow to Friedlaender, 13 (26) December 1913, in Davis, "Jewry, East and West," 27.

[38] Ibid., 28.

[39] Ibid., 27.

government and to the international community. During the crucible of war, Russian Jewry came to hope that the war's end also would solve its own anomalous situation.[40] At the same time, the first years of the war witnessed the de facto, if not the de jure, end of the Pale of Settlement. With hundreds of thousands of Jews expelled from the front, Russian Jewry experienced its first mass taste of the Russian interior not as emancipated citizens but rather as war refugees. Ideologues of Jewish national emancipation could not fail to take note of this historical irony.[41] As a compact group living on contiguous territory under the same political regime, Russian Jewry no longer existed. Rather, the forced migration of Jews to the Russian interior coupled with the loss of areas of the Pale to foreign armies indicated yet another step in the creation of a Russian-Jewish diaspora, begun thirty-five years before with the onset of large-scale emigration.[42]

These political and national realities granted Dubnow's and Friedlaender's work a new sense of timeliness and urgency. Soon after the war's outbreak, Dubnow expressed to Friedlaender his hope for an expedited timetable for the publication of the translation, arguing that the project now assumed "a special social significance, serving as material for a question that is destined to become an object of international discussion."[43] The urgent political plight of Russian Jewry during the war led Dubnow to propose the publication of the part of the book dealing with the period beginning in 1881 as a separate pamphlet to serve as a "*Vademecum* for the contemporary Jewish problem in its entire historic complication."[44] The JPS leaders rejected this request but agreed to publish Dubnow's work even before its translation of the Bible, due to its pressing political relevance.[45] Significantly, Dubnow informed

---

[40] Frankel, "An Introductory Essay: The Paradoxical Politics of Marginality. Thoughts on the Jewish Situation During the Years 1914–1921," *Studies in Contemporary Jewry* 4 (1988): 4.

[41] For an example of an autonomist's ambivalence over the de facto abolition of the Pale, see Elias Tcherikower, "Yidishe proyekten vegn sibir," *Yidisher kongres* 1, 14 (12 November 1915): 2–3.

[42] Litvak, *Conscription and the Search for Modern Russian Jewry*, 172–74.

[43] Dubnow to Friedlaender, 1 September 1914, quoted in both the Russian original and in English translation in Davis, "Jewry, East and West," 33–34. For Friedlaender's concurring response, see Friedlaender to Dubnow, 14 May 1915, as quoted in Davis, "Jewry, East and West," 40.

[44] Dubnow to Friedlaender, 21 June 1915, as quoted in both Russian and English in Davis, "Jewry, East and West," 41–43.

[45] See letter from Israel Friedlaender to Henrietta Szold, 27 July 1915, as quoted in Davis, "Jewry, East and West," 43–44 n. 12. Also see Davis's comments there about the reasons behind the JPS's decision.

Friedlaender that he intended to title his section on the period from 1881 to 1911 "The Thirty Years' War."[46]

During the second half of 1915 and the first half of 1916, Dubnow worked feverishly on this last section, never before having written about the past thirty years from a historical perspective.[47] Although the tsarist censor withheld this last section, Dubnow sent Friedlaender the rest of the manuscript by 1916. In the immediate aftermath of the February Revolution, he sent Friedlaender the final section. Even though volumes 2 and 3 did not appear until 1918 and 1920, Dubnow had completed them in the final days of the *ancien régime*.[48]

Dubnow's Metahistorical Schema in *History of the Jews of Russia and Poland*

Dubnow himself best articulated the heightened meaning of his metahistorical narrative of lachrymose history and national renaissance during World War I:

> At the end of the eighteenth century, when Western Europe had just begun the emancipation of the Jews, the latter were subjected in the East of Europe to every possible medieval experiment... His [Alexander II's] tragic death in 1881... has again thrown millions of Jews into the dismal abyss of medievalism.
>
> ... Russia created a lurid antithesis to Jewish emancipation at a time when the latter was consummated not only in Western Europe, but also in the semi-civilized Balkan States... But Russian Judaeophobia... produced a system aiming not only at the disfranchisement, but also at the direct physical annihilation of the Jewish people... The year 1881 marks the starting-point of this systematic war against the Jews, which has continued until our own days, and is bound to reach a crisis upon the termination of the great world struggle.[49]

---

[46] Dubnow to Friedlaender, 30 September 1915, quoted in both the original Russian and in English translation in Davis, "Jewry, East and West," 46–47.

[47] Dubnow to Friedlander, 16 April 1915; Dubnow to Friedlaender, 30 September 1915; Dubnow to Friedlaender, 8 December 1915; Dubnow to Friedlaender, 10 February 1916, quoted in both the Russian original and in English translation in Davis, "Jewry, East and West," 36–39, 46–47, 48–49, 50–52.

[48] See Dubnow to Friedlaender, 21 June 1916, in both the Russian original and English translation; Dubnow to Friedlaender, 12 August 1916; and Friedlaender to Dubnow, 15 June 1917—all in Davis, "Jewry, East and West," 55–58; 59–60; 61–62.

[49] Quoted in Friedlaender, "Translator's Preface," in Dubnow, *History of the Jews of Russia and Poland*, 2:6–7.

Dubnow thus envisioned the history of Russian Jewry from the late eighteenth century through World War I as serving as a tragic counternarrative to the emancipation of West European Jewry. In this contrast of Western Europe with Russia, Dubnow continued in the historiographical tradition of his Russian-Jewish lawyer predecessors. The fact that the triumph of emancipation in Western and Central Europe occurred simultaneously with the Russian government's partial retreat from its experiment of selective integration made this historiographical contrast all but inevitable.[50] Dubnow's labeling of tsarist policies as an example of "medievalism" demonstrates the extent to which he had imbibed the *Wissenschaft des Judentum*'s lachrymose portrayal of Jewish history, since it was the Middle Ages that German-Jewish historians had depicted as the darkest era in Jewish history.[51] As Dubnow had indicated in his correspondence to Friedlaender, his narrative history concentrated largely upon anti-Tsarist legislation, with separate chapters dedicated to Jewish cultural and intellectual history.[52] Dubnow thus applied to the Russian-Jewish experience Graetz's depiction of medieval Jewry reacting to its persecution through spiritual ennoblement, now transmuted into overtly national terms.[53]

The comparison of Jewish suffering under successive tsars to medieval persecution, particularly to that of medieval Spain, appears throughout Dubnow's narrative. Dubnow, for instance, labeled the section regarding the Cantonists, "Military Martyrdom."[54] Admitting that he had relied not on official documents but rather on "traditions current among the people," Dubnow credulously reported a popular story of an entire regiment of Cantonists who deliberately drowned themselves while on the way to their baptism.[55] According to Olga Litvak, Dubnow based his account on a story that was first told in the 1840s about two Jewish recruits who deliberately drowned themselves rather than endure forcible baptism together with the rest of their regiment. First reported in an 1845 issue of the German-Jewish *Allgemeine Zeitung des Judentums*, this story achieved popular acclaim through its retelling in the 1847 epic poem by Ludwig Wihl titled "Die beiden Matrosen" (The Two Sailors). Whereas Wihl spoke only of two victims and set the story in Odessa, Dubnow changed the scene to Kazan and depicted

---

[50] Nathans, "On Russian-Jewish Historiography," 402–3; and Nathans, *Beyond the Pale*, 375–76.
[51] Baron, "Ghetto and Emancipation"; Engel, *Historians of the Jews and Holocaust*, 29–84, especially 67.
[52] Dubnow, *History of the Jews of Russia and Poland*, 2:203–42, 3:40–65.
[53] Schorsch, "Ideology and History in the Age of Emancipation," 56–57.
[54] Dubnow, *History of the Jews of Russia and Poland*, 2:22.
[55] Ibid., 27.

the entire regiment as choosing death over conversion.⁵⁶ What probably so attracted Dubnow to this story and led him to embellish it was its echo of an old Jewish literary motif dealing with acts of martyrdom committed in bodies of water. First appearing in the Babylonian Talmud in reference to the aftermath of the Roman destruction of Judea, this theme resurfaced in different forms in medieval and early modern Jewish texts dealing with martyrdom.⁵⁷

Dubnow, the champion of secular history, turned not to historical sources but rather to religious literature and liturgy in enshrining the Cantonists into the pantheon of Jewish martyrs who had chosen death over forced conversion. Cantonist loyalty to Judaism both posed as a foil in Dubnow's imagination to acculturating Russian Jews' alleged abandonment of tradition and national identity and served as an inspiration for contemporary Russian-Jewish soldiers fighting in World War I. Cantonist memoirists, in contrast, often depicted their military service as the arena in which they ambivalently left their old allegiances to traditional Jewish society behind even as they refused to convert to Christianity.⁵⁸

Returning to the comparison of tsarist Russia to medieval Spain that he had first invoked in a letter to Friedlaender, Dubnow wrote that most Cantonist children withered away in the barracks that functioned as "inquisitorial dungeons."⁵⁹ Comparing the events of 1881 to 1492, Dubnow found irony in the fact that "Ancient Catholic Spain held forth a welcoming hand to the victims of modern Greek-Orthodox Spain."⁶⁰ Alexander III thus became a modern-day Ferdinand, with modern Russia reenacting the persecutory role of medieval Spain. Rather than berate those Jews who had converted to Christianity to stay in Moscow following the expulsion of its Jews in 1891, Dubnow compared their fate to that of the Marranos.⁶¹

It is no coincidence that Dubnow increasingly compared tsarist Russia to medieval Spain. Litvak has argued that Dubnow and other Jewish historians writing during World War I sought to weave the history of Russian Jews into the seamless web of Jewish destiny, particularly at a moment when Russian

---

[56] Litvak, *Conscription and the Search for Modern Russian Jewry*, 191–93.
[57] For the Talmudic passage, see Babylonian Talmud Gittin 57a. For the most notable examples of this literary motif in the Middle Ages and early modern era, see Robert Chazan, *European Jewry and the First Crusade* (Berkeley, CA, 1996); Abraham ibn Daud, *Sefer ha-Qabbalah*, ed. and trans. Gerson Cohen (Philadelphia, 1967), 46–48; Nathan Hannover, *Abyss of Despair (Yeven Metzulah): The Famous 17th-Century Chronicle Depicting Jewish Life in Russia and Poland during the Chmielnicki Massacres of 1648–1649*, trans. Abraham J. Mesch (New Brunswick, NJ, 1983), 53.
[58] Litvak, *Conscription and the Search for Modern Russian Jewry*, 187–93.
[59] Dubnow to Friedlaender, 13 (26) December 1913, as quoted in Davis, "Jewry, East and West," 28; Dubnow, *History of the Jews of Russia and Poland*, 2:27.
[60] Dubnow, *History of the Jews of Russia and Poland*, 2:27.
[61] Ibid., 425.

10. Between External Persecution and National Renaissance

Jewry was ceasing to exist as a geographically compact unit. Just as Jewish chroniclers in the sixteenth century reacted to the expulsion from Spain with a historiographical reconstruction of Sefarad, so too during World War I did Dubnow imagine a Russian Jewry united by national and cultural values. Indeed, during the years of mass emigration, Russian Jews demonstrated an interest in the story of Spanish Jewry, as manifested in the ever-popular Yiddish translations of Solomon in Verga's classic sixteenth-century work, *Shevet Yehudah*. The twin images of expulsion and Marranism fit well with Dubnow's attempt to sacralize the historical experiences of his generation of Russian Jews.[62]

Dubnow's desire to view victims of pogroms and of Russian anti-Jewish policy as martyrs led him to other comparisons taken from traditional Jewish sources and collective memory. Following the death of Alexander III, "the martyred nation stood at the threshold of the new reign with a silent question on its lips: 'What next?'"[63] This statement echoed Exodus 2:23, which described the Children of Israel as crying at the death of Pharaoh. Similarly, Dubnow noted that the expulsion from Moscow coincided with Passover, "as if the eternal people needed to be reminded of the new bondage and of the new Pharaohs."[64] In a clear reference to the biblical account of Pharaoh's decree to kill all first-born male Israelites but to spare the females, Dubnow wrote that, like the ancient Pharaoh, the quota system in Russian pregymnasia applied only to Jewish male students, not to women.[65] He decried this quota system, imposed by "the educational Hamans" as "the spiritual murder of Jewish school children."[66]

As in his 1912 article, in this history, Dubnow expressed his hope that the martyrs of the pogroms and of discriminatory legislation would inspire contemporary Jews to action. He found a modern analogue to the Ten Martyrs of the liturgy in the dramatic tale of ten Jews murdered on their way to defend fellow Jews against a pogrom, whose memory, he declared, should "become sacred to the entire Jewish people."[67] Here we have an example of

---

[62] Litvak, *Conscription and the Search for Modern Russian Jewry*, 191.
[63] Dubnow, *History of the Jews of Russia and Poland*, 2:429.
[64] Ibid., 401.
[65] Ibid., 3:30.
[66] Ibid., 159. Nathans addressed this passage, observing its similarity to "the archetypal approach to Jewish history." He noted that Dubnov later admitted that the quota was extended to Jewish girls. See Nathans, "On Russian-Jewish Historiography," 416 and 430 n. 72.
[67] Ibid., 118. The story of the Ten Martyrs, killed both at the time of the destruction of the Second Temple and during the Hadrianic persecutions, appears most famously in the liturgical poems, "Eleh ezk'rah" and "Arzei Levanon," recited respectively on Yom Kippur and on Tisha B'av.

Dubnow's understanding of martyrdom as inspiration for national heroism.[68] This example also demonstrated how Dubnow transmuted the religious conception of martyrdom into modern, nationalist terms.

In his portrayal of the legal status of Russian Jewry, Dubnow built on Graetz's scholarship as well as his Russian-Jewish predecessors. One of Baron's central arguments regarding the lachrymose conception was that *Wissenschaft* scholars presented Jewish legal status in the Middle Ages in a historical vacuum, without comparing Jewish privileges to the far less advantageous legal status of serfs. The first Russian-Jewish lay historian to produce a narrative history of Russian Jewry, Il'ia Grigor'evich Orshanskii (1846–1875) compared Russian-Jewish legal status to that of emancipated Western Jews rather than to other groups within Russian society. Consequently, he imagined a united Russian citizenry, minus the Jews, possessing uniform legal rights that did not in reality exist. Orshanskii's cohort of lawyer-historians fluctuated between an image of Russian-Jewish exceptionalism under tsarist law and a view of Russian Jewry's legal status as a "barometer" of Russia's political climate.[69]

All these features of this early Russian-Jewish historiography entered into Dubnow's history. For instance, he wrote that the Jews, "the most hapless section of Russian subjects," bore the brunt of Nicholas I's oppression.[70] From this description, the reader would never have realized that the largest group of tsarist subjects, the serfs, had far fewer rights of mobility under Nicholas I than did the Jews. Dubnow also unfavorably compared the legal status of the "three million Jewish serfs" of the Pale of Settlement to the actual serfs whom Alexander II emancipated.[71] When commenting on the irony that Jews died in the Crimean and then in the Russo-Japanese wars when they still suffered from "the whip of rightlessness" at home, Dubnow conjured the image of a Russian citizenry in the Western sense of the word.[72] In his description of the pogroms that followed the declaration of the October Manifesto, Dubnow wrote, "The principal victims of this protracted St. Bartholomew night were the new Huguenots of the emancipation movement—the Jews."[73] The Jews appeared not only as the most persecuted of the tsar's subjects but also as the foremost sacrifices for the liberation of Russia.

In contrast to this depiction of a unified Russian citizenry along Western lines, late tsarist Russia, in reality, functioned on an estates system that determined the different privileges and responsibilities of tsarist subjects.

---

[68] Dubnov, "Nokh draysik-yorikn krig," 7–8.
[69] Nathans, *Beyond the Pale*, 318–20.
[70] Dubnow, *History of the Jews of Russia and Poland*, 2:141.
[71] Ibid., 154.
[72] Ibid., 149 and 3:95.
[73] Ibid., 3:127.

When the government of Alexander II sought to acculturate Jews whom it deemed useful to the state, it did so by incorporating them into the various existing estates. This selective integration led to the creation of a highly stratified Russian Jewry, in which a visible minority possessed the right to live a relatively privileged life outside the Pale while the majority in the Pale enjoyed little access to the world of Russian high society.[74]

Dubnow's motivation for dwelling on tsarist persecution of the Jews and their lack of political rights was, as in his 1912 essay, to argue that external oppression had awakened the Jewish national spirit. Invoking Pushkin's famous metaphor of the hammer both shattering glass and forging steel, Dubnow explained that tsarist persecution "had only helped to steel it [the Jewish people] and to harden its indestructible spiritual self."[75] Russian Jewry survived the stormy years of 1903–1906 only because it reacted to its oppression through the development of a national consciousness. In Dubnow's triumphalist vision, the early Jewish nationalism of the 1880s led inexorably to the adoption of his vision of autonomism by all Jewish political parties between 1905 and 1907.[76] The flowering of Hebrew and Yiddish literature during this period remarkably demonstrated the Jewish ability to react to oppression with cultural renaissance: "As in all previous critical moments in the history of the Jews, the spirit of the nation, defying its new tormentors, has grown stronger in the worn-out body. The Hamans of Russia who have attempted to crush the Eternal People have failed as signally as their predecessors in Persia, Syria, and Byzantium."[77] Contemporary historians, of course, would debate the direct line of cause and effect that Dubnow posited between tsarist oppression and the Jewish national renaissance in *fin-de-siècle* Russia.[78]

Dubnow's history reached its polemical climax in its last several pages, which summarized the fate of Russian Jewry from 1911 to 1916. Compared to

---

[74] Nathans, *Beyond the Pale*, 367–81.
[75] Ibid., 40.
[76] Ibid., 143–45, 53–55.
[77] Ibid., 163–64.
[78] For a more contemporary historical view that perpetuated Dubnov's causal nexus between the tsarist embrace of antisemitism in the 1880s and the rise of Jewish nationalism, see Frankel, *Prophecy and Politics*. Other contemporary historians have sought the origins of Jewish nationalism in the Russian Haskalah movement. See Charles H. Freundlich, *Peretz Smolenskin, His Life and Thought: A Study of the Renascence of Jewish Nationalism* (New York, 1965). Bartal in his "Neither a Future, nor a Past,'" traced the nationalist tendency as far back as the mid-nineteenth century. Bartal and David Fishman argued that the rise of modern Hebrew and Yiddish culture resulted from East European Jewry's modernization during the era of Alexander II's Great Reforms. The proliferation of the Yiddish press occurred similarly as a result of the lifting of tsarist censorship in the wake of the 1905 revolution. See Bartal, *The Jews of Eastern Europe, 1772–1881*, trans. Chaya Naor (Philadelphia, 2002), 102–11; and David E. Fishman, *The Rise of Modern Yiddish Culture* (Pittsburgh, 2005), 18–32.

the pogroms and expulsions that Polish and Russian Jewries endured during the first two years of World War I, "the ancient annals of Jewish martyrdom faded into insignificance."[79] Reaching a rhetorical crescendo, Dubnow concluded his history with a summary of the Jewish people's encounter with tsarist Russia:

> Here the power that dominates history opened up before the Jewish people a black abyss of medievalism in the midst of the blazing light of modern civilization, and finally threw it into the flames of the gigantic struggle of nations. What may the World War be expected to bring to the World-Nation? Full of agitation, the Jew is looking into the future, and the question of his ancient prophet is trembling on his lips: "Ah Lord God! wilt Thou make a full end of the remnant of Israel?" ... Let the entire past of the Jewish people serve as an answer to this question—a people which, in the maelstrom of human history, has succeeded in conquering the two cosmic forces: Time and Space.[80]

Beneath the surface of Dubnow's historiographical and ideological schema rests a barely buried theological belief in Jewish exceptionalism. At the height of World War I, he romantically presented this belief to his American readers in the hope that they would fight for Jewish rights at the end of the war. This dramatic affirmation of faith in the survival of the Jewish people was also directed inward toward Russian Jews both home and abroad to instill in them the faith that they would survive the current conflagration.

After Revolution: Tsarist Persecution as Motivation for Jewish Emancipation

In the immediate aftermath of the February Revolution, Dubnow continued to argue that the Jews had borne the brunt of tsarist despotism; this time to make the case for an amelioration of the Jews' legal status by the provisional government. Dubnow expressed these opinions in a political essay titled *Chego khotiat evrei* ("What Do the Jews Want?"). This essay appeared as a pamphlet in "What Do the Nations of Russia Want?" a series that addressed the national demands of the Ukrainians, the Poles, the Lithuanians, the Georgians, the Muslims, and other such groups. Dubnow began the pamphlet by asserting the Jewish claim to be the most oppressed group under the old regime, attacked by the tsars "not only with the stick of rightlessness" but also

---

[79] Dubnow, *History of the Jews of Russia and Poland*, 3:168.
[80] Ibid., 168–69.

with the stick of pogroms.[81] Alexander III and Nicholas II, argued Dubnow, turned the Russian people against the Jews to distract them from their misery.[82]

Unlike in his history, where Dubnow qualified his portrayal of Jews in the revolutionary movement with a depiction of Jews as loyal, albeit unappreciated, imperial subjects, he now wholeheartedly celebrated Jewish opposition to the tsarist regime. The tsarist regime together with the Black Hundreds, he asserted, unleashed the pogroms of October 1905 as a punishment for the Jews' disproportionate participation in the revolution. With particular pathos, Dubnow described the expulsions and pogroms that Russian Jewry suffered during World War I. After thirty months of war, however, the Russian people finally recognized the tsar as their true enemy, at last understanding antisemitism as the divisive tactic employed by the tsar to maintain his rule.[83] Whereas the old regime's pogroms perpetuated the same kind of persecution that the Jews experienced at the stakes of the Inquisition, the newly liberated Russia would protect Jewish internal freedom.[84] Legalization of Jewish national autonomy would restore a form of historical Jewish self-government that flourished under Polish rule but was crushed by the Romanovs after the Polish partitions.[85] By offering the Jews broad civil and national rights, the new regime could best right the historical wrongs perpetrated by tsarist policy and repay the Jews for their role in the revolution.[86]

Between Graetz and Dubnow: A Reassessment

Studies of Dubnow's historiography have examined the ways in which Dubnow both drew inspiration from and rebelled against Heinrich Graetz and *Wissenschaft des Judentums*.[87] From his debut as a national Jewish historian, Dubnow recognized his debt to Graetz but at the same time argued for a shift

---

[81] S. M. Dubnov, *Chego khotiat evrei* (Petrograd, 1917), 1, 3.
[82] Ibid.
[83] Ibid., 5–10.
[84] Ibid., 31.
[85] Ibid., 14–15.
[86] It is noteworthy that two years after the appearance of this pamphlet, it appeared in a much-abridged English translation as "The Demands of the Jews." Originally thirty pages, the piece now appeared as an eight-page pamphlet. Absent entirely was the first section that dealt with the history of Jewish oppression in the reigns of Alexander III and Nicholas II. The translators clearly hoped that American readers, particularly Jews, would learn about and therefore lobby for Jewish national rights in Russia. In the preface, the translator introduced Dubnov as the author of the three-volume *History of the Jews of Poland and Russia*, published by the Jewish Publication Society during the same years. See S. M. Dubnov, *The Demands of the Jews* (New York, 1919).
[87] Frankel, "S. M. Dubnov"; Seltzer, "From Graetz to Dubnow."

in some of Graetz's historiographical methods and priorities.[88] This recent scholarship, however, has largely remained silent regarding the ways that Dubnow perpetuated Graetz's schema of *lernen und leiden* in his portrayal of the Russian-Jewish experience and in his conception of Jewish national renaissance.[89]

This chapter reveals that Dubnow adopted Graetz's lachrymose conception largely because it fit with his battle for Russian Jewry's political emancipation and his triumphal historiographical conception of national renaissance. I have shown that there were continuities as well as ruptures between the German *Wissenschaft des Judentums* and the national Jewish historical scholarship that Dubnow inaugurated. Like his German predecessors, Dubnow was fighting for Jewish emancipation, albeit now defined in terms of national as well as personal political rights. Also like *Wissenschaft* historians, Dubnow sought to depict Jewish suffering as a means of preventing the erosion of Jewish identity in its encounter with modernity. Dubnow diverged from Graetz both in his imagery, which envisioned tsarist Russia as at war with its Jews, and in his emphasis on the connection between a Jewish cultural renaissance and the ultimate attainment of national political rights.

The next generation of historians of the Russian-Jewish experience, both in tsarist Russia and in the Russian-Jewish Diaspora, perpetuated this historiographical tradition. One of Dubnow's immediate disciples, Elias Tcherikower (1881–1943), for instance, wrote during World War I about the exceptionalism of Jewish legal status under the tsars and for the linkage of Jewish cultural renaissance to persecution.[90]

Later, to American and Israeli Jews, tsarist Russia symbolized the inferno from which their parents and grandparents had escaped.[91] Soviet Jewish ideology, moreover, contrasted the oppression of the Jews under the tsars with their liberation under the Soviets.

---

[88] Frankel, "S. M. Dubnov," 12, 14–17.

[89] One scholar to address this schema in terms of the conflict between Dubnov's historiographical belief in the rise and fall of diaspora hegemonic centers and his belief in historical progress was Jonathan Frankel. See Frankel, "S. M. Dubnov," 18–20.

[90] Tcherikower, "Di yidishe rekhtlozinkeyt in rusland," in *In kampf far yidishe rekht: a blik in der yidisher rekhtlozinkeyt un in der geshikhte fun der yidisher emantsipatsions bavegung*, ed. Ber Borochov (New York, 1916), 33–45; Tcherikower, "Ven der malokh hamoves hot keyn shlite nit," *Der yidisher kempfer* 3 (12 May 1916), 8.

[91] As an example of how this view persisted in American-Jewish historiography, see Louis Greenberg, *The Jews in Russia: The Struggle for Emancipation*, 2 vols. (New Haven, 1944, 1951). The Broadway musical *Fiddler on the Roof* enshrined this view of the Russian-Jewish past in American-Jewish collective memory. See Steven J. Zipperstein, *Imagining Russian Jewry: Memory, History, Identity* (Seattle, 1999), 33–39.

10. Between External Persecution and National Renaissance

It is ironic that Dubnow's ideological agenda prevented him from applying his own vision of objective social history based on archival evidence to the nineteenth- and early-twentieth-century Russian-Jewish experience. Falling prey to the politicized collective memories of American, Israeli, and Soviet Jews, the Jewish experience under the tsars would have to wait until the last quarter of the twentieth century to receive the kind of objective historical treatment that Dubnow had first demanded for it nearly one hundred years earlier.

11. Soviet Holocaust Photography and Landscapes of Emptiness

David Shneer

> I used to live in the cities,
> And happily lived among the living,
> Now on empty vacant lands
> I must dig up the graves.
> Now every ravine is a sign
> And every ravine is now my home.
>
> —Ilya Ehrenburg, "Babi Yar," 1944

On 22 June 1941, the German army invaded the Soviet Union, launching a war that claimed about twenty-seven million Soviet lives. On 9 May 1945, with Soviet army troops in Berlin, the Germans capitulated, and the Soviets celebrated. In between, Soviet journalists and photographers were charged with telling the story of the war to the public as it was unfolding. Soviet photojournalists had to make sense of the war visually and walk a fine line between the many overlapping stories that the press had to tell: the triumph of Soviet heroism, the population's persistence in the face of potential defeat, and Nazi atrocities committed against the Soviet population generally, and its Jewish population specifically.

Nazi atrocity and Holocaust photography are generally defined by two canonical sets of images. The first are perpetrator photographs taken by the Nazis themselves, like the photograph of the young Jewish boy with hands raised from the Warsaw Ghetto, whose photo was taken as part of the Stroop Report, or the grim pictures of Einsatzgruppen shooting campaigns on the eastern front. The second set of images are so-called liberation images coming from photographers documenting Dachau and Buchenwald and other concentration camps that American and British armies liberated in April 1945. These two bodies of photography usually illustrate permanent exhibitions in Holocaust museums and are the ones most often studied by those who write about Holocaust photography.[1] By moving beyond the canonical and looking

---

[1] See cultural theorists such as Ulrich Baer, *Spectral Evidence: Photography of Trauma* (Boston, 2002); Andrea Liss, *Trespassing through Shadows: Memory, Photography, and the Holocaust* (Minneapolis, MN, 1998); Brett Kaplan, *Unwanted Beauty: Aesthetic Pleasure in Holocaust*

11. Soviet Holocaust Photography and Landscapes of Emptiness

at Soviet liberation photography that was widely circulated from early 1942 on, we have a better understanding of how the Holocaust was visualized in the Soviet Union as it was unfolding and of how the Soviet population made sense of the unprecedented violence that the war brought to the western regions of the Soviet Union. We will see that the Soviet press used images propagandistically to mobilize the population to fight a war that in its early years was going terribly. The press and its photographers suggested to readers that German occupation would in no way bring peace. Perhaps more important, documenting Nazi atrocities with the seductive, seemingly mimetic power of a camera gave the Soviet Union forensic evidence of war crimes committed against the Soviet people. Finally, the aesthetics of liberation photography from the East European borderlands reveal a radically different Holocaust landscape from that of concentration camps with emaciated survivors.

The Soviet press published gruesome images of Nazi atrocities from the first days of the war, nearly all taken by photographers working for the Germans or German soldiers themselves. Not infrequently, after a German soldier was killed in battle, Soviet troops would find the bodies and retrieve the cameras documenting the atrocities. They were then delivered to the relevant Soviet authorities, in this case the political commissar of the unit, as "trophy photographs." Most major Soviet press outlets published photographs like "Punishment in Poland," which appeared in *Ogonek*, the leading illustrating magazine in the country (Figure 11-1). These so-called perpetrator images—those taken by the Germans and their accomplices, initially coming out of Poland—shaped the Soviet understanding of the Nazi extermination campaign from its first days. It documented the naked brutality of the Nazis, who openly and proudly murdered civilians, including women and children, and it suggested to the Soviet reading audience what Soviet citizens' fate might be if they did not fight against the German war machine.

Soviet photographers did not witness scenes of Nazi atrocities with their own eyes until late 1941, when the Red Army began reconquering cities near Moscow that had been under Nazi occupation for a brief time. Most of what Soviet photographers saw were gruesome scenes of corpses in the streets, public hangings, looting, and burning—Nazi atrocities that had everything

---

Representation (Urbana-Champaign, IL, 2006). Journalists and photographers who have written critically about Holocaust photography include Barbie Zelizer, *Remembering to Forget: Holocaust Memory through the Camera's Eye* (Chicago, 2000); and Janina Struk, *Photographing the Holocaust: Interpreting the Evidence* (London, 2004). See also Susan Sontag, *Regarding the Pain of Others* (New York, 2004).

to do with total war but little to do with the specific Nazi war against the Jews.[2] But no Soviet photographer had witnessed the gruesome scenes of mass murder of Jews that were going on throughout the occupied Soviet Union in 1941.

FIGURE 11-1. *Ogonek* Coverage of Nazi Atrocities, 25 June 1941. German "trophy" photograph. Caption: "Punishment in Poland. Those sentenced are forced to dig their own graves."

In January 1942, seven months after the German invasion of the Soviet Union, Dmitrii Baltermants flew over the Black Sea and descended into the region around the newly liberated city of Kerch. Baltermants already had experience photographing the heat of battle and the brutality of war at the front just kilometers from the western edge of Moscow in the fall of 1941, but this new assignment in the south would reveal something new about the enemy.[3] The German army had occupied Kerch, a small peninsula that juts into the Sea of Azov in southern Russia, in mid-November 1941, but held it

---

[2] The Baltermants Archive in Scarsdale, NY, holds many photographs from November and December 1941 of liberated villages in the Moscow region that had been under Nazi occupation. See the notebook labeled "War Photography, 1941," The Dmitrii Baltermants Archive. In addition, the archive of Semen Fridlyand, who was special war correspondent for *Ogonek* shows similar photographs from late 1941. In the press, the two biggest stories about early Nazi atrocities broke after the liberation of Volokolamsk, eighty miles northwest of Moscow, and Rostov, in southern Russia. About the Germans' eight-day occupation of Rostov, journalists and photographers wrote about mass shootings on the streets. See, for example, "Ne zabudem, ne prostim: Fotodokumenty o krovavykh zverstvakh fashistskikh merzavtsev v Rostove-na-Donu," *Krasnaia zvezda*, 11 December 1941.

[3] See the notes in Baltermants Archive, Scarsdale, NY. The archive does not have a finding aid.

11. Soviet Holocaust Photography and Landscapes of Emptiness

for only six weeks. In the first week of December, the Gestapo, the German State Secret Police, registered 7,500 Jews who remained in the city after the arrival of German forces. It then ordered Kerch's Jews to Sennaia Square, from which they were deported to an antitank ditch on the outskirts of town and shot.[4] On 31 December, the city was one of the first places with a significant prewar Jewish population to be liberated from Nazi occupation. This made it one of the first places where Soviet soldiers, journalists, and photographers saw the effects of Nazi occupation and the war against European Jewry with their own eyes.[5]

Baltermants's plane landed at an airfield on the outskirts of town near a place called Bagerov Trench (Bagerovskii Rov). The photographer saw older women and families wandering around crying, searching for something (Figure 11-2).

FIGURE 11-2. Dmitrii Baltermants, "Residents of Kerch Search for Their Loved Ones," 1942. Scanned from the maquette for Baltermants's unpublished book *Tak eto bylo*. Courtesy of Paul and Teresa Harbaugh

---

[4] There are conflicting stories about the Nazi mass murders at Kerch. Andrej Angrick's work on Einsatzgruppen D, which carried out the murders, is based on German archives and trial testimony taken in the 1960s. His report says that only 2,500 Jews were murdered in that first week of December. The remainder was murdered in the reoccupation of the city in June 1942. See Andrej Angrick, *Besatzungspolitik und Massenmord: Die Einsatzgruppe D in der südlichen Sowjetunion 1941–1943* (Hamburg, 2003). Soviet sources, based on survivor testimony, put the number at 7,000–7,500. See Leonid Mel'kov, *Kerch: Povest'-khronika v dokumentakh, vospominaniiakh i pis'makh uchastnikov geroicheskoi zashchity i osvobozhdeniia goroda v 1941–1944 godakh* (Moscow, 1981). According to one survivor, Jews were rounded up over the course of two weeks and trucked out to Bagerov trench to be shot. Sinti/Roma (Gypsies) were then rounded up and brought to the same site to be shot. See "Testimony of Neisha Kemilev," Yad Vashem Archives, group M33, file 88, p. 102.

[5] The cities to be liberated before Kerch were primarily in the Moscow region (Klin and Volokolamsk) and did not have large Jewish populations, as well as Rostov, which was occupied for too short a time for mass executions. For a list and dates of cities liberated by the Red Army, see militera.lib.ru. For the demographics of prewar Soviet Jewry, see Mordechai Altshuler, *Soviet Jewry on the Eve of the Holocaust: A Social and Demographic Profile* (Jerusalem, 1998).

And then, amid the wailing, Baltermants saw dozens of corpses littering the bleak, frozen wintertime landscape. "Were they [the bodies of] Red Army soldiers or prisoners of war?" he asked himself. "The clothing on the corpses suggested that they were civilians, brought out to this field and shot en masse." His colleague Lev Borodulin recalled many years later, "Now we know exactly whose corpses those were, but in that distant January 1942, one had to guess: were these Red Army soldiers or prisoners; how did all these relatives get here; if they were Communists, how come there were so many; and if they were Communist Youth, how come there were so many small children?"[6]

On that frozen field near Kerch, Baltermants and the other photojournalists assigned to Kerch became the first liberators to photograph the mass murder of Jews by the Nazi special killing units, the Einsatzgruppen, on Soviet soil. Baltermants knew that he was not just photographing for tomorrow's newspaper but was bearing witness to something important. He used two rolls of precious film to photograph the scene before him. After delays due to the exigencies of transporting film across long distances during wartime, two months later, several of his photographs were published in *Ogonek*.[7]

Evgenii Khaldei, an up-and-coming photographer working for the Telegraph Agency of the Soviet Union (TASS), had been sent south after his tour of duty with the Northern Fleet and was also one of the first to bear witness to Nazi mass murder in Kerch (Figure 11-3). "The trench was two kilometers long," opens the section of his diary about the discovery at Bagerov Trench of the Nazis' mass murder of Jews. Khaldei refers to them in his diary as the "7,000 women, children, and elderly," omitting the word "Jew." Khaldei interviewed townspeople about the Germans' six-week occupation of the city, and he also went directly to the trench to interview witnesses.[8] We know, then, that at the time, Khaldei understood that these were Jewish bodies and that Nazi atrocities targeted Jews differently from others. But both his diary and the framing of the pictures in the press elided the Jewishness of the event.

Although Baltermants and Khaldei were among the first photographers at the scene, the first Kerch photographs to appear in the press were by another Jewish photographer working for TASS, Mark Redkin. His photos appeared in *Ogonek* on 4 February 1942.[9] On the top, the magazine published a landscape

---

[6] Lev Borodulin, "Lev Borodulin o Dmitrii Baltermantse," www.sem40.ru. See also the interview with Tat'iana Baltermants, June 2004.
[7] See "Interview with Dmitrii Baltermants," in V. A. Nikitin, *Rasskazy o fotografakh i fotografiiakh* (Leningrad, 1991), 175–76.
[8] Evgenii Khaldei, "Ianvar' 1942 g.," *Dnevnik Evgeniia Khaldeiia*, in the Evgenii Khaldei Archives, housed at Fotosoiuz in Moscow.
[9] *Ogonek*, 4 February 1942, 4. The original photograph can be found in Yad Vashem Archives, photograph 4331/16.

228

11. Soviet Holocaust Photography and Landscapes of Emptiness

of bodies strewn along an antitank ditch at the center of the composition. Two Soviet soldiers standing on the right investigate the scene as the white of the sky and the white of the snow in the ditch blend together in the top left. The photo beneath the landscape image shows a close-up of the dead, in this case a mother surrounded by dead children. At the time, no one could have imagined a more horrible image, especially one captured by Soviet photographers as opposed to German trophy photographs.

The caption beneath the photographs suggests how Redkin and the *Ogonek* editors placed the photograph within an evolving narrative of the war and of Nazi atrocities: "Hitler ordered his bandits to annihilate the peaceful Soviet population. Wherever the Germans found themselves, they murdered thousands of women and children. The bodies of the murdered were dumped in a pit (top of the photograph). Among the murdered were many women and children (lower part of the photograph). The Hitlerite thugs showed no one any mercy." The caption writers obscured the perpetrators of the crimes. In one sentence, it is followers of Hitler, in another Germans. And no mention is made of the fact that most of the dead women and children so grotesquely splashed on the pages of the magazine were Jewish.[10]

FIGURE 11-3. Evgenii Khaldei, "Kerch," January 1942, image scanned from original negative. Courtesy of Fotosoiuz, Moscow.

---

[10] Angrick suggests that the roundup and mass murder of the city's remaining Jewish population took place over three days, 3–5 December 1941 (*Besatzungspolitik und Massenmord*, 356).

One month later, *Ogonek* followed up its earlier Kerch photographs with a two-page layout of photographs by Baltermants and Israel Ozerskii, and an article by the journalist I. Antselovitch. The paragraph introducing the large photo layout: "These photographs were taken at a moment after the German occupiers drove [the people] out to this place. Seventy-five hundred residents from the very elderly to breast-feeding babies were shot from just a single city. They were killed in cold blood in a premeditated fashion. They were killed indiscriminately—Russians and Tatars, Ukrainians and Jews. The Hitlerites have indiscriminately murdered the Soviet population in many other cities, villages, and the countryside."

It is clear from the caption that by the 1940s, the use of ethnicity in the captions to the photographs reflects a larger shift in the way populations were categorized, away from class background from the 1920s and 1930s to ethnic and racial definitions of identity.[11] Jews were clearly included among Soviet ethnicities. In addition, photographers were also expected to keep careful track of the names and ethnic identities of the people they photographed.[12] So Baltermants would have known the ethnic identity of those bearing witness to the crime and, probably, of the victims in his photographs. Many years after the war, Baltermants claims to have understood that the German occupiers did not, as the caption states, kill Kerch residents "indiscriminately." He recognized that Jews and other politically suspect people were targeted for murder. From an interview with Baltermants recounting how he took the Kerch photographs, "In the fall of 1941 the Germans drove 7,000 residents—partisans, Communists, and Jews—to the trench. They drove out whole families—women, the elderly, and children. They drove all of them to an antitank ditch and shot them."[13]

The writers, photographers, and editors insinuated in other ways that this was a massacre of Jews. In Figure 11-2, the photographer has pictured a woman wailing over a pile of corpses, the first photograph in a two-page montage, captioned as "Residents of Kerch Search for Their Relatives. In the photo: V. S. Tereshchenko digs under bodies for her husband." The photo editor has embedded a second photograph next to Tereshchenko's, occupying the same visual field on the page, whose caption reads, "On the right: the body of 67-year-old I. Kh. Kogan." By placing these two photographs side by side, the editors suggest that the Jewish Kogan (Russian for Cohen) is, in

---

[11] For more on the rise of ethnic and racial notions of Soviet identity, see David Brandenberger, *National Bolshevism: Stalinist Mass Culture and the Formation of Modern Russian National Identity, 1931–1956* (Cambridge, MA, 2002); and Amir Weiner, *Making Sense of War: The Second World War and the Fate of the Bolshevik Revolution* (Princeton, NJ, 2002).

[12] David Shneer, *Through Soviet Jewish Eyes: Photography, War, and the Holocaust* (New Brunswick, NJ, 2010), chap. 2.

[13] Nikitin, *Rasskazy*, 153.

fact, the husband for whom the very Ukrainian-sounding Tereshchenko was searching. Although this couple reflected the idealized Soviet multiethnic family, the fact could not have been lost on the reader that after the Nazis left town, the Ukrainian Tereshchenko was alive, and the Jewish Kogan was dead.

Finally, the *Ogonek* editor back in Moscow and Antselovitch hint at the Jewishness of the story when Antselovitch says that according to orders from Berlin, the first to be shot were "Soviet citizens of one particular ethnicity." In an effort to universalize Nazi atrocities, Soviet editors rarely labeled the victims of Nazi atrocities explicitly as Jews or included Jews in a list of peoples who were targeted. Although some readers may have missed the allusion, many, Jews among them, would have understood exactly which ethnicity the writer had in mind.

From the published record and from many internal memoranda between editors and photographers working for the Soviet press, it is clear that photographing Nazi atrocities was a central mission for Soviet photographers. The impetus to document atrocities only increased with the founding of the Extraordinary State Commission for the Establishment and Investigation of Atrocities Committed by the German-Fascist Invaders and Their Accomplices in November 1942. This was the official state body charged with investigating and documenting Nazi war crimes and then circulating the material for war crimes trials and for public propaganda purposes. These commissions investigated crimes that took place in each and every city that the Red Army liberated, although Marina Sorokina and Niels Paulson argue that the primary purpose of the extraordinary commissions was not to discover the truth of the crimes but to deflect attention from the Soviets' own war crimes and to publicize Nazi atrocities as part of the Soviet propaganda campaign.[14]

In most liberated cities, the investigators—along with journalists and commission photographers, whose names did not make the front page of the Soviet press—found pits, ravines, or trenches on the outskirts of town where the mass murders took place and the victims were haphazardly buried. The name of Kiev's Babi Yar, referenced in the quotation from Ehrenburg's poem that opens this article, was only the most visible site of the Nazi war against the Soviet Union and its Jewish population after the city's liberation on 6 November 1943.[15] These pits were regarded as crime scenes, and it was

---

[14] For more on the establishment of the Extraordinary Commission, see Marina Sorokina, "People and Procedures: Toward a History of the Investigation of Nazi Crimes in the USSR," *Kritika: Explorations in Russian and Eurasian History* 6, 4 (2005): 797–831. See also Kiril Feferman, "Soviet Investigation of Nazi War Crimes," *Journal of Genocide Research* 5, 4 (2003): 587–602.

[15] The Extraordinary Commission files document more precise locations of the Nazi shootings and almost always include a pit near town. In Lugansk, then called Voroshilovgrad, mass burial pits were found at Ivanishchev Ravine; in Artemovsk at Chasov Ravine, and so on.

the extraordinary commission's task to prepare materials for war crimes trials against the Germans and their collaborators. Commission photographers, who were not generally the same as the well-known photographers working for the central press, were thus documenting crime scenes. They were forensic photographers.

In most liberated cities, Extraordinary Commission investigators excavated the sites where the mass murders had taken place. Photographers documented both the investigation and the crime scene. Because of the repetitive nature of the photographs, Extraordinary Commission photography became more "generic" as city after city had its war crimes' scene photographed.

As we will see, the genre of Soviet forensic photography developed by commission photographers intersected with the more crafted aesthetic conventions of Soviet photojournalists when certain liberation sites made it to the front pages of the newspapers. Whereas commission photographers aimed their work at a narrow audience of those reading crime reports, photojournalists were telling a compelling story for a wide public. Together, the two define Soviet Holocaust liberation photography.

Soviet Holocaust liberation photography most often began with a "general view [*obshchii vid*]" image. Some are empty landscapes meant to be filled in by a reader's imagination or by articles accompanying the photograph. Others, like Baltermants's photographs from Kerch, include either mourners or researchers. Carol Zemel has written about American liberation photography: "Nowhere is the Nazi reduction of persons to despised matter more visible [than in images of tumbled heaps of corpses piled in the camps]. In some, the disturbing presence of the bodies is alleviated by the view of Allied soldiers—merging the viewer with the rescuer once again, and providing some sense of closure, some end to the tale."[16] Because the commission photographer documented crimes for a private audience, closure was not necessarily the goal of these photographs. Instead, the photographer bears witness, and documents others bearing witness, to *crimes*, not to a human story about loss.

After the "general view" image, commission photographers frequently produced close-ups of the work being done at the crime scene. In documenting the September 1943 liberation of the eastern Ukrainian city of Artemovsk, the photographer took pictures of: "a row of children," "a mother with two children who have been shot," and "excavations." The first two closely match the Redkin photographs from Kerch, showing that commission photographers and photojournalists were not necessarily photographing in entirely different

---

[16] Carol Zemel, "Emblems of Atrocity: Holocaust Liberation Photographs," in *Image and Remembrance: Representation and the Holocaust*, ed. Shelley Hornstein and Florence Jacobowitz (Bloomington, IN, 2003), 214.

11. Soviet Holocaust Photography and Landscapes of Emptiness

genres. The final one, excavations (*raskopki*), is the least descriptive and most haunting title of them all.

To conduct its research after a city was liberated, the extraordinary commission exhumed bodies from the ravines, trenches, and pits that dotted the blackened landscape of Ukraine to determine what happened. Researchers counted bodies, checked clothing, examined bullet wounds to determine how and when people were killed. Like forensic researchers who study murder scenes day in and day out, these photographers captioned their photographs in a hauntingly dry manner.[17] Such photo essays of general views, close-ups of corpses, and landscapes of exhumed bodies appear over and over again in Extraordinary Commission reports.

On 20 November 1943, shortly after the liberation of Kiev and the discovery of Babi Yar, *Ogonek* published photographs from a Nazi camp for Soviet POWs called Khorol' in the Poltava region. It was *Ogonek*'s first use of the term "death camp" (Figure 11-4). The photographic essay followed some of the now-established tropes from Soviet Nazi atrocity liberation photography—a large open pit, investigators sifting through remains of people. But the photographs of barracks, bones, and graffiti suggested something new to the reader. The presence of a camp suggested that the Nazis established permanent places in which to commit Nazi atrocities, not just ravines on the outskirts of town in which to dump bodies. The notion of a "death camp" as opposed to a ravine, pit, or trench, pushed the visual narrative of death in a new direction, one that would prepare the population for the future discoveries of the death camps on Polish soil.

---

[17] U.S. Holocaust Memorial Museum (USHMM) RG 22.002, reel 7, page 95. The reproductions of these photographs are not of sufficiently high quality to reproduce here.

FIGURES 11-4a-b. "Death Camp." *Ogonek*, 20 November 1943

11. Soviet Holocaust Photography and Landscapes of Emptiness

When imagining extermination and concentration camps, most people think of two sites: Auschwitz, with its iconic gate "Arbeit Macht Frei," and Dachau and Buchenwald, with piles of bodies and emaciated survivors, whom American journalists photographed extensively in April 1945.[18] In the Soviet Union, however, the first visual images of extermination camps came not from Auschwitz or Dachau, but from the liberation of Majdanek in July 1944.

One of the things that distinguished the visual record of Majdanek from those of the dozens of other sites of atrocities was that the Soviet press, and on occasion the foreign press, published an extensive photographic record. Each major press outlet as well as the extraordinary commissions had photographers at Majdanek. Iakov Riumkin photographed for *Pravda*, Oleg Knorring for *Krasnaia zvezda* (Red Star, the Soviet army's newspaper), Boris Tseitlin for *Ogonek*. Viktor Tiomin had several photos published in *LIFE Magazine* and the *Illustrated London News*.[19] Several other photographers, including a second *Izvestiia* correspondent from Stalingrad, Georgii Zelma, have Majdanek photos in their archives; and one other, Mikhail Trakhman, has a whole series of hauntingly beautiful landscapes of the camp. At Majdanek, the documentary nature of the Extraordinary Commission photographs confronted the more aesthetically interesting and compelling photographs that had graced the pages of the Soviet press since 23 June 1941. Unlike in Artemovsk, where the anonymous commission photographer did not take poetic license by making beautiful photographs; at Majdanek, all the most important photojournalists were vying for the "best" photographs of the camp, the metaphoric and literal "money shot." Soviet Nazi atrocities moved from the realm of forensic photography to that of Soviet photojournalism.

Samarii Gurarii's photographs adorned *Izvestiia* when the newspaper broke the story about the camp on 12 August 1944, shortly after the well-known Soviet writer Konstantin Simonov's long reports began appearing in the Soviet and Western press. The 12 August layout in *Izvestiia* occupied page 1. The photographs were arrayed as a triptych of objects or scenes that would eventually become emblematic of Nazi atrocities—piles of shoes, gas canisters, and corpses. They were clearly arranged for a Soviet audience that had become accustomed to seeing photographs of Nazi atrocities, and sometimes witnessing them when, for example, people returned home from their places of evacuation. With the discovery of Majdanek, the role of bearing witness, of showing the viewers that the nightmare of atrocities was over, became even more important.

---

[18] On Auschwitz as icon, see Oren Stier, "Different Trains: Holocaust Artifacts and the Ideologies of Remembrance," *Holocaust and Genocide Studies* 19, 1 (2005): 81–106.

[19] Struk, *Photographing the Holocaust*, 141.

11. Soviet Holocaust Photography and Landscapes of Emptiness

In the many photographs that lay in Extraordinary Commission reports from dozens of cities across Ukraine, Russia, and Belorussia, the most typical photographs are like Gurarii's first photograph in the upper left—the witnessed uncovering of mass burial pits. The only thing that distinguishes this photograph is the large number of people witnessing the exhumation of bodies.

But Gurarii's *Izvestiia* triptych forced viewers to see things they had probably never seen before: a bizarre photograph of canisters, for example, one of the few photographs in the visual narrative of Nazi atrocities that begged explanation. A reader would need to turn to the article accompanying the photographs to learn that these somber men holding canisters were in fact holding in their hands the tools that killed people. It was not a gun or a knife, something easily recognizable as a murder weapon. It was a canister of gas— in fact, a disinfectant used to kill lice—that in the case of Majdanek (and the other extermination camps that the Red Army and its photographers would soon uncover) was instead used to mass murder hundreds of thousands of human beings, most of them Jews. These canisters would have been the most difficult photographs to stand alone in 1944, because they had no meaning independent of the text explaining what they were.

The third published Gurarii photograph, of a warehouse overflowing with empty shoes, has more meaning built into the image. The image of the field of shoes became the most important iconic image representing Majdanek— the absence of eight hundred thousand people who once stood in the eight hundred thousand pairs of shoes that accompanying articles said were discovered. This new iconography broke with the images that Soviet readers had come to associate with Nazi atrocities—burial sites, burned down villages, and corpses.

This photograph (Figure 11-5) moves far beyond forensic photography. These are local Poles from Lublin, a large city that is visible just beyond the barbed wire fence of Majdanek. They are either searching for dead relatives, mourning their local losses, or present as part of a Soviet campaign to have the local townspeople bear witness to atrocities that took place in their backyards. Unlike American photos in Germany that have locals witnessing atrocities as a form of punishment, Soviet liberation photographs show Polish witnesses in times of mourning. These photographs allowed the Poles (and all Soviet readers of *Izvestiia*) to see Poland as a place of mourning and loss, as a victim of atrocities, not like Germany, which was a place that perpetrated violence and had earned retribution and punishment.

237

FIGURE 11-5. Mikhail Trakhman, "Local Visitors at Majdanek." August 1944. Courtesy of U.S. Holocaust Memorial Museum.

11. Soviet Holocaust Photography and Landscapes of Emptiness

At Majdanek, the genre of photographing the Soviet liberators with Jewish, Polish, and other victims was taken to a new extreme. In Figure 11-6, most likely taken by the Soviet Jewish photographer Mikhail Trakhman, we see in the foreground a pile of human skulls, labeled "10," presumably the tenth item that the extraordinary commission had marked and labeled as evidence. Just beyond the skulls are skeletons of the dead. But the point of the photograph is not the victims' bones. The photograph is arrayed around the witnesses to the crime, Lublin residents standing and staring blankly at the pile of bones. The women are dressed modestly, mostly in black, although one woman who occupies more than her share of the visual field is dressed in white and appears to be standing *on* the bones. To the left is a young girl, maybe ten years old, dressed in her Sunday best, having even put on a simple gold bracelet for the occasion—an outing to a concentration camp. The faces are somber, but not that somber. It does not seem as if anyone has recently shed tears at this site. In the background, we see the city of Lublin, which fades into the distance and shadows of other townspeople who were visiting Majdanek on the day the photograph was taken.[20]

In perhaps the most arresting picture, Trakhman photographed townspeople visiting Majdanek. This is a different angle from the above-mentioned

FIGURE 11-6. Unattributed, but most likely Mikhail Trakhman, "Poles Watching Germans Bearing Witness to Corpses," August 1944. Yad Vashem Archives 4212/16

---
[20] Yad Vashem Archives, photograph 3031/13.

Gurarii photograph that was published in *Izvestiia*. This new angle shows an entirely different scene. Unlike the Gurarii image, which is clearly still operating in the forensic genre that puts the dead bodies at the center of the image and suggests that Poles are mourning the dead, Trakhman has put an unfolding drama *among the living* on display.

The sky is flat, gray, and empty. The only objects breaking up the gray expanse are two brick chimneys off to the right, jutting into the sky, one looking over the crowds, one tiny and off in the distance. Like Gurarii's, the photograph is centered on the burial pit. But that is not what captures the eye. The trench rips the photograph in two. On the left, the townspeople of Lublin line the edge of the trench, but most of them do not look at the pit. To what are they bearing witness if not to the murdered before them? If one follows their eyes, they are looking across the pit to the right side of the frame where German POWs are being paraded by.

German soldiers were brought to Majdanek, as in this picture, to bear witness to their crimes. The BBC's Moscow correspondent, Alexander Werth, reported: "A crowd of German prisoners had been taken through the camp. Around stood crowds of Polish women and children, and they screamed at the Germans, and there was a half-insane old Jew who bellowed frantically in a husky voice: 'Kindermörder, Kindermörder!'" and the Germans went through the camp, at first at an ordinary pace, and then faster and faster, till they ran in a frantic panicky stampede, and they were green with terror, and their hands shook and their teeth chattered."[21] But what role do the Polish witnesses play? Unlike photographs from the Soviet Union where the investigators and mourners bearing witness to the crime are figured as "good" liberators, and unlike similar photographs from Germany where local townspeople were brought to see the dead and dying as a form of punishment, the photographer has brilliantly figured the local Poles as ambiguous characters in this dramatic encounter. They are victims mourning their dead, as in the Soviet Union. But they are also passive bystanders who simply watch the Germans parade by, just as they may have watched what was happening at Majdanek from their homes in Lublin during the war.[22] Crossing the border from the Soviet Union into Poland made all the difference in how photographers pictured liberation.

Although the photographers may have given Poles at Majdanek an ambiguous treatment, their presence, coupled with the absence of Jews, rendered Majdanek a non-Jewish place—aside from the many Jews documenting its liberation from behind their cameras, including Trakhman and Tseitlin. In fact, Majdanek was rendered so "not Jewish" that the funeral

---

[21] Werth, *Russia at War*, 895.
[22] Yad Vashem Archives, photograph 4212/16.

procession photographs, another convention of Soviet liberation photography, show crowds lining the streets and rows of coffins being led to the burial ground. But rather than having a Soviet star on a staff leading the way, the Polish, mostly Catholic, crowd is led through the town by crosses and a priest making a eulogy.[23]

More important, however, than what Trakhman and other Soviet photojournalists photographed is what they did *not* picture, as Figure 11-7 suggests. As the critic Luc Sante describes in his study of urban police photography from the turn of the twentieth century: "The uninhabited pictures are pregnant with implication . . . And there are incidental factors that influence the viewer but may or may not be germane to the deed associated with the site: shadows, stains, footprints in the snow. The stains may be blood, the footprints may be those of the escaped murderer, or they may not be. Every detail of these pictures, relevant or not, has a weight, as if it had been chosen, and the compositions can seem impossibly definitive. The empty pictures may lack the unifying presence of death, but their power of suggestion derives from their preternatural stillness . . . Empty photographs have no reason to be except to show that which cannot be shown"—in this case, the mass murder of Jews and others in Trakhman's still landscape.[24]

FIGURE 11-7. Mikhail Trakhman, Majdanek, July–August 1944. Courtesy of U.S. Holocaust Memorial Museum.

---

[23] Photographs of the Majdanek procession can be found at the Yad Vashem Archives in Jerusalem, photo series 3013 and in Mikhail Trakhman's private archives, managed by his widow, Elena Sitnina, in Moscow.
[24] Luc Sante, *Evidence* (New York, 1992), 61–62.

The more common ravine photographs, like many that appeared in *Ogonek*, left everything to the imagination. Without a caption telling the reader that people were shot and dumped in a ravine or in the above landscape of Majdanek, a reader would be forgiven for simply skipping over a photograph of an empty landscape. The goal of such photographs was to document a crime scene, and in crime scene photography, a photographer conjures what was once in the scene, not simply what one sees in the photograph at the moment it was taken. Luc Sante argues that police photographs show "only that something happened, and that the occurrence left behind a body, a relic, or a site. Their function, therefore, must have been literally as souvenirs, memory aids, records for records' sake."[25]

Janina Struk argues that the photographs of Majdanek were less compelling liberation images than those coming out of Dachau and Buchenwald. In her words, "[i]n comparison to the emotive images of human suffering which would be used to represent the camps liberated by the Western allies, those which were released to represent Majdanek showed the industrial scale of the camp—Zyklon B cylinders, the interior of gas cells, the interior of barracks, piles of shoes and boots, ashes of human remains in the crematoria, and a pile of identity cards—the kind of detailed photographic evidence that police photographers might take in the course of a criminal investigation. *Time* and *LIFE* correspondent Richard Lauterbach, one of the few foreign correspondents to have visited Majdanek, wrote that he was largely unaffected by seeing the gas-chambers and open graves."[26]

Seeing Soviet liberation photography as crime or police photography helps us understand why the images feel less compelling than some of the material produced in 1945 by American liberation photographers, such as Margaret Bourke-White or Lee Miller. Struk is correct in pointing out Soviet photographers' interest in *how* the killing occurred. The *Ogonek* layout of Majdanek in Figure 11-8 gives an overview of the Soviet Nazi atrocity visual essay, based on the photographic genre that had been developed by the extraordinary commissions. There are photographs of the means of carrying out the atrocities—chimneys, crematoria, and, on the top right, the room where victims undressed. We then move to remnants of the actual bodies—skulls and bones from incompletely incinerated corpses. As we move from left to right, we see the remnants of the victims—passports and personal photographs, the warehouse of shoes.[27] It is less about the identity of the victims, and more about the crime committed.

---

[25] Ibid., 97.

[26] Struk, *Photographing the Holocaust*, 142.

[27] Similar photographs can be found in many private archives. They are also available at Yad Vashem Archives, 5318/189, as well as series 3031.

11. Soviet Holocaust Photography and Landscapes of Emptiness

Zemel has argued that Bourke White and Miller took photographs that lent themselves to becoming icons of the Holocaust, images that were detached from any historical context and lacked temporal and spatial anchors.[28] These Soviet photographers were operating in a radically different aesthetic and political universe, one in which documentation took precedence over aestheticization, and that drew on a two-year history of Soviet war crimes photography.

In fact, in Soviet liberation photographs we seldom see close-ups of human faces. One is more likely to see a close-up of the dead than of survivors. Not until Auschwitz, which was *not* widely covered in the Soviet media, did images of survivors become a dominant form of representing liberation. Unlike the other extermination camps, upon whose liberation the Red Army discovered a few dozen survivors, if any, at Auschwitz there were an estimated seven thousand survivors.[29] As we see in photographs from the Auschwitz funerals, among those walking the frozen streets from the exhumation area to the burial site were prisoners in striped clothing.[30]

FIGURE 11-8. Mikhail Trakhman and Boris Tseitlin, "Majdanek Death Camp." *Ogonek*, 31 August 1944, 8–9.

---

[28] Zemel, "Emblems of Atrocity," 209–10.

[29] For basic information about Auschwitz, see "Auschwitz," in *Holocaust Encyclopedia* (Washington, DC), found online at www.ushmm.org.

[30] Yad Vashem Archives, photographs 4201/36–53. The archival series 4201 contains photographs taken at Majdanek and Auschwitz that were acquired from the State Photography and Film Archive in Kiev.

243

The late appearance of the survivor in Soviet Holocaust photography also suggests that the figure of the survivor posed particular challenges for the Soviet understanding of the war and Nazi atrocities. For more than two years, Nazi atrocities had been presented as the total destruction of the local occupied population, of "peaceful Soviet citizens." Few of the articles that accompanied Soviet Holocaust photography asked how bystanders in the photographs managed to remain alive after Nazi occupation. Had Soviet newspapers consistently figured victims as Jews, which they did not, then one could have easily explained that those left alive were simply not Jewish. Since the published record more often framed Nazi atrocities as crimes against *peaceful Soviet citizens*, however, a reader could be forgiven for asking how some people survived the occupation.

The presence of survivors would have posed additional challenges for readers trying to make sense of the war. How did someone survive Nazi occupation? And, more important, who counts as a survivor, worthy of sympathy, and who a bystander—or worse, a collaborator, deserving of retribution—when "peaceful Soviet citizens" were lying in mass burial pits? Only after the military and its photographers cross into Polish territory do survivors—almost always clearly marked by their striped prisoners' garb or their emaciated bodies—appear in Soviet Holocaust photography.

In addition to the problematic role the survivor played in the Soviet narrative, American liberation photographers at places like Dachau, Belsen, and Buchenwald had an entirely different scene in front of their cameras, which also demanded a different approach. The extermination camps in Poland did a more complete job of extermination—of both bodies and the relics of destruction—than did the concentration camps in Germany. When American liberators arrived, they found thousands of starving survivors and piles of relatively fresh corpses instead of the empty landscapes and traces of mass murders at burial sites and extermination camps.

But here we reach the limits of seeing Soviet Holocaust photography just through the lens of forensics, especially as liberation photography moved from the realm of the extraordinary commissions to photojournalism that appeared in newspapers. If each image in an Extraordinary Commission photograph was an image documenting a specific crime, as liberation photography moved into the newspapers, it became part of an evolving *narrative*, a story of Nazi atrocities against Jews, Soviets, and humanity. In this way, the images transcend police photography and function as memorial devices, art, and photojournalism, as much as they document the absence that viewers of these photographs had to fill in with their imaginations.

Susan Sontag, one of the best-known critics and theorists of photography, has argued that images "do not tell [people] anything . . . they were not already

11. Soviet Holocaust Photography and Landscapes of Emptiness

primed to believe. In contrast, images offering evidence that contradicts cherished pieties are invariably dismissed as having been staged for the camera."[31] In her words, "photographs cannot create a moral position."[32] They merely reinforce what we already believe. These are powerful, and contestable, words, but Sontag reminds us that we situate photographs in our own ideological world and amid our prior experience. A reading audience contextualizes a photograph by what it has already seen and cannot contextualize an image by what it has not yet seen.

The Soviet reading audience could integrate photographs of the Holocaust into the already developing canon of Soviet liberation photography of Nazi atrocities. American newspapers and other press outlets had shunned graphic battle images (let alone atrocities against civilians) in order to present a sanitized picture of the war effort. Because of this, in the words of the historian Paul Fussell, the American home front had a "deep deficiency in imagination."[33] That is, until Dachau, Nordhausen, and Buchenwald. Unlike Dachau photographs by American and British photographers, which documented the emotional revulsion and shock the army and these journalists felt upon discovering concentration camps, Soviet photojournalists had already spent three years both documenting *and* experiencing atrocities. They were the first Holocaust liberator photographers, who created a photographic genre to help them and those who would see and use their photographs make sense of the genocide that unfolded before their cameras.

---

[31] Sontag, *Regarding the Pain of Others*, 10.
[32] Susan Sontag, *On Photography* (New York, 2001, originally published in 1977), 17–19.
[33] Paul Fussell, *Wartime: Understanding and Behavior in the Second World War* (New York, 1989), 11–13, 269.

12. Transformed Myths in Verse

Boris Slutsky's Three Holocaust Poems and the Question of Violence

Marat Grinberg

> Poetry is a knife cutting through the ego's control over language. Thus, it is a violence, but a healing violence, one that opens the wound to release what has been hidden and sequestered.
>
> —Joel Kovel, *"Poetry after the Holocaust"*

For post-Holocaust poetry, the question of violence takes on a specifically metapoetic meaning. The problem is not how to depict the atrocities in verse (the impossibility of doing so is clear to most of the poets of the destruction), but rather what happens to language, the language of poetic tradition and diction, once it comes into contact with the historical reality and memory of the catastrophe. For Celan, to employ one definitive case, the issue took on personal life-shattering connotations due to his choice of German for his verse. For Boris Slutsky, whose poems on the Holocaust, I would argue, yield fresh paradigms for grasping the relationship between the event and the poetic word, the problem ultimately acquired a cautiously transformative meaning. Born in 1919 in Ukraine and raised in Soviet Kharkov, Slutsky became a prominent member of the group of young poets in Moscow in the late 1930s. Fighting in Russia's war against Hitler proved to be one of the most decisive and transformative experiences of his life. He fully emerged as a poet after the war. Recognized as a significant figure during his lifetime, most of his verse remained unpublished during his productive years. The last nine years of his life—he died in 1986—he remained creatively silent, writing not a single line of poetry.

It seems that from early on, Slutsky was supremely conscious of two factors: he was born a Jew, which for him meant that he would walk a specific historical, existential, and personal path in life; and he was born in Russia at a crucial historical point. The two facts forcefully and fruitfully merged in his poetic vocation. This essay offers close readings of three of Slutsky's poems, "I was a liberator of Ukraine...," "Now I often dream of Auschwitz...," and "The rabbis walked onto the plains." All three ponder violence: in the first piece, violence perpetrated against language; in the second one, psychological and emotional violence, which the speaker compulsively inflicts on himself by reinserting himself into the destruction scenery; and finally, in the third poem, both physical and metaphysical violence, which the Jewish civilization suffers as a result of its encounter with the non-Jewish realm. In each poem, Slutsky works as both a poet-exegete, who comments obliquely and openly on Jewish and non-Jewish sacred and secular texts, and a metapoetic thinker, whose engagement with history and texts ultimately produces a statement on the meaning of poetic language. Of course, this statement itself takes the form of Slutsky's own poems, whose postulates waver between a language's failure to adequately grasp the catastrophe and a promise of redemption, which springs forth from this very failing language. Thus these poems stand both as what I would call transformed myths and transformed history. The key is that the transformation occurs via language or, more specifically, formal poetic devices. This chapter intends to show how, through the usage of parallelisms (syntactic, rhythmic, and phonic), Slutsky reveals what occurs within language—poetic, metaphysical, historical—as it attempts to speak to the effects of the catastrophe.

"I was a liberator of Ukraine": The Murdered Language

"I was a liberator of Ukraine" occupies a singular place in the annals of Holocaust poetry, offering a requiem to Yiddish, the language the Nazis murdered.[1] Only a poet with a keen and profound awareness of language could write a memorial so intricate. It reads:

> Ia osvobozhdal Ukrainu,
> Shel cherez evreiskie derevni.
> Idish, ikh iazyk,—davno ruina
> Vymer on i goda tri kak drevnii.

---

[1] The history of Soviet Jewish poetic responses to the Holocaust is only now being written. It is clear, however, that some Russian poets, such as Slutsky and Ian Satunovskii, responded to the destruction already on its eve; some, such as Il'ia Erenburg and Il'ia Sel'vinskii, among others, responded to it during the war and continued to powerfully do so after the war. For a selection of prominent Holocaust poems, see Ada Kolganova, ed., *Menorah: Evreiskie motivy v russkoi poezii* (Moscow, 1993), 117–72.

Net, ne vymer—vyrezan i vyzhzhen.
Slishkom byli, vidno, iazykaty.
Vse pogibli, i nikto ne vyzhil.
Tol'ko ikh voskhody i zakaty

V ikh stikhakh, to sladkikh, to goriuchikh,
To goriachikh, gorech'iu goriashchikh,
V proshlom slishkom, mozhet byt', koliuchikh,
V nastoiashchem—nastoiashchikh.

Markishem opisan i Gofshteinom,
Bergel'sonom tshchatel'no rasskazan
Etot mir, kotoryi i Einshteinom
Nesposoben k zhizni byt' priviazan.

No ne kak zerno, ne kak polovu,
A kak pepel chernyi rassevaiut,
Chtob sam-sto vzoshlo liuboe slovo
Tam, gde rty ruiny razevaiut.

Goda tri kak dreven, kak antichen
Tot iazyk, kak chelovek, ubityi.
Goda tri perstami v knigi tychem,
V alfavit, kak klinopis', zabytyi.[2]

I was a liberator of Ukraine,
And passed through her Jewish villages.
Yiddish, their language, became a ruin long ago.
It died out and has been ancient for about three years.

No, not died out—it was slaughtered and burned.
Its folk must have been too garrulous.
Everyone perished and none survived.
Only their dawns and dusks survived

In their poems, either sweet or burning,
Sometimes hot burning with grief,
In the past perhaps too prickly,
But today completely true.

Described by Markish and Gofshtein,
Told scrupulously by Bergel'son,
This world even by Einstein

---

[2] Published in *God za godom*, no. 5 (1989): 85–86.

12. Transformed Myths in Verse

> Cannot be tied back to life.
> Neither like a seed, nor like chaff,
> But like ashes we spread them,
> So that any word would rise a hundred times more
> Where now ruins gape their mouths.
>
> For about three years it's been antique and ancient—
> That language, murdered like a human being.
> About three years we've been poking fingers into its books,
> Into the alphabet, forgotten like cuneiform.[3]

To give a proper burial to Yiddish, Slutsky strives to extract all the resources from his Russian. The poem's language is rich in assonances (-r and the hashers), parallelisms (the morphological *nastoiashchem-nastoiashchikh*—in the present-true, *dreven/antichen*—ancient/antique), archaisms (*persty* for fingers), folk sayings (*ne kak zerno, ne kak polovu*—neither like a seed nor like chaff), and an agricultural term (*sam-sto*—reaping the harvest a hundred times more than was sown). Its chronotope is multifaceted. On the one hand, the "three years" suggest 1944, the year of Slutsky's participation in the battles for Ukraine, particularly his native city of Kharkov. It was then "three years" since most of the killings of the Jews in Ukraine by death squads in 1941. On the other hand, the "three years" indicate the time spent since the end of the war, placing the poem's composition circa 1948 (Slutsky rarely dated his poems). Written, as I suggest, before 1952, the year of Stalin's murder of the Yiddish poets and writers, some of whom Slutsky mentions, in the reader's historical consciousness, the poem, nevertheless, begins to speak to this catastrophe as well, intensifying its effect of a requiem to the language and its culture. With the comprehensive imperfective past tense of the opening line of the poem (I was liberating Ukraine), Slutsky stresses that it is a recollection, but also that for him the war has never ended. In turn, this retrospective stand becomes essential to the poet's transformation of the "three years" into antiquity. Such is the chrono part of the text. The tope aspect, its topography, is no less significant. The traditional landscape of Soviet war poems is the Russian villages. Slutsky reverses this paradigm in making "the Jewish villages" (the shtetlakh) the sole location of the poem. Thus, he embodies the Holocaust both in Russian linguistic and geographical locations of memory as well as, of course, his own poetics. His choice of "the Jewish villages" as the site of destruction of *Yiddishkeit* is crucial in the context of the overall representation and commemoration of the Holocaust. According to Timothy Snyder, "Auschwitz as symbol of the Holocaust excludes those who were at the

---

[3] All translations from Slutsky in this chapter are mine.

center of the historical event": "Yiddish-speaking Jews of Poland . . . and the Soviet Jewish populations . . . Relatively few Polish Jews and almost no Soviet Jews died there. The two largest groups of victims are nearly missing from the memorial symbol."[4] I would argue that the poem's sound design subtly reinforces its memorializing intent. The jarring and indeed violent –g, –ch and –sh in the third stanza stress the force of its adjectives. The preponderance of the –r sound throughout the poem encompasses the most potent symbol of the murder of Soviet Jewry: ia*r*—ravine, as in Babii Iar (often rendered Babi Yar in English), along with many others, turned killing sites, and scattered all over Ukraine and Belorussia. Slutsky would return to this device in the later "Rabbis walked onto the plains."

While clearly the poem is about Yiddish as both the metonymy of East European Jewish civilization and the organic part of its murdered speakers, as well as a supreme value in itself, it is most fundamentally about poetry and its ability or inability to measure the catastrophe. In the first stanza's last line, the poet, it seems almost inadvertently, slips into restating a prewar expectation, both official and popular, that Yiddish would die out, only to immediately correct himself and, in pronouncing Yiddish's murder in the next stanza, implicitly condemn those who wished for its "natural" erasure. The enjambment between the second and the third stanzas breaks open Slutsky's poetic preoccupation. On the one hand, "their" in "their dawns and ducks" refers as expected to Yiddish speakers, whose garrulousness was the "excuse" for the language's and the people's slaughter, but on the other, it fundamentally points to Yiddish poems. The enjambment, along with the absence of the verb ("survived" is not stated but assumed in the Russian original at the end of the second stanza), morphs the first "their," which modifies the people, into the second one, which now, through syntactic parallelism, begins to describe the poems ("in their poems"). Indeed, the poems still belong to the people. What is more important is that everything—both the people and the very metaphoric core of their existence in the world ("dawns and dusks")—thus must be viewed as elements of the poetic word. The survivors here, to use the loaded post-Holocaust term, are the personified poems themselves. Hurriedly, Slutsky shifts the focus from the victims, whom nothing can revive, to the preservation of poetic texts, the sole remnants of the burned planet, that themselves speak of that planet's hopes and despairs, passions, and sorrows. On the one hand, this shift constitutes a thoroughly Judaic move, considering Judaism's centeredness on the preservation of and commenting on specific texts, but on the other, it radically departs from it, for he does not preserve a

---

[4] See in Timothy Snyder, "Holocaust: The Ignored Reality," *New York Review of Books* 56, 12 (2009): 14.

sacred canon but a body of secular poetry, admittedly imperfect ("prickly") but made true by the very fact of remaining in the postcatastrophe universe. Slutsky's own skepticism toward such a position, redolent of the whole Modernist project, seeps through the poem's messianic and proleptic visions.

The verse's messianic hope is encompassed within the poetic remnant as well. It is the national and, indeed, the mimetic content of Yiddish rhymes that the poet polemically plants like the martyrs' ashes so that they would bear multiple fruit where there are now only ruins. The refusal to sow them like a seed can be interpreted as referring to the famous passage from the Gospel of John (12:24), used by Dostoevsky as the epigraph to *The Brothers Karamazov*, which states that if a seed falls into the ground and dies, it will produce much fruit; hence the redemption through Christ's death.[5] The chaff, I would argue, alludes to Anna Akhmatova's programmatic lines, "*if you* only *knew* from what *refuse* / the *poems grow*, knowing no shame / like a yellow dandelion by the fence, / like burdocks and goosefoot."[6] Like Akhmatova, Slutsky also talks about nature's waste, but if her burdocks and goosefoot grow by themselves, without human involvement, his chaff points back to the human-manufactured catastrophe. As an agricultural term, it describes a byproduct of grain harvesting, used as fodder for animals or ploughed into the soil or burnt. Thus Slutsky dissociates both from Christian apocalypticism and Modernist aestheticism, which turn away from the manmade historical world. In their stead, he offers a promise of an almost messianic era of the future. The problem is that unlike the classical Jewish messianic idea—or at least one strand of it, which Gershom Scholem has famously called "restorative"—Slutsky's messianic age lies here by definition outside the zone of the temporal, for no laws of physics—even the groundbreaking ones of Einstein—can revive the destroyed villages.[7] Also, as a fruit of the ashes—a very non-Jewish image—this messianic vision has death perpetually ingrained into its backbone. Thus the poet makes sure to specify through a simile (a rare device in his poetry) that we spread them like ashes. One should also keep in mind that "ashes" here is a symbol, since he does not talk about Auschwitz with its gas chambers but Ukraine with its ravines.

---

[5] I am grateful to Harriet Murav for pointing out this allusion to me.
[6] My translation. The fact that Anna Akhmatova's poem ("Mne ni k chemu odicheskie rati...") was published in 1940 stresses its relevance for Slutsky. It was fresh on his mind when he was writing "I was a liberator of Ukraine." See *Zvezda*, no. 3-4 (1940): 75; and Anna Akhmatova, *Sochineniia* (Moscow, 1990), 277, 422.
[7] Gershom Scholem, *The Messianic Idea in Judaism and Other Essays on Jewish Spirituality* (New York, 1971), 1-36. See also David Biale, *Gershom Scholem: Kabbalah and Counter-History* (Cambridge, MA, 1979), 148-70.

For Slutsky, the Holocaust casts an enveloping shadow over the totality of Jewish history. Like Klee's Angelus Novus from Benjamin's "Theses on the Philosophy of History," the poet "sees one single catastrophe which keeps piling wreckage upon wreckage and hurls it in front of his feet." Like the angel, he "would like to stay, awaken the dead, and make whole what has been smashed," but unlike him, he also faces the wind of time to which the angel turns his back by chaining his lyrical word to the historical, even at its most disrupted.[8] The poetic component within Slutsky's messianism challenges the unfeasibility of its fulfillment in the confines of time. He refuses to consider the actual resurrection of the people, since that would constitute a desecration—turning the victims into a fodder for commemorative visions. Instead, in a nonapocalyptic fashion—Scholem classically views "utopian-catastrophic" or apocalyptic messianism as "a sudden rupture in historical continuity"—the Yiddish poetic line retains its historicity through being a repository of the people's collective and individual paths.[9] Again, Slutsky is speaking at a symbolic level; in the poem, the Yiddish poets are mentioned, but there is no serious engagement with them on his part.[10] The "any word" refers to the poet's own rhyme and reason, whose major projections are historiographic. Furthermore, it describes the ideal poetic language as such. In the poem, "Poetic language is not a Lutheran sermon . . . ," he sums up:

>   Poeticheskii iazyk—soldatskii miting pered boem.
>   Net vremeni dlia boltovni, a slovo—govori liuboe,
>   Lish' by khvatalo za serdtsa, lish' by doshlo,
>   Lish' by prozhglo,
>   Lish' by pobede pomoglo.[11]

>   Poetic language is a soldiers' meeting before battle.
>   There is no time for blabbery—say any word,
>   As long as it grabs by the heart, as long as it reaches,
>   As long as it burns,
>   As long as it helps the victory.

---

[8] Walter Benjamin, *Illuminations*, trans. Harry Zohn (New York, 1968), 257. At the same time, Benjamin's Angelus remains within history since the "storm," which blows at him from Paradise, "we call progress."

[9] Biale, *Gershom Scholem*, 149.

[10] Bergel'son, mainly a prose writer, is actually the most intricate figure in the poem. In one version, provided here, of which there is Slutsky's handwritten manuscript (Figure 12-1), line 14 states, "Bergel'sonom tshchatel'no rasskazan"—scrupulously told by Bergel'son. Another manuscript, published in *Menorah*, has "Bergel'sonom tshchatel'no razyskan"—scrupulously discovered by Bergel'son. If the second version is valid, Slutsky suggests that the Yiddish world became lost but was still locatable prior to the war (*Menorah*, 123).

[11] Boris Slutsky, *Sobranie sochinenii* (Moscow, 1991), 1: 343 (hereafter *SS*).

Slutsky's vision of the ultimate poetic expression recalls, first and foremost, Yiddish; the fourth line unquestionably alludes to the "burning" Yiddish poems, whose language was burnt, while victory speaks not just to the Soviet triumph in the war but to the messianic resurrection of Yiddish verse and, through it, poetry as such. Thus any word is necessarily metapoetic and Jewish in the Slutskian fashion. His historiography, however, problematizes its potential—its reach.

Throughout his oeuvre, Slutsky routinely canonizes his contemporaneity, turning its epochs into archetypes, each with a life of its own and yet linked with all the others. The fact that in "I was a liberator of Ukraine," the three years become the ancient, and the antique is not unexpected. Writing in the immediate aftermath of the event, the poet extracts himself from history to exhume the language's dead body and convey the enormity of what transpired through speaking from within tradition. Because this tradition lacks specificity, however, the code to unlocking the contents of the Jewish world, slaughtered and burned, is not to be found. The traditional sources and paradigms have been dislodged in response both to the scope of the Holocaust and to the poet's resistance to offer any remedies that would minimize the horrible reality of what took place. "Can poetry be such new tradition?" is the question that Slutsky both haltingly but positively answers and instantly undercuts.

The pitfalls of this dialectic are particularly visible in the last stanza. There, in one of the most powerful images in twentieth-century poetry, the desecrated language is compared to a man who was killed. Since three years here equal eternity, it is for eternity that "we" poke fingers into Yiddish books. Slutsky uses the Church Slavonic *persty*, which suggests the sacredness of this act, evocative of what scribes and monks do.[12] Its obscurity may imply the readers' blindness in front of the text and the inability to read it—if the texts are ancient, the commentators are estranged from them. But it could also signify the incessant and obsessive touching of the Torah scroll's script with the finger of a yad—a sacred pointer, at the top of which extends a hand, through which the Jew derives holiness from the scroll's "cuneiform" signs. The problem is that the Torah in the poem is just that—an illusive symbol—rather than a meaningful intertext. The cuneiform of Yiddish also evokes the original script of the Assyrians and the demise of the great Babylonian civilization. Like the Fall of Babylon, the fall of the Pale is irrevocable. While Jeremiah was the prophet of the Babylonian exile, hence his Lamentations, Slutsky is an idiosyncratic Jeremianic "forecaster" of his own time.[13] The problem is

---

[12] Harriet Murav has suggested to me that *persty* contains a polemical allusion to the doubting Thomas narrative in the Gospels (John 20:27).

[13] See his poem "Proroki i prognozisty" (Prophets and Forecasters), in Slutsky, *SS*, 2:263.

that for him, the scripture here is, if not absent, then at best concealed as an indecipherable and removed realm and at worst made superfluous in an almost Kafkaesque fashion.[14] Without it, the poet is unable to imbue the ruins with the (or a) meaning.

For Slutsky, "ruins" is an important term with a moral and an archetypical dimension. In the poem "Farewell," which describes a dinner encounter between Good and Evil, in Good's mouth the teeth, knocked out by Evil, stand like ruins.[15] In another poem, "The First Century," ruins, contrasted with the more mundane *razvaliny* (wreckage), designate the first century—the defining moment of the West—with its Rome and Christ.[16] In the requiem to Yiddish, they convey the incommensurability of coming to terms with the burned planet. Harold Bloom's concept of proleptic—that is, anachronistic—representation sheds a broader theoretical light on Slutsky's exegetical and metapoetic crisis. Bloom comments: "Proleptic representation is the inevitable rhetorical resource of all canonizing discourse, which means that all canonizing must be done at the expense of the presence of the present moment. When you declare a contemporary work a permanent, classic achievement, you make it suffer an astonishing, apparent, immediate loss in meaning."[17] Hence, any canonization contains an element of "misreading." The fact that the demolished Yiddish tradition can be approached only from afar, like a dead fossil and principally as a sacred object, makes its actual revival impossible and any redemption incomplete and divorced from life. Once the dead civilization has been sanctified, it can never be fully accessed and represented. It becomes morally irreproachable and actually unapproachable. In his comprehensive work on catastrophe in Hebrew literature throughout the ages, Alan Mintz insightfully claims, "Catastrophe in Jewish tradition is best understood not in terms of physical and material devastation; a destructive event becomes a catastrophe when it convulses or vitiates shared assumptions about the destiny of the Jewish people in the world."[18] Slutsky conceives of the Holocaust as devastating precisely because it has created an irreparable chasm in the Jewish cultural and collective memory, symbolized

---

[14] In a 1934 letter to Gershom Scholem, who writes that for Kafka, the law is not absent but unfulfillable, Benjamin retorts: "Kafka ... had no answers to these questions [of the Law and God's judgment]. But the form in which they presented themselves to him ... contains indications of a state of the world in which such questions no longer have a place, because their answers, far from being instructive, make the questions superfluous." See Gershom Scholem, ed., *The Correspondence of Walter Benjamin and Gershom Scholem 1932–1940*, trans. Gary Smith and Andre Lefevere (Cambridge, MA, 1992), 128.

[15] Slutsky, *SS*, 1:263.

[16] Ibid., 1:463.

[17] Harold Bloom, *Kabbalah and Criticism* (New York, 2005), 52.

[18] Alan Mintz, *Hurban: Responses to Catastrophe in Hebrew Literature* (Syracuse, NY, 1996), 2.

by the destruction of Yiddish. Thus, this catastrophe's singularity turns "I was a liberator of Ukraine" into an ongoing hermeneutic failure. In "Now I often dream of Auschwitz," it attains an elegiac emotional charge.

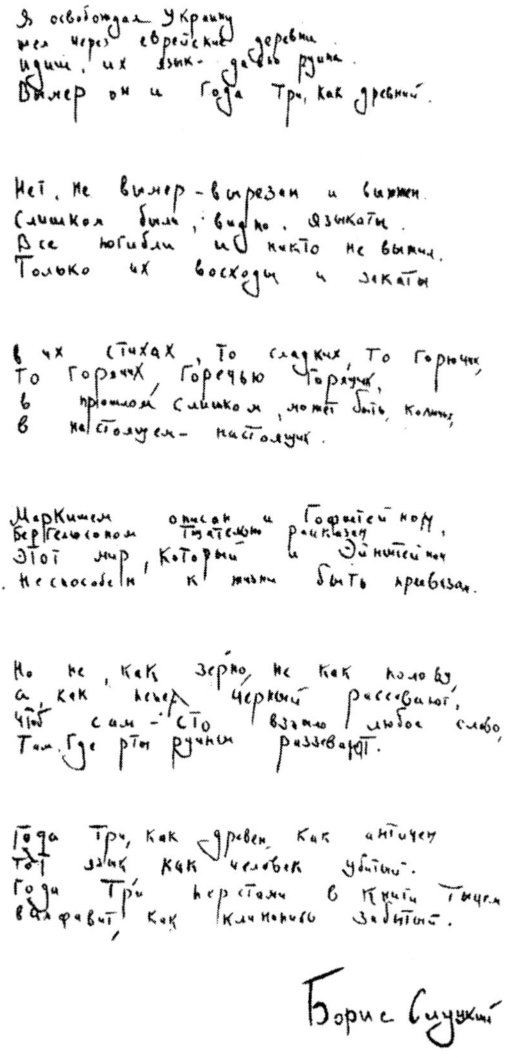

FIGURE 12-1. Slutsky's handwritten copy of "I was a liberator of Ukraine."

"Now I often dream of Auschwitz": The Unending Dream

Surprisingly, "Now I often dream of Auschwitz" was officially published in 1969. It deserves to be quoted in full.

> Teper' Osventsim chasto snitsia mne:
> Doroga mezhdu stantsiei i lagerem.
> Idu, bredu s tolpoiu bednym Lazarem,
> A chemodan kolotit po spine.
>
> Naverno, chto-to ia podozreval
> I vzial udobnyi, legkii chemodanchik,
> Ia shel s tolpoiu nalegke, kak dachnik.
> Shel i okrestnosti obozreval.
>
> A liudi chemodany i uzly
> Nesli s soboi,
> I kofry, i bauly,
> Vysokie, kak gornye auly,
> Im byli te bauly tiazhely.
>
> Doroga cherez son kuda dlinnei,
> Chem naiavu, i tiagostnei, i dlitel'nei.
> Kak budto ne idesh'—plyvesh' po nei,
> I kazhdyi vzmakh vse tishe i medlitel'nei.
>
> Idu kak vse: spesha i ne spesha,
> I ne stuchit zastynuvshee serdtse.
> Davnym-davno zamerzshaia dusha
> Na tom shosse ne smozhet otogret'sia.
>
> Nekhitraia promyshlennost' dymit
> Navstrechu nam
> Pogannym sladkim dymom,
> I medlennym poletom
> Lebedinym
> Ostatki dush pogannyi dym tomit.[19]

> Now I often dream of Auschwitz:
> The road between a station and a camp.
> I am walking, wandering with the crowd like a poor Lazarus,
> While a suitcase beats against my back.

---

[19] Slutsky, *SS*, 2:134.

12. Transformed Myths in Verse

> Perhaps I something did suspect
> And brought along a small suitcase, light and convenient.
> Like a vacationer, I walked with the crowd lightly packed,
> Walked and the surroundings observed.
>
> But people carried
> Bundles and suitcases,
> As well as heavy bags,
> High like villages in the southern mountains.
> Those bags were heavy for them.
>
> A road through dream is longer than
> In an awakened state, as well as more burdened and protracted.
> It is as if you're not walking—but swimming along it,
> And every stroke is slower and calmer.
>
> I walk like all the rest: in haste and not in haste,
> My frozen heart beats not.
> For a long, long time my frozen soul
> Has not been able to warm up on that highway.
>
> The simple industry puffs smoke
> In our way,
> A vile sweet smoke,
> And with a swan's slow
> Flight
> The vile smoke torments the souls' remainders.

This poem is one of the most chiseled in Slutsky's oeuvre. Exemplary of his technique, it reveals a provocative usage of paronomasia, namely the repetition of words, which are similar in sound, but not always in meaning. Most noteworthy is a daring paronomastic parallelism in the third stanza between the very mundane *bauly* and the exotic sounding *auly* and then syntactically back, in the manner of biblical parallelism, to *bauly*. The objects here break at the seams: the bags are loaded with the sufferings of millennia, which draw their carriers down. There is an enormous contrast between the equanimity of the speaker's voice and the horror he is witnessing in this recurrent dream, in which he is a participant. Its images are iconoclastic: crowds of Jews, as in Slutsky's "How They Killed My Grandmother,"[20] and the Auschwitz smoke, ironically sweet as in his "The Pale's impaled."[21] The poem acquires its calmness through the speaker's contentment with his Jewish path

---

[20] Ibid., 2:29.
[21] Boris Slutsky, *Things That Happened*, trans. G. S. Smith (Moscow, 1999), 19:187–88.

and the poetic image of Lazarus that it generates. The poet is a poor Lazarus. Why employ a character from the gospels, a testament to Jesus's miraculous power, in a Jewish memorial poem? Slutsky boldly chooses to do so in order to reverse Lazarus's image. While the New Testament character is resurrected to affirm Jesus' divinity, the poet is "resurrected," awoken after each dream, to bear the memory of Auschwitz in his veins and poems. He becomes a survivor who can never divorce himself from the experiences that he, without having lived through them physically, is meant to undergo existentially and poetically as a Jew.

The dreams are not redemptive and can never absolve the poet from facing the experience. They cannot warm his heart, frozen by the catastrophe; their terror is only prolonged, as if shot in slow motion. The poet is aware of the enormity of the situation while everyone else remains hopeful. This knowledge, however, does not grant him any particular spiritual or historical exemption. On the contrary, professing some hope as well, he appears too lightly packed for this final passage. This self-reproachful and ironic Romantic journeyman figure drastically differs from his position as a scribe and commentator in his other memorial texts. Whereas there he responds to the catastrophe by peering at it both from within and without, here he is solely in the midst of it, defenseless and out of reach with the coolheaded tools of his own poetics. The people in the crowd carry their riches, which are of a spiritual—poetic—nature. It is as if responding to their poeticity that the smoke of crematoria (savagely defined by Slutsky as "simple industry") deliberately greets the Jews with its "swan's flight" and thus tricks them as to its final intentions. The Jews have only the remainders of their souls. The poet knows that the camp system destroyed its inmates by depriving them of any traces of human nature. In preserving parts of their souls, they persist in their humanity and Jewishness and thus, in both biblical and Slutskian manner, sanctify life. In "The Rabbis walked onto the plains," Slutsky turns again to this implicit notion of sanctification, cautiously transforming a hermeneutic abyss and personal terror into a new poetic word.

"The Rabbis walked onto the plains": Dwelling in Life

"The Rabbis walked onto the plains" was published only once, in a narrowly Jewish anthology *God za godom,* a Russian-language supplement to *Sovetish Heymland,* the only postwar Soviet journal in Yiddish. Strikingly, the poem was not included in the authoritative three-volume edition of Slutsky's work. Other than myself, only Maxim Shrayer mentions it, and he provides a succinct and perceptive evaluation of its importance. Shrayer poignantly writes, "'The rabbis came down to the valley . . .,' belongs with the greatest poems about the Shoah, and translation does but partial justice to Slutsky's clairvoyance of diction and verbal artistry."[22] This neglected masterpiece reads:

> Ravviny vyshli na ravniny,
> Byt' mozhet, v pervyi v zhizni raz.
> Prirodu videli ravviny
> Vpervye v svoi poslednii chas.
> Za chas pred tem, kak chernyi dym
> Ravvinov uletuchil v dali,
> Oni vpervye uvidali
> Vesennikh iablon' belyi dym.[23]

> The rabbis walked onto the plains,
> Perhaps for the first time in their lives.
> The rabbis saw nature
> For the first time in their last hour.
> An hour before the black smoke
> Flew the rabbis away to far reaches,
> For the first time they saw
> The spring apples' white smoking haze.

The rabbis are Slutsky's metonymic sign of the Jewish civilization, the most laconic and yet the most profound in its encompassing of the biblical dictum and promise to the Israelites, "'And as for you, you will become for me a kingdom of priests and a holy nation'" (Exod. 19:6). In Richard Friedman's commentary, "'holy nation' . . . means that Israel will be consecrated if the people will live the life that their divine covenant requires of them."[24] In this way, Slutsky upholds the sanctity of Judaism. This in turn enables his conception of the relationship between poetry and the unspeakable horror of the Holocaust.

"How do we speak of the Jewish catastrophe so that it becomes a part of the Russian literary code?" is the question that the poem poses. To resolve this question, Slutsky sings of the catastrophe through primordial Russian archetypes, which imbue the poem with a biblical intonation. The parallel relationship between "rabbis"—*ravviny*—and "plains"—*ravniny*—is

---

[22] Maxim Shrayer, ed., *An Anthology of Jewish-Russian Literature: Two Centuries of Dual Identity in Prose and Poetry* (Armonk, NY, 2007), 2:794.
[23] *God za godom*, no. 5 (1989): 95.
[24] Richard Friedman, *Commentary on the Torah* (New York, 2001), 232.

paronomastic. Shrayer notices it, writing, "Only a poet of God's grace could hear in the paronomastic collision of the rhyming pair *ravviny* (rabbis)—*ravniny* (valleys) the double tragedy of Soviet Jewry." Undoubtedly, Slutsky is contemplating here not just the tragedy of Soviet Jewry but also the demise of Jewish civilization as such. Pointedly, he does so with the linguistic tools and poetic tradition(s) he has at his disposal. Paronomastic parallelism, as noted above, is a pivotal feature of Slutsky's poetry in general, one that chains it to the parallelistic nature of biblical poeticity. Thus "the rabbis walked onto the plains" is not a simple parabolic phrase, but the literal encounter between "the rabbis," the translation of the Hebrew *rabbanim,* and "the plains," the inherently mythological Russian space.

Indeed, as Mikhail Epshtein argues, "The national landscape plays a unique, in many respects a central and organizing role in Russian poetry."[25] *Ravnina* is this landscape's indelible and major part in both old and modern Russian verse, most prominently starting with Pushkin. In the lyrical spread of eight lines, essentially predicated on the repetition of the same few words, Slutsky reaches deep into Russian literary and mythological history, creating a *bylina*. The rabbis walk onto the plains, as the epic heroes do in *byliny*. Having stepped onto the plains for the first time in their lives, the rabbis confront another universe and world order: Russian, Christian—the whole non-Jewish realm. For them, this encounter proves to be fatal. Significantly, in Russian tradition, "plains" denote an ambiguous space. M. M. Kail' notes: "The semantics of the Russian field is a spacious, naked, vast, and uncultivated plain. In Russian tradition, field is a dangerous and pernicious expanse... Such open spaces challenge their inhabitants, and demand from them maximal efforts for survival. The danger that emanates from the field is reflected in numerous Russian proverbs."[26] From another perspective, the archetype of the plain includes an element of existential freedom. As a result, "precisely in the field does man draw strength and wisdom to contemplate his own nature."

In light of the poem's intertexts, to be explicated below, Sergei Esenin appropriates both the ruinous aspects of the plain ("Snezhnaia ravnina, belaia luna...") and its native comfort ("Spit kovyl'. Ravnina dorogaia..."),[27] while Tsvetaeva, in the programmatic Russian poem of destruction, decries the world as one malicious ravnina, "S akulami ravnin/ otkazyvaius' plyt'—/ vniz—po techen'iu spin" (With the sharks of plains / I refuse to swim / down—

---

[25] Mikhail Epshtein, *Stikhi i stikhii* (Samara, 2007), 171.
[26] M. M. Kail', "Evropeiskie paralleli v obrazakh prostranstva v skazke P. P. Ershova 'Konek-Gorbunok.'" Accessed at http://library.ikz.ru/georg-steller/aus-sibirien-2013-2005/kail-m.m.-ishim-rossiya-evropeiskie-paralleli-v on 12 February 2010.
[27] Sergei Esenin, *Stikhotvoreniia. Poemy. Povesti. Rasskazy* (Moscow, 2008), 296, 258.

the streams of backs).[28] Slutsky's archetypical plains absorb these divergent permutations, refracting them through a specifically Jewish lamentful and potentially redemptive lens. Indeed, the "–r" of *ravviny* and *ravniny* has the "–r" of "I was a liberator of Ukraine" embedded in it, with its allusion to *iary*—the killing ravines. The rabbis' plains already contain in themselves the memory of the future destruction; they are desolate and gaping, silent and eerily peaceful. There is a profound affinity between Slutsky's imagery and Soviet Holocaust photography, mainly produced by photographers who were Jews, as David Shneer argues (Figure 12-2). Like Slutsky's language, they look at the chasm that opens in nature as a result of the obliteration of the Jews.

FIGURE 12-2. Unattributed, "General View of the Shooting Area at Babi Yar." Source: Yad Vashem Archives, photo no. 4147/20. I am grateful to David Shneer for providing me with this photograph.

In eyeing nature, the rabbis commit an act that breaks with rabbinic ethics. At its most famous, the Mishnah stipulates, "Rabbi Yaakov said: He who is walking by the way and studies and breaks off his study and exclaims: 'How beautiful is this tree!' 'How fine is this field!' is regarded as if he had sinned against his own soul" (Chapters of the Fathers 3:9).[29] It is, of course, fascinating that both Slutsky and the Mishnah speak of the "field." However much Slutsky responded deliberately or intuitively to this passage, his Judaic

---

[28] Marina Tsvetaeva, *Sobranie sochinenii* (Moscow, 1995), 2:360.
[29] *Chapters of the Fathers*, trans. Samson Raphael Hirsch (Jerusalem, 1989), 47.

thinking shines here. Hayim Nahman Bialik famously commented on the rabbinic statement in his "Halachah and Aggadah," stating, "Our aestheticists have spent all their ammunition on this unfortunate mishnah: but even here the sympathetic ear will detect, between the lines, the apprehension, the trembling anxiety for the future, of a wandering people which has nothing to call its own but a Book, and for which any attachment of its soul to one of the lands of its sojourn means mortal danger."[30] Precisely in this "trembling anxiety," the core of Slutsky's poem is located, its correspondence with Bialik's commentary almost uncanny.

Both Slutsky and Bialik treat the damaging relationship between the Jew and nature not as a cliché but as a principal feature of the Jewish mind. In this, they are joined by Celan, who states in "Conversations in the Mountains," "because the Jew, you know, what does he have that is really his own, that is not borrowed, taken and not returned ... because the Jew and nature are strangers to each other, have always been and still are, even today, even here."[31] In Celan's polemic/defense of *Yiddishkeit*, the archetypical Russian plains are substituted with the equally archetypical mountains. The discourse on nature brings into Slutsky's poem another possible intertext, that of Celan's "blood brother"—Osip Mandelstam. The plains constitute one of the predominant images in Mandelstam's late Voronezh poetry. For him, they bear an unmistakably fateful omen, paradigmatically both destructive and freeing. The most relevant text for Slutsky's poem is "Ne sravnivai: zhyvushchii nesravnim ..." (Do not compare: the living is incomparable ...), which also exhibits a striking use of parallelism.[32] Slutsky consciously polemicizes with his Russian-Jewish interlocutor, whose poem stands out as an almost pantheistic embrace of nature by the hounded artist. While Scripture prohibits any portrayal of its deity, the poet reversely commands: do not dare to create a semblance of any living creature, entity, or simply natural element. The artist, who once likened composing poetry to an imitation of Christ, becomes a wandering pagan under the duress of time.[33]

For Slutsky, the Jew's sojourn in history inevitably and fundamentally touches on the experience of solitude—*odinochestvo*—where *odin* (one) is not merely a morpheme but a central concept. On the one hand, the poem's linguistic fabric forms an entrenched Russian-Jewish field. On the other, it collapses the coexistence of the two spheres and traditions; stepping over the boundaries of solitude results in one of these realms' demise. Once again, the sign of the plains holds both ends of the poem together, safeguarding

---

[30] Hayyim Nachman Bialik, *Revealment and Concealment: Five Essays* (Jerusalem, 2000), 67.
[31] Paul Celan, *Collected Prose*, trans. Rosemarie Waldrop (New York, 1986), 17, 18.
[32] Osip Mandel'shtam, *Sobranie sochinenii* (Moscow, 1994), 3:111–12.
[33] See "Skriabin i khristianstvo," in ibid., 1:201–6.

12. Transformed Myths in Verse

its indeterminacy from falling into the abyss of silence, whose resolution spells out very real repercussions for Slutsky's own poetic fate—he wrote not a single line of poetry in the last nine years of his life. Having rooted the destroyed Jewish civilization linguistically and mythologically in the Russian space, Slutsky immediately cuts the cord, which binds them, thus producing a commentary not only on the last hour of the Jewish world but also on its continuous core. Emblematically, Slutsky creates an equally mythological and quotidian picture, where "an hour before" simultaneously signifies the temporal second, minute, hour, year before the demise and the supratemporal parameters of the Jewish world's encounter with history and nature. The latter emerges in the poem in the image of the white smoke (haze) of spring apples, through which Slutsky directly quotes from Esenin's lyric masterpiece, "Ne zhaleiu, ne zovu, ne plachu . . ." (I do not regret, nor call, nor cry . . .), thus turning his poem's intertextual map into a blueprint of its hidden meanings.

Slutsky's citing of Esenin is deeply ironic and compromises the source's tone and worldview. In his poem, Esenin pines over his spent youth, perpetuating the preoccupations of Russian elegy.[34] Ultimately, he does not grumble at life, blessing the gift of life as well as that of death. In turning to Esenin, with his normative lyricisms, Slutsky insists how inadequate and unacceptable they are in the world that bears the mark of the destruction. Their presence in the poem points to their fundamental irreconcilability with the grasp of horror, experienced by the rabbis at the threshold of the end. For the first time, the rabbis glance at the spring apples' white haze—the poet stops here. The Jews' adoring of and bemusement at the apples leads neither to a blessing nor to a curse, so they should not be viewed as a replica of the fruit of the tree of knowledge. The world order alters as the result of what has transpired, but how?

Slutsky does not recreate a traditional—in Homeric (*The Iliad*), biblical (the book of Lamentations), and Pushkinian (*The Bronze Horseman*) terms— scheme of an ironic contrast between indifferent nature and man-made evil, the paradigmatic example of which in modern Jewish poetry comes from Bialik's "In the City of Slaughter" (which, I would argue, Slutsky knew well), where "the sun rose, rye bloomed, and the slaughterer slaughtered . . . / and the sun like the day before yesterday throws its light to the earth."[35] Like Bialik, Slutsky does not describe the indescribable: the actual murder of the people. However, unlike Bialik, he abstains from the diction of an ironic prophet, who imbues nature (and thus, by extension, God), with the malicious uninvolvement in

---

[34] Esenin, *Stikhotvoreniia. Poemy. Povesti. Rasskazy*, 156. For a translation, see http://vagalecs.narod.ru/yes-chron-eng.htm.

[35] *Songs from Bialik*, trans. Atar Hadari (Syracuse, NY, 2000), 1, 2.

human fate. None of the hermeneutic models, Bialik's prophesies, devoid of redemption, or Esenin's jovial acceptance of life's cyclicity, satisfy Slutsky. His "apples" are the sign of the breakdown of language, in its poetic, exegetical, and scriptural expressions, in the face of the catastrophic historical moment. Fundamentally, they are the sign of the mystery of the birth of a new language, overflowing with semantic incompleteness and a promise of hope.

Is there a probability of some deliverance in the far reaches, into which the rabbis, burned by Auschwitz, metamorphose?—the poet leaves this question hermeneutically open. Yet, it is the poem's parallel structure that reveals Slutsky's intent. The last four lines are encased between the seemingly tautological and syntactic parallelism of "black smoke"/ "white smoke." Yet, as typically occurs in Slutsky's poetry, his tautologies act as homonyms. Clearly, the black smoke of the chimneys is radically different from the white smoke of the blossoming apples, and yet the two are interwoven, functioning similarly to a photomontage, in which every image is positioned as an archive of another.[36] Slutsky's smoke should be comprehended as an enantiosemia, a word that designates both itself and its opposite. If in "Now I often dream of Auschwitz," the smoke was a lecherous and tempting tool of destruction, here it touches on something far more fundamental to Slutsky's poetics and metaphysics.[37] On the one hand, the correlation of "smokes" suggests that the seed and reality of the ruin are ingrained in Jewish life, and the cataclysm's consequences cannot be overturned. On the other hand, the impulse of rebirth runs as an undercurrent in the ruinous landscape. Thus "The rabbis walked onto the plains" presents the most resolute yet open-ended version of what I term Slutsky's concept of incomplete messianism. The exodus does not take place in the rabbis' spring, but death does not overpower all either.[38]

Slutsky, as I have pointed out, knows that death in Auschwitz was preceded by a thorough dehumanization of the victims, so he leaves the question of afterlife open. What is astonishing, however, is that his rabbis remain perpetually alive in their consciousness, unceasingly staring at the smoke of the end and perhaps renewal. "The hour before" never ends for them. They do not die but rather vanish. The violence done to them remains ingrained in our memories, language, and psyches, but they, to quote the psalm, "dwell" in life—this is, at least, what the poet hopes.

---

[36] See in Sven Spieker, *The Big Archive: Art from Bureaucracy* (Cambridge, MA, 2008).

[37] In the poem "Domoi" (Homeward), Slutsky compares his and his generation's aging to "black smokes, flying over cities" (*SS*, 3:310). Here again he links his fate with that of the Holocaust, emphasizing the special meaning of "smoke" in his oeuvre.

[38] In the poem "Nemedlennaia spravedlivost' …" (Immediate Justice), Slutsky imagines a messianic scenario in which the "plain of his existence" would turn into a paradise (*SS*, 2:527). He finds the prospect of such perfection nauseating and opts instead for imperfect history.

A Bibliography of John D. Klier's Works

Books

Russia Gathers Her Jews: The Origins of the Jewish Question in Russia (DeKalb: Northern Illinois University Press, 1985).

With Shlomo Lambroza, eds. *Pogroms: Anti-Jewish Violence in Modern Jewish History* (Cambridge: Cambridge University Press, 1992).

Imperial Russia's Jewish Question, 1885–1881 (Cambridge: Cambridge University Press, 1995).

With Helen Mingay. *The Quest for Anastasia: Solving the Mystery of the Lost Romanovs* (Secaucus, NJ: Carol Publishing Group, 1997).

Rossiia sobiraet svoikh evreev (Moscow: Mosty kul'tury; Jerusalem: Gesharim, 2000) [the Russian translation of *Russia Gathers Her Jews*].

Russians, Jews, and the Pogroms of 1881–1882 (Cambridge: Cambridge University Press, 2011).

Articles

"Alexander I, Soldier's Cloth, and the Jews," *Canadian–American Slavic Studies* 9, 4 (1975): 463–71.

"The Ambiguous Legal Status of Russian Jewry in the Reign of Catherine II," *Slavic Review* 35, 3 (1976): 504–17.

"The *Illiustratsiia* Affair of 1858: Polemics on the Jewish Question in the Russian Press," *Nationalities Papers* 5, 2 (1977): 117–35.

"The Jewish Question in the Reform-Era Russian Press, 1855–1865," *Russian Review* 39, 3 (1980): 301–20.

"*Kievlianin* and the Jews: A Decade of Disillusionment, 1864–1873," *Harvard Ukrainian Studies* 5, 1 (1981): 83–101.

"*Odesskii vestnik*'s Annus Mirabilis of 1858," *Canadian Slavonic Papers* 23, 1 (1981): 41–55.

"*Zhid*: The Biography of a Russian Pejorative," *Slavonic and East European Review* 60, 1 (1982): 1–15.

"The Jewish *Den'* and the Literary Mice, 1869–71," *Russian History* 10, 1 (1983): 31–49.

"The Russian Press and the Anti-Jewish Pogroms of 1881," *Canadian-American Slavic Studies* 17, 1 (1983): 199–221.

"The *Times* of London, the Russian Press, and the Pogroms of 1881-2," *Carl Beck Papers* 308 (1984): 1–26.

"1855–1894 Censorship of the Press in Russian and the Jewish Question," *Jewish Social Studies* 48, 3–4 (1986): 257–68.

"The Origins of the 'Blood Libel' in Russia," *Newsletter of the Study Group on Eighteenth Century Russia*, no. 14 (1986): 12–22.

"The Polish Revolt of 1863 and the Birth of Russification: Bad for the Jews?" *Polin: Studies in Polish Jewry* 1 (1986): 91–106.

"Russian Judeophobes and German Antisemites: Strangers and Brothers," *Jahrbucher für Geschichte Osteuropas* 37, 4 (1989): 524–40.

"*Pamiat'* and the 'Jewish Menace': Remembrance of Things Past," *Nationalities Papers* 19, 2 (1991): 214–27.

"The Russian Jewish Intelligentsia and the Concept of *Sliianie*," *Ethnic Studies* 10 (1993): 157–74.

"Krug Gintsburgov i politika shtadlanuta v imperatorskoi Rossii," *Vestnik Evreiskogo universiteta v Moskve* 3, 10 (1995): 38–55.

"'Popular Politics' and the Jewish Question in the Russian Empire, 1881–2," *Transactions of the Jewish Historical Society of England* (1995): 155–85.

"Evreiskii vopros v slavianofil'skoi presse, 1862–1886: I. S. Aksakov i ego izdaniia," *Vestnik Evreiskogo universiteta v Moskve* 1, 17 (1998): 41–60.

"I. S. Aksakov and the Jewish Question, 1862–1886," *Evrei v Rossii: Istoriia i kul'tura: Sbornik nauchnykh trudov* 5 (1998): 155–69.

"Traditional Russian Religious Antisemitism," *The Jewish Quarterly* 174 (Summer 1999): 29–34.

"From *Soviet Jews Affairs* to *East European Jewish Affairs*: A 24-Year Retrospective on the Shifting Priorities of Jews in East-Central Europe," *East European Jewish Affairs* 30, 1 (2000): 1–16.

"The Jew as Russifier: Lev Levanda's *Hot Times*," *Jewish Culture and History* 4, 1 (2001): 31–52.

"New Politics for Old: A Reassessment of the Traditional Jewish Political Leadership in 1881–1882," *Jewish Studies at the Central European University* 2 (2002): 125–35.

"Solzhenitsyn and the Kishinev Pogrom: A Slander against Russia?" *East European Jewish Affairs* 33, 1 (2003): 49–59.

"Why Were Russian Jews Not Kaisertreu?" *Ab Imperio*, no. 4 (2003): 41–58.

"Polish Shtetls under Russian Rule, 1772–1914," *Polin: Studies in Polish Jewry* 17 (2004): 97–108.

"'Two Synagogues' in Moscow: Jewish Books in the Russian Capital," *East European Jewish Affairs* 34, 2 (2004): 171–77.

"The *Kahal* in the Russian Empire—Life, Death, and Afterlife of a Jewish Institution, 1772–1882," *Jahrbuch des Simon-Dubnow-Instituts* 5 (2006): 33–50.

Book Chapters

"Muscovite Faces and Petersburg Masks: The Problem of Religious Judeophobia in 18th-Century Russia," in *Russia and the World of the Eighteenth Century*, ed. R. P. Bartlett et al. (Columbus, OH: Slavica Publishers, 1988), 125–39.

"The Concept of 'Jewish Emancipation' in a Russian Context," in *Civil Rights in Imperial Russia*, ed. Olga Crisp and Linda Edmondson (Oxford: Clarendon Press; New York: Oxford University Press, 1989), 121–44.

"Russian Jewry on the Eve of the Pogroms," 3–12, and "The Pogrom Paradigm in Russian History," 13–38, in *Pogroms: Anti-Jewish Violence in Modern Russian History*, ed. Klier and Lambroza.

"Russkaia voina protiv 'Khevra kadisha,'" in *Istoriia evreev v Rossii: Problemy istorichnikovedeniia i istoriografii*, ed. D. A. El'iashevich (St. Petersburg: Peterburgskii evreiskii universitet, 1993), 109–15.

"Russian Jewry as the 'Little Nation' of the Russian Revolution," in *Jews and Jewish Life in Russia and the Soviet Union*, ed. Yaacov Ro'i (Ilford, UK: Frank Cass, 1995), 146–56.

"Emigration Mania in Late-Imperial Russia: Legend and Reality," in *Patterns of Migration, 1850–1914*, ed. Aubrey Newman and Stephen W. Massil (London: Jewish Historical Society of England, 1996), 21–30.

"Judaizing without Jews: Novgorod and Moscow, 1480–1505," in *Culture and Identity in Muscovy, 1359–1584*, ed. A. M. Kleimola and G. D. Lenhoff (Moscow: ITZ-Garant, 1997), 336–49.

"The Myth of Zion among East European Jewry," in *Myths and Nationhood*, ed. George Schöpflin and Geoffrey Hosking (New York: Routledge in association with the School of Slavonic and East European Studies, University of London, 1997), 170–81.

"The Dog That Didn't Bark: Antisemitism in Post-Communist Russia," in *Russian Nationalism Past and Present*, ed. Geoffrey Hosking and Robert Service (Basingstoke, UK: MacMillan in association with the School of Slavonic and East European Studies, University of London; New York: St. Martin's Press, 1998), 129–47.

"S. M. Dubnov and the Kiev Pogrom of 1882," in *A Missionary for History: Essays in Honor of S. M. Dubnow*, ed. K. Groberg and A. Greenbaum (Minneapolis: University of Minnesota, 1998), 65–71.

"Russian Jews and the Soviet Agenda," in *Reinterpreting Russia*, ed. Geoffrey Hosking and Robert Service (Oxford: Oxford University Press, 1999), 183–97.

"Velikii Oktiabr': Khorosho dlia evreia, plokho dlia evreev," in *Evrei i russkaia revoliutsiia: Materialy i issledovaniia*, ed. O. V. Budnitskii (Moscow: Mosty kul'tury; Jerusalem: Gesharim, 1999), 443–50.

"*Westjuden*: Germany and German Jews through East European Eyes," in *The German Lands and Eastern Europe*, ed. Roger Bartlett and Karen Schönwälder (London: MacMillan, 1999), 136–56.

"Mesjanism zydowski w wieku Mickiewicza," in *Duchowosc Zydowska w Polsce: materiały z międzynarodowej konferencji dedykowaneamięci Profesora Chone Shmeruka, Kraków, 26–28 kwietnia*, ed. Michał Galas (Krakow: Księg. Akademicka, 2000), 219–27.

"The Russian Jewish Intelligentsia and the Search for National Identity," in *Ethnic and National Issues in Russian and East European History*, ed. John Morison (London: Macmillan, 2000), 131–45.

"What Exactly Was a Shtetl?" in *The Shtetl: Image and Reality*, ed. Gennady Estraikh and Mikhail Krutikov (Oxford: Legenda, 2000), 23–35.

"'Manuscripts Don't Burn': The Significance of Open Archives in the FSU," in *Preserving Jewish Archives as Part of the European Cultural Heritage*, ed. Jean-Claude Kuperminc and Rafaele Arditt (Paris: Nadir de l'alliance israélite universelle, 2001), 76–82.

"State Policy and the Conversion of Jews in Imperial Russia," in *Of Religion and Empire: Missions, Conversion, and Tolerance in Russia*, ed. Robert Geraci and Michael Khodarkovsky (Ithaca, NY: Cornell University Press, 2001), 92–112.

"Christians and Jews and the 'Dialogue of Violence' in Late Imperial Russia," in *Religious Violence between Christians and Jews: Medieval Roots, Modern Perspectives*, ed. Anna Sapir Abulafia (Basingstoke, UK: Palgrave Macmillan, 2002), 157–70.

"'Exit, Pursued by a Bear': Russian Administrators and the Ban on Yiddish Theatre in Imperial Russia," in *Yiddish Theatre: New Approaches*, ed. Joel Berkowitz (Oxford: The Littman Library of Jewish Civilization, 2003), 159–74.

"From Elisavetgrad to Broadway: The Strange Odyssey of Iakov Gordon," in *Extending the Borders of Russian History: Essays in Honor of Alfred J. Rieber*, ed. Marsha Siefert (Budapest: Central European University Press, 2003), 113–25.

"The Jewish Press and Jewish Identity: Leningrad/St. Petersburg, 1989–1992," in *New Jewish Identities: Contemporary Europe and Beyond*, ed. Zvi Gitelman et al. (Budapest: Central European University Press, 2003), 139–57.

"*Aliyah, Goldene Medina* or *Neues Vaterland*: Emigration Choices in the Late Soviet Jewish Press," in *Der Ort des Judentums in der Gegenwart, 1989–2002*, ed. Hiltrud Wallenborn et al. (Berlin: Be.Bra, 2004), 29–46.

"The Holocaust and the Soviet Union," in *The Historiography of the Holocaust*, ed. Dan Stone (Basingstoke, UK: Palgrave Macmillan, 2004), 276–95.

"'Otkuda i kuda idem': Izuchenie dorevoliutsionnoi istorii rossiiskogo evreistva v Soedinennykh Shtatakh v XX veke," in *Istoriia i kul'tura rossiiskogo i vostochnoevropeiskogo evreistva*, ed. O. V. Budnitskii et al. (Moscow: Dom evreiskoi knigi, 2004), 40–65.

"Traditions of the Commonwealth: Lithuanian Jewry and the Exercise of Political Power in Tsarist Russia," in *The Vanished World of Lithuanian Jews*, ed. Alvydas Nikzentaitis, Stefan Schreiner, and Darius Staliunas (Amsterdam: Rodopi, 2004), 5–20.

"From 'Little Man' to 'Milkman': Does Jewish Art Reflect Jewish Life?" *Studies in Jewish Civilization* 16: *The Jews of Eastern Europe*, ed. Leonard J. Greenspoon, Ronald A. Simkins, and Gerald Shapiro (Omaha: Creighton University Press, 2005), 217–31.

"Jewry in the Former Soviet Union," in *Modern Judaism: An Oxford Guide*, ed. Nicholas de Lange and Miri Freud-Kandel (Oxford: Oxford University Press, 2005), 178–90.

"Kazaki i pogromy: Chem otlichalis' 'voennye' pogromy?" in *Mirovoi krizis 1914–1920 i sud'ba vostochnoevropeiskogo evreistva*, ed. O. V. Budnitskii et al. (Moscow: ROSSPEN, 2005), 47–70.

"Iskusstvo i pogromy: Khudozhestvennoe otobrazhenie antievreiskogo nasiliia v imperskoi Rossii, 1871–1903," in *Russko-evreiskaia kul'tura*, ed. O. V. Budnitskii et al. (Moscow: ROSSPEN, 2006), 437–52.

"Russification and the Jews Reconsidered," in *Central and East European Jews at the Crossroads of Tradition and Modernity*, ed. Jurgita Siauciunaite-Verbickiene and Larisa Lempertiene (Vilnius: Center for Studies of the Culture of East European Jews, 2006), 11–32.

"Kontrabanda liudei: Pravitel'stvo Rossii i emigratsiia iz Tsarstva Pol'skogo v 1881–1892 gg.," in *Evreiskaia emigratsiia, 1881–2005*, ed. O.V. Budnitskii (Moscow: ROSSPEN, 2008), 20–33.

"Russland bis 1917," in *Handbuch des Antisemitismus. Judenfeindschaft in Geschichte und Gegenwart* 1: *Länder und Regionen*, ed. Wolfgang Benz (Munich: de Gruyter, 2008), 298–306.

"Speaking the Language of the Streets: The Press and the Narrative of Russia's Urban Pogroms of 1881–82," in *Presse und Stadt. City and Press*, ed. Susanne Marten-Finnis and Markus Winkler (Bremen: Édition Lumière, 2009), 173–82.

Review Articles

"The Former Soviet Union and Its Jews," *Studies in Contemporary Jewry* 9 (1993): 183–87.

"Unravelling the Conspiracy Theory: A New Look at the Pogroms," *East European Jewish Affairs* 23, 2 (1993): 79–89.

"Hunter's Notebooks," *East European Jewish Affairs* 27, 1 (1997): 85–95.

"Polemics with Encyclopedias: Aleksandr Solzhenitsyn's *Dvesti let vmeste*," *Ab Imperio*, no. 2 (2002): 589–604.

"Sapper in a Minefield—Russians Read Solzhenitsyn's *Two Hundred Years Together*," *Jahrbuch des Simon-Dubnow-Instituts* 2 (2003): 491–515.

"Cry Bloody Murder," *East European Jewish Affairs* 36, 2 (2006): 213–29.

Short Notes

"Archival Sources for the Study of East European Jewry in Kiev," *Soviet Jewish Affairs* 21, 2 (1991): 39–44.

"Kiev Archival Materials on East European Jewry," *Soviet Jewish Affairs* 21, 2 (1991): 39–43.

"Sources of Liberal Judeophobia in Reform-Era Russia," in *Istoricheskie sud'by evreev v Rossii i SSSR*, ed. I. Krupnik and M. Kupovskii (Moscow: Evreiskoe istoricheskoe obshchestvo, 1991), 72–77.

"O russko-evreiskoi intelligentsii: K postanovke voprosa," in *Evrei v Rossii: Istoriia i kul'tura*, ed. D. A. El'iashevich (St. Petersburg: Peterburgskii evreiskii universitet, 1995).

"A Port, Not a Shtetl: Reflections on the Distinctiveness of Odessa," *Jewish Culture and History* 4, 2 (2001): 169–74.

"Hans Rogger, 1923–2002," *East European Jewish Affairs* 32, 1 (2002), 149–52.

"Introduction: Two Epochal Anniversaries—The Death of Stalin and the Kishinev Pogrom," *East European Jewish Affairs* 33, 1 (2003): 1–3.

INDEX

Page numbers followed by letter *f* indicate figures.

A

Abraham of Bohemia, 142
Abramovich, Sh. J., 84–85, 89, 103; *The Wishing Ring*, 96
Adler, Cyrus, 211
Afrikaners population growth, 135–36
Ahad ha'am, 88, 211
Akhmatova, Anna, 251, 251n6
Aksenfeld, Yisroel, 103
Aleksandra Petrovna Romanova (Grand Duchess of Russia), 35
Alekseev, Aleksandr, 49
Alexander II (Tsar of Russia): emancipation of serfs under, 218; pogroms after assassination of, 73, 160, 167; selective integration under, 51, 52, 219. *See also* Great Reforms
Alexander III (Tsar of Russia), 216, 217, 221
Alexandria (Egypt), pogrom in, 150
Allgemeine Zeitung des Judentums, 215
Altshuler, Mordechai, 192n20
America. *See* immigration to America; United States
American Jewish Joint Distribution Committee (JDC), 66
American liberation photography, 232, 236; vs. Soviet liberation photography, 242, 243
Anna Karenina (Tolstoy), 90, 91–92, 100
An-sky, Semyon Akimovich: assimilationism of, resentment of, 77; "Behind a Mask," 68; childhood of, 74–75; *The Destruction of Galicia*, 191n13, 197; and *Evreiskii mir* (journal), 76, 76n24, 78; Kiev archive of, 68–69; letters to Zhitlowsky, 69–70; and Lilienblum, 74–75, 78; Lozno diary of, 67, 68–69, 70–73, 81–82; narrative of return, 69; revision of memoir, 78–79, 81; Russian and Yiddish literature influencing, 68, 79–81; as self-promoter, 69, 78–79, 82; "Sins of Youth and Sins of Age," 67, 72–73, 75–76, 78–79, 81

antisemitism: nationalism and, 176; racialism and, 168, 169–70, 186; resistance to political liberalization and, 167, 168, 175; in Russia, Klier on, 169, 169n6, 172–73; in Russia, origins of, 173–74; in Russia, spread in 19th century, 174–75; in Russian army, 189–93, 196, 201; traditional vs. modern, 167–69, 171–72; transnational quality of, 185; and visual depiction of Jews in rightwing newspapers, 167, 171, 175, 176–84, 179*f*, 180*f*, 183*f*, 184*f*, 186; in Western and Central Europe, 169–70, 185–86. *See also* pogrom(s)
Antselovitch, I., 230, 231
apology, letters of, 115–16
Argentine steppes, Jewish colonization of, 53
army, Russian: antisemitism in, 189–93, 196, 201; role in pogroms, 188, 189, 189n5
army service, Jews and: desire to avoid, 121–22, 122n48. *See also* Cantonists
Aronson, Michael, 152
artisans, Jewish, 51–52; and Yiddish language, 65. *See also* ORT
Ashkenazi Jews. *See* East European Jewry
Aslanov, Cyril, 140
assimilation: An-sky and, resentment of, 77; of West European Jewry, Dubnow on, 210
Associated Press, 159, 163
Auschwitz: photographic images of, 236, 243–44; poem about, 247, 256–58; as symbol of Holocaust, limitations of, 249–50
autobiography. *See* memoirs
autocracy: extreme right and defense of, 179–80, 180*f*; Jews and opposition to, 221
Avi Chai Foundation, 18
Aviezer (Guenzburg), 74
Avrutin, Eugene, 57, 170

B

Babel', Isaac Emmanuilovich, 200
Babi Yar, 250, 261*f*
"Babi Yar" (Ehrenburg), 224, 231
Bakinovskii, Pavel, 29, 31

Index

Bakst, Isaac, 53
Bakst, Nikolai (Noah), 52–54
Bałaban, Majer, 137, 142
Baltermants, Dmitrii, 226–28, 230, 232; photographs of Nazi atrocities, 227f
Bankanovich, Meier, 155n29
Baring, Maurice, 162n53
Baron, Salo W.: and conspiratorial theory of pogroms, 149; on Jewish migration, 130–31, 142; on lachrymose conception of Jewish history, 149, 203, 207, 218; on victims of Civil War pogroms, 187n1
Bartal, Israel, 203n2, 219n78
bats, depiction of Jews as, 179–82, 180f
"Behind a Mask" (An-sky), 68
Beider, Alexander, 140–41
Beilis, Mendel, 169, 182
Belorussia, 1915 pogroms in, 193–94
Benjamin, Walter, 251, 254n14
Bergelson, David, 55, 65, 248, 252n10
Bernshteyn, Arn Dovid, 114
Bhabha, Homi, 28
Bialik, Hayim Nahman, 88, 89, 262, 263, 264
Białystok, pogroms in, 162, 199
Biloxi Blues (Simon), 80n39
Birch, Mariia Noevna, 27, 28
Birnboym, Y., 109n9
Black Death: and end of *Ostsiedlung*, 132, 144; impact on Eastern Europe, 144–45; Jews during, 132–33
Black Hundreds, 176; French antisemites compared to, 185; membership in, 176; perception of Jews as threat, 177–84, 179f, 180f, 183f, 184f; and pogroms of October 1905, 221
blood libel, 169; appearance in Russia, 174, 182; Klier on, 174n18
Bloom, Harold, 254
bogatyr, depiction in political cartoons, 179, 180f
Bohemian Jews. *See* Czech Jews
Bolshevism: Jewish participation in, pogroms as retribution for, 188, 200. *See also* socialism
Bonnell, Victoria, 177n26
Börne, Karl Ludwig, 70
Borodulin, Lev, 228

Bourke-White, Margaret, 242, 243
Brafman, Yaakov, 49
Bramson, Leon, 54, 59
Brenner, Michael, 205
Briantsev, Nikandr, 27, 29–35, 37, 40, 43, 45, 49
British press: on pogroms in tsarist Russia, 154, 155, 156, 157, 159–61, 211; on Warsaw pogrom of Christmas 1881, 155–56
brivnshteler (Jewish anthology of model letters), 106, 107–8; anxieties in, 117–18, 119, 124–26; authors of, 107; bi- or trilingualism in, 110, 111n15, 113; emigration to America in, 108, 119–20, 120n41, 122–25; modernizing trends in, 113–15, 119; and "paper life," 119, 126; parent-child relations in, 116–18, 120, 124–25; *pis'movnik* compared to, 106, 108–18, 126; politics in, 108, 108n4; readers of, 107; romance in, 112, 113–15
The Brothers Karamazov (Dostoevsky), 251
Brutskus, Boris (Ber), 54, 58
Brzhenkovskaya, Bronislava, 194
Buber, Shlomo, 203n2
Buchenwald, images of, 224, 236, 242
Bulak-Balakhovich, Stanislav Nikodimovich, 188–89
Bund (political party), 208; and Yiddish language, 59, 63
Buxtorf the Elder, Johann, 143
Byzantium: iconography of, representation of Jews in, 172; Jewish migration to Eastern Europe from, 128, 129n2, 138n34

C

Cantonists, loyalty to Judaism, 215–16
Caron, Vicki, 168
Catherine the Great (Empress of Russia), 174, 182
Celan, Paul, 246, 262
censorship: of *brivnshtelers*, 122; of Dubnow's work, 214; of Jewish press, 76n24; relaxation during Great Reforms, 219n78; of Yiddish books, 108
Central Europe. *See* Western and Central Europe

273

Central Jewish Committee for the Relief of War Victims (EKOPO), 64
Central Zionist Organization, 163
charitable organizations *(hevras)*, 52, 54
Chechen War, First, 197–98
Chego khotiat evrei (Dubnow), 220–21
Chelishchev, Mikhail Nikolaevich, 30
Chrysostom, Saint John, 173
cities: pogroms in, 153. *See also specific cities*
civil rights movement, influence on Klier, 15
civil-society institutions, Jewish: components of government in, 60; failure of integration reforms and, 58; "generation of 1905" and, 64; intellectuals in, 54; mutual-aid organizations, 55–58, 63–64; philanthropic organizations, 51–54; in post-World War I Eastern Europe, 64–65; and Yiddish language, 59, 65, 66
Civil War, Russian: atamans of, 188–89, 189n6. *See also* pogroms of Civil War period
Cohen, Israel, 148n3
Cold War era, Russian historical research in, 17
concentration camps: photographic images of, 224, 225, 233–42, 234f–235f, 238f, 239f, 241f, 243f, 245; poetry about, 247, 256–58
Confessions (Rousseau), 86, 92n22, 97
consumer cooperatives, and Jewish trade, 57
conversion/converts, Jewish: ambivalence toward, 28, 38, 40, 168n1; Cantonist resistance to, Dubnow on, 215–16; Christian neglect of, 48–49; dishonesty of, 40, 42, 43; educational and professional choices for, 45–46; in medieval Christian society, 172; modern antisemitism and rejection of, 168, 171; poverty and, 38–39; racialization of, 49, 57; traditional antisemitism and acceptance of, 172; women, 33, 43–44. *See also* Mariinsko Sergievskii Shelter for Baptized Jewish Children
cooperatives: consumer, 57; credit, 55–58, 65–66; Second Congress in Kiev, 63–64; and Yiddish language, 61, 64, 66
correspondence. *See* letters
Cossacks, role in pogroms, 189, 194, 195, 197, 200
craftsmen. *See* artisans
credit cooperatives, Jewish, 55–58; at Second Congress of All-Russian Cooperatives, 63–64; in Soviet Union, 65–66; and Yiddish language, 61, 64, 66
Crusades, 132, 172, 209
Czech Jews, 136–37, 141; migration into Polish lands, 137–38, 142, 143, 145; population growth among, 144–45
Czernowitz Yiddish Language Conference, 62, 63

D

Dachau, images of, 224, 236, 242, 245
Davitt, Michael, 158n42, 211
Dawn (Jewish weekly), 92
death camps. *See* concentration camps
Demidov, Igor' Petrovich, 197
Denikin, Anton Ivanovich, 199
deportations of Jews, during World War I, 192, 192n20, 193, 213
Desert Evening News (newspaper), 162
desire *(heyshek/heshek)*, in Sholem-aleichem's *The Penknife*, 92–94, 97, 98
The Destruction of Galicia (An-sky), 191n13, 197
devil, visual association of Jews with, 171, 172, 185n39
diaries: An-sky's, 67, 68–69, 70–73, 81–82; artistic considerations in, 81–82; reading out loud, 79–80, 80n39
diaspora: emancipation of Western Jewry and reinterpretation of, 207; Russian-Jewish, creation of, 213
diaspora nationalism: Dubnow and, 203, 205, 207, 208, 222; ORT and, 65; Zhitlowsky and, 67
Dietrich-Löwe, Heinz, 152
Dik, Aizik-Meyer (Ayzik Meyer), 80, 81, 85, 103, 104
Diner, Hasia, 211
Dinezon, Yankev, 78
Dmowski, Roman, 148
Dolgorukov, Pavel Dmitrievich, 192
"Domoi" (Slutsky), 264n37
Dostoevsky, Fyodor, 104; *The Brothers*

Karamazov, 251; *The Idiot*, 90–92, 100
Dov, Tsvi, 125
Dracula (Stoker), 181
Dreyfus Affair, 185
Dubnow, Simon Markeevich: belief in Jewish exceptionalism, 202, 220; *Chego khotiat evrei* ("What Do the Jews Want?"), 220–21; disciples of, 222; on emancipation of Jews, 210, 222; and *Evreiskii mir* (journal), 208; after February Revolution, 220–21; Friedlaender and, 211, 212; Graetz and, 221–22; and historiography of Russian Jewry, 202–6, 203n2; *History of the Jews*, 210; *History of the Jews of Russia and Poland*, 205, 211–20; ideological schema of, 60, 203, 207, 214–20; and lachrymose conception of Jewish history, 149, 203, 205, 207–8, 214–15, 218, 222; metaphor of "thirty years' war," 206, 214; on persecution and national renaissance, 205, 206, 207–10, 215–20, 222; on pogroms, 149, 218; publications in U.S., 205, 210–12; on Sholem-aleichem's *The Penknife*, 92, 93; *Wissenschaft des Judentums* and, 203–5, 206, 215, 221, 222; on Yiddish language, 50; and *Yidishe velt* (journal), 208–10
Dundes, Alan, 168n1
Dzagiler, P. D., 28, 34

E

Eastern Europe: Black Death in, 144–45; German migration into *(Ostsidelung)*, 130n4, 131–32, 144; medieval Jewish population in, 133–34. *See also* East European Jewry
East European Jewish Affairs (journal), 18
East European Jewry: genetic background of, 129n2, 140, 140n40; individual/family migration and origins of, 137–38, 141–42, 145; Khazar origins of, hypothesis of, 129n3, 138n34, 139; migration creating, 127–33, 134n15; onomastic evidence for origins of, 140–42; population growth among, 135, 135n20, 136; religious customs *(minhag)* of, 137–38; resistance to new waves of Jewish migration, 130–31; source population of, 128–29; source regions for, 136–37; Yiddish dialect of, 138–40, 143. *See also* migration of Jews into Eastern Europe
education: for converted Jews, 34–35; Jewish, Sholem-aleichem's *The Penknife* on, 86, 94, 95, 99; Jewish philanthropy and, 52, 53; and language instruction, debate about, 62–63
Egypt: first antisemitic pogrom in, 150; Israelites' exile in, tsarist Russia compared to, 217
Ehrenburg, Ilya, 247n1; "Babi Yar," 224, 231
Einsatzgruppen, 224, 228
Einstein, Albert, 238, 251
EKOPO (Central Jewish Committee for the Relief of War Victims), 64
Elisavetgrad pogrom (1881), 154, 156
Elkun, Jonathan, 172
emancipation, Jewish: Dubnow on, 210, 222; historiography of struggle for, 204, 206, 207; lachrymose conception as tool in battle for, 207; in Western and Central Europe, 207, 210, 214, 215, 218
emancipation of serfs, 218
emigration: and national renewal, Dubnow on, 210. *See also* immigration to America
Emily's New Moon (Montgomery), 80n39
Engel, David, 145, 207
England: Jewish studies in, 18. *See also* British press; English language
English language: Russian words absorbed in, 153n20; term "pogrom" in, 153–54, 162; and Yiddish language, 125
Epshtein, Mikhail, 260
eroticism: in Sholem-aleichem's *The Penknife*, 93, 95, 96–97, 98, 100–101. *See also* love letters; sexual imagery
Esenin, Sergei, 260, 263, 264
espionage suspects, Jews as, 192–93, 196
Ettinger, S., 187n1
Even the Wise Can Err (Ostrovskii), 79–80
Evreiskaia nedelia (journal), 196
Evreiskii mir (journal), 208; An-sky and, 76, 76n24, 78; Dubnow and, 208
Extraordinary State Commission for the Establishment and Investigation of Atrocities Committed by the German-

275

Index

Fascist Invaders and Their Accomplices, 231–32, 236, 244

F
family correspondence, 106n1, 120–21, 120n42, 124, 125–26
family/individual migration of Jews, 137–38, 141–42, 145
"Farewell" (Slutsky), 254
February Revolution. *See* Revolution of 1917
Fiddler on the Roof (musical), 222n91
fields. *See* plains/fields
Fink, Carole, 149
"The First Century" (Slutsky), 254
First Chechen War, 197–98
Fishman, David, 219n78
Fitzhugh, Louise, 68
Flaubert, Gustave, 90
Folkists, and Yiddish language, 59
forensic photography, Soviet, 231–32, 233, 236, 244
Fort Hays State University, 16
Forverts (newspaper), 62, 65, 66; advice column in, 115
France: antisemitism in, 168, 185. *See also* French Revolution; Western and Central Europe
Frankel, Jonathan, 20, 192n20, 219n78, 222n89
Fraynd (newspaper), 61
Fredrickson, George, 170
French Revolution: and modern antisemitism, 167; reevaluation of diaspora experience after, 207
French-speaking population of Quebec, 136
Freundlich, Charles H., 219n78
Fridlyand, Semen, 226n2
Friedlaender, Israel, 205, 206, 207, 210–14
Friedman, Dov Arye, 122
Friedman, Richard, 259
Frishman, Dovid, 111
From the Fair (Sholem-aleichem), 80–81
Fuenn, Shmuel Yosef, 203n2
Fussell, Paul, 245

G
Galaka, Ivan, 189n6

Galicia, pogroms in, 195, 197
Garfield, James, 154
Garnier, Théodore, 185
Gassenschmidt, Christoph, 64
Gergel, N., 187n1
German-speaking lands: migration into Eastern Europe from, 130n4, 131–32, 144; persecution and expulsion of Jews from, 133
Germany: concentration camps in, 244; historiography of Jews in, 204; pogroms in, 154; *Reichskristallnacht* in, 150. *See also* Nazism; Western and Central Europe
Gilman, Sander, 184
Gintsburg family, 51
Gobineau, Arthur de, 170
Gogol, Nikolai, 104; *The Inspector General*, 68, 79
Goldstein, David, 140n40
Golubova, Vera, 29, 31
Gomel: 1903 pogrom in, 159; savings-and-loan association in, 55
Gordon, Judah Leib, 103
Gorelik, Shmarye, 77
Gornfel'd, Arkady, 77–78
Goscilo, Helena, 179
Gossman, Lionel, 86–87
Gotlober, Abraham, 103
government: components of, in Jewish civil-society institutions, 60; role in pogroms, assertions regarding, 149–52, 155, 156–57, 161–63
Graetz, Heinrich, 215, 218; and Dubnow, 221–22
Great Reforms, era of: censorship in, 219n78; emancipation of serfs in, 218; extreme Right's resistance to, 176; Jewish question in, 17–18, 175; pogroms in, 73, 152, 160, 167; selective integration in, 51, 52, 219
Grigor'ev, Nikifor Aleksandrovich, 188, 189n6
Grossman, Vladimir, 59
Guenzburg, Mordecai Aaron, 74
Gurarii, Samarii, 236–37, 240
Gusev-Orenburgskii, S., 187n1

H
Ha'am, Ahad, 88, 211

Index

Handl un Melokhe (journal), 64
Harkavy, Alexander, 111
Hasid, Rabbi Judah Ha, 137n28
Hebraists, language wars with Yiddishists, 62–63
Hebrew: in *brivnshtelers* (letter-writing manuals), 110; Jewish cultural renaissance and, 219
heder: corporal punishment in, 94, 95, 99; and literacy, 109; in Sholem-aleichem's *The Penknife*, 86, 94, 95, 99, 102
hevras (charitable organizations), 52, 54
heyshek/heshek (desire), in Sholem-aleichem's *The Penknife*, 92–94, 97, 98
Hilbrenner, Anke, 209
Hirsch, Baron Maurice de, 53
Hirshkan, Tsvi, 77
History of the Jews (Dubnow), 210
History of the Jews of Russia and Poland (Dubnow), 205, 211–20
Holocaust, poetic responses to, 246–64, 247n1
Holocaust photography: American, 232, 236, 242, 243, 245; concentration camp images in, 224, 225, 233, 236, 242, 245; perpetrator images in, 224, 225; Soviet, 225, 227–45, 227f, 229f, 234f, 235f, 238f, 239f, 241f, 243f; survivor figure in, 243–44
Homer, 263
Horowitz (Hurwitz), Khaim Dov, 61
"How They Killed My Grandmother" (Slutsky), 257
Hundert, Gershon, 113n24, 134
Hurwitz (Horowitz), Khaim Dov, 61

I

The Idiot (Dostoevsky), 90–92, 100
Illustrated London News (newspaper), 236
immigration to America: in family correspondence, 106n1, 120–21, 120n42, 124, 125–26; in model letters *(brivnshteler)*, 108, 119–20, 120n41, 122–25; motivations for, 121–22; and national renewal, Dubnow on, 210; *pis'movnik* on, 111
Imperial Philanthropy Society, 30
Imperial Russia: government conspiracy against Jews in, theories of, 157–58; Jewish experience in, Dubnow and lachrymose conception of, 203, 205, 207–8, 214–15, 218, 222; notion of race in, 170–71; pogroms in, Anglo-American press on, 151, 154–63, 165–66; rightwing press in, visual depiction of Jews in, 167, 171, 175, 176–84, 179f, 180f, 183f, 184f, 186
Imperial Russia's Jewish Question (Klier), 17–18, 83–84
industrialization, antisemitism as backlash against, 167, 175
The Inspector General (Gogol), 68, 79
integration of Jews: vs. disaggregation from larger society, 57; failure of state-sponsored efforts, 58; selective, 51–53, 219. *See also* conversion/converts, Jewish
International Research and Exchanges Board (IREX), 17
Isserles, Rabbi Moses, 138
Italy, Jewish migration to, 133
Ivan IV (Ivan the Terrible), 173
Ivanov, Alexander, 161n51
"I was a liberator of Ukraine" (Slutsky), 247–55, 255f
Izvestiia (newspaper), 236–37

J

Jackson, Robert Louis, 102
Jacobs, Joseph, 156
Janville, Sibylle Martel de, 185
Japan, Russia's war with, 170
JDC (American Jewish Joint Distribution Committee), 66
Jewish Chronicle, on pogroms, 159, 162, 162n53
Jewish Colonization Association (JCA), 53, 54, 59–60; and credit cooperatives, 61, 66; and Yiddish language, 63
Jewish People's Fraternal Order, 66
Jewish People's Gazette, 86
Jewish Publication Society of America (JPS), 210–11, 213
Jewish question: emergence of, 174; evolution of, 17–18; public debate on, 48–49, 175
Jewish World (weekly), 155, 156
John Chrysostom, Saint, 173

277

K

Kafka, Franz, 254n14
Kahanovitsch, Pinkhes, 76–77
Kail', M. M., 260
Kapel, Alexander, 77
Karaites, 139
Keane, John, 59
Kedrov, P. I., 34
Kel'ner, Viktor, 19
Kennan, George, 150n8
Kerch: German occupation in World War II, 226–27; Nazi mass murders at, 227–28, 227f, 227n4, 229f
Kerenskii, Alexandre Fedorovich, 196
Khaldei, Evgenii, 228–29; images of Nazi atrocities, 229f
Khazars, and East European Jews, 129n3, 138n34, 139
kheder. See heder
Kiev: An-sky archive in, 68–69; Babi Yar in, 224, 231, 250, 261f; during Civil War, 198–99; Klier's research in, 18; medieval Jewish community in, 128; pogrom of 1881 in, 163; Second Congress of All-Russian Cooperatives in, 63–64
King, Robert, 139
Kirschrot, Jan, 62
Kishinev pogrom (1903), Anglo-American press coverage of, 154, 158–59, 211
Klee, Paul, 251
Klier, John Doyle: on antisemitism in Russia, 169, 169n6, 172–73; bibliography of works by, 265–72; biography of, 14–20; on blood libel, 174n18; conference in honor of, 20; on conversion of Jews, 57; and field of Russian-Jewish history and culture, 14, 15–16, 20; on Gintsburg Circle, 51; *Imperial Russia's Jewish Question*, 17–18, 83–84; on integration of Jews, 58; and new generation of Jewish studies scholars, 19; on pogroms, 19, 152–53, 156n34; research after collapse of Soviet Union, 18–19; research in Soviet Union, 17; *Russia Gathers Her Jews*, 16, 26; *Russians, Jews, and the Pogroms of 1881-1882*, 19, 152; use of fiction for understanding of Jewish history, 84
Knorring, Oleg, 236
Der Kooperativer Kredit in Mayerev-kant (journal), 64
Kotik, Abraham Hersh, 64
Kovel, Joel, 246
Kraków, Czech Jews in, 137–38, 143
Krasnaia zvezda (newspaper), 236
Krogh, Steffen, 139
Kutrzeba, Stanisław, 145
Kuzmin, Mikhail, 80n39

L

Labor Zionists, and Yiddish language, 59
lachrymose conception of Jewish history: Baron on, 149, 203, 207, 218; Dubnow and, 149, 203, 205, 207–8, 214–15, 218, 222
land. *See* plains/fields
land speculation, association of Jews with, 183, 184f
languages: in *brivnshteler*, 110, 111n15, 113; Turkic, East European Jews and, 139. *See also* English language; Hebrew; Russian language; Yiddish language
Latski-Bertoldi, Wolf, 60, 64
Lauterbach, Richard, 242
Lazarus, image of, 256, 258
Lenepveu, V., 185
lernen und leiden (study and persecution), in Jewish historiography, 204, 205, 222
Lestschinsky, Jacob, 60, 62, 64, 65
letters: European cross-linguistic manuals, 110; family, 106n1, 120–21, 120n42, 124, 125–26. *See also brivnshteler; pis'movnik*
Levin, Nora, 187n1
Levinsohn, Isaac-Baer, 103
liberalism, antisemitism as backlash against, 167, 168, 175
LIFE Magazine, 236, 242
Lifshits, Yeshue-Mordkhe, 53
Lilienblum, Moshe Leib: An-sky and, 74–75, 78; *Sins of Youth*, 68, 73–76
Linetskii, Yitskhok Yoyel, 103
Liozno, 67; An-sky on, 70–71
literacy: *brivnshteler* and, 109–10; *pis'movnik* and, 111

Index

literature: and understanding of Jewish history, 84. *See also* poetry; Russian literature; Yiddish literature

Lithuania: Ashkenazi Jews in, origins of, 141; medieval Jewish population in, 133; pogroms of 1915, 193–94; resistance to new waves of Jewish migration in, 131

Litvak, Olga, 210n31, 215, 216

Litvin, A., 65

locusts, depiction of Jews as, 178, 179*f*, 185

Los Angeles Herald (newspaper), 163

love letters: in *brivnshteler,* 112, 113–15; in *pis'movnik,* 111–12, 113

Löwe, Heinz-Dietrich, 175

Lublin, 238*f*, 239, 241*f*

luftmentshn, 52

M

Madame Bovary (Flaubert), 90

Maimon, Solomon, 92n22

Majdanek concentration camp, images of, 236–42, 238*f*, 239*f*, 241*f*, 243*f*

Manchester Guardian (newspaper), 151, 159

Mandelstam, Osip, 262

Maria Aleksandrovna Romanova (Empress of Russia), 30n9, 32

Mariinsko Sergievskii Shelter for Baptized Jewish Children: diet at, 29–31; education at, 34–35; imperial patronage of, 30n9, 32–33, 48; mission of, 27–28, 31, 49; origins of, 28–29; placement of children after graduation from, 35–37; profiles of wards and parents, 37–48; trend toward racialization at, 49

Marranism, 216, 217

marriage: broken, 115; early, 74, 75

martyrdom, Jewish: Cantonists', 215–16; and national renewal, Dubnow on, 205, 206, 207–10, 215–20; Ten Martyrs story, 217, 217n67

maskilim: and An-sky, 68, 71, 75, 76, 81; and model letters *(brivnshteler),* 107, 113, 119; and social satires, 80, 81

mass migration: definition of, 130; of Jews, evidence for/against, 130n4, 142

Meir, Natan, 57

memoirs: An-sky's, 67, 72–73, 75–76, 78–79, 81; conflicting impulses in, 86–87; Jewish, importance of literacy in, 109

Memoirs of a Russian Governor (Urusov), 163–64

migration: mass, 130, 142; short- vs. long-distance, characteristics of, 130, 144; waves of, 130

migration of Jews into Eastern Europe, 127–33, 134n15; end of, 143–44; individual/family, 137–38, 141–42, 145; mass, conditions for, 130n4, 142; population growth and, 144–45; source regions for, 136–37, 144; violence and, 127, 132–33, 141, 144, 146

Miller, A., 117

Miller, Jaroslav, 143n50

Miller, Lee, 242, 243

minhag (religious customs), of East European Jewry, 137–38

Mintz, Alan, 254

Miron, Dan, 85, 105

model letters. *See brivnshteler; pis'movnik*

Moment (newspaper), 61

Mongol invasion, 128

monsters, depiction of Jews as, 182, 183*f*

Montgomery, Lucy Maud, 80n39

Morgenthau, Henry, 148n3

Morgn-Frayhayt (newspaper), 66

Morning Post (newspaper), 166

Motzkin, Leo, 163

Mukdoyni, Alexander, 77

Munro, H. H., 164–65, 166

Mussorgsky, Modest, 15

mutual-aid organizations, Jewish, 55–58

N

Nathans, Benjamin, 51, 203n2

Nathans, Paul, 163n57

nationalism, and antisemitism, 176

national renaissance, Dubnow on, 205, 206, 207–10, 215–20, 222

nature: in Jewish tradition, 261–62; and man-made evil, contrast between, 263; in Russian poetry, 260

Nazism: Einsatzgruppen, 224, 228; modern antisemitism and, 168. *See also* Holocaust photography

New York Times, on pogroms in tsarist Russia, 156–57
Nicholas I (Tsar of Russia), 218
Nicholas II (Tsar of Russia): difficulties encountered by, 167; extreme Right and, 176; policies on Jews, 221
Niger, Shmuel, 76
Nikolai Nikolaevich Romanov (Grand Duke of Russia), 191
Nikon, Patriarch, 173
Nister, Der, 76–77
"Now I often dream of Auschwitz" (Slutsky), 247, 256–58, 264

O

October Days of 1905. *See* Revolution of 1905
October manifesto, and Yiddish press, 61
Odessa: pogrom of 1881, 156; pogrom of 1905, 162; rightwing publication in, 176
Ogonek (magazine), images of Nazi atrocities in, 225, 226*f*, 228–29, 233, 234*f*–235*f*, 236, 242, 243*f*
Old Believer schismatic sects, 173
Olesha, Iurii, 81–82
onomastics, East European Jewish, 140–42
Opatoshu, Joseph, 66
OPE (Society for the Promotion of Enlightenment among the Jews of Russia), 51, 53, 60; and Yiddish language, 63, 65
Orshanskii, Il'ia Grigor'evich, 218
ORT (Society for the Promotion of Artisanal and Agricultural Work among the Jews in Russia), 52, 53, 54, 60; internationalization of, 65; and Yiddish language, 63, 65
Orthodox Christianity: representation of Jews in, 172–73. *See also* Russian Orthodoxy
Ostrovskii, Aleksandr, 79–80
Ostsiedlung, 130n4, 131–32, 144
Ozerskii, Israel, 230

P

Pale of Settlement: artisans in, 51–52; confusion about boundaries of, 147; de facto abolition of, 213; expulsions of 1890-1891 and, 157; relaxation of rules regarding residence in, 51, 52; Russian as foreign language in, 61; during World War I, 192, 192n20, 193, 213
Paperna, Avrom, 111
parallelisms: in Mandelstam's poetry, 262; in Slutsky's poems, 247, 249, 257, 259–60, 264
parent-child relations: *brivnshteler* on, 116–18, 120, 124–25; *pis'movnik* on, 115–16
Pares, Bernard, 162n53
Paulson, Niels, 231
peasants: emancipation of serfs, 218; and Jews, anxieties about influence of, 178, 179*f*; in *Ostsiedlung*, 130n4, 131; and pogroms, 153, 154–55, 194
The Penknife (Sholem-aleichem), 85–105; contemporary Russian literature and, 90–92, 100; desire *(heyshek/heshek)* in, 92–94, 97, 98; Dubnow on, 92, 93; elliptical conclusion of, 99–100, 102, 105; eroticism in, 93, 95, 96–97, 98, 100–101; mis/communication in, 104–5; questions about autobiographical sources of, 101–2; rebellion against tradition in, 103, 104; re-writing of, 87–89, 94–95; violence in, 94, 95, 99
Peretz, I. L., 50, 76, 77
Perl, Joseph, 103
persecution: and national renaissance, Dubnow on, 205, 206, 207–10, 215–20; study and *(lernen und leiden)*, in Jewish historiography, 204, 205, 222
Peter the Great (Tsar of Russia), 173
Petliura, Simon Vasil'evich, 188, 198
Petrovsky-Shtern, Yohanan Mironovich, 189
philanthropy: Jewish, pillars of, 51–54; and Yiddish language, transformation of, 50. *See also* Mariinsko Sergievskii Shelter for Baptized Jewish Children
photography: American liberation, 232; ideological beliefs and, 245; in Kishinev pogrom, 158; police, 241, 242; and Slutsky's poetic imagery, 261; Soviet liberation, 225, 227–44, 227*f*, 229*f*, 234*f*, 235*f*, 238*f*, 239*f*, 241*f*, 243*f*. *See also* Holocaust photography
physical stereotypes of Jews, 171, 179,

Index

185n39
Pińsk pogrom (1919), 148, 149
Pisarev, Dmitrii, 74
Piskorski, Jan M., 131–32
pis'movnik (Russian anthology of model letters), 106; *brivnshteler* compared to, 106, 108–18, 126; love letters in, 111–12, 113; parent-child relations in, 115–16; social literacy in, 111
plague. *See* Black Death
plains/fields: in Jewish tradition, 261–62; in Mandelstam's poetry, 262; in Russian tradition, 260; in Slutsky's poetry, 259–60, 262–63
"Poetic language is not a Lutheran sermon" (Slutsky), 252
poetry: post-Holocaust, 246–64, 247n1; Russian, nature in, 260; and violence, 246, 247. *See also* Slutsky
pogrom(s): assassination of Alexander II and, 73, 160, 167; authorities' role in, 149–52, 155, 156–57, 161–63, 189, 189n5; causes of, 152, 187–88, 200–201; "classic" definition of, 189; conspiratorial theory of, 149; Cossacks and, 189, 194, 195, 197, 200; Dubnow on, 149, 218; ethnic/religious riots labeled as, 150–52; etymology of term, 161; in Germany, 154; ironic take on, 164–65; Klier on, 19, 152–53; literary use of term, 163–64; misunderstanding surrounding, 147–48; myth of, universal acceptance of, 163; peasants and, 153, 154–55, 194; in Poland, Christmas 1881, 155–56; in Poland, pre-World War II, 148–49; Revolution of 1905 and, 162, 167, 197, 218, 221; term, adoption in English language, 153–54, 162; *Times* definition of, 159–61; in tsarist Russia, Anglo-American press on, 151, 154–63, 165–66, 211; women in, 194, 195, 197, 200. *See also* pogroms of 1881-1882; pogroms of Civil War period (1918-1921)
pogroms of 1881-1882: Anglo-American press on, 153–57; Dubnow on, 209; firearms used by Jews in, 197; Klier on, 19, 156n34; religious conservatism in response to, 73

pogroms of Civil War period (1918-1921), 187, 193–95, 198–200; causes of, 187–88, 200–201; as military phenomenon, 188–89; suspicions underlying, 189–91, 196, 198; victims of, 187, 187n1
Poland: images of Nazi atrocities in, 225, 226f, 236–42, 238f, 239f, 241f, 243f; partitioning of, antisemitism after, 174; pogroms in pre-World War II period, 148–49, 198; Warsaw pogrom of Christmas 1881, 155–56. *See also* Polish lands
Poliak-Gilman, 113, 114–15
police, role in pogroms, 189, 189n5
police photographs, 241, 242
Polish lands: early Jewish settlers of, 128, 129n3, 133; migration of Czech Jews into, 137–38, 142, 143, 145; *Ostsiedlung* in, 131–32
Polish-Lithuanian Commonwealth, Russian incorporation of, 174
political liberalization, resistance to, and antisemitism, 167, 168, 175
political parties: rightwing, 176; and Yiddish language, 59, 63
politics: *brivnshtelers* and, 108, 108n4; Russian-Jewish, after Revolution of 1905, 178, 208
population growth: exponential, 134; and Jewish migration to Eastern Europe, 144–45; and *Ostsiedlung*, 131; rapid, documented cases of, 135–36
Potemkina, Tat'iana Borisovna, 49
poverty: and conversion to Christianity, 38–39, 46; education as route out of, 52, 109
Poznanski, Renée, 207
Pozner, Solomon, 196
Pravda (newspaper), 236
press: Anglo-American, on pogroms, 151, 154–63, 165–66, 211; French rightwing, visual representations of Jews in, 185; Jewish, censorship of, 76n24; Russian rightwing, visual representations of Jews in, 167, 171, 175, 176–84, 179f, 180f, 183f, 184f; Soviet, images of Nazi atrocities in, 224, 225, 227–44, 227f, 229f, 234f, 235f, 238f, 239f, 241f, 243f; U.S., coverage of

281

World War II in, 245; U.S., images of Nazi atrocities in, 232, 236, 242, 243, 245; world, interconnectedness of, 163; Yiddish-language, 61–62, 64, 66, 86, 208, 219n78, 258

Pushkin, Alexander, 219, 260, 263

Q

Quebec, French-speaking population of, 136

R

"The rabbis walked onto the plains" (Slutsky), 247, 258–64

Rabinovich, Naum, 101–2

Rabinovich, Solomon Naumovich, 93. *See also* Sholem-aleichem

race, concept of: growing influence of, 49, 57; in late imperial Russia, 170–71

racialism: and antisemitism, 168, 169–70, 186; and attitudes toward Jewish converts, 49, 57, 168, 171

Ransel, David, 32

Rappoport, Shloyme-Zanvl. *See* An-sky, Semyon Akimovich

Ravnitskii, Y. Kh., 88, 89

Red Army: officers of, in Civil War, 189n6; and pogroms, 188, 189

Redkin, Mark, 228–29, 233

Reichskristallnacht, 150

Reiner, Elchanan, 138

religious customs *(minhag)*, of East European Jewry, 137–38

residency restrictions, for Jews, 51, 52. *See also* Pale of Settlement

revolutionary movement, antisemitism as backlash against, 175

Revolution of 1905: pogroms concurrent with, 162, 167, 197, 218, 221; political mobilization after, 178, 208; Yiddish press after, 61

Revolution of 1917, impact on Jews, 196, 220–21

rightwing press: French, visual representations of Jews in, 185; Russian, visual representations of Jews in, 167, 171, 175, 176–84, 179*f*, 180*f*, 183*f*, 184*f*

La Rire (journal), 185

Riumkin, Iakov, 236

Rogger, Hans, 20, 152

Roitberg, Joseph, 62

Romanov, Nikolai Nikolaevich (Grand Duke of Russia), 191

Romanov, Sergei Aleksandrovich (Grand Duke of Russia), 32, 33, 42

Romanova, Aleksandra Petrovna (Grand Duchess of Russia), 35

Romanova, Maria Aleksandrovna (Empress of Russia), 30n9, 32

Rostov, German occupation of, 226n2

Rothschild Foundation, 18

Rousseau, Jean-Jacques, 86, 92n22, 97

Rubin, Israel, 65

Russia Gathers Her Jews (Klier), 16, 26

Russian-Jewish history and culture, field of: after collapse of Soviet Union, 20; Klier and, 14, 15–16, 20

Russian language: in *brivnshtelers*, 110; as foreign language in Pale of Settlement, 61; translation of Yiddish literature into, 76–78; words absorbed in English, 153n20

Russian literature: influence on An-sky, 68, 79–80; influence on Sholem-aleichem, 90–92

Russian Orthodoxy: attitudes toward Jews in, 172–74, 191, 201; and Jewish conversion, 30, 48–49

Russians, Jews, and the Pogroms of 1881-1882 (Klier), 19, 152

Russo-Jewish Committee, 156

S

Saltykov-Shchedrin, Mikhail, 80, 81

Samuel, Stuart, 148n3

Sante, Luc, 241, 242

Satunovskii, Ian, 247n1

savings-and-loan associations. *See* credit cooperatives

Schechtman, Joseph, 188

Schellekens, Jona, 135n18, 136n24

Schiff, Jacob, 158, 211

Schiper, Ignacy, 133

Scholem, Gershom, 103n43, 251, 252, 254n14

Second Congress of All-Russian

Index

Cooperatives, Kiev, 63–64
selective integration of Jews, 51–53, 219
Sel'vinskii, Il'ia, 247n1
Semenov, E. P., 163
Semesenko, Ivan, 189n6
serfs: emancipation of, 218. *See also* peasants
Sergei Aleksandrovich Romanov (Grand Duke of Russia), 32, 33, 42
sexual imagery: in cartoons depicting Jews, 180, 180f, 184, 184f. *See also* eroticism
Sforim, Mendele Moykher, 50, 76
Shaftensbury, Lord, 155n30
Shandler, Jeffrey, 109
Shargorodskaia, Frida, 68
Shaykevitsch, N. M. (Shomer), 107n3, 125n53
Shma, Israel Ta, 137n28
Shnayder, Mordechai Betsalel, 108n4
Shneer, David, 261
Sholem-aleichem (Sholem Aleichem): contemporary Russian literature and, 90–92, 100, 104; discussion of name, 83n; on everyday life, 87, 93; and *Evreiskii mir* (journal), 76; *From the Fair*, 80–81; father of, 101–2; *Tevye* cycle, first part of, 89; and Yiddish language, 50, 84, 103–4. *See also The Penknife*
Shomer's briefenshteler, 107n3, 124, 125n53
Shrayer, Maxim, 258–59, 260
Siedlce pogrom (1906), 162, 163
Sigismund I, 142
Simon, Neil, 80n39
Simonov, Konstantin, 236
Sins of Youth (Lilienblum), 68, 73–76
"Sins of Youth and Sins of Age" (An-sky), 67, 72–73, 75–76, 78; revision for second edition, 78–79, 81
Slutsky, Boris, 246–47; "Domoi," 264n37; "Farewell," 254; "The First Century," 254; "How They Killed My Grandmother," 257; "I was a liberator of Ukraine," 247–55, 255f; messianism of, 251–52, 264, 264n38; "Now I often dream of Auschwitz," 247, 256–58, 264; parallelisms in poetry of, 247, 249, 257, 259–60, 264; "Poetic language is not a Lutheran sermon," 252; "The rabbis walked onto the plains," 247,
258–64
Smorgon' pogrom (1915), 194
Snel, Harmen, 135n18
Snyder, Timothy, 249
socialism: antisemitism as backlash against, 168, 175, 188, 200; early forms of, Jewish savings-and-loan associations and, 56; Jewish, and Yiddish language, 59, 66
social satire, in Yiddish literature, 80–81, 84
Society for the Promotion of Artisanal and Agricultural Work among the Jews in Russia. *See* ORT
Society for the Promotion of Enlightenment among the Jews of Russia. *See* OPE
socioeconomic rivalry, and pogroms, 152, 188, 200
Sol'skii, V., 34
Sontag, Susan, 225, 244, 245
Sorokina, Marina, 231
Sovietish Heymland (journal), 258
Soviet liberation photography, 225, 227–44, 227f, 229f, 234f, 235f, 238f, 239f, 241f, 243f; vs. American liberation photography, 242, 243, 245; effort to universalize Nazi atrocities in, 230–31; Extraordinary State Commission and, 231–32, 233, 236, 244; journalists and, 227–31; and Slutsky's poetic imagery, 261; survivor figure in, 244
Soviet Union: collapse of, Russian-Jewish studies after, 18–19, 20; Jewish credit cooperatives in, 65–66; Jewish ideology in, 222; Jewish studies in, 18–19; research on Jewish history in, 17; Yiddish-language press in, 258. *See also* Soviet liberation photography
Spain, medieval: comparison of tsarist Russia to, 214, 216; expulsion of Jews from, 209, 217
Spanish Inquisition, 168
Spectator (magazine), 157
Stalin, Joseph, 249
Stanislawski, Michael, 81
Stoker, Bram, 181
Stolypin, P. A., 208
St. Petersburg: Jewish community in, 51. *See also* Mariinsko Sergievskii Shelter for

283

Baptized Jewish Children
St. Petersburg Missionary Society, 28, 29
Strannik (journal), 28, 29, 34, 35, 37, 48–49
Strickland, Debra Higgs, 172
Struck, Il'ko Timofeevich, 189n6
Struk, Janina, 242
survivors: in Holocaust photography, 243–44; poems as, 250, 258

T

Talmud: antisemites on, 168, 169n5; violence in, 94, 95
Tcherikower, Elias, 149, 222
Telegraph Agency of the Soviet Union (TASS), 228
Ten Martyrs, story of, 217, 217n67
Terpilo, Daniil Ilyich (Zeleny), 189n6
The Times of London, on pogroms in tsarist Russia, 156, 159–61
Tiomin, Viktor, 236
Toch, 134n15
Tolstoy, Lev, 80n39, 104; *Anna Karenina*, 90, 91–92, 100
Trachtenberg, Barry, 64
trade unions, early Jewish savings-and-loan associations and, 56, 65
Trakhman, Mikhail, 236; photographs of Nazi concentration camp, 238*f*, 239–41, 239*f*, 241*f*, 243*f*
Trotskii, Matvei, 31
Trotsky, Leon, 185n39, 188
Tsederbaum, Alexander, 86
Tseitlin, Boris, 236, 243*f*
Tsvetaeva, Marina, 260
Turkic language, East European Jews and, 139

U

Ukraine: massacres of 1648, 209. *See also* Kiev; Odessa
Union of Russian People, 176; depiction in political cartoons, 179, 180*f*
United States: Dubnow's publications in, 205, 210–12; Holocaust photography in, 232, 236; press coverage of pogroms in tsarist Russia, 154, 155, 156–57, 162–63; Yiddish press in, 62, 65, 66, 115. *See also* immigration to America
University College London (UCL), 18
University of Illinois at Urbana-Champaign, 20
urbanization: and antisemitism, 175, 183; and pogroms, 153
Urusov, S. D., 163–64

V

vampires: Jews compared to, 181, 185; in Russian folklore, 181, 181n30
van Straten, Jits, 129n2, 129n3, 135n18
Varshavskii, Mark Abramovich, 191
Vasil'chikov, Ivan Alexeevich, 189n6
Veche (newspaper), 176, 177; depiction of Jews in, 178–82, 179*f*, 180*f*, 186; meaning of name, 176n21
Veniamin, O., 34
Verdery, Katherine, 177
Verga, Joseph ibn , 217
Vilna, cooperatives in, 55
violence: anti-Jewish, during World War I, 192–95; in *heder*, 94, 95, 99; interethnic, in tsarist Russia, 152–53; and Jewish migration to Eastern Europe, hypothesis of, 127, 132–33, 141, 144, 146; and mass migration, 130; poetry and, 246, 247; in Talmud, 94, 95. *See also* pogrom(s)
visual imagery: representations of Jews in rightwing newspapers, 167, 171, 175, 176–84, 179*f*, 180*f*, 183*f*, 184*f*. *See also* photography
Vladimir, medieval Jewish community in, 128
Volokolamsk, German occupation of, 226n2
Voßische Zeitung, 163

W

Warsaw pogrom of Christmas 1881, 155–56
waves of migration, 130
Weinberg, Jaime, 121n46
Weinreich, Max, 59
Weinryb, Bernard, 132, 133
Werth, Alexander, 240
Western and Central Europe: antisemitism in, 169–70, 185–86; emancipated Jewries of, 207, 210, 214, 215, 218; letter-writing

manuals in, 110; migration into Eastern Europe from, 130n4, 131–32
Wexler, Paul, 129n3
"What Do the Jews Want?" (Dubnow), 220–21
"White Pantyhose" (female snipers), 197–98
Whites, in Russian Civil War, 189n6; pogroms carried out by, 188; suspicion of Jews, 198–99
white slave trade, purported role of Jews in, 180
Wihl, Ludwig, 215
The Wishing Ring (Abramovich), 96
Wisse, Ruth, 102
Wissenschaft des Judentums movement: and Dubnow, 203–5, 206, 215, 221, 222; and lachrymose history, 207, 218
Wolf, Lucien, 163
women, in First Chechen War, 197–98
women, Jewish: conversion to Christianity, 33, 43–44; educational choices for, 45–46; fertility among, 135n18; pogroms and, 194, 195, 197, 200
World ORT Union, 65
World War I: anti-Jewish violence during, 192–95; deportations of Jews during, 192, 192n20, 193; execution of Jews for suspected espionage during, 192–93; Jewish civil-society institutions after, 64–65; Russian Jewry's hopes during, 212–13; suspicion of Jews during, 189–91, 196, 198, 201; veterans of, in Russian Civil War, 189
World War II: American press coverage of, 245. *See also* Holocaust photography; Nazism

Y

Yanushkevich, Nikolai Nikolaevich, 191
Yiddish language: in *brivnshtelers* (letter-writing manuals), 107, 107n3, 110; civil-society institutions and, 59, 65, 66; cooperative movement and, 61, 64, 66; destruction of, poem about, 247–55; eastern vs. western, 138–40, 143; English words in, 125; Jewish writers and, 76–78, 103–4; mis/communication in, 104–5; origins of, theories of, 139; periodicals in, 61–62, 64, 66, 86, 208; in postwar Soviet Union, 258; rise in status, and language wars, 62–63; rules for writing in, 107n3, 110; Russian's privileged position relative to, 76–78; Sholem-aleichem and, 50, 84, 103–4; transformation from jargon to national language, 50, 59–64; "triumph and tragedy" of, 65
Yiddish literature: apologism in, 84–85; censorship of, 108; descriptions of everyday life in, 84; flowering of, 219, 219n78; social satire in, 80–81, 84
Di Yidishe Kooperatsye (journal), 64
Yidishe velt (journal), 208–10

Z

Zalman, Shneur, 67
Zeleny (Daniil Ilyich Terpilo), 189n6
Zelma, Georgii, 236
Zemel, Carol, 232, 243
Zemkropski, Meyshe Abba, 124
zhargon, Yiddish as, 21, 62, 64, 107n3, 110
zhargon committees, 59
zhid (pl. *zhidy*), 177n25
Zhitlowsky, Chaim, 67, 68; An-sky's letters to, 69–70
Ziegler, Philip, 144
Zimman, Morris, 124
Zionism, *brivnshtelers* and, 108n4
Zionist Congress (1906), 61
Zionist Socialists, 208; and ORT, 65; and Yiddish language, 59
Znamia (newspaper), 176, 177; depiction of Jews in, 182–84, 183f, 184f, 186
Zoossmann-Diskin, Avshalom, 140n40

285

PUBLISHED IN THE SERIES
Borderlines: Russian and East European Jewish Studies

EXEMPLARY BODIES
Constructing the Jew in Russian Culture since the 1880s

Henrietta MONDRY

300 pages
Cloth 978-1-934843-39-0
$58.00 / £39.50
Electronic 978-1-61811-026-8
$40.00 / £24.50

This book explores the construction of the Jew's physical and ontological body in Russian culture as represented in literature, film, and non-literary texts from the 1880s to the present. With the rise of the dominance of biological and racialist discourse in the 1880s, the depiction of Jewish characters in Russian literary and cultural productions underwent a significant change, as these cultural practices recast the Jew not only as an archetypal "exotic" and religious or class Other (as in Romanticism and realist writing), but as a biological Other whose acts, deeds, and thoughts were determined by racial differences. This Jew allegedly had physical and psychological characteristics that were genetically determined and that could not be changed by education, acculturation, conversion to Christianity, or change of social status. This stereotype has become a stable archetype that continues to operate in contemporary Russian society and culture.

Henrietta Mondry is Professor and Director of the Russian Program at University of Canterbury, New Zealand. Her recent books include *Populist Writers and the Jews: In the Footsteps of 'Two Hundred Years Together,'* St. Petersburg: Akademicheskii proekt, 2005 (in Russian) and *Pure, Strong and Sexless: Russian Peasant Woman's Body and Gleb Uspensky*, Amsterdam: Rodopi, 2006.

> "Henrietta Mondry's *Exemplary Bodies: Constructing the Jew in Russian Culture since the 1880s* is one of the most important books to appear in the burgeoning field of Russian-Jewish studies this decade. Taking seriously the problematics of real Jews in the Russianspeaking lands, Mondry examines the fantasies about their bodies in writings from Anton Chekhov to the new Russian racial science of the 2000s. This is a readable and engaging study offering methodological and critical insights into antisemitism and its images. It provides the reader with a detailed understanding of the function of such images over the past century from Romanoff Russia through the short and bloody history of the USSR to Putin's Russia. It gives one pause about the continuities in Russian images of the Jew into the future."
> —Sander Gilman, Author, *The Jew's Body*

"I AM TO BE READ NOT FROM LEFT TO RIGHT, BUT IN JEWISH: FROM RIGHT TO LEFT"
The Poetics of Boris Slutsky

Marat GRINBERG
486 pages
Cloth 978-1-934843-73-4
$65.00 / £44.25
Electronic 978-1-61811-133-3
$65.00 / £44.25

Boris Slutsky (1919-1986) is a major original figure of Russian poetry of the second half of the twentieth century whose oeuvre has remained unexplored and unstudied. The first scholarly study of the poet, Marat Grinberg's book substantially fills this critical lacuna in the current comprehension of Russian and Soviet literatures. Grinberg argues that Slutsky's body of work amounts to a Holy Writ of his times, which daringly fuses biblical prooftexts and stylistics with the language of late Russian Modernism and Soviet newspeak. The book is directed toward readers of Russian poetry and pan-Jewish poetic traditions, scholars of Soviet culture and history and the burgeoning field of Russian Jewish studies. Finally, it contributes to the general field of poetics and Modernism.

Marat Grinberg (PhD University of Chicago) is an assistant professor of Russian and humanities at Reed College in Portland, Oregon.

> "Boris Slutsky, according to this brilliant book, accomplished the seemingly impossible: a poet of Soviet times, he reforged the totality of Russian literary culture, from Church Slavonic to Pushkin to Khlebnikov and beyond, within the crucible of Jewish self-understanding. Marat Grinberg, author of this impressive study, has also accomplished the seemingly impossible. He demonstrates how this supremely Russian poet can and must be read in his totality: "from right to left," from beginning to end, and from his desk drawer to Red Square."
> —David G. Roskies, Sol and Evelyn Henkind Professor of Yiddish Literature, Jewish Theological Seminary. Director, Center for Yiddish Studies, Ben Gurion University of the Negev

> "In this erudite and insightful book, Marat Grinberg rescues a great poet from a numbing set of mid-century clichés. No longer a "war poet," or "Soviet diarist," or sometime Jew, Boris Slutsky emerges as he was in fact—a sometimes playful, sometimes anguished heir to Russian modernism, who read Jewish catastrophe through Jewish texts."
> —Alice Nakhimovsky, Professor of Russian and Jewish Studies, Colgate University

JACOB'S LADDER
Kabbalistic Allegory in Russian Literature

Marina APTEKMAN
250 pages
Cloth 978-1-934843-38-3
$70.00 / £47.50
Electronic 978-1-61811-115-9
$70.00 / £47.50

Jacob's Ladder discusses the reflection of kabbalistic allegory in Russian literature and provides a detailed analysis of the evolution of the perception of Kabbalah in Russian consciousness. Aptekman investigates the questions of when, how and why Kabbalah has been used in Russian literary texts from Pre-Romanticism to Modernism and what particular role it played in the larger context of the Russian literary tradition. The correct understanding of this liaison helps the reader to clarify many enigmatic images in Russian literary works of the last two centuries and to understand the roots of a particular cultural falsification that played an important role in the anti-Semitic mythology of the twentieth century.

Marina Aptekman (PhD Brown University) is an assistant professor of Russian Language and Literature at Hobart and William Smith Colleges. Her recent publications include articles "Forward to the Past or Two Radical Views on Russian Nationalist Future: Pyotr Krasnov's *Behind the Thistle* and Vladimir Sorokin's *Day of Oprichnik*" (SEEJ), and "Kabbalah, Judeo-Masonic Conspiracy and Post-Soviet Literary Discourse: from Political Tool to Virtual Reality."(Russian Review).

> "Marina Aptekman makes skillful use of rich and diverse source materials, some new and others interpreted in an original and innovative way. This is an important and thought-provoking contribution to the field of Russian-Jewish cultural relations."
> —Mikhail Krutikov, associate professor of Slavic languages and literature, University of Michigan

> "This book is a fascinating study of a largely unexplored subject—the role of Kabbalah in Russian literature from the mid 17th to the 20th century and the larger context in which literature developed. Focusing on images and allegories that derive, directly and indirectly, from Kabbalah, Aptekman shows how and why it became an important element in mystical freemasonry, Romanticism, and Modernism. In addition, she limns the alternation between mystical and magical (or occult) interpretations of kabbalah and reveals how the occult interpretation came to be associated with black magic and, eventually, with the myth of a Judeo-Masonic conspiracy."
> —Bernice Glatzer Rosenthal, professor of history, Fordham University